LONGMAN

Second Edition

Introductory Course
for the
TOEFL® Test

iBT

DEBORAH PHILLIPS WITHDRAWN

PEARSON
Longman

TOEFL® is the registered trademark of Educational Testing Service (ETS). This publication is not endorsed or approved by ETS. No endorsement of this publication by Educational Testing Service should be inferred.

Longman Introductory Course for the TOEFL Test: iBT, Second Edition

Pearson Education, 10 Bank Street, White Plains, NY 10606

Staff credits: The people who made up the *Longman Introductory Course for the TOEFL Test: iBT, Second Edition* team, representing editorial, production, design, and manufacturing, are: Pietro Alongi, Rhea Banker, Dave Dickey, Warren Fischbach, Nancy Flaggman, Patrice Fraccio, Lester Holmes, Katherine Keyes, Melissa Leyva, Lise Minovitz, Linda Moser, Michael Mone, Barbara Sabella, Kenneth Volcjak, Sarah Wales-McGrath

Project editor: Helen B. Ambrosio
CD-ROM project manager: Helen B. Ambrosio
CD-ROM technical manager: Evelyn Fella
CD-ROM technical development editor: Lisa Hutchins
Text design adaptation: Page Designs International
Text composition: Page Designs International
Text photography: Hutchings Photography, Pearson Learning Group
Additional photograph credits: London Bridge in U.K. on page 117 © *Bettmann/CORBIS*; London Bridge in U.S. on page 117 © *Nik Wheeler/CORBIS*; James Fenimore Cooper on page 134 © *CORBIS*; Theodore Roosevelt on page 158 © *CORBIS*; Franklin D. Roosevelt on page 158 © *CORBIS*; Eleanor Roosevelt on page 158 © *Oscar White/CORBIS*; Niagara Falls on page 294 © *Gary W. Carter/CORBIS*; Angel Falls on page 294 © *James Marshall/CORBIS*; Victoria Falls on page 294 © *natureimmortal/Fotolia*; Stone Mountain on page 312 © *Kevin Fleming/CORBIS*; Confederate Memorial Carving on page 312 © *Raymond Gehman/CORBIS*; Leland Stanford on page 328 © *Bettmann/CORBIS*; Hoover Tower on page 328 © *Morton Beebe, S.F./CORBIS*; Neptune on page 346 © *CORBIS*; Overhead of Pentagon on page 372 © *Bettmann/CORBIS*; Molly Brown on page 374 © *Bettmann/CORBIS*; Olympus Mons on page 376 © *CORBIS*; Hoover Dam on page 378 © *Dave G. Houser/CORBIS*; US Pavilion at 1967 World's Fair on page 400 © *Bettmann/CORBIS*.

Library of Congress Cataloging-in-Publication Data

Phillips, Deborah
  Longman Introductory Course for the TOEFL Test : iBT / Deborah Phillips. — 2nd ed.
      p. cm.
    Rev. ed. of: 2004.
    Includes bibliographical references.
  ISBN 978-0-13475272-3 (student bk. with Cd-rom & iTests with AK, 2e) —
  1. Test of English as a Foreign Language—Study guides.
  2. English language—Textbooks for foreign speakers.
  3. English language—Examinations—Study guides. I. Title.
  II. Title: Introductory course for the TOEFL test.
  PE1128.P44 2008
  428.0076—dc22

                                                          2008028427

Printed in the United States of America
1   17

CONTENTS

SECTION TWO: LISTENING 97

SECTION THREE: SPEAKING   161

TOEFL-LEVEL TEST   392

To the Teacher:

HOW TO VIEW YOUR STUDENTS' DATA ON THE WEBSITE

Follow these steps to view your students' data on **www.longmantestprep.com**.

STEP 1: Choose a class name and e-mail address.

Decide on a unique class name, such as TOEFL 101 or Prep 07. Then choose an e-mail address or create a new one only for student data. Give this information to your students.

STEP 2: Go to www.longmantestprep.com.

After your students have submitted their data, go to this website: **www.longmantestprep.com**.

STEP 3: Enter information.

Type the information requested in each box: *E-mail Address* and *Password*. You must use the same e-mail address that you gave your students. You can use any password.

STEP 4: Click on "Login" to enter the website.

After you enter the website, you can choose REVIEW BY STUDENTS to see the results of an individual student. You can also choose REVIEW BY ACTIVITY to see the results of a particular activity.

To the Student:

HOW TO SEND YOUR DATA FROM THE CD-ROM

Get your class name and teacher's e-mail address from your teacher. Then follow these steps after you complete any exercises on the enclosed CD-ROM.

STEP 1: Start the process.

To start the process, click on SEND DATA on the Main Menu.

STEP 2: Select recordings (if you have made any).

When you send data, your Results Reports, Skills Reports, and written responses will be sent automatically. However, you must select your recordings (if you have any).

STEP 3: Enter information.

Type the information requested in each box: *Your Name, Your E-mail Address, Your Teacher's E-mail Address,* and *Your Class Name.* Then click on CONTINUE to send the data.

STEP 4: Wait for data to send.

You will see a message when the computer connects to the Internet and starts sending data. You will also see a message when the data has been sent.

INTRODUCTION

ABOUT THIS COURSE

PURPOSE OF THE COURSE

This course is intended to prepare students for the TOEFL® iBT (Internet-Based Test). It is based on the most up-to-date information available on the TOEFL iBT.

Longman Introductory Course for the TOEFL® Test: iBT, 2E can be used in a variety of ways, depending on the needs of the reader:

- It can be used as the *primary classroom text* in a course emphasizing preparation for the TOEFL iBT.

- It can be used as a *supplementary text* in a more general ESL/EFL course.

- Along with its companion audio program, it can be used as a tool for *individualized study* by students preparing for the TOEFL iBT outside of the ESL/EFL classroom.

LEVEL OF THE BOOK

Longman Introductory Course for the TOEFL Test: iBT, 2E is intended for intermediate-level students. The text starts *below* the level of the TOEFL test and continues up to the level of the *easier* tasks on the TOEFL iBT. It presents and practices those language skills that appear regularly on the TOEFL iBT and that are appropriate to this level.

This book is intended for those students who are interested in preparing for the TOEFL iBT but who are not yet ready for all the materials found on the actual test. It can be used most effectively to introduce lower-level TOEFL skills and strategies prior to the study of the more advanced *Longman Preparation Course for the TOEFL Test: iBT, 2E.*

WHAT IS IN THE BOOK

The book contains a variety of materials that together provide a comprehensive preparation course:

- **Diagnostic Pre-Tests** for each section of the TOEFL iBT (Reading, Listening, Speaking, Writing) measure students' level of performance and allow students to determine specific areas of weakness.

- **Language Skills** for each section of the test provide students with a thorough understanding of the language skills that are regularly tested on the TOEFL iBT.

- **Test-Taking Strategies** for each section of the test provide students with clearly defined steps to maximize their performance on the test.

- **Exercises** provide practice of one or more skills in a non-TOEFL format.

- **TOEFL Exercises** provide practice of one or more skills in a TOEFL format.

- **TOEFL Review Exercises** provide practice of all of the skills taught up to that point in a TOEFL format.
- **TOEFL Post-Tests** for each section of the test measure the progress that students have made after working through the skills and strategies in the test.
- Four **Mini-Tests** allow students to simulate the experience of actual tests using shorter versions (approximately 1.5 hours each) of the test.
- A **Complete Test** allows students to simulate the experience of taking an actual test using a full-length version (approximately 3.5 hours) of the test.
- A **TOEFL-Level Test** allows students to understand the level of the actual test using a shorter-length test.
- **Scoring Information** allows students to determine their approximate TOEFL score on the TOEFL-Level Test.
- **Skill-Assessment Checklists** and **Diagnostic Charts** allow students to monitor their progress in specific language skills on the Pre-Tests, Post-Tests, Mini-Tests, Complete Test, and TOEFL-Level Test so that they can determine which skills require further study.

WHAT IS ON THE CD-ROM

The CD-ROM, with test items that are completely different from the questions in this book, includes a variety of materials that contribute to an effective preparation program for the TOEFL iBT.

- An **Overview** describes the features of the CD-ROM.
- **Skills Practice** for each of the sections (Reading, Listening, Speaking, Writing) provide students with the opportunity to review and master each of the language skills on the test.
- Four **Mini-Tests** allow students to simulate the experience of taking actual tests using shorter versions (approximately 1.5 hours each) of the test.
- A **Complete Test** allows students to review all of the lower-level skills taught throughout the course in a TOEFL-format test.
- A **TOEFL-Level Test** allows students to understand the level of the actual test using a shorter-length test.
- **Answers** and **Explanations** for all the skills practice and test items allow students to understand their errors and learn from their mistakes.
- **Skills Reports** relate the test items on the CD-ROM to the language skills presented in the book.
- **Results Reports** enable students to record and print out charts that monitor their progress on all the skills practice and test items.

The following chart describes the contents of the CD-ROM:

	SKILLS PRACTICE		TESTS	
READING	Skills 1–2 Skills 3–4 Skills 5–6 Skills 7–8 Skills 9–10	26 questions 24 questions 29 questions 25 questions 17 questions	Mini-Test 1 Mini-Test 2 Mini-Test 3 Mini-Test 4	13 questions 13 questions 13 questions 13 questions
			Complete Test TOEFL-Level Test	39 questions 13 questions
LISTENING	Skills 1–2 Skills 3–4 Skills 5–6	16 questions 14 questions 16 questions	Mini-Test 1 Mini-Test 2 Mini-Test 3 Mini-Test 4	11 questions 11 questions 11 questions 11 questions
			Complete Test TOEFL-Level Test	34 questions 11 questions
SPEAKING	Skills 1–2 Skills 3–4 Skills 5–8 Skills 9–12 Skills 13–15 Skills 16–18	3 questions 3 questions 3 questions 3 questions 3 questions 3 questions	Mini-Test 1 Mini-Test 2 Mini-Test 3 Mini-Test 4	3 questions 3 questions 3 questions 3 questions
			Complete Test TOEFL-Level Test	6 questions 6 questions
WRITING	Skills 1–8 Skills 9–14	32 questions 43 questions	Mini-Test 1 Mini-Test 2 Mini-Test 3 Mini-Test 4	1 question 1 question 1 question 1 question
			Complete Test TOEFL-Level Test	2 questions 2 questions

AUDIO RECORDINGS TO ACCOMPANY THE BOOK

The audio program that can be purchased to accompany this book includes all of the recorded materials from the Listening, Speaking, and Writing skills sections and the Mini-Tests, Complete Test, and TOEFL-Level Test.

MATERIALS TO FOLLOW THIS BOOK

After completing the introductory materials in this course, students are ready to move on to more advanced materials in the Longman program:

- ***Longman Preparation Course for the TOEFL Test: iBT, 2E*** is a book and CD-ROM package that thoroughly prepares students for the iBT version of the TOEFL test.
- ***Longman Preparation Course for the TOEFL Test: iBT, 2E Audio CDs*** contain the recorded material from the Listening, Speaking, and Writing sections as well as the Mini-Tests and Complete Tests.

OTHER AVAILABLE MATERIALS

Longman publishes a full suite of material for TOEFL preparation: materials for the paper TOEFL test and the iBT (Internet-Based Test). Please contact Longman's website at www.pearsonlongman.com for a complete list of available TOEFL products.

ABOUT THE TOEFL iBT

OVERVIEW OF THE TOEFL iBT

The TOEFL iBT is a test to measure the English proficiency and academic skills of nonnative speakers of English. It is required primarily by English-language colleges and universities. Additionally, institutions such as government agencies, businesses, or scholarship programs may require this test.

DESCRIPTION OF THE TOEFL iBT

The TOEFL iBT currently has the following four sections:

- The **Reading** section consists of three long passages and questions about the passages. The passages are on academic topics; they are the kind of material that might be found in an undergraduate university textbook. Students answer questions about stated details, inferences, sentence restatements, sentence insertion, vocabulary, pronoun reference, function, and overall ideas.

- The **Listening** section consists of six long passages and questions about the passages. The passages consist of two student conversations and four academic lectures or discussions. The questions ask the students to determine main ideas, details, function, stance, inferences, and overall organization.

- The **Speaking** section consists of six tasks: two independent tasks and four integrated tasks. In the two independent tasks, students must answer opinion questions about some aspect of academic life. In two integrated reading, listening, and speaking tasks, students must read a passage, listen to a passage, and speak about how the ideas in the two passages are related. In two integrated listening and speaking tasks, students must listen to long passages and then summarize and offer opinions on the information in the passages.

- The **Writing** section consists of two tasks: one integrated task and one independent task. In the integrated task, students must read an academic passage, listen to an academic passage, and write about how the ideas in the two passages are related. In the independent task, students must write a personal essay.

The probable format of a TOEFL iBT is outlined in the following chart:

	TOEFL iBT	TIME
READING	3 passages and 39 questions	60 minutes
LISTENING	6 passages and 34 questions	60 minutes
SPEAKING	6 tasks and 6 questions	20 minutes
WRITING	2 tasks and 2 questions	60 minutes

It should be noted that at least one of the sections of the test will include extra, uncounted material. Educational Testing Service (ETS) includes extra material to try out material for future tests. If you are given a longer section, you must work hard on all of the materials because you do not know which material counts and which material is extra. (For example, if there are four reading passages instead of three, three of the passages will be counted and one of the passages will not be counted. It is possible that the uncounted passage could be any of the four passages.)

REGISTRATION FOR THE TEST

It is important to understand the following information about registration for the TOEFL test:

- The first step in the registration process is to obtain a copy of the *TOEFL Information Bulletin*. This bulletin can be obtained by downloading it or by ordering it from the TOEFL website at www.toefl.org.
- From the bulletin or the website, it is possible to determine when and where the TOEFL iBT will be given.
- Procedures for completing the registration form and submitting it are listed in the *TOEFL Information Bulletin*. These procedures must be followed exactly.

HOW THE TEST IS SCORED

Students should keep the following information in mind about the scoring of the TOEFL iBT:

- The TOEFL iBT is scored on a scale of 0 to 120 points.
- Each of the four sections (Reading, Listening, Speaking, Writing) receives a scaled score from 0 to 30. The scaled scores from the four sections are added together to determine the overall score.
- Speaking is initially given a score of 0 to 4 and Writing is initially given a score of 0 to 5. These scores are converted to scaled scores of 0 to 30. Criteria for the 0 to 4 Speaking scores and 0 to 5 Writing scores are included on pages 454–472.
- After students complete the TOEFL-Level Test in the book, it is possible for them to estimate their scaled scores. A description of how to determine the scaled scores of the various sections of the TOEFL-Level Test is included on pages 447–472. (Please note that it is not possible to provide scores for the Pre-Tests, Post-Tests, Mini-Tests, and Complete Test because they are below the level of the TOEFL iBT.)
- After students complete the TOEFL-Level Test on the CD-ROM, scaled scores are provided.

HOW iBT SCORES COMPARE WITH PAPER SCORES

Both versions of the TOEFL test (the PBT or Paper-Based Test and the iBT or Internet-Based Test) have different scaled score ranges. The paper TOEFL test has scaled scores ranging from 200 to 677; the iBT has scaled scores ranging from 0 to 120. The following chart shows how the scaled scores on the two versions of the TOEFL test are related:

iBT Internet-Based Test	PBT Paper-Based Test
120	677
115	650
110	637
105	620
100	600
95	587
90	577
85	563
80	550
75	537
70	523
65	513
60	497
55	480
50	463
45	450
40	433
35	417
30	397
25	377
20	350

TO THE STUDENTS

HOW TO PREPARE FOR THE TOEFL iBT

The TOEFL iBT is a standardized test of English and academic skills. To do well on this test, you should therefore work in these areas to improve your score:

- You must work to improve your knowledge of the English *language skills* that are covered on the TOEFL iBT.
- You must work to improve your knowledge of the *academic skills* that are covered on the TOEFL iBT.
- You must understand the *test-taking strategies* that are appropriate for the TOEFL iBT.
- You must take *practice tests* with the focus of applying your knowledge of the appropriate language skills and test-taking strategies.

This book can familiarize you with the English language skills, academic skills, and test-taking strategies necessary for the TOEFL iBT, and it can also provide you with a considerable amount of test practice. A huge amount of additional practice of the English language skills, academic skills, test-taking strategies, and tests is found on the CD-ROM.

HOW TO USE THIS BOOK

This book provides a variety of materials to help you prepare for the TOEFL iBT. Following these steps can help you to get the most out of this book:

1. Take the Diagnostic Pre-Test at the beginning of each section. When you take the Pre-Test, try to reproduce the conditions and time pressure of a real TOEFL test.
   a. Take each section of the test without interruption.
   b. Time yourself for each section so that you can experience the time pressure that exists on an actual TOEFL test.
   c. Play the listening audio one time only during the test. (You can play it more times when you are reviewing the test.)

2. After you complete the Reading or Listening Diagnostic Pre-Test, you should diagnose your errors and record your results.
   a. Complete the appropriate Diagnosis and Scoring charts on pages 448–453 to determine which language skills you have mastered and which need further study.
   b. Record your results on the Test Results charts on pages 450 and 453.

3. After you complete the Speaking or Writing Diagnostic Pre-Test, you should assess and score it and record your results.
   a. Complete the appropriate Skill-Assessment Checklists on pages 454–468 to assess the skills used in the test.

b. Score your results using the Speaking Scoring Criteria on pages 461–462 or the Writing Scoring Criteria on pages 469–470.

c. Record your scores on the Test Results charts on pages 464–465 and page 472.

4. Work through the presentation and exercises for each section, paying particular attention to the skills that caused you problems in a Pre-Test. Each time that you complete a TOEFL-format exercise, try to simulate the conditions and time pressure of a real TOEFL test.

   a. For reading questions, allow yourself one and one-half minutes for one question. (For example, if a reading passage has ten questions, you should allow yourself 15 minutes to read the passage and answer the questions.)

   b. For listening questions, play the recording one time only during the exercise. Do not stop the recording between questions.

   c. For speaking, allow yourself 15 to 20 seconds to prepare your response and 45 to 60 seconds to give your response.

   d. For writing, allow yourself 20 minutes to write an integrated writing response and 30 minutes to write an independent writing response.

5. When further practice on a specific point is included in an Appendix, a note in the text directs you to this practice. Complete the Appendix exercises on a specific point when the text directs you to those exercises and the point is an area that you need to improve.

6. When you have completed all the skills exercises for a section, take the Post-Test for that section. Follow the directions above to reproduce the conditions and time pressure of a real TOEFL test. After you complete the Post-Test, follow the directions above to diagnose your answers and record your results.

7. As you work through the course material, periodically schedule Mini-Tests. There are four Mini-Tests in the book. As you take each of the tests, follow the directions above to reproduce the conditions and time pressure of a real test. After you finish each test, follow the directions above to diagnose your answers and record your results.

8. Near the end of the course, take the Complete Test under the conditions and time pressure of a real test. Diagnose your answers, and record your results.

9. Near the end of the course, take the TOEFL-Level Test. Diagnose and assess your answers, and record your results. Determine your TOEFL score using the charts on pages 447–472.

HOW TO USE THE CD-ROM

The CD-ROM provides additional practice of the language skills and iBT-version tests to supplement the language skills and tests in the book. The material on the CD-ROM is completely different from the material in the book to provide the maximum amount of practice. Following these steps can help you get the most out of the CD-ROM:

1. After you have completed the language skills in the book, you should complete the related Skills Practice exercises on the CD-ROM.

	AFTER THIS IN THE BOOK	COMPLETE THIS ON THE CD-ROM
READING	Vocabulary and Reference Sentences Details Inferences Reading to Learn	Vocabulary and Reference Sentences Details Inferences Reading to Learn
LISTENING	Basic Comprehension Pragmatic Understanding Connecting Information	Basic Comprehension Pragmatic Understanding Connecting Information
SPEAKING	Independent Tasks Integrated Tasks (Reading and Listening) Integrated Tasks (Listening)	Independent Tasks Integrated Tasks (Reading and Listening) Integrated Tasks (Listening)
WRITING	Integrated Tasks Independent Tasks	Integrated Tasks Independent Tasks

2. Work slowly and carefully through the Reading and Listening Skills Practice exercises. These exercises are not timed but are instead designed to be done in a methodical and thoughtful way.

   a. Answer a question on the CD-ROM using the skills and strategies that you have learned in the book.

   b. Use the *Check Answer* button to determine whether the answer to that question is correct or incorrect.

   c. If your answer is incorrect, reconsider the question, and choose a different answer.

   d. Use the *Check Answer* button to check your new response.

   e. When you are satisfied that you have figured out as much as you can on your own, use the *Explain Answer* button to see an explanation.

   f. Then move on to the next question, and repeat this process.

3. Work slowly and carefully through the Speaking and Writing Skills Practice exercises. These exercises are not timed but are instead designed to be done in a methodical and thoughtful way.

   a. Complete a Speaking or Writing task using the skills and strategies that you have learned in the book. Take good notes as you work on a task.

   b. Play back your spoken response in Speaking or review your written response in Writing.

   c. Use the *Sample Notes* button to compare your notes to the sample notes provided on the CD-ROM.

   d. Use the *Sample Answer* button to see an example of a good answer and to compare your response to this answer.

   e. Complete the *Skill-Assessment Checklist* to evaluate how well you completed your response.

4. As you work your way through the Skills Practice exercises, monitor your progress on the charts included in the program.

   a. The *Results Reports* include a list of each of the exercises that you have completed and how well you have done on each of the exercises. (If you do an exercise more than once, the results of each attempt will be listed. In Speaking, only the final attempt will be saved.) You can print the *Results Reports* if you would like to keep them in a notebook.

   b. The *Skills Reports* include a list of each of the language skills, how many questions related to each language skill you have answered, and what percentage of the questions you have answered correctly. In this way, you can see clearly which language skills you have mastered and which language skills require further work. You can print the *Skills Reports* if you would like to keep them in a notebook.

5. Use the four Mini-Tests on the CD-ROM periodically throughout the course to determine how well you have learned to apply the language skills and test-taking strategies presented in the course. Use the Complete Test and TOEFL-Level Test near the end of the course to determine your progress in the course.

6. Take the tests in a manner that is as close as possible to the actual testing environment. Choose a time when you can work on a section without interruption.

7. Work straight through each test section. The *Check Answer, Explain Answer, Sample Notes,* and *Sample Answer* buttons are not available during the test sections.

8. After you complete a Reading or Listening test section, do the following:

   a. Follow the directions to go to the *Results Report* for the test that you have just completed. The number correct is given in the upper right hand corner of the *Results Report* for the Mini-Test or Complete Test section that you have just completed. A TOEFL equivalent score is given in the upper right hand corner of the *Results Report* for the TOEFL-Level Test section that you have just completed.

   b. In the *Results Report,* see which questions you answered correctly and incorrectly, and see which language skills were tested in each question. Print the *Results Report* if you would like to keep it in a notebook or turn it in to your teacher.

   c. In the *Results Report,* review each question by double-clicking on a particular question. When you double-click on a question in the *Results Report,* you can see the question, the answer that you chose, the correct answer, and the *Explain Answer* button. You may click on the *Explain Answer* button to see an explanation.

d. Return to the *Results Report* for a particular test whenever you would like by entering the *Results Report* through the *Results* button on the Main Menu. You do not need to review a test section immediately but may instead wait to review the test section.

9. After you complete a Speaking or Writing test section, do the following:

   a. Complete the *Skill-Assessment Checklist* as directed.

   b. Play back your spoken response in Speaking or review your written response in Writing.

   c. Use the *Sample Notes* button to compare your notes to the sample notes provided on the CD-ROM.

   d. Use the *Sample Answer* button to see an example of a good answer and to compare your response to this answer.

TO THE TEACHER

HOW TO GET THE MOST OUT OF THE SKILLS EXERCISES IN THE BOOK

The skills exercises are a vital part of the TOEFL preparation process presented in this book. Maximum benefit can be obtained from the exercises if the students are properly prepared for the exercises and if the exercises are carefully reviewed after completion. Here are some suggestions:

- Be sure that the students have a clear idea of the appropriate skills and strategies involved in each exercise. Before beginning each exercise, review the skills and strategies that are used in that exercise. Then, when you review the exercises, reinforce the skills and strategies that can be used to determine the correct answers.

- After you review the exercises, be sure to discuss each answer, the incorrect answers as well as the correct answers. Discuss how students can determine that each correct answer is correct and each incorrect answer is incorrect.

- The exercises are designed to be completed in class rather than assigned as homework. The exercises are short and take very little time to complete, particularly since it is important to keep students under time pressure while they are working on the exercises. Considerably more time should be spent in reviewing exercises than in actually doing them.

HOW TO GET THE MOST OUT OF THE TESTS IN THE BOOK

There are five different types of tests in this book: Diagnostic Pre-Tests, Post-Tests, Mini-Tests, a Complete Test, and a TOEFL-Level Test. When the tests are given, it is important that the test conditions be as similar to actual TOEFL test conditions as possible; each section of the test should be given without interruption and under the time pressure of the actual test. Giving the speaking tests in the book presents a unique problem because the students need to respond individually during the tests. Various ways of giving the speaking tests are possible; you will need to determine the best way to give the speaking tests for your situation. Here are some suggestions:

- You can have the students come in individually and respond to the questions as the teacher listens to the responses and evaluates them.

- You can have a room set up where the students come in individually to take a speaking test and record their responses on a cassette recorder. Then either the student or the teacher will need to evaluate the responses.

- You can have a room set up where students come in in groups of four to take a speaking test and record the responses on four cassette recorders, one in each corner of the room. Then either the students or the teacher will need to evaluate the responses.

- You can have the students sit down in an audio lab or computer lab where they can record their responses on the system or on cassette recorders. Then either the students or the teacher will need to evaluate the responses.

Review of the tests should emphasize the function served by each of these different types of tests:

- While reviewing the Diagnostic Pre-Tests, you should encourage students to determine the areas where they require further practice.
- While reviewing the Post-Tests, you should emphasize the language skills and strategies involved in determining the correct answer to each question.
- While reviewing the Mini-Tests, you should review the language skills and test-taking strategies that are applicable to the tests.
- While reviewing the Complete Test and TOEFL-Level Test, you should emphasize the overall strategies for the tests and review the variety of individual language skills and strategies taught throughout the course.

HOW TO GET THE MOST OUT OF THE CD-ROM

The CD-ROM is designed to supplement the practice that is contained in the book and to provide an alternate modality for preparation for the TOEFL iBT. Here are some ideas to consider as you decide how to incorporate the CD-ROM into your course:

- The CD-ROM is closely coordinated with the book and is intended to provide further practice of the skills and strategies that are presented in the book. This means that the overall organization of the CD-ROM parallels the organization of the book but that the exercise material and test items on the CD-ROM are different from those found in the book. It can thus be quite effective to teach and practice the language skills in the book and then use the CD-ROM for further practice and assignments.
- The CD-ROM can be used in a computer lab during class time (if you are lucky enough to have access to a computer lab during class time), but it does not need to be used in this way. It can also be quite effective to use the book during class time and to make assignments from the CD-ROM for the students to complete outside of class, either in the school computer lab or on their personal computers. Either method works quite well.
- The CD-ROM contains a Skills Practice section, four Mini-Tests, one Complete Test, and one TOEFL-Level Test. In the Skills Practice section, the students can practice and assess their mastery of specific skills. In the various kinds of test sections, the students can see how well they are able to apply their knowledge of the language skills and test-taking strategies to test sections.
- The CD-ROM scores the various sections in different ways. The Skills Practice exercises, Mini-Test sections, and Complete Test sections are given scores that show the percentage correct. The TOEFL-Level Test sections are given TOEFL-equivalent scaled scores.
- The CD-ROM contains printable *Skills Reports* and *Results Reports* so that you can easily and efficiently keep track of your students' progress. You may want to ask your students to print the *Results Report* after they complete each exercise or test and keep the *Results Reports* in a notebook; you can then ask the students to turn in their notebooks periodically so that you can easily check that the assignments have been completed and monitor the progress that the students are making.

- The Speaking tasks can be reviewed by the students immediately after the students have completed them. Each speaking task is also saved and can be accessed through the *Results Menu*, though only the most recent version of each speaking task is saved. The speaking tasks can also be saved to a disk and submitted to the teacher. (You could also have the students record their responses on a cassette recorder as they complete a test instead of having them record their responses on the computer. Then you could have the students turn in their cassettes for review instead of turning in computer disks.)

- The Writing tasks can be printed when they are written so that they can be reviewed and analyzed. Each of the writing tasks is also automatically saved and can be accessed through the *Results Menu*. It is also possible for students to copy their writing tasks into a word processing program so that they can make changes, corrections, and improvements to their writing tasks.

HOW MUCH TIME TO SPEND ON THE MATERIAL

You may have questions about how much time it takes to complete the materials in this course. The numbers in the following chart indicate approximately how many hours it takes to complete the material[1]:

	BOOK		CD-ROM	
READING SKILLS	Pre-Test	2		
	Skills 1–2	6	Skills 1–2	2
	Skills 3–4	6	Skills 3–4	2
	Skills 5–6	6	Skills 5–6	2
	Skills 7–8	6	Skills 7–8	2
	Skills 9–10	6	Skills 9–10	2
	Post-Test	2		
LISTENING SKILLS	Pre-Test	1		
	Skills 1–2	5	Skills 1–2	2
	Skills 3–4	5	Skills 3–4	2
	Skills 5–6	5	Skills 5–6	2
	Post-Test	1		
SPEAKING SKILLS	Pre-Test	2		
	Skills 1–4	4	Skills 1–4	2
	Skills 5–8	4	Skills 5–8	2
	Skills 9–12	4	Skills 9–12	2
	Skills 13–15	3	Skills 13–15	2
	Skills 16–18	3	Skills 16–18	2
	Post-Test	2		

---

[1] The numbers related to the book indicate approximately how much time it takes to introduce the material, complete the exercises, and review the exercises. The numbers related to the CD-ROM indicate approximately how much time it takes to complete the exercises and review them.

	BOOK		CD-ROM	
WRITING SKILLS	Pre-Test Skills 1–8 Skills 9–14 Post-Test	2 10 10 2	Skills 1–8 Skills 9–14	2 2
MINI-TEST 1	Reading Listening Speaking Writing	1 1 1 1	Reading Listening Speaking Writing	1 1 1 1
MINI-TEST 2	Reading Listening Speaking Writing	1 1 1 1	Reading Listening Speaking Writing	1 1 1 1
MINI-TEST 3	Reading Listening Speaking Writing	1 1 1 1	Reading Listening Speaking Writing	1 1 1 1
MINI-TEST 4	Reading Listening Speaking Writing	1 1 1 1	Reading Listening Speaking Writing	1 1 1 1
COMPLETE TEST	Reading Listening Speaking Writing	2 2 2 2	Reading Listening Speaking Writing	2 2 2 2
TOEFL-LEVEL TEST	Reading Listening Speaking Writing	1 1 2 2	Reading Listening Speaking Writing	1 1 2 2
APPENDIX	Appendix A Appendix B	4 9		
	140 hours		**60 hours**	

HOW TO DIVIDE THE MATERIAL

You may need to divide the materials in this course so that they can be used over two sessions. The following is one suggested way to divide the materials into two sessions:

SESSION 1	BOOK		CD-ROM	
READING SKILLS	Pre-Test Skills 1–2 Skills 3–4 Skills 5–6	2 6 6 6	 Skills 1–2 Skills 3–4 Skills 5–6	 2 2 2
LISTENING SKILLS	Pre-Test Skills 1–2 Skills 3–4	1 5 5	 Skills 1–2 Skills 3–4	 2 2
SPEAKING SKILLS	Pre-Test Skills 1–4 Skills 5–8	2 4 4	 Skills 1–4 Skills 5–8	 2 2
WRITING SKILLS	Pre-Test Skills 1–8	2 10	 Skills 1–8	 2
MINI-TEST 1	Reading Listening Speaking Writing	1 1 1 1	Reading Listening Speaking Writing	1 1 1 1
MINI-TEST 2	Reading Listening Speaking Writing	1 1 1 1	Reading Listening Speaking Writing	1 1 1 1
MINI-TEST 3	Reading Listening Speaking Writing	1 1 1 1	Reading Listening Speaking Writing	1 1 1 1
APPENDIX	Appendix A	4		
		69 hours		**28 hours**

SESSION 2	BOOK		CD-ROM	
READING SKILLS	Skills 7–8	6	Skills 7–8	2
	Skills 9–10	6	Skills 9–10	2
	Post-Test	2		
LISTENING SKILLS	Skills 5–6	5	Skills 5–6	2
	Post-Test	1		
SPEAKING SKILLS	Skills 9–12	4	Skills 9–12	2
	Skills 13–15	3	Skills 13–15	2
	Skills 16–18	3	Skills 16–18	2
	Post-Test	2		
WRITING SKILLS	Skills 9–14	10	Skills 9–14	2
	Post-Test	2		
MINI-TEST 4	Reading	1	Reading	1
	Listening	1	Listening	1
	Speaking	1	Speaking	1
	Writing	1	Writing	1
COMPLETE TEST	Reading	2	Reading	2
	Listening	2	Listening	2
	Speaking	2	Speaking	2
	Writing	2	Writing	2
TOEFL-LEVEL TEST	Reading	1	Reading	1
	Listening	1	Listening	1
	Speaking	2	Speaking	2
	Writing	2	Writing	2
APPENDIX	Appendix B	9		
		71 hours		**32 hours**

READING

READING DIAGNOSTIC PRE-TEST

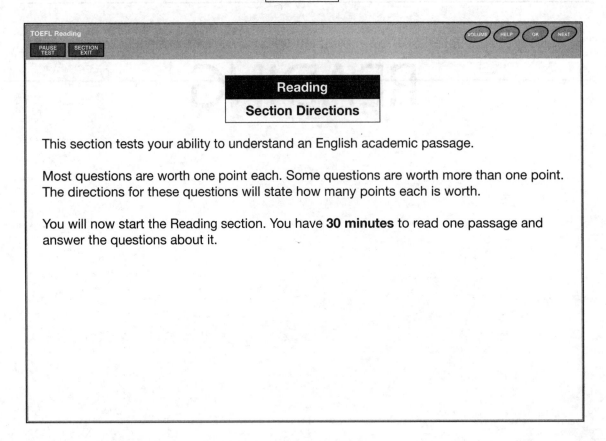

TOEFL Reading

PAUSE TEST | SECTION EXIT

VOLUME | HELP | OK | NEXT

Reading
Section Directions

This section tests your ability to understand an English academic passage.

Most questions are worth one point each. Some questions are worth more than one point. The directions for these questions will state how many points each is worth.

You will now start the Reading section. You have **30 minutes** to read one passage and answer the questions about it.

Read the passage.

Paragraph   **George Washington Carver**

▶1   Scientist and inventor George Washington Carver was born into slavery during the American Civil War. After the war, he worked diligently to get an education. He managed to get an advanced degree in botany, which is the study of plants. After he finished his college degree, he worked in the South. He taught people about botany and about how it could be used to improve farming.

▶2   Carver learned that there was a problem with cotton farming in the South. Cotton takes nutrients from the soil. If cotton is planted year after year, the quality of the soil decreases. Carver knew that plants like peanuts and sweet potatoes are different from cotton. They add nutrients to the soil rather than take nutrients from the soil. Carver told farmers that it was a bad idea to grow only cotton and no other crops each year. He told them that they should also grow plants like peanuts and sweet potatoes, which improve the quality of the soil. Many farmers followed the advice that Carver offered them. The result was that the production on their farms increased.

▶3   The increased production of peanuts and sweet potatoes improved the quality of the soil. However, when production of peanuts and sweet potatoes increased, a new problem developed. The new problem was that there were too many peanuts and sweet potatoes. To solve this problem, Carver began working in a laboratory to find new uses for peanuts and sweet potatoes. He developed hundreds of products that could be made from peanuts and sweet potatoes. These hundreds of products included food products, medicines, plastics, and fertilizer.

Refer to this version of the passage to answer the questions that follow.

Paragraph
George Washington Carver

1 ▶ **5A** Scientist and inventor George Washington Carver was born into slavery during the American Civil War. **5B** After the war, he worked diligently to get an education. **5C** He managed to get an advanced degree in botany, which is the study of plants. **5D** After he finished his college degree, he worked in the South. He taught people about botany and about how it could be used to improve farming.

2 ▶ Carver learned that there was a problem with cotton farming in the South. Cotton takes nutrients from the soil. If cotton is planted year after year, the quality of the soil decreases. Carver knew that plants like peanuts and sweet potatoes are different from cotton. They add nutrients to the soil rather than take nutrients from the soil. Carver told farmers that it was a bad idea to grow only cotton and no other crops each year. He told them that they should also grow plants like peanuts and sweet potatoes, which improve the quality of the soil. Many farmers followed the advice that Carver offered them. The result was that the production on their farms increased.

3 ▶ This increased production of peanuts and sweet potatoes improved the quality of the soil. **15A** However, when production of peanuts and sweet potatoes increased, a new problem developed. **15B** The new problem was that there were too many peanuts and sweet potatoes. **15C** To solve this problem, Carver began working in a laboratory to find new uses for peanuts and sweet potatoes. **15D** He developed hundreds of products that could be made from peanuts and sweet potatoes. These hundreds of products included food products, medicines, plastics, and fertilizer.

Questions

1. Which of the following is NOT stated in paragraph 1 about George Washington Carver?

   Ⓐ The period when he was born
   Ⓑ Who his parents were
   Ⓒ What he studied in school
   Ⓓ What kind of work he did

2. The word "diligently" in paragraph 1 is closest in meaning to

   Ⓐ very hard
   Ⓑ only a little
   Ⓒ very easily
   Ⓓ occasionally

3. In botany, one would most likely study

   Ⓐ rocks
   Ⓑ sharks
   Ⓒ painting
   Ⓓ roses

4. The word "it" in paragraph 1 refers to

   Ⓐ college degree
   Ⓑ the South
   Ⓒ botany
   Ⓓ farming

5. Look at the four squares [■] that indicate where the following sentence could be added to paragraph 1.

   This was a war that was fought from 1861 to 1865.

   Where would the sentence best fit? Click on a square [■] to add the sentence to the paragraph.

6. Which of the sentences below best expresses the essential information in the first highlighted sentence in paragraph 2?

   Ⓐ The soil will get worse due to repeated planting of cotton.
   Ⓑ The same soil is used when cotton is planted year after year.
   Ⓒ The amount of soil decreases if cotton is planted over again.
   Ⓓ The quality of the cotton decreases if it is planted over again.

7. It can be inferred from paragraph 2 that

   Ⓐ peanuts and sweet potatoes are good for the soil, while cotton is not
   Ⓑ peanuts and sweet potatoes and cotton are all good for the soil
   Ⓒ cotton is good for the soil, while peanuts and sweet potatoes are not
   Ⓓ neither peanuts and sweet potatoes nor cotton is good for the soil

8. Which of the sentences below best expresses the essential information in the second highlighted sentence in paragraph 2?

   Ⓐ Farmers told Carver that it was not good to grow cotton.
   Ⓑ Carver told farmers not to plant cotton with other crops.
   Ⓒ Carver knew that it was best to plant cotton with no other crops.
   Ⓓ Farmers learned from Carver that it was not good to grow only cotton.

9. The word "them" in paragraph 2 refers to

   Ⓐ nutrients
   Ⓑ farmers
   Ⓒ plants
   Ⓓ peanuts

10. The word "offered" in paragraph 2 could best be replaced by

ⓐ showed
ⓑ asked
ⓒ made
ⓓ gave

11. Why does the author begin paragraph 3 with the expression "This increased production of peanuts and sweet potatoes"?

ⓐ To introduce new ideas into paragraph 3
ⓑ To announce the topic for paragraph 3
ⓒ To summarize the ideas from paragraph 2
ⓓ To ask a question to be answered in paragraph 3

12. The author uses the word "However" to begin the second sentence of paragraph 3 in order to show that

ⓐ everything was not good when the production of certain crops increased
ⓑ the production of peanuts and sweet potatoes was a result of a previously mentioned idea
ⓒ an example of a previously mentioned idea will follow
ⓓ two ideas that are in agreement are presented

13. According to paragraph 3, what problem developed from the production of peanuts and sweet potatoes?

ⓐ There were too many ways that peanuts and sweet potatoes could be used.
ⓑ Carver did not have a laboratory where he could study peanuts and sweet potatoes.
ⓒ Peanuts and sweet potatoes did not actually improve the quality of the soil.
ⓓ There were too many peanuts and sweet potatoes, and there was nothing to do with them.

14. It is stated in paragraph 3 that Carver was working in a laboratory to find new

ⓐ ways to grow peanuts and sweet potatoes
ⓑ kinds of peanuts and sweet potatoes
ⓒ products that can be made from peanuts and sweet potatoes
ⓓ ways to turn peanuts into sweet potatoes

15. Look at the four squares [■] that indicate where the following sentence could be added to paragraph 3.

It added nutrients back to the soil.

Where would the sentence best fit? Click on a square [■] to add the sentence to the paragraph.

16. Which of the following is NOT listed in paragraph 3 as a product that can be made from peanuts and sweet potatoes?

ⓐ Food
ⓑ Clothing
ⓒ Medicine
ⓓ Plastic

17.

Directions: An introductory sentence for a brief summary of the passage is provided below. Complete a summary of the ideas in the passage by selecting the THREE answer choices that express the most important ideas in the passage. **This question is worth 2 points** (2 points for 3 correct answers, 1 point for 2 correct answers, and 0 points for 1 or 0 correct answers).
George Washington Carver was successful in many ways during his life.
•   •   •

Answer Choices (choose 3 to complete the chart):

(1) Carver was successful as a farmer.

(2) Carver learned about a problem and a solution in relation to the planting of cotton.

(3) Carver learned about new ways to use cotton.

(4) Carver learned to solve the problem of too many peanuts and sweet potatoes.

(5) Carver was born during the Civil War.

(6) Carver worked very hard to become well educated.

18.

Directions:	Select the appropriate answer choices about George Washington Carver's accomplishments, and match them to the correct category. **This question is worth 3 points** (3 points for 5 correct answers, 2 points for 4 correct answers, 1 point for 3 correct answers, 0 points for 2, 1, or 0 correct answers).

in education	•
in solving a problem in cotton farming	• •
in solving a problem in the production of peanuts	• •

Answer Choices (choose 5 to complete the table):

(1) He learned about many new ways to use peanuts and sweet potatoes.

(2) He got an advanced degree in botany.

(3) He held many jobs while he was in college.

(4) He learned that planting cotton helped to improve the soil.

(5) He learned that planting cotton took nutrients from the soil.

(6) He learned that planting peanuts and sweet potatoes added nutrients to the soil.

(7) He learned that there was a problem when too many peanuts and sweet potatoes were produced.

Turn to pages 448–450 to *diagnose* your errors and *record* your results.

READING OVERVIEW

The first section on the TOEFL *iBT* is the Reading section. This section consists of three passages, each followed by a number of questions. All of the questions accompanying a passage are worth one point each, except for the last question in the set, which is worth more than one point.

- The **passages** are lengthy readings on academic topics.

- The **questions** may ask about vocabulary, pronoun reference, the meanings of sentences, where sentences can be inserted, stated and unstated details, inferences, rhetorical purpose, and overall organization of ideas.

The following strategies can help you in the Reading section.

STRATEGIES FOR READING

1. **Be familiar with the directions.** The directions on every test are the same, so it is not necessary to spend time reading the directions carefully when you take the test.

2. **Dismiss the directions as soon as they come up.** The time starts when the directions come up. You should already be familiar with the directions, so you can click on Continue as soon as it appears and save all of your time for the passages and questions.

3. **Do not worry if a reading passage is on a topic that is not familiar to you.** All of the information that you need to answer the questions is included in the passages. You do not need any background knowledge to answer the questions.

4. **Do not spend too much time reading the passages.** You do not have time to read each passage in depth, and it is quite possible to answer the questions correctly without first reading the passages in depth.

5. **Skim each passage to determine the main idea and overall organization of ideas in the passage.** You do not need to understand every detail in each passage to answer the questions correctly. It is therefore a waste of time to read each passage with the intent of understanding every single detail before you try to answer the questions.

6. **Look at each question to determine what type of question it is.** The type of question tells you how to proceed to answer the question.

   - For *vocabulary questions,* the targeted word will be highlighted in the passage. Find the highlighted word, and read the context around it.

   - For *reference questions,* the targeted word will be highlighted in the passage. Find the targeted word, and read the context preceding the highlighted word.

- For *sentence insertion questions,* there will be darkened squares indicating where the sentence might be inserted. Read the context around the darkened squares carefully.

- For *sentence restatement questions,* the targeted sentence will be highlighted in the passage. Read the highlighted sentence carefully. It may also be helpful to read the context around the highlighted sentence.

- For *detail questions, unstated detail questions,* and *inference questions,* choose a key word in the question, and skim for the key word (or a related idea) in order in the passage. Read the part of the passage around the key word (or related idea).

- For *rhetorical purpose questions,* the targeted word or phrase will be highlighted in the passage. Read the highlighted word or phrase and the context around it to determine the rhetorical purpose.

- For *overall ideas questions,* focus on the main ideas rather than details of the passages. The main ideas are most likely explained in the introductory paragraph and at the beginning or end of each supporting paragraph.

7. **Choose the best answer to each question.** You may be certain of a particular answer, or you may eliminate any definitely incorrect answers and choose from among the remaining answers.

8. **Do not spend too much time on a question you are completely unsure of.** If you do not know the answer to a question, simply guess and go on. You can return to this question later (while you are still working on the same passage) if you have time.

9. **Monitor the time carefully on the title bar of the computer screen.** The title bar indicates the time remaining in the section, the total number of questions in the section, and the number of the question that you are working on.

10. **Guess to complete the section before time is up.** It can only increase your score to guess the answers to questions that you do not have time to complete. (Points are not subtracted for incorrect answers.)

READING SKILLS

The following skills will help you to implement these strategies in the Reading section of the TOEFL *iBT*.

VOCABULARY AND REFERENCE

Reading Skill 1: UNDERSTAND VOCABULARY FROM CONTEXT

In the Reading section of the TOEFL *iBT*, you may have to decide on the meaning of a word or phrase. You may be given a difficult word or phrase that you have never seen before. You may also be given an easier-looking word or phrase with a number of meanings. The context (the words around the vocabulary word) will probably help you understand what the word or phrase means. Look at an example of a difficult word that you may not have seen before. The context around the word helps you understand the meaning of the word.

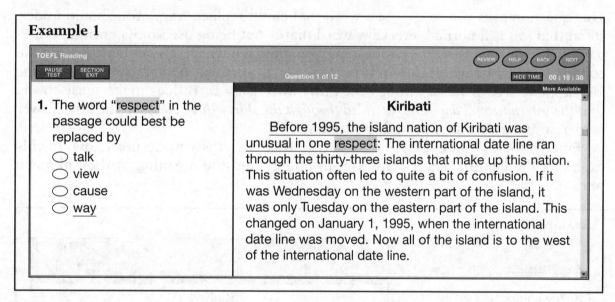

Example 1

TOEFL Reading

PAUSE TEST | SECTION EXIT

Question 1 of 12   HIDE TIME 00 : 18 : 38

REVIEW | HELP | BACK | NEXT

More Available

1. The word "respect" in the passage could best be replaced by
   - ○ talk
   - ○ view
   - ○ cause
   - ○ <u>way</u>

Kiribati

    Before 1995, the island nation of Kiribati was unusual in one respect: The international date line ran through the thirty-three islands that make up this nation. This situation often led to quite a bit of confusion. If it was Wednesday on the western part of the island, it was only Tuesday on the eastern part of the island. This changed on January 1, 1995, when the international date line was moved. Now all of the island is to the west of the international date line.

This question asks about the meaning of the word "respect." The passage states that *the island nation of Kiribati was unusual in one respect*. From this, you need to understand that *respect* could best be replaced by *way*. The last answer is therefore the best answer to this question.

Next, look at an example of a word that you often see in everyday English. In this type of question, you should *not* give the normal everyday meaning of the word. Instead, a secondary meaning is being tested, so you must study the context to determine the meaning of the word in this situation.

Example 2

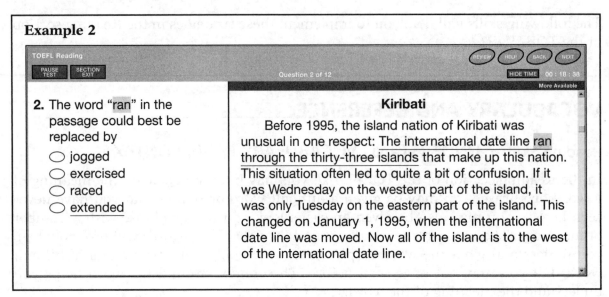

This question asks you to choose a word that could replace "ran." You should understand that *ran* is a normal, everyday word that is not being used in its normal, everyday way. To answer this type of question, you must see which answer best fits into the context in the passage. It does not make sense to say that *the international date line jogged, exercised, or raced through the thirty-three islands.* It does make sense to say that *the international date line extended through the thirty-three islands.* The last answer is therefore the best answer to this question.

Finally, look at an example of a phrase that perhaps you do not know. In this example, the context again helps you to understand the meaning of the unknown phrase.

Example 3

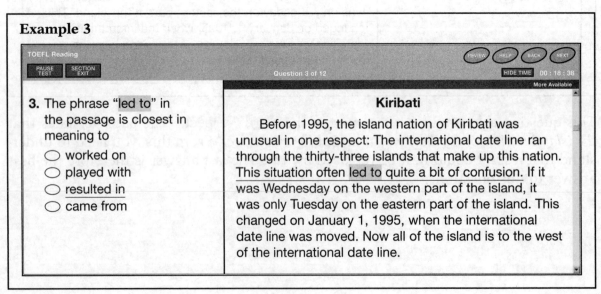

This question asks about the meaning of the phrase "led to." The passage states that *this situation often led to quite a bit of confusion.* From this, you need to understand that *led to* is closest in meaning to *resulted in.* The third answer is therefore the best answer to this question.

The following chart outlines the key information that you should remember about questions testing vocabulary from context.

QUESTIONS ABOUT VOCABULARY FROM CONTEXT	
HOW TO IDENTIFY THE QUESTION	The word (or phrase) X **is closest in meaning to ...** The word (or phrase) X **could best be replaced by ...**
WHERE TO FIND THE ANSWER	Information to help you to understand the meaning of an unknown word or phrase can often be found in the context surrounding the word or phrase.
HOW TO ANSWER THE QUESTION	1. Find the word or phrase in the passage. 2. Read the sentence that contains the word or phrase carefully. 3. Look for context clues to help you to understand the meaning. 4. Choose the answer that the context indicates.

READING EXERCISE 1: Study each of the passages, and choose the best answers to the questions that follow.

PASSAGE ONE (Questions 1–7)

Paragraph   **The Tournament of Roses**

▶1   The Tournament of Roses today is quite famous for the parade and football game that take place every year on January 1. On New Year's morning every year, a parade of flower-covered floats moves through the streets of Pasadena, California. Then, in the afternoon, a football game is contested between a university team from the western states and a rival team from farther east.

▶2   In its early days, the Tournament of Roses was quite different from the tournament of today. It had its beginning in 1890, when New Year's Day was celebrated in Pasadena with burro races and a parade of carriages covered with flowers.

▶3   A football game was not part of the Tournament of Roses until 1902. In that year, the west coast team lost the game badly. In fact, the team lost by a score of 49 to nothing. Because of the defeat, another football game was not played as a part of the Tournament of Roses for another fourteen years.

1. The word "famous" in paragraph 1 is closest in meaning to
   Ⓐ well-done
   Ⓑ well-known
   Ⓒ well-lit
   Ⓓ well-played

2. The phrase "take place" in paragraph 1 could best be replaced by
   Ⓐ run
   Ⓑ open
   Ⓒ occur
   Ⓓ locate

3. The word "contested" in paragraph 1 could best be replaced by
   Ⓐ argued
   Ⓑ watched
   Ⓒ studied
   Ⓓ played

4. The phrase "different from" in paragraph 2 could best be replaced by
   Ⓐ unlike
   Ⓑ after
   Ⓒ near
   Ⓓ like

5. The word "beginning" in paragraph 2 is closest in meaning to
   Ⓐ entrance
   Ⓑ start
   Ⓒ movement
   Ⓓ set

6. The word "badly" in paragraph 3 is closest in meaning to
   Ⓐ interestingly
   Ⓑ wonderfully
   Ⓒ importantly
   Ⓓ terribly

7. The word "defeat" in paragraph 3 is closest in meaning to
   Ⓐ loss
   Ⓑ start
   Ⓒ fun
   Ⓓ win

PASSAGE TWO (Questions 8–14)

Paragraph

Mark Twain

1▶ From the start of his career as a writer, Mark Twain was fascinated with inventions. As a result, he chose to spend much of his available income on various inventions, generally without much success. In fact, he lost a lot of the money he invested. By 1887, the forty-nine-year-old author had invested most of his money on one project, the Paige typesetting machine.

2▶ Twain expected the Paige machine to be completed in 1889. Unfortunately, the machine was never completely finished, and by the early 1890s, Twain knew he was in a serious financial situation. He worked hard to take care of his problems by producing a number of books in a row. He wrote *A Connecticut Yankee in King Arthur's Court* (1892), *An American Claimant* (1892), *Tom Sawyer Abroad* (1893), and *Pudd'nhead Wilson* (1894). However, all of this work did not solve his financial problems, and he was forced to declare bankruptcy.

8. The expression "As a result" in paragraph 1 could best be replaced by
   - Ⓐ Also
   - Ⓑ Furthermore
   - Ⓒ Therefore
   - Ⓓ However

9. The word "income" in paragraph 1 is closest in meaning to
   - Ⓐ time
   - Ⓑ money
   - Ⓒ work
   - Ⓓ space

10. The word "fact" in paragraph 1 is closest in meaning to
    - Ⓐ preparation
    - Ⓑ action
    - Ⓒ reality
    - Ⓓ motion

11. The word "completed" in paragraph 2 is closest in meaning to
    - Ⓐ finished
    - Ⓑ taken
    - Ⓒ interested
    - Ⓓ started

12. The word "serious" in paragraph 2 could best be replaced by
    - Ⓐ great
    - Ⓑ tired
    - Ⓒ pretty
    - Ⓓ grave

13. The expression "take care of" in paragraph 2 could best be replaced by
    - Ⓐ increase
    - Ⓑ exercise
    - Ⓒ comfort
    - Ⓓ solve

14. The expression "in a row" in paragraph 2 could best be replaced by
    - Ⓐ one after another
    - Ⓑ very slowly
    - Ⓒ on time
    - Ⓓ in a straight line

PASSAGE THREE (Questions 15–21)

Paragraph   **Copernicus**

1 From the early history of man, people believed that we lived in a geocentric universe. That is, they believed that the Earth was the center of the universe. They believed that the Sun, the Moon, and the planets revolved around the Earth. They had good reasons for these beliefs. It appeared to them that the Earth was stationary. It also appeared to them that the Sun, the Moon, and the planets were moving across the sky.

2 Nicolaus Copernicus (1473–1543) did not believe that the universe was geocentric; he did not accept the idea that the Earth was the center of the universe. He studied the movement of the stars and the planets carefully. He came to believe that our Earth was part of a heliocentric system. In a heliocentric system, planets revolve around a sun. Copernicus believed that our Earth revolved around the Sun. Most of the people living at that time believed the opposite. Today, we recognize that Copernicus was accurate.

15. In a "geocentric" universe in paragraph 1,

Ⓐ the Earth is in the middle of the universe

Ⓑ the Moon is in the middle of the universe

Ⓒ the Sun is in the middle of the universe

Ⓓ the Earth revolves around the Moon

16. In paragraph 1, "revolved around" could best be replaced by

Ⓐ lined up with

Ⓑ were different

Ⓒ outlined

Ⓓ circled

17. The word "stationary" in paragraph 1 is closest in meaning to

Ⓐ not dark

Ⓑ not moving

Ⓒ not quiet

Ⓓ not circular

18. The phrase "accept the idea" in paragraph 2 could best be replaced by

Ⓐ buy

Ⓑ think

Ⓒ remember

Ⓓ take

19. In a "heliocentric" universe in paragraph 2,

Ⓐ the Earth is in the middle of the universe

Ⓑ the Moon is in the middle of the universe

Ⓒ the Sun is in the middle of the universe

Ⓓ the Earth revolves around the Moon

20. The word "recognize" in paragraph 2 could best be replaced by

Ⓐ doubt

Ⓑ forget

Ⓒ understand

Ⓓ intend

21. The word "accurate" in paragraph 2 is closest in meaning to

Ⓐ wrong

Ⓑ nice

Ⓒ upset

Ⓓ correct

Reading Skill 2: RECOGNIZE REFERENTS

In the Reading section of the TOEFL *iBT,* you may have to find the referent for a particular pronoun (a referent is the noun that a pronoun refers to). You may be asked to find the referent for a third person subject pronoun (*he, she, it, they*). You may be asked to find the referent for a third person object pronoun (*him, her, it, them*). A referent generally precedes the pronoun in the passage. You should therefore look in front of the pronoun or adjective to find its referent. Look at an example of a question that asks for the referent of the subject pronoun *they*.

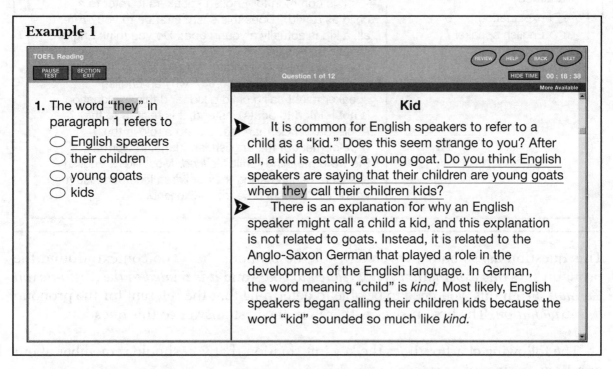

Example 1

TOEFL Reading

Question 1 of 12   00 : 18 : 38

1. The word "they" in paragraph 1 refers to
- ○ English speakers
- ○ their children
- ○ young goats
- ○ kids

Kid

1   It is common for English speakers to refer to a child as a "kid." Does this seem strange to you? After all, a kid is actually a young goat. Do you think English speakers are saying that their children are young goats when they call their children kids?

2   There is an explanation for why an English speaker might call a child a kid, and this explanation is not related to goats. Instead, it is related to the Anglo-Saxon German that played a role in the development of the English language. In German, the word meaning "child" is *kind.* Most likely, English speakers began calling their children kids because the word "kid" sounded so much like *kind.*

This question asks about the referent for the pronoun "they." The context around the pronoun asks *do you think English speakers are saying that their children are young goats when they call their children kids.* From this, you need to be able to determine that the referent for the pronoun *they* is *English speakers.* The first answer is therefore the best answer to this question.

Next, look at an example of a question that asks for the referent of the subject pronoun *it*.

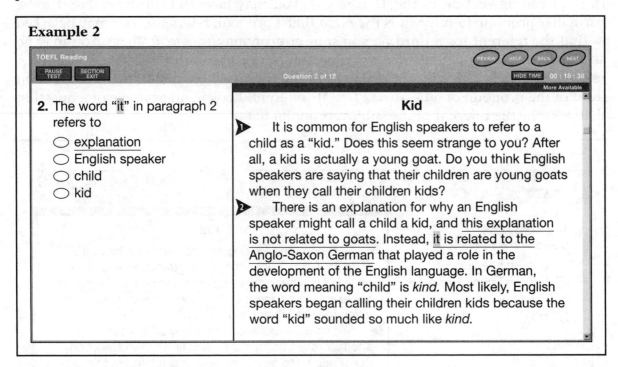

Example 2

TOEFL Reading
PAUSE TEST   SECTION EXIT
REVIEW   HELP   BACK   NEXT
Question 2 of 12
HIDE TIME   00 : 18 : 38
More Available

2. The word "it" in paragraph 2 refers to

○ explanation
○ English speaker
○ child
○ kid

Kid

▶ It is common for English speakers to refer to a child as a "kid." Does this seem strange to you? After all, a kid is actually a young goat. Do you think English speakers are saying that their children are young goats when they call their children kids?

▶ There is an explanation for why an English speaker might call a child a kid, and this explanation is not related to goats. Instead, it is related to the Anglo-Saxon German that played a role in the development of the English language. In German, the word meaning "child" is *kind*. Most likely, English speakers began calling their children kids because the word "kid" sounded so much like *kind*.

This question asks about the referent for the pronoun "it." The context around the pronoun says *this explanation is not related to goats* and *it is related to the Anglo-Saxon German*. From this, you need to be able to determine that the referent for the pronoun *it* is *explanation*. The first answer is therefore the best answer to this question.

The following chart outlines the key information that you should remember about questions testing referents.

QUESTIONS ABOUT REFERENTS	
HOW TO IDENTIFY THE QUESTION	The word X **refers** to ...
WHERE TO FIND THE ANSWER	The pronoun or adjective is highlighted in the passage. The referent generally comes before the highlighted pronoun or adjective.
HOW TO ANSWER THE QUESTION	1. Locate the highlighted pronoun or adjective. 2. Look for nouns *before* the highlighted word. 3. Try each of the nouns in the context around the highlighted word. 4. Choose the best answer.

READING EXERCISE 2: Study each of the passages, and choose the best answers to the questions that follow.

PASSAGE ONE *(Questions 1–3)*

Paragraph

Oxygen at High Altitudes

▶**1** There is less oxygen at high altitudes than there is at low altitudes. This lowered oxygen at high altitudes has an effect on people and animals that spend time visiting places at high altitudes. It makes them feel tired and out of breath at all times.

▶**2** Living beings who spend all of their time at high altitudes are able to adapt to shortages of oxygen. They adapt by producing more red blood cells or by having blood cells that live longer than average.

1. The word "It" in paragraph 1 refers to
   Ⓐ lowered oxygen
   Ⓑ an effect
   Ⓒ time
   Ⓓ breath

2. The word "them" in paragraph 1 refers to
   Ⓐ high altitudes
   Ⓑ people and animals
   Ⓒ places
   Ⓓ all times

3. The word "They" in paragraph 2 refers to
   Ⓐ living beings
   Ⓑ high altitudes
   Ⓒ shortages
   Ⓓ red blood cells

PASSAGE TWO (Questions 4–8)

Lascaux Cave

1 A few decades ago, four French schoolboys made an exciting discovery. They discovered a cave full of prehistoric paintings. The paintings were from 17,000 to 20,000 years ago.

2 The boys regularly spent their days in the outdoors. They discovered the cave one day while they were wandering around outside with their dog. The dog disappeared down a hole. The boys followed it down the hole and discovered the paintings.

3 The cave that the boys found has a number of rooms. It has one big main cave and a number of smaller rooms. There are passageways that connect the various rooms.

4 There are paintings on the walls throughout the cave. They show various animals, including bison, horses, rhinoceroses, and wolves. The animals are painted in red, yellow, brown, and black colors.

4. The word "They" in paragraph 1 refers to
   Ⓐ decades
   Ⓑ schoolboys
   Ⓒ paintings
   Ⓓ years

5. The word "They" in paragraph 2 refers to
   Ⓐ paintings
   Ⓑ boys
   Ⓒ days
   Ⓓ outdoors

6. The word "it" in paragraph 2 refers to
   Ⓐ cave
   Ⓑ day
   Ⓒ dog
   Ⓓ hole

7. The word "It" in paragraph 3 refers to
   Ⓐ dog
   Ⓑ hole
   Ⓒ cave
   Ⓓ number

8. The word "They" in paragraph 4 refers to
   Ⓐ rooms
   Ⓑ paintings
   Ⓒ walls
   Ⓓ animals

PASSAGE THREE (Questions 9–12)

Paragraph   **Pepper**

1   White and black pepper come from the same plant. They both come from the berry of a climbing vine called *Piper nigrum L.*

2   The berry of the *Piper nigrum L* is called a peppercorn. The peppercorn itself is not either black or white. When the peppercorn is on the vine, it has a green hue in the beginning. It first changes from green to yellow. Then it changes from yellow to red.

3   If you want to make black pepper, you must use younger berries. You pick the young berries and dry them. When you dry the berries, the outside skin becomes dark. At this point, the outside skin is dark, but the peppercorn inside is white. You then grind the peppercorn with the outside skin to make black pepper. Black pepper is really a ground mixture of the black skin and the white peppercorn. It looks black even though it is a mix of black and white.

4   If you want to make white pepper, you use older berries. You pick the older berries and then soak them in water. You soak the berries to remove the skin from the outside of the berries. When all of the pieces of skin are removed from the peppercorns, only the white berries from inside remain. You dry the white berries and then grind them to make batches of white pepper.

9. The word "They" in paragraph 1 refers to
   Ⓐ white and black pepper
   Ⓑ same plant
   Ⓒ the berry
   Ⓓ a climbing vine

10. The word "it" in paragraph 2 refers to
   Ⓐ the peppercorn
   Ⓑ the vine
   Ⓒ a green hue
   Ⓓ the beginning

11. The word "It" in paragraph 3 refers to
   Ⓐ black pepper
   Ⓑ a ground mixture
   Ⓒ the black skin
   Ⓓ the white peppercorn

12. The word "them" in paragraph 4 refers to
   Ⓐ the pieces
   Ⓑ the peppercorns
   Ⓒ the white berries
   Ⓓ batches

READING EXERCISE (Skills 1–2): Read the passage.

Paragraph
El Niño

▶ 1   El Niño conditions seem to take place approximately every three to seven years. They typically start in December, and they last around eighteen months, or a year and a half. During a regular El Niño event, trade winds are at below-average strength, and the patterns of temperature and precipitation on and around ocean waters are changed.

▶ 2   The changing temperature patterns involve temperature increases in some locales and temperature decreases in others. In the western part of the Pacific Ocean, the water becomes cooler than average; in the eastern part of the Pacific Ocean, it becomes warmer.

▶ 3   As the warm water moves east across the Pacific Ocean, wet weather accompanies it. The outcome is that countries to the west of the Pacific, such as China, are drier and chillier than usual during an El Niño event. Countries to the east of the Pacific, such as Peru, are wetter and hotter than normal.

Refer to this version of the passage to answer the questions that follow.

Paragraph
El Niño

▶ 1   El Niño conditions seem to take place approximately every three to seven years. They typically start in December, and they last around eighteen months, or a year and a half. During a regular El Niño event, trade winds are at below-average strength, and the patterns of temperature and precipitation on and around ocean waters are changed.

▶ 2   The changing temperature patterns involve temperature increases in some locales and temperature decreases in others. In the western part of the Pacific Ocean, the water becomes cooler than average; in the eastern part of the Pacific Ocean, it becomes warmer.

▶ 3   As the warm water moves east across the Pacific Ocean, wet weather accompanies it. The outcome is that countries to the west of the Pacific, such as China, are drier and chillier than usual during an El Niño event. Countries to the east of the Pacific, such as Peru, are wetter and hotter than normal.

1. The phrase "take place" in paragraph 1 is closest in meaning to
   Ⓐ live
   Ⓑ happen
   Ⓒ put
   Ⓓ open

2. The word "They" in paragraph 1 refers to
   Ⓐ conditions
   Ⓑ years
   Ⓒ months
   Ⓓ winds

3. The phrase "temperature and precipitation" in paragraph 1 is closest in meaning to
   Ⓐ travel
   Ⓑ change
   Ⓒ movement
   Ⓓ weather

4. The word "locales" in paragraph 2 is closest in meaning to
   Ⓐ measures
   Ⓑ places
   Ⓒ choices
   Ⓓ seasons

5. The word "part" in paragraph 2 could best be replaced by
   Ⓐ height
   Ⓑ pair
   Ⓒ section
   Ⓓ motion

6. The word "it" in paragraph 2 refers to
   Ⓐ the western part
   Ⓑ the water
   Ⓒ the eastern part
   Ⓓ the Pacific Ocean

7. The word "it" in paragraph 3 refers to
   Ⓐ the eastern part
   Ⓑ the warm water
   Ⓒ the Pacific Ocean
   Ⓓ wet weather

8. The word "outcome" in paragraph 3 is closest in meaning to
   Ⓐ result
   Ⓑ entrance
   Ⓒ idea
   Ⓓ cause

9. The word "chillier" in paragraph 3 is closest in meaning to
   Ⓐ wetter
   Ⓑ softer
   Ⓒ higher
   Ⓓ colder

10. The word "normal" in paragraph 3 is closest in meaning to
    Ⓐ usual
    Ⓑ here
    Ⓒ even
    Ⓓ expected

SENTENCES

Reading Skill 3: SIMPLIFY MEANINGS OF SENTENCES

In the Reading section of the TOEFL *iBT,* you may have to simplify the meaning of a long and difficult sentence. In this type of question, you must choose the one answer that is closest to the meaning of a sentence that is highlighted in the passage. Look at an example that asks how to simplify the meaning of a highlighted sentence.

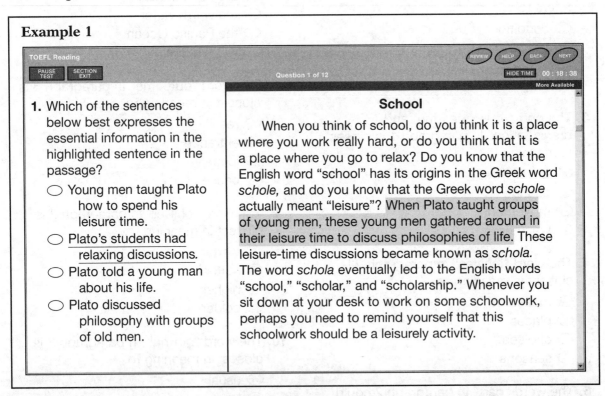

Example 1

TOEFL Reading

PAUSE TEST | SECTION EXIT

Question 1 of 12

HIDE TIME 00 : 18 : 38
More Available

REVIEW HELP BACK NEXT

1. Which of the sentences below best expresses the essential information in the highlighted sentence in the passage?

- ○ Young men taught Plato how to spend his leisure time.
- ○ Plato's students had relaxing discussions.
- ○ Plato told a young man about his life.
- ○ Plato discussed philosophy with groups of old men.

School

When you think of school, do you think it is a place where you work really hard, or do you think that it is a place where you go to relax? Do you know that the English word "school" has its origins in the Greek word *schole,* and do you know that the Greek word *schole* actually meant "leisure"? When Plato taught groups of young men, these young men gathered around in their leisure time to discuss philosophies of life. These leisure-time discussions became known as *schola.* The word *schola* eventually led to the English words "school," "scholar," and "scholarship." Whenever you sit down at your desk to work on some schoolwork, perhaps you need to remind yourself that this schoolwork should be a leisurely activity.

This question asks about the meaning of a difficult sentence. To answer this question, you should break the sentence down into parts. *When Plato taught groups of young men* in the passage refers to *Plato's students* in the second answer. *These young men gathered around in their leisure time to discuss philosophies of life* in the passage refers to *had relaxing discussions* in the second answer. From this, you can determine that the second answer is the best answer to this question.

Now look at another example that asks how to simplify the meaning of a high-lighted sentence.

Example 2

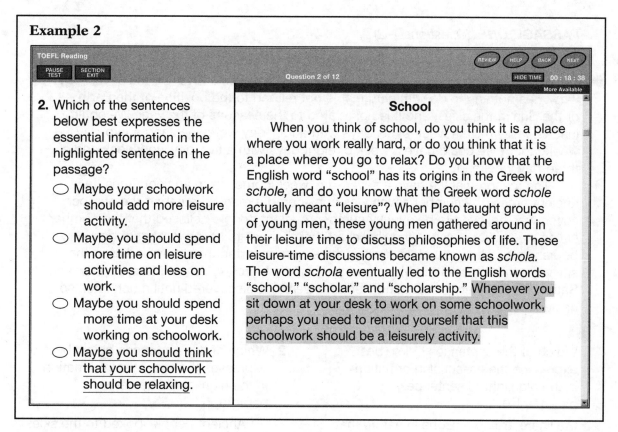

This question also asks about the meaning of a difficult sentence. To answer this question, you should break the sentence down into parts. *Whenever you sit down at your desk to work on some schoolwork* in the passage refers to *your schoolwork* in the last answer. *Perhaps you need to remind yourself* in the passage refers to *maybe you should think* in the last answer. *That this . . . should be a leisurely activity* in the passage refers to *should be relaxing* in the last answer. From this, you can determine that the last answer is the best answer to this question.

The following chart outlines the key information that you should remember about questions testing the simplified meanings of sentences.

QUESTIONS ABOUT SIMPLIFYING THE MEANINGS OF SENTENCES	
HOW TO IDENTIFY THE QUESTION	Which of the **sentences below** best expresses the **essential information** ...?
WHERE TO FIND THE ANSWER	The targeted sentence is highlighted in the passage. Information to answer the question is in the highlighted sentence and may also be in the context around the highlighted sentence.
HOW TO ANSWER THE QUESTION	1. Study the highlighted sentence carefully. 2. Break the sentence down into meaningful parts. 3. Read the context around the highlighted sentence. 4. Choose the best answer to the question.

READING EXERCISE 3: Study each of the passages, and choose the best answers to the questions that follow.

PASSAGE ONE (Questions 1–2)

Paragraph

Seven Days in a Week

➊ You may wonder why there are seven days in a week. After all, the seven-day week has nothing to do with nature; it is not related to the position of the Earth or the Sun in the skies, and it is not related to the seasons of the year. We could just as easily have a week of six days with a four-day workweek and a two-day weekend, or we could have a week of eight days with a five-day workweek and a three-day weekend.

➋ The reason that we have a seven-day week comes from ancient times. In ancient times, the number seven was considered a magical number; the number seven was believed to be a lucky number. Ancient people believed that the number seven was lucky because they believed that there were seven important heavenly bodies in the sky. To ancient people, the seven important heavenly bodies in the sky were the Sun and the Moon and the planets Mercury, Venus, Mars, Jupiter, and Saturn. The planets Uranus and Neptune were not discovered until much later, so ancient people did not know about them.

1. Which of the sentences below best expresses the essential information in the highlighted sentence in paragraph 1?

   Ⓐ There are no reasons in nature that a week has seven days.
   Ⓑ Because of the position of the Sun in the sky, we have a seven-day week.
   Ⓒ The position of the Earth in the sky is not related to the seasons of the year.
   Ⓓ The seven-day week is related to the seasons of the year.

2. Which of the sentences below best expresses the essential information in the highlighted sentence in paragraph 2?

   Ⓐ Ancient people looked to the skies because heavenly bodies were there.
   Ⓑ The number seven is in the shape of the heavenly bodies.
   Ⓒ Ancient people believed that there were seven heavenly bodies, and they were correct.
   Ⓓ People in ancient times thought that certain bodies in the sky made the number seven lucky.

PASSAGE TWO (Questions 3–5)

Paragraph

Communication Satellites

1   Today, many satellites are in orbit around Earth. Radio, telephone, and television signals are beamed up to satellites from transmitters on the ground. The signals are then beamed down from the satellites to receivers on Earth. The transmitters and receivers can be far apart on Earth, and signals can still be transmitted successfully.

2   Satellites have been around for only a relatively short period of time. The first communications satellite was launched in 1960. Up until 1960, there were not any rockets that were powerful enough to send a satellite into orbit.

3   Today, the space shuttle plays a big role with satellites. Satellites do not need to be launched from Earth because they can be launched from the space shuttle. The space shuttle also helps if a satellite breaks down. The space shuttle can be used to recapture satellites so that they can be repaired.

3. Which of the sentences below best expresses the essential information in the highlighted sentence in paragraph 1?

   Ⓐ Television signals can be seen on satellites.

   Ⓑ Many satellites send beams to transmitters.

   Ⓒ Many kinds of signals are sent from the ground to satellites.

   Ⓓ Satellites send radio, telephone, and television signals to the ground.

4. Which of the sentences below best expresses the essential information in the highlighted sentence in paragraph 2?

   Ⓐ Since 1960, all satellites have traveled on rockets.

   Ⓑ No rocket was able to push a satellite into space before 1960.

   Ⓒ There were not many rockets until 1960.

   Ⓓ Satellites in use before 1960 were not very powerful.

5. Which of the sentences below best expresses the essential information in the highlighted sentence in paragraph 3?

   Ⓐ Today, satellites are sent from Earth to the space shuttle.

   Ⓑ The space shuttle does not need to be launched from Earth.

   Ⓒ Today, there are fewer satellites because of the space shuttle.

   Ⓓ Because of the space shuttle, it is not necessary to send satellites from Earth.

PASSAGE THREE (Questions 6–9)

Paragraph

Alexander's Gold

▶ 1 Alexander the Great was one of the greatest gatherers of gold in history. Alexander inherited the kingdom of Macedonia in northern Greece at a young age. He gathered a huge army and advanced from Macedonia through Persia, much of western Asia, Egypt, and India. He conquered an extraordinary amount of land; he conquered more land than anyone who came before him.

▶ 2 As Alexander traveled and conquered, he was always on the hunt for gold. Some of his men were experts in finding deposits of gold. However, finding deposits of gold was not the only way that Alexander got gold. He also took the public wealth of the cities he conquered and the private wealth of the citizens of those cities. Throughout his travels, he gathered huge amounts of gold.

▶ 3 It was a problem for Alexander's men to transport so much gold because the huge amount of gold Alexander possessed was so heavy. To solve this problem, Alexander had his men dig holes and bury some of the gold in hidden places along his route. Some of this gold has been found by treasure hunters, but experts believe that much of Alexander's gold is still hidden.

6. Which of the sentences below best expresses the essential information in the highlighted sentence in paragraph 1?

Ⓐ Alexander conquered many of the conquerors who came before him.

Ⓑ Alexander was an extraordinary man who conquered many people.

Ⓒ Alexander was the first person to conquer so much land.

Ⓓ Alexander wanted to travel through more lands than any other person.

7. Which of the sentences below best expresses the essential information in the highlighted sentence in paragraph 2?

Ⓐ Alexander took gold from cities and from people.

Ⓑ Alexander gave the wealth of private citizens to the cities.

Ⓒ Alexander became wealthy because he was a private citizen.

Ⓓ Alexander used the wealth of citizens to conquer cities.

8. Which of the sentences below best expresses the essential information in the first highlighted sentence in paragraph 3?

Ⓐ Alexander's men found it hard to travel because they were heavy.

Ⓑ Alexander solved a problem by finding a lot of gold.

Ⓒ Alexander's gold was much heavier than other gold.

Ⓓ It was hard to carry so much gold because of the weight of the gold.

9. Which of the sentences below best expresses the essential information in the second highlighted sentence in paragraph 3?

Ⓐ Alexander did not do a good job of hiding his gold.

Ⓑ People have probably found only part of Alexander's gold.

Ⓒ Treasure hunters have found all of Alexander's gold.

Ⓓ Alexander has not yet been found by treasure hunters.

Reading Skill 4: INSERT SENTENCES INTO THE PASSAGE

In the Reading section of the TOEFL *iBT,* you may have to decide where to insert sentences into a passage. In this type of question, you must click on one of a number of squares in a passage to show that the sentence should be added there. Look at an example that asks where to insert a sentence.

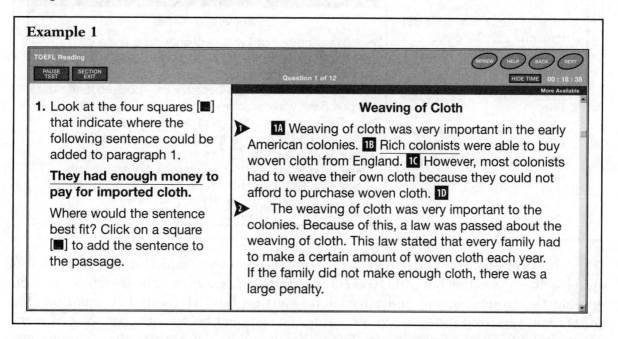

This question asks you to decide where a sentence could be added to one of the paragraphs. To answer this question, you should study the sentence to be inserted and then look at the context before and after each insertion box. The sentence states that *they had enough money,* and the context before insertion box **1C** mentions *rich colonists.* From this, it can be determined that the sentence should be added at insertion box **1C**. You should click on **1C** to answer this question.

Now look at another example that asks where to insert a sentence.

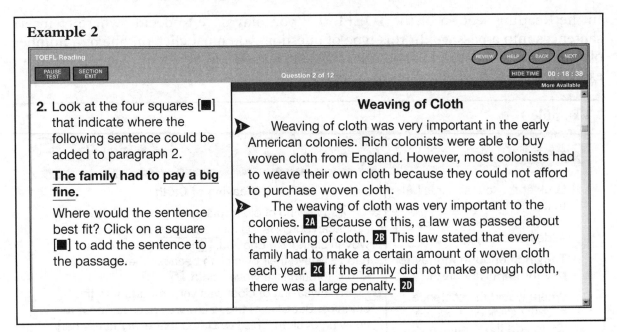

Example 2

TOEFL Reading

PAUSE TEST   SECTION EXIT

REVIEW   HELP   BACK   NEXT

Question 2 of 12

HIDE TIME   00 : 16 : 38

More Available

2. Look at the four squares [■] that indicate where the following sentence could be added to paragraph 2.

The family had to pay a big fine.

Where would the sentence best fit? Click on a square [■] to add the sentence to the passage.

Weaving of Cloth

1 ▶ Weaving of cloth was very important in the early American colonies. Rich colonists were able to buy woven cloth from England. However, most colonists had to weave their own cloth because they could not afford to purchase woven cloth.

2 ▶ The weaving of cloth was very important to the colonies. **2A** Because of this, a law was passed about the weaving of cloth. **2B** This law stated that every family had to make a certain amount of woven cloth each year. **2C** If the family did not make enough cloth, there was a large penalty. **2D**

This question asks you to decide where a sentence could be added to one of the paragraphs. To answer this question, you should study the sentence to be inserted and then look at the context before and after each insertion box. The sentence mentions *the family* and says that it has to *pay a big fine*. The context before insertion box **2D** mentions *the family* and *a large penalty*. From this, it can be determined that the sentence should be added at insertion box **2D**. You should click on **2D** to answer the question.

The following chart outlines the key information that you should remember about questions that ask where to insert a sentence.

QUESTIONS ABOUT INSERTING SENTENCES	
HOW TO IDENTIFY THE QUESTION	Look at the **four squares [■]** ...
WHERE TO FIND THE ANSWER	The places where the sentence may be inserted are marked in the passage.
HOW TO ANSWER THE QUESTION	1. Look at the sentence to be inserted. Look for any key words or ideas at the beginning or the end of the sentence. 2. Read the context before and after the insertion squares for any ideas that relate to the sentence to be inserted. 3. Choose the insertion square that is most related to the sentence to be inserted.

READING EXERCISE 4: Study each of the passages, and choose the best answers to the questions that follow.

PASSAGE ONE (Questions 1–2)

Paragraph
Dinosaur Footprints

1 　　**1A** The first dinosaur footprints in America were discovered by a twelve-year-old boy in 1802. **1B** The boy, named Pliny Moody, was working on his family farm in western Massachusetts when he saw something very strange. **1C** He saw a flat piece of stone with huge footprints on it. **1D**

2 　　Pliny told his family and friends that he had discovered something unusual. **2A** However, no one at the time knew that these were dinosaur footprints. **2B** This was some time before the word "dinosaur" had been created. **2C** Today, we know that the footprints that Pliny discovered and reported were made by the dinosaurs that had lived in the area millions of years earlier. **2D**

1. Look at the four squares [■] that indicate where the following sentence could be added to paragraph 1.

The footprints were in the shape of the footprints of a bird, but they were much bigger.

Where would the sentence best fit? Click on a square [■] to add the sentence to the paragraph.

2. Look at the four squares [■] that indicate where the following sentence could be added to paragraph 2.

The word "dinosaur" was not invented until 1841.

Where would the sentence best fit? Click on a square [■] to add the sentence to the paragraph.

PASSAGE TWO *(Questions 3–5)*

The Washington Monument

Paragraph

➤ 1   **3A** The Washington Monument in Washington, D.C., was built to honor the first president of the United States. **3B** The monument dedicated to George Washington is a tall, thin structure built in the shape of an obelisk. **3C** At a height of 555 feet, it is the tallest stone structure in the world. **3D**

➤ 2   **4A** The monument was first planned in 1783. **4B** However, it actually took more than a century to finish. **4C** The monument took so long to build, in part, because of how money was collected to build it. **4D**

➤ 3   **5A** The money for the monument came from donations. **5B** Work on the monument progressed slowly because the money came in slowly. **5C** As money was raised, more work was done. **5D** The monument was not completely built until 1884.

3. Look at the four squares [■] that indicate where the following sentence could be added to paragraph 1.

An obelisk is a four-sided stone pillar with a pyramid shape on top.

Where would the sentence best fit? Click on a square [■] to add the sentence to the paragraph.

4. Look at the four squares [■] that indicate where the following sentence could be added to paragraph 2.

This was the year when the Revolutionary War officially ended.

Where would the sentence best fit? Click on a square [■] to add the sentence to the paragraph.

5. Look at the four squares [■] that indicate where the following sentence could be added to paragraph 3.

These gifts from individual people were limited to one dollar each.

Where would the sentence best fit? Click on a square [■] to add the sentence to the paragraph.

PASSAGE THREE (Questions 6–8)

Paragraph

Alex Haley

1　　American author Alex Haley (1921–1992) became very famous as the author of the book *Roots: The Saga of an American Family.* In this book, Haley described the history of his family through a combination of fact and fiction.

2　　**6A** Throughout his youth, Haley had heard stories of his family history. **6B** These stories were about an ancestor of his called "The African." **6C**

3　　**7A** While Haley was in Washington, D.C., one day, he went to the National Archives. **7B** He went there to find information about early family members, and he succeeded in his search. **7C** This success encouraged him to spend the next twelve years researching and making his family history. **7D**

4　　When Haley's book appeared in 1976, it received a large amount of praise and recognition. **8A** The book was also awarded the Pulitzer Prize in that year. **8B** Then it was made into a television series, which was shown in 1977 and 1979. **8C** This series attracted a large number of viewers. **8D**

6. Look at the four squares [■] that indicate where the following sentence could be added to paragraph 2.

This ancestor had been brought to America two centuries earlier on a slave ship.

Where would the sentence best fit? Click on a square [■] to add the sentence to the paragraph.

7. Look at the four squares [■] that indicate where the following sentence could be added to paragraph 3.

He found some information there about his great-grandfather.

Where would the sentence best fit? Click on a square [■] to add the sentence to the paragraph.

8. Look at the four squares [■] that indicate where the following sentence could be added to paragraph 4.

More than 130 million people watched the "Roots" series.

Where would the sentence best fit? Click on a square [■] to add the sentence to the paragraph.

READING EXERCISE (Skills 3–4): Read the passage.

Paragraph   **3D Movies**

▶ ① To accomplish a three-dimensional, or 3D, effect in a movie, two steps are necessary. First, the movie needs to be shot in a special way. Then, the movie needs to be viewed in a special way.

▶ ② To shoot a 3D movie, it is necessary to use two cameras at the same time. The two cameras are placed next to each other. The placement of the cameras imitates how two eyes each see one scene from a different perspective. The same picture is shot by each of the cameras at the same time, but each of the cameras films the scene from a different angle because of the position of the cameras.

▶ ③ When you go to a theater to view a 3D film, you must wear special glasses to get the three-dimensional effect. Both pieces of film are projected simultaneously; when the pieces of film are projected at the same time, the special glasses then force each of your eyes to see the film in a different way. Your left eye sees the film shot with the left camera, and your right eye sees the film shot with the right camera. If you try to watch the movie without the special glasses, it will seem like you have double vision.

Refer to this version of the passage to answer the questions that follow.

Paragraph   **3D Movies**

▶ ① To accomplish a three-dimensional, or 3D, effect in a movie, two steps are necessary. First, the movie needs to be shot in a special way. Then, the movie needs to be viewed in a special way.

▶ ② **2A** To shoot a 3D movie, it is necessary to use two cameras at the same time. **2B** The two cameras are placed next to each other. **2C** The placement of the cameras imitates how two eyes each see one scene from a different perspective. **2D** The same picture is shot by each of the cameras at the same time, but each of the cameras films the scene from a different angle because of the position of the cameras.

▶ ③ When you go to a theater to view a 3D film, you must wear special glasses to get the three-dimensional effect. **4A** Both pieces of film are projected simultaneously; when the pieces of film are projected at the same time, the special glasses then force each of your eyes to see the film in a different way. **4B** Your left eye sees the film shot with the left camera, and your right eye sees the film shot with the right camera. **4C** If you try to watch the movie without the special glasses, it will seem like you have double vision. **4D**

1. Which of the sentences below best expresses the essential information in the highlighted sentence in paragraph 1?

   Ⓐ Two steps are needed to make a movie.
   Ⓑ A 3D effect is impossible to do.
   Ⓒ Two things are needed to create a 3D movie.
   Ⓓ If a movie is in 3D, two things are needed to watch it.

2. Look at the four squares [■] that indicate where the following sentence could be added to paragraph 2.

   This is different from a regular movie, which is shot with only one camera.

   Where would the sentence best fit? Click on a square [■] to add the sentence to the paragraph.

3. Which of the sentences below best expresses the essential information in the highlighted sentence in paragraph 2?

   Ⓐ Two cameras shoot the same picture at the same time but from different angles.
   Ⓑ Two cameras shoot different pictures at different times and from different angles.
   Ⓒ Two cameras shoot different pictures at different times but from the same angle.
   Ⓓ Two cameras shoot the same picture at the same time and from the same angle.

4. Look at the four squares [■] that indicate where the following sentence could be added to paragraph 3.

   The movie will seem very unclear and fuzzy.

   Where would the sentence best fit? Click on a square [■] to add the sentence to the paragraph.

5. Which of the sentences below best expresses the essential information in the highlighted sentence in paragraph 3?

   Ⓐ The picture will be clear if you watch a 3D movie without special glasses.
   Ⓑ The picture will not be clear if you watch a 3D movie with 3D glasses.
   Ⓒ The picture will be clear if you watch a 3D movie with 3D glasses.
   Ⓓ The picture will not be clear if you watch a double movie with special glasses.

READING REVIEW EXERCISE (Skills 1–4): Read the passage.

Paragraph

Paul Revere in Longfellow's Poem

1 Paul Revere was recognized in Longfellow's poem "The Midnight Ride of Paul Revere" for his act of heroism during Revolutionary times. In this well-known poem, Longfellow describes how Paul Revere made a nighttime ride on horseback. The purpose of this famous ride was to warn the Concord militia that the British were planning to attack.

2 However, Longfellow's poem does not recount the historical events accurately. In reality, Paul Revere did not travel alone on his important ride. Instead, he met up with William Dawes in Lexington. These two set out for Concord with a Dr. Samuel Prescott, who was on his way home.

3 On the way between Lexington and Concord, the three were stopped by some British soldiers. Revere became a prisoner of the British soldiers, and Dawes managed to escape from them. It was Dr. Prescott rather than Paul Revere who got through to Concord to warn the American defenders of the British attack that was coming. However, it was Paul Revere and not Dr. Prescott who received the credit for the heroic deed in Longfellow's poem.

Refer to this version of the passage to answer the questions that follow.

Paragraph

Paul Revere in Longfellow's Poem

1 **3A** Paul Revere was recognized in Longfellow's poem "The Midnight Ride of Paul Revere" for his act of heroism during Revolutionary times. **3B** In this well-known poem, Longfellow describes how Paul Revere made a nighttime ride on horseback. **3C** The purpose of this famous ride was to warn the Concord militia that the British were planning to attack. **3D**

2 However, Longfellow's poem does not recount the historical events accurately. In reality, Paul Revere did not travel alone on his important ride. Instead, he met up with William Dawes in Lexington. These two set out for Concord with a Dr. Samuel Prescott, who was on his way home.

3 **10A** On the way between Lexington and Concord, the three were stopped by some British soldiers. **10B** Revere became a prisoner of the British soldiers, and Dawes managed to escape from them. **10C** It was Dr. Prescott rather than Paul Revere who got through to Concord to warn the American defenders of the British attack that was coming. **10D** However, it was Paul Revere and not Dr. Prescott who received the credit for the heroic deed in Longfellow's poem.

1. The word "well-known" in paragraph 1 is closest in meaning to
   (A) wonderful
   (B) historic
   (C) long
   (D) famous

2. Which of the sentences below best expresses the essential information in the highlighted sentence in paragraph 1?
   (A) The British made the ride to warn the Concord militia of an attack.
   (B) The ride was made because a warning of a planned attack was needed.
   (C) The ride occurred during an attack of the British on the Concord militia.
   (D) The purpose of the ride was to tell the militia about an attack that had happened.

3. Look at the four squares [■] that indicate where the following sentence could be inserted into paragraph 1.

   This ride was from Lexington to Concord.

   Where would the sentence best fit? Click on a square [■] to add the sentence to the paragraph.

4. The word "recount" in paragraph 2 is closest in meaning to
   (A) remember
   (B) number
   (C) describe
   (D) add

5. The word "he" in paragraph 2 refers to
   (A) Longfellow
   (B) Paul Revere
   (C) William Dawes
   (D) Dr. Samuel Prescott

6. The phrase "set out for" in paragraph 2 could best be replaced by
   (A) headed toward
   (B) arrived from
   (C) located
   (D) positioned

7. The word "way" in paragraph 3 could best be replaced by
   (A) manner
   (B) purpose
   (C) trip
   (D) walk

8. The word "them" in paragraph 3 refers to
   (A) these two
   (B) the three
   (C) British soldiers
   (D) American defenders

9. Which of the sentences below best expresses the essential information in the highlighted sentence in paragraph 3?
   (A) Dr. Prescott was not the hero in Longfellow's poem, and Paul Revere was.
   (B) Both Dr. Prescott and Paul Revere were considered heroes in Longfellow's poem.
   (C) In Longfellow's poem, Dr. Prescott was considered a hero, and Paul Revere was not.
   (D) In Longfellow's poem, neither Dr. Prescott nor Paul Revere was considered a hero.

10. Look at the four squares [■] that indicate where the following sentence could be inserted into paragraph 3.

    Dr. Prescott was the only one who continued on his way.

    Where would the sentence best fit? Click on a square [■] to add the sentence to the paragraph.

DETAILS

Reading Skill 5: FIND FACTUAL INFORMATION

In the Reading section of the TOEFL *iBT,* you may have to answer questions about factual information. The answers to these multiple-choice questions are often restatements of words in the passage. This means that the correct answer has the same idea as something in the passage but uses different words to express the idea. The answers to these questions are generally given in order in the passage, and the questions generally tell you which paragraph contains the answers. Because of this, it is not too difficult to find answers in the passage. Look at an example of a factual information question.

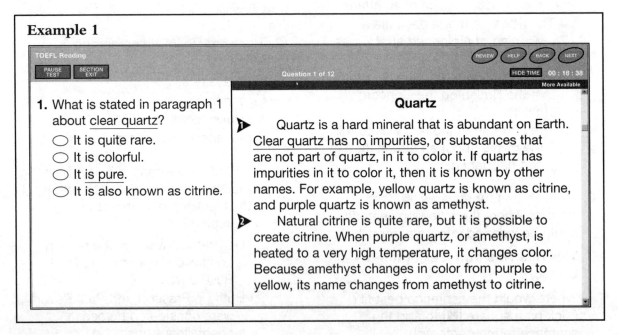

This question asks about what is stated in paragraph 1. It is stated in paragraph 1 that *clear quartz has no impurities.* From this, you need to understand that *clear quartz . . . is pure.* The third answer is therefore the best answer to this question.

Now look at another example of a factual information question.

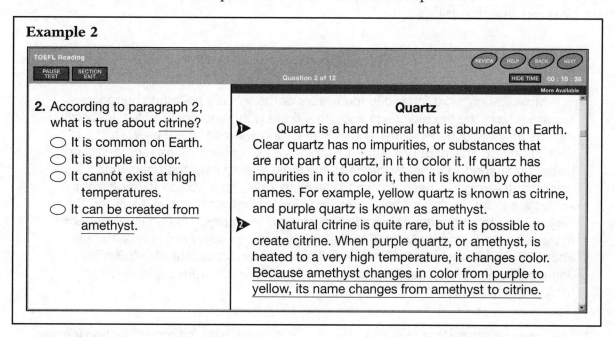

Example 2

2. According to paragraph 2, what is true about citrine?
  ○ It is common on Earth.
  ○ It is purple in color.
  ○ It cannot exist at high temperatures.
  ○ It can be created from amethyst.

Quartz

Quartz is a hard mineral that is abundant on Earth. Clear quartz has no impurities, or substances that are not part of quartz, in it to color it. If quartz has impurities in it to color it, then it is known by other names. For example, yellow quartz is known as citrine, and purple quartz is known as amethyst.

Natural citrine is quite rare, but it is possible to create citrine. When purple quartz, or amethyst, is heated to a very high temperature, it changes color. Because amethyst changes in color from purple to yellow, its name changes from amethyst to citrine.

This question asks about what is true according to paragraph 2. It is stated in paragraph 2 that *because amethyst changes in color from purple to yellow, its name changes from amethyst to citrine.* From this, you need to understand that *citrine can be created from amethyst.* The last answer is therefore the best answer to this question.

The following chart outlines the key information that you should remember about questions testing details.

QUESTIONS ABOUT FACTUAL INFORMATION	
HOW TO IDENTIFY THE QUESTION	**According to** paragraph X ... It is **stated** in paragraph X ... It is **indicated** in paragraph X ... It is **mentioned** in paragraph X ...
WHERE TO FIND THE ANSWER	These answers are generally found in order in the passage, and the paragraph where the answer is found is generally indicated in the question.
HOW TO ANSWER THE QUESTION	1. Choose a key word or phrase in the question. 2. Scan the appropriate paragraph for the key word or phrase (or related idea). 3. Read the sentence that contains the key word or phrase (or related idea) carefully. 4. Choose the best answer.

READING EXERCISE 5: Study each of the passages, and choose the best answers to the questions that follow.

PASSAGE ONE *(Questions 1–5)*

Icebergs

Most icebergs are formed in the waters of the world's polar and subpolar regions. These are the regions in and around the north and south poles. Icebergs melt as they encounter warmer ocean waters and warmer ocean breezes closer to the equator. This happens with most, but not all, icebergs. One record-setting iceberg managed to travel farther from the frigid waters near the poles than any other iceberg has been known to travel. In 1894, an iceberg broke off from Antarctica in the south and began moving slowly northward. It eventually left the very cold waters near the pole and entered warmer waters. This unusual iceberg managed to get amazingly close to the equator. It was observed at a latitude of about 26 degrees south of the equator. This is on the same latitude as Rio de Janeiro, Brazil, which is famous for its comfortably warm waters and weather throughout the year.

1. The passage states that icebergs form
   - Ⓐ only in the north
   - Ⓑ only in the south
   - Ⓒ near the equator
   - Ⓓ in both the north and south

2. According to the passage, where are subpolar regions located?
   - Ⓐ At the North Pole
   - Ⓑ Close to the poles
   - Ⓒ Close to the equator
   - Ⓓ At the equator

3. The record-setting iceberg mentioned in the passage traveled
   - Ⓐ into unusually warm waters
   - Ⓑ unusually close to the North Pole
   - Ⓒ unusually far south
   - Ⓓ unusually far from the equator

4. When did the record-setting iceberg mentioned in the passage exist?
   - Ⓐ In the first half of the eighteenth century
   - Ⓑ In the last half of the eighteenth century
   - Ⓒ In the first half of the nineteenth century
   - Ⓓ In the last half of the nineteenth century

5. According to the passage, the iceberg was seen
   - Ⓐ in Rio de Janeiro
   - Ⓑ far north of Rio de Janeiro
   - Ⓒ as far north as Rio de Janeiro
   - Ⓓ far south of Rio de Janeiro

PASSAGE TWO *(Questions 6–12)*

Paragraph

Submarines

1▶   Some people have a mistaken belief. They mistakenly believe that submarines are a fairly recent invention. However, the truth is different. The truth is that submarines have actually been around, and in use, for hundreds of years.

2▶   Submarines were actually used during the American Revolutionary War, though they were not very successful. The *Turtle* was a one-man wooden submarine that was used by the American side during the Revolutionary War. In 1776, the Americans used the submarine to try to attach a mine to an English ship to blow it up. They wanted to do this because the ship was in New York Harbor to block the Americans from using the harbor. In order to attach the mine to the English ship, an American man went underwater in a submarine in the harbor. However, when the man was underwater in the submarine, too much carbon dioxide built up inside the submarine, and the man could not think clearly. Because he was not able to think clearly, he was not able to attach the mine properly to the English ship. The man did manage to return to the surface of the water; the man, the submarine, and the English ship all came out of this situation successfully.

6. According to paragraph 1, what mistaken belief do some people have?

Ⓐ That submarines were never invented

Ⓑ That submarines took hundreds of years to invent

Ⓒ That submarines were used during the American Revolution

Ⓓ That submarines were not invented long ago

7. According to the passage, what is the real situation?

Ⓐ That submarines were never invented

Ⓑ That submarines took hundreds of years to invent

Ⓒ That submarines were not used during the American Revolution

Ⓓ That submarines were invented long ago

8. What is stated in the passage about the *Turtle*?

Ⓐ It was an underwater boat.

Ⓑ It was made of metal.

Ⓒ It held two people.

Ⓓ It was used by the British against the Americans.

9. What did the Americans want to do with the *Turtle,* according to the passage?

Ⓐ Open a mine

Ⓑ Destroy a British ship

Ⓒ Block New York Harbor

Ⓓ Blow up an American ship

10. The passage states that the man inside the *Turtle*

Ⓐ refused to go underwater

Ⓑ went swimming in the harbor

Ⓒ developed a problem in his head

Ⓓ blew up the British ship

11. According to the passage, what caused the man's problem?

Ⓐ An excess of carbon dioxide

Ⓑ Too much water in the submarine

Ⓒ Too little carbon dioxide

Ⓓ Too little time underwater

12. The passage indicates that the English ship

Ⓐ sank in New York Harbor

Ⓑ was not damaged

Ⓒ hit the submarine

Ⓓ was blown up

PASSAGE THREE *(Questions 13–19)*

Paragraph   **Sugar**

▶1   There are many kinds of sugar. Some of the many kinds are cane sugar, beet sugar, maple sugar, palm sugar, and corn sugar. The two most widely used kinds of sugar are cane sugar and beet sugar.

▶2   It is generally believed that sugarcane was first grown in India. Sugarcane is the plant that is used to make sugar from cane, or cane sugar. From India, the sugarcane plant moved into other parts of Asia as well as North Africa and Europe. Christopher Columbus was well acquainted with sugarcane because his wife's mother owned a sugarcane plantation on the island of Madeira. It was Christopher Columbus who introduced sugarcane to the Americas on his second voyage there. The production of sugarcane grew rapidly in the Americas after its introduction there.

▶3   Sugar beets are another major source of sugar in addition to the sugar obtained from sugarcane. Napoleon is often given credit for the increased use of sugar from sugar beets. After the French lost a sea battle to the British in 1805, the British fleet created a blockade that stopped supplies of sugarcane from coming into France. Napoleon offered a large prize to someone who could develop a good method of producing sugar from sugar beets. As a result, huge crops of sugar beets were grown by farmers, and forty factories to produce sugar from sugar beets were created.

13. It is stated in paragraph 1 that palm sugar is

- Ⓐ one of four kinds of sugar
- Ⓑ one of the kinds of sugar that is used least
- Ⓒ one of the two most widely used kinds of sugar
- Ⓓ the most widely used kind of sugar

14. According to paragraph 2, sugar originally came from

- Ⓐ India
- Ⓑ northern Asia
- Ⓒ North Africa
- Ⓓ Europe

15. Which of the following is true, according to paragraph 2?

- Ⓐ Sugarcane is a kind of sugar.
- Ⓑ Cane sugar is a kind of plant.
- Ⓒ Sugarcane is made from cane sugar.
- Ⓓ Cane sugar is made from sugarcane.

16. It is indicated in paragraph 2 that Christopher Columbus

- Ⓐ knew nothing about sugarcane
- Ⓑ owned a sugarcane plantation
- Ⓒ brought sugarcane from the Americas
- Ⓓ brought sugarcane to the Americas

17. According to paragraph 3, sugar beets

Ⓐ provide a lot of sugar

Ⓑ provide more sugar than sugarcane

Ⓒ do not provide much sugar

Ⓓ come from sugarcane

18. What is stated in paragraph 3 about Napoleon?

Ⓐ He won a battle in 1805.

Ⓑ He created a blockade.

Ⓒ He stopped sugarcane from coming into France.

Ⓓ He wanted to increase the production of sugar from sugar beets.

19. According to paragraph 3, what happened after Napoleon offered a certain prize?

Ⓐ The French lost a sea battle to the British.

Ⓑ Farmers began working in factories.

Ⓒ The production of sugar from sugar beets increased.

Ⓓ Factories began producing sugar from sugarcane.

Reading Skill 6: UNDERSTAND NEGATIVE FACTS

In the Reading section of the TOEFL *iBT,* you may have to find an answer that is *not stated,* or *not mentioned,* or *not true* in the passage. This type of question really means that three of the answers are *stated, mentioned,* or *true* in the passage, while one answer is NOT.

You should note that there are two kinds of answers to this type of question. First, there are three answers that are true and one that is *not true* according to the passage. Second, there are three true answers and one that is *not stated* or *not mentioned* in the passage. Look at an example that asks you to find the one answer that is *not true.*

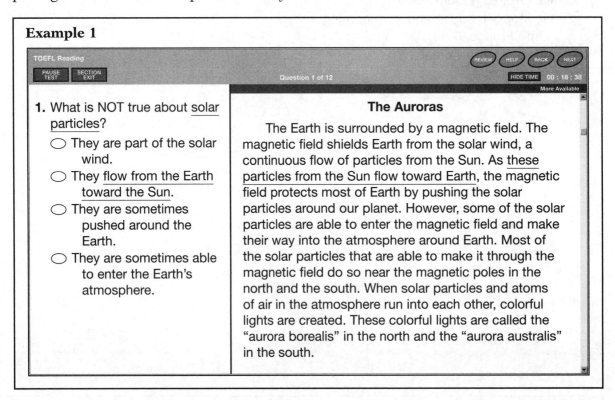

Example 1

TOEFL Reading REVIEW HELP BACK NEXT

PAUSE TEST | SECTION EXIT | Question 1 of 12 | HIDE TIME 00 : 18 : 38

More Available

1. What is NOT true about solar particles?
- ○ They are part of the solar wind.
- ○ They flow from the Earth toward the Sun.
- ○ They are sometimes pushed around the Earth.
- ○ They are sometimes able to enter the Earth's atmosphere.

The Auroras

The Earth is surrounded by a magnetic field. The magnetic field shields Earth from the solar wind, a continuous flow of particles from the Sun. As these particles from the Sun flow toward Earth, the magnetic field protects most of Earth by pushing the solar particles around our planet. However, some of the solar particles are able to enter the magnetic field and make their way into the atmosphere around Earth. Most of the solar particles that are able to make it through the magnetic field do so near the magnetic poles in the north and the south. When solar particles and atoms of air in the atmosphere run into each other, colorful lights are created. These colorful lights are called the "aurora borealis" in the north and the "aurora australis" in the south.

This question asks you to determine which of the answers is NOT true. This means that three of the answers are true and one is NOT. To answer this type of question, you must find the one answer that is NOT true according to the information in the passage. It is stated in the passage that *these particles from the Sun flow toward Earth.* This means that it is NOT true that *solar particles flow from the Earth toward the Sun.* The second answer is therefore the best answer to this question.

The next example asks you to find the one answer that is *not mentioned.*

Example 2

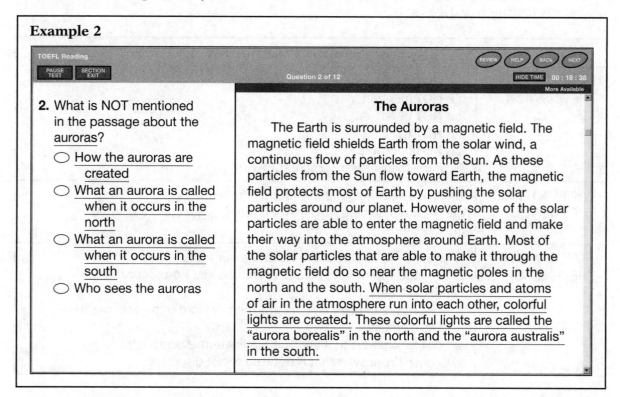

TOEFL Reading

PAUSE TEST   SECTION EXIT

Question 2 of 12

REVIEW   HELP   BACK   NEXT

HIDE TIME   00 : 18 : 38
More Available

2. What is NOT mentioned in the passage about the auroras?
   ○ How the auroras are created
   ○ What an aurora is called when it occurs in the north
   ○ What an aurora is called when it occurs in the south
   ○ Who sees the auroras

The Auroras

The Earth is surrounded by a magnetic field. The magnetic field shields Earth from the solar wind, a continuous flow of particles from the Sun. As these particles from the Sun flow toward Earth, the magnetic field protects most of Earth by pushing the solar particles around our planet. However, some of the solar particles are able to enter the magnetic field and make their way into the atmosphere around Earth. Most of the solar particles that are able to make it through the magnetic field do so near the magnetic poles in the north and the south. When solar particles and atoms of air in the atmosphere run into each other, colorful lights are created. These colorful lights are called the "aurora borealis" in the north and the "aurora australis" in the south.

This question asks you to determine which of the answers is NOT mentioned in the passage. This means that three of the answers are mentioned in the passage and one of the answers is NOT mentioned. To answer this kind of question, you must find the three answers that are in the passage and then choose the remaining answer as the correct answer. The passage states that *when solar particles and atoms of air in the atmosphere run into each other, colorful lights are created,* which describes *how the auroras are created* in the first answer. The passage also states that *these colorful lights are called the "aurora borealis" in the north and the "aurora australis" in the south,* which explains *what an aurora is called when it occurs in the north* in the second answer and *what an aurora is called when it occurs in the south* in the third answer. The last answer is the one that is NOT mentioned and is therefore the best answer to this question.

The following chart outlines the key information that you should remember about questions testing negative facts.

QUESTIONS ABOUT NEGATIVE FACTS	
HOW TO IDENTIFY THE QUESTION	It is **NOT** stated … It is **NOT** mentioned … It is **NOT** discussed … It is **NOT** true … It is **NOT** indicated … All of the following are **true EXCEPT** …
WHERE TO FIND THE ANSWER	These answers are generally found in order in the passage, and the paragraph where the answer is found is generally indicated in the question.
HOW TO ANSWER THE QUESTION	1. Choose a key word or phrase in the question. 2. Scan the appropriate paragraph for the key word or phrase (or related idea). 3. Read the sentence that contains the key word or phrase (or related idea) carefully. 4. Look for answers that are true. Eliminate these answers. 5. Choose the answer that is not true or not discussed.

READING EXERCISE 6: Study each of the passages, and choose the best answers to the questions that follow.

PASSAGE ONE *(Questions 1–4)*

Paragraph   **The Penguin**

▶1   A penguin is a bird that is generally found in the colder regions of the world. The back of its body and its head are black, while the front of its body is white. This coloring makes the penguin look like it is dressed for a formal occasion.

▶2   The name "penguin" comes from the Welsh words *pen* ("head") and *gwyn* ("white"). The name "penguin" actually means "white head." This does not seem to make sense because a "penguin" has a black head and not a white head.

▶3   There is a different bird, the auk, that looks much like the penguin. One difference is that the auk has white spots on its head. Welsh fishermen called the auk a penguin. This was because of the white spots that the auk had on its head.

▶4   Something happened many years after the Welsh sailors gave the auk the name "penguin." Other sailors near Antarctica saw a bird that looked something like the auk, so they called it a penguin. Now the bird with a black head has a name that means "white head."

1. What is NOT discussed in paragraph 1 about the penguin?
   Ⓐ Where it is found
   Ⓑ What it eats
   Ⓒ What its body looks like
   Ⓓ What its head looks like

2. All of the following are true about the name "penguin" EXCEPT that
   Ⓐ it comes from a Welsh language
   Ⓑ *pen* means "head"
   Ⓒ *gwyn* means "white"
   Ⓓ "penguin" means "black head"

3. According to paragraph 3, what is NOT true about the auk?
   Ⓐ It is a kind of fish.
   Ⓑ It looks something like a penguin.
   Ⓒ Its head has white spots on it.
   Ⓓ It was called a penguin by fishermen.

4. It is NOT stated in paragraph 4 that sailors
   Ⓐ called the auk a penguin
   Ⓑ saw a bird that was similar to the auk
   Ⓒ called a bird with a black head a name that means "white head"
   Ⓓ called a bird with a white head a name that means "black head"

PASSAGE TWO (Questions 5–8)

Paragraph

Fingerprints

▶ 1   A fingerprint is a record of the markings on the surface of the thumb or on any of the fingers on a hand. Police detectives first began keeping records of fingerprints of criminals around the end of the nineteenth century, and fingerprinting was first used to solve a murder in 1902.

▶ 2   In that year, a man named Reibel was murdered in his apartment in Paris, France. The police detective who was in charge of solving the murder was someone who had already started collecting the fingerprints of known criminals. In the dead man's apartment, the detective found some broken pieces of glass with blood on them. The detective believed that the criminal had cut himself and had left some fingerprints on the pieces of glass. When the detective found some fingerprints on the broken glass, he matched the fingerprints from the glass to the fingerprints that he had recorded from a known criminal. The criminal was arrested by the police, and he admitted his guilt. He confessed after he saw that he had left his fingerprints in the home of the murdered man.

5. What is NOT true about fingerprints, according to paragraph 1?

  Ⓐ That they were first collected around the end of the 1800s

  Ⓑ That they were first used to solve a murder in the early twentieth century

  Ⓒ That they were first collected around the end of the 1900s

  Ⓓ That they were used to solve a crime soon after they were first collected

6. What is NOT indicated in paragraph 2 about Reibel?

  Ⓐ What happened to him

  Ⓑ What his job was

  Ⓒ Where he was murdered

  Ⓓ When he was murdered

7. What is NOT stated in paragraph 2 about the broken pieces of glass?

  Ⓐ They were found in Reibel's apartment.

  Ⓑ They had blood on them.

  Ⓒ They had Reibel's fingerprints on them.

  Ⓓ They had the criminal's fingerprints on them.

8. What is NOT mentioned in paragraph 2 about the criminal?

  Ⓐ The police took him to jail.

  Ⓑ He learned that he had left his fingerprints on the glass.

  Ⓒ He said that he was guilty.

  Ⓓ He broke the glass before he entered Reibel's apartment.

PASSAGE THREE *(Questions 9–13)*

Paragraph

The Tarantella and the Tarantula

▶**1**   The tarantella is a lively dance, while the tarantula is a large and hairy spider. Both the tarantella, the dance, and the tarantula, the spider, are named after the Italian city of Taranto.

▶**2**   There is actually an explanation why these two different things, a dance and a spider, have related names. The story of how both the dance and the spider got their names from an Italian city goes back to the Middle Ages. At the time, the citizens of Taranto were known for a lively dance they performed, and this dance was named the tarantella, after the name of the city. The dance was so energetic that the dancers sometimes danced until they collapsed and became unconscious. The city leaders did not like the dance because it was so wild, so they created a law saying that it was illegal to dance the tarantella. When this law was created, the people of the city were unhappy because they loved their dance so much.

▶**3**   In order to continue dancing even though the dance was illegal, the townspeople came up with a story. The story was that a large, hairy spider that lived in the area had bitten them, and they had to dance the tarantella so that they would not become sick from the spider bite. The large, hairy spider became known as the tarantula, the spider that supposedly caused people to dance the tarantella.

9. What is NOT discussed in paragraph 1?

Ⓐ What the tarantella is

Ⓑ What the tarantula is

Ⓒ Where the tarantella and tarantula got their names

Ⓓ When the tarantella and tarantula got their names

10. According to paragraph 2, it is NOT true that the tarantella

Ⓐ was a dance

Ⓑ was very slow

Ⓒ was performed by people who lived in Taranto

Ⓓ was named after the city of Taranto

11. It is stated in paragraph 2 that city leaders did NOT

Ⓐ think the tarantella was a good thing

Ⓑ think the tarantella was too wild

Ⓒ make a law against the tarantella

Ⓓ make the citizens of Taranto unhappy

12. According to the story in paragraph 3, it is NOT true that

Ⓐ there was a large spider

Ⓑ the spider had bitten some townspeople

Ⓒ the spider had to dance the tarantella

Ⓓ the dance kept people healthy

13. It is NOT indicated in paragraph 3

Ⓐ who made up the story

Ⓑ what the spider looked like

Ⓒ why the people had to dance the tarantella

Ⓓ when the people in the story danced

READING EXERCISE (Skills 5–6): Study the passage, and choose the best answers to the questions that follow.

Paragraph
Medford's Attempted Silk Industry

➤ A little more than 100 years ago, a scientist in Medford, Massachusetts, was trying to help local industry. Instead of helping local industry, however, he caused a major problem with the local environment.

➤ The scientist thought that it would be a good idea to try to develop the silk-making industry in Medford. He knew that the silk industry in Asia was successful because of the silkworm, a caterpillar that ate only mulberry leaves. Mulberry trees did not grow in Medford, so the scientist decided to work on developing a type of silk-making worm that would eat the type of tree leaves in Medford.

➤ His plan was to create a worm that was a cross between the Asian silkworm and another type of imported worm that would eat the types of leaves around Medford. Unfortunately, his plan did not turn out as he wanted. He was not able to come up with a silk-producing worm. However, the worms that he imported did like to eat the tree leaves around Medford. Many of the trees around Medford lost their leaves to these worms and died.

1. According to paragraph 1, the situation described in this passage took place approximately
   Ⓐ a decade ago
   Ⓑ two decades ago
   Ⓒ a century ago
   Ⓓ two centuries ago

2. According to paragraph 1, the scientist
   Ⓐ had no effect on Medford
   Ⓑ hurt rather than helped Medford
   Ⓒ helped rather than hurt Medford
   Ⓓ did not actually live in Medford

3. All of the following are mentioned in paragraph 2 about the scientist EXCEPT
   Ⓐ that he worked in the silk industry in China
   Ⓑ that he wanted to develop the silk industry in Medford
   Ⓒ that he knew something about the silk industry in China
   Ⓓ that he wanted to develop a certain kind of worm

4. Which of the following is NOT stated about the silkworm?
   Ⓐ It is a type of caterpillar.
   Ⓑ It likes only mulberry leaves.
   Ⓒ It grows successfully in Asia.
   Ⓓ It grows successfully in Medford.

5. It is stated in paragraph 3 that the scientist wanted to create a worm
   Ⓐ that was just like the Asian silkworm
   Ⓑ that could be imported from Asia
   Ⓒ that would eat the leaves in Asia
   Ⓓ that was a mix of two other worms

6. According to paragraph 3, it is NOT true that the scientist
   Ⓐ planned to create a new kind of worm
   Ⓑ created silkworms
   Ⓒ imported worms
   Ⓓ was unsuccessful

7. According to paragraph 3, what did the scientist's worms do?
   Ⓐ They made silk.
   Ⓑ They turned into silkworms.
   Ⓒ They killed a lot of trees.
   Ⓓ They died immediately.

READING REVIEW EXERCISE (Skills 1–6): Read the passage.

Paragraph   **The War of 1812**

▶ 1   When the United States went to war against England in 1812, the U.S. navy was much weaker than the British navy. In fact, the British navy at the time had over 800 warships. The entire U.S. navy had only 16 warships in its fleet, so it was almost nonexistent.

▶ 2   To increase its naval power, the United States tried to convert merchant ships into warships. When a merchant ship was converted into a warship, two big changes were made. First, the cargo hold was emptied. Then, heavy cannons to fight the enemy were added to the top of the deck.

▶ 3   This type of conversion of merchant ships into warships was not always successful, for a very good reason. The changes that were made to convert a ship from a merchant ship to a warship made the ship much less stable. A heavy cargo in the hold at the bottom of a merchant ship allowed the ship to stay balanced in the water. When the cargo was removed, the ship became less stable. Then, when the heavy metal cannons were added to the deck of the ship, the ship became even less stable. As a result, a number of these converted merchant ships tipped over and sank.

Refer to this version of the passage to answer the questions that follow.

Paragraph   **The War of 1812**

▶ 1   When the United States went to war against England in 1812, the U.S. navy was much weaker than the British navy. In fact, the British navy at the time had over 800 warships. The entire U.S. navy had only 16 warships in its fleet, so it was almost nonexistent.

▶ 2   **6A** To increase its naval power, the United States tried to convert merchant ships into warships. **6B** When a merchant ship was converted into a warship, two big changes were made. **6C** First, the cargo hold was emptied. **6D** Then, heavy cannons to fight the enemy were added to the top of the deck.

▶ 3   This type of conversion of merchant ships into warships was not always successful, for a very good reason. The changes that were made to convert a ship from a merchant ship to a warship made the ship much less stable. A heavy cargo in the hold at the bottom of a merchant ship allowed the ship to stay balanced in the water. When the cargo was removed, the ship became less stable. Then, when the heavy metal cannons were added to the deck of the ship, the ship became even less stable. As a result, a number of these converted merchant ships tipped over and sank.

1. It is stated in the passage that the U.S. navy was

    Ⓐ not as strong as the British navy
    Ⓑ stronger than the British navy
    Ⓒ as weak as the British navy
    Ⓓ equal in strength to the British navy

2. The word "entire" in paragraph 1 could best be replaced by

    Ⓐ tiny
    Ⓑ tired
    Ⓒ even
    Ⓓ whole

3. The word "it" in paragraph 1 refers to

    Ⓐ the British navy
    Ⓑ time
    Ⓒ the U.S. navy
    Ⓓ its fleet

4. The word "convert" in paragraph 2 is closest in meaning to

    Ⓐ buy
    Ⓑ build
    Ⓒ change
    Ⓓ sell

5. According to paragraph 2, what was added to a merchant ship when it was converted?

    Ⓐ A cargo hold
    Ⓑ Cannons
    Ⓒ A deck
    Ⓓ The enemy

6. Look at the four squares [■] that indicate where the following sentence could be added to paragraph 2.

    The hold needed to be emptied to increase the ship's speed.

    Where would the sentence best fit? Click on a square [■] to add the sentence to the paragraph.

7. Which of the sentences below best expresses the essential information in the highlighted sentence in paragraph 3?

    Ⓐ It is understandable why a certain change did not work well.
    Ⓑ There were good reasons why warships were changed into merchant ships.
    Ⓒ Trying to change warships into merchant ships was not a success.
    Ⓓ Putting merchant ships into a war zone was successful.

8. According to paragraph 3, all of the following made a merchant ship less stable EXCEPT

    Ⓐ being converted to a warship
    Ⓑ having a heavy cargo in the hold
    Ⓒ having heavy cannons on deck
    Ⓓ having an empty cargo hold

9. According to the passage, what happened to many converted merchant ships?

    Ⓐ They became part of the British navy.
    Ⓑ They went to the bottom of the ocean.
    Ⓒ They carried large cargoes.
    Ⓓ They filled their holds with cannons.

10. The expression "As a result" in paragraph 3 is closest in meaning to

    Ⓐ However
    Ⓑ Also
    Ⓒ Afterwards
    Ⓓ Therefore

INFERENCES

Reading Skill 7: MAKE INFERENCES FROM STATED FACTS

In the Reading section of the TOEFL *iBT*, you may sometimes have to answer a multiple-choice question by drawing a conclusion from a specific detail or details in the passage. Questions of this type contain the words *implied, inferred, likely,* or *probably* to let you know that the answer to this question is not directly stated. In this type of question, it is important to understand that you do not need to "pull the answer out of thin air." Instead, some information will be given in the passage, and you will draw a conclusion from that information. Look at an example of an inference question.

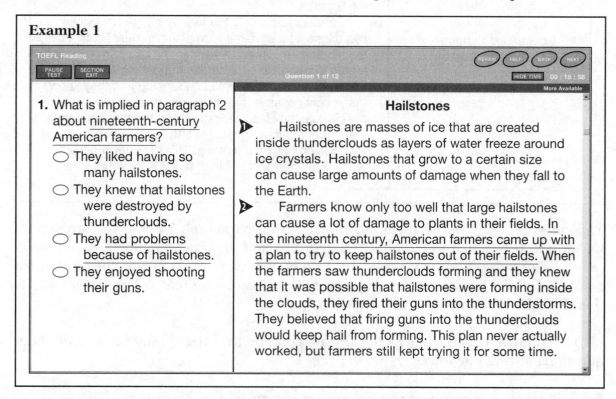

Example 1

TOEFL Reading

Question 1 of 12

00 : 18 : 38

1. What is implied in paragraph 2 about nineteenth-century American farmers?

○ They liked having so many hailstones.
○ They knew that hailstones were destroyed by thunderclouds.
○ They had problems because of hailstones.
○ They enjoyed shooting their guns.

Hailstones

Hailstones are masses of ice that are created inside thunderclouds as layers of water freeze around ice crystals. Hailstones that grow to a certain size can cause large amounts of damage when they fall to the Earth.

Farmers know only too well that large hailstones can cause a lot of damage to plants in their fields. In the nineteenth century, American farmers came up with a plan to try to keep hailstones out of their fields. When the farmers saw thunderclouds forming and they knew that it was possible that hailstones were forming inside the clouds, they fired their guns into the thunderstorms. They believed that firing guns into the thunderclouds would keep hail from forming. This plan never actually worked, but farmers still kept trying it for some time.

This question asks about what is implied in paragraph 2 about American farmers. It is stated in paragraph 2 that *in the nineteenth century, American farmers came up with a plan to try to keep hailstones out of their fields.* From this, you need to draw the conclusion that *nineteenth-century American farmers . . . had problems because of hailstones.* The third answer is therefore the best answer to this question.

Now look at another example of an inference question.

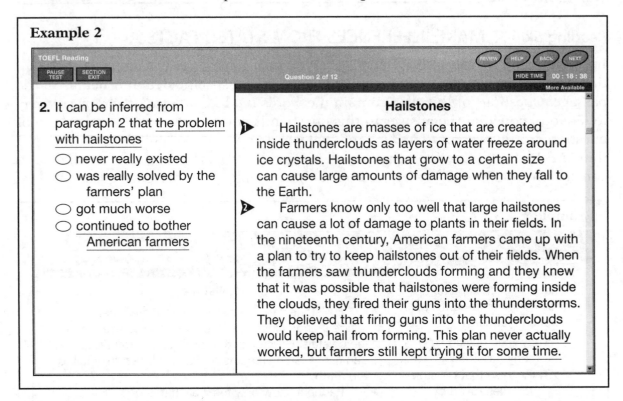

Example 2

2. It can be inferred from paragraph 2 that <u>the problem with hailstones</u>

- ○ never really existed
- ○ was really solved by the farmers' plan
- ○ got much worse
- ○ <u>continued to bother American farmers</u>

Hailstones

▷ Hailstones are masses of ice that are created inside thunderclouds as layers of water freeze around ice crystals. Hailstones that grow to a certain size can cause large amounts of damage when they fall to the Earth.

▷ Farmers know only too well that large hailstones can cause a lot of damage to plants in their fields. In the nineteenth century, American farmers came up with a plan to try to keep hailstones out of their fields. When the farmers saw thunderclouds forming and they knew that it was possible that hailstones were forming inside the clouds, they fired their guns into the thunderstorms. They believed that firing guns into the thunderclouds would keep hail from forming. <u>This plan never actually worked, but farmers still kept trying it for some time.</u>

This question asks you what can be inferred from paragraph 2 about the problem of hailstones. It is stated in paragraph 2 that *this plan never actually worked, but farmers still kept trying it for some time.* From this, you can draw the conclusion that *the problem with hailstones . . . continued to bother American farmers.* The last answer is therefore the best answer to this question.

The following chart outlines the key information that you should remember about questions testing inferences.

QUESTIONS ABOUT INFERENCES FROM STATED FACTS	
HOW TO IDENTIFY THE QUESTION	It is **implied** in paragraph X ... It can be **inferred** from paragraph X ... It is most **likely** that ... What **probably** happened ...?
WHERE TO FIND THE ANSWER	The answers to these questions are generally found in order in the passage.
HOW TO ANSWER THE QUESTION	1. Choose a key word or phrase (or related idea). 2. Scan the passage for the key word or phrase (or related idea). 3. Carefully read the sentence that contains the key word or phrase (or related idea). 4. Draw a conclusion based on the sentence. 5. Choose the best answer.

READING EXERCISE 7: Study each of the passages, and choose the best answers to the questions that follow.

PASSAGE ONE *(Questions 1–3)*

Paragraph

Flour

▶1 There are two types of wheat flour, and these two types of wheat flour are hard and soft flour. If a kind of flour is hard flour, it is not called hard flour because the flour feels hard. Instead, the hardness of the flour is based on how much protein the flour has. Wheat flour that has a high percentage of protein is called hard wheat flour, while wheat flour that has a low percentage of protein is called soft wheat flour.

▶2 Two kinds of wheat that are grown in the United States are durum wheat and red winter wheat. Durum wheat provides a particularly hard wheat flour with a very high percentage of protein in it, while red winter wheat provides a particularly soft wheat flour. The most commonly purchased flour in the United States is called all-purpose flour. It is actually made from a combination of hard and soft wheat flour.

1. It is implied in paragraph 1 that wheat
   Ⓐ may or may not have a lot of protein
   Ⓑ always has a lot of protein
   Ⓒ always has a low amount of protein
   Ⓓ never has any protein

2. It can be inferred from paragraph 2 that red wheat has
   Ⓐ no protein
   Ⓑ a low percentage of protein
   Ⓒ a moderate amount of protein
   Ⓓ a really high percentage of protein

3. All-purpose flour most likely has
   Ⓐ no protein
   Ⓑ a low percentage of protein
   Ⓒ a moderate amount of protein
   Ⓓ a really high percentage of protein

PASSAGE TWO *(Questions 4–6)*

Paragraph   **Machu Picchu**

▶1   In 1911, when explorer Hiram Bingham was out hiking in some tall mountains in South America, the Andes in Peru, he came across an amazing discovery. He came across the ruins of an ancient city high in the Andes that no one had seen for some time. This city was situated on a ridge between two mountains. The place was called Machu Picchu, after one of the two mountains.

▶2   Machu Picchu was an ancient religious fortress-city. It contained many temples and houses, and it was well fortified. It was surrounded by terraces for farming, and there were aqueducts that supplied water to the city and the farming terraces. There was a stone road through the Andes Mountains that connected Machu Picchu to other ancient cities.

▶3   Machu Picchu was originally a city built by the Incas. It is not known exactly how old the city is, but it is at least 500 years old.

4. It can be inferred from paragraph 1 that, in 1911, Machu Picchu was
   Ⓐ full of people
   Ⓑ recently built
   Ⓒ very modern
   Ⓓ deserted

5. It is implied in paragraph 2 that citizens in the ancient city of Machu Picchu
   Ⓐ interacted with people from other cities
   Ⓑ carried water to the top of the mountain
   Ⓒ ate only fish and hunted animals for food
   Ⓓ lived outside without any shelter

6. Based on the information in paragraph 3, Machu Picchu was probably built
   Ⓐ in 3000 B.C.
   Ⓑ in 500 A.D.
   Ⓒ in 1500 A.D.
   Ⓓ in 1850 A.D.

PASSAGE THREE *(Questions 7–9)*

Paragraph

1   When astronauts go into space, they are weightless. When they are in space, they need to do simple tasks like eating and drinking in weightlessness. Because they need to do these things in space, astronauts need to practice completing tasks when they are weightless. They need this practice before they actually go into space.

2   The National Aeronautics and Space Administration (NASA) has found a way for astronauts to experience weightlessness before they go into space. Astronauts go up in a jet plane that flies in a parabolic pattern. Flying in a parabolic pattern means that the jet plane goes up rapidly and then suddenly goes down. When the jet plane is at the top of the curve, the people inside the plane are weightless.

3   The astronauts go up inside an empty cargo jet. A cargo jet is a jet that is used to carry things rather than people. When the astronauts go up inside the empty cargo jet, they can move around. When the jet plane comes close to the top and begins turning downward, the astronauts are weightless for 30 to 60 seconds. The astronauts can spend this time practicing skills that they will need when they actually go into space.

7. It is implied in paragraph 1 that astronauts need to practice completing tasks in weightlessness because the tasks are

  Ⓐ hard to do
  Ⓑ fun to do
  Ⓒ exciting to do
  Ⓓ easy to do

8. It can be inferred from paragraph 2 that one is weightless in the period when he or she is

  Ⓐ rising
  Ⓑ falling
  Ⓒ in the period between rising and falling
  Ⓓ in the period between falling and rising

9. Based on the information in paragraph 3, cargo planes are most likely used because

  Ⓐ they are not expensive
  Ⓑ NASA has a lot of them available for use
  Ⓒ it is enjoyable for astronauts to fly in them
  Ⓓ they have a lot of room for movement

Reading Skill 8: INFER RHETORICAL PURPOSE

In the Reading section of the TOEFL *iBT,* you may sometimes have to explain *why* the author has included certain words, phrases, or sentences in a passage. A word, phrase, or sentence is highlighted in the passage. You must decide which of four multiple-choice answers best explains why the author has included the highlighted information. You must look at how the highlighted information fits into the overall presentation of ideas in the passage rather than looking at the highlighted information only.

Look at an example of a question that asks you to determine the rhetorical purpose of a phrase.

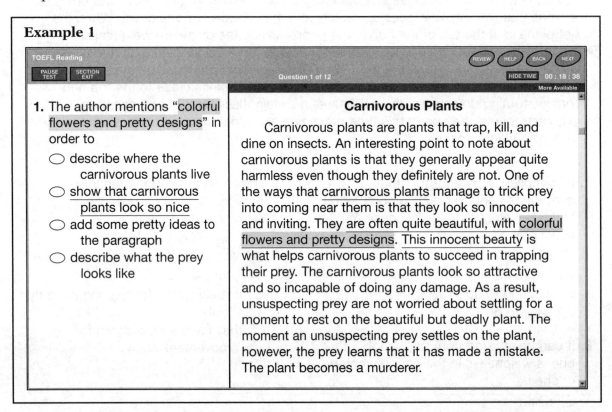

This question asks you to explain why the author mentions "colorful flowers and pretty designs." The author states that *carnivorous plants . . . are often quite beautiful, with colorful flowers and pretty designs* and mentions *this innocent beauty.* From this, it can be determined that the author mentions *colorful flowers and pretty designs* in order to *show that carnivorous plants look so nice.* The second answer is therefore the best answer to this question.

Now look at another example, one that asks you about the rhetorical purpose of a certain word.

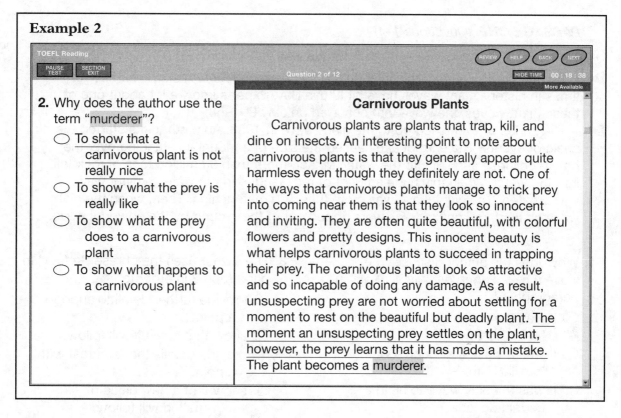

Example 2

More Available

2. Why does the author use the term "murderer"?
- ⃝ To show that a carnivorous plant is not really nice
- ⃝ To show what the prey is really like
- ⃝ To show what the prey does to a carnivorous plant
- ⃝ To show what happens to a carnivorous plant

Carnivorous Plants

Carnivorous plants are plants that trap, kill, and dine on insects. An interesting point to note about carnivorous plants is that they generally appear quite harmless even though they definitely are not. One of the ways that carnivorous plants manage to trick prey into coming near them is that they look so innocent and inviting. They are often quite beautiful, with colorful flowers and pretty designs. This innocent beauty is what helps carnivorous plants to succeed in trapping their prey. The carnivorous plants look so attractive and so incapable of doing any damage. As a result, unsuspecting prey are not worried about settling for a moment to rest on the beautiful but deadly plant. The moment an unsuspecting prey settles on the plant, however, the prey learns that it has made a mistake. The plant becomes a murderer.

This question asks you to explain why the author uses the term "murderer." The author states that *the moment an unsuspecting prey settles on the plant, however, the prey learns that it has made a mistake* and that *the plant becomes a murderer*. From this, it can be determined that the author mentions a *murderer* in order *to show that a carnivorous plant is not really nice*. The first answer is therefore the best answer to this question.

The following chart outlines the key information that you should remember about questions testing rhetorical purpose.

QUESTIONS ABOUT RHETORICAL PURPOSE	
HOW TO IDENTIFY THE QUESTION	**Why** does the **author** ... The **author** mentions X **in order to** ...
WHERE TO FIND THE ANSWER	The important information is highlighted in the passage.
HOW TO ANSWER THE QUESTION	1. Study the highlighted information carefully. 2. Study the context around the highlighted information. Ask yourself how the highlighted information is related to the context around it. 3. Draw a conclusion about the purpose of the highlighted information. 4. Choose the best answer.

READING EXERCISE 8: Study each of the passages, and choose the best answers to the questions that follow.

PASSAGE ONE (Questions 1–4)

Paragraph

Lituya Bay

▶ 1   Lituya Bay is a long, thin inlet on the southern coast of Alaska. A number of times in history, giant waves have hit Lituya Bay. Experts know a lot about one of these giant waves, the wave that occurred on July 9, 1958.

▶ 2   A series of events led up to the giant wave in 1958. An earthquake started the chain of events. The earthquake caused the side of a mountain standing over the bay to collapse and fall into the water. In fact, more than 90 million tons of rock fell into the water. When this huge amount of rock landed in the water, a giant wave was created. The giant wave was more than 500 meters high. Then, when the giant wave hit land, millions of trees were ripped out of the ground by the powerful wave.

1. Why does the author discuss "the wave that occurred on July 9, 1958" in paragraph 1?
   - Ⓐ It was the only huge wave ever to hit Lituya Bay.
   - Ⓑ It was a wave that people were familiar with.
   - Ⓒ It was the only wave to hit in a certain decade.
   - Ⓓ It was a wave that caused an earthquake.

2. Why does the author mention an "earthquake" in paragraph 2?
   - Ⓐ It was caused by the giant wave.
   - Ⓑ It was the last step in a series of events.
   - Ⓒ It happened when the rock fell into the water.
   - Ⓓ It caused the great wave described in the passage.

3. The author uses the phrase "In fact" in paragraph 2 in order to
   - Ⓐ provide further detail to support a point
   - Ⓑ show that a result will follow
   - Ⓒ provide details that contrast with a point
   - Ⓓ show that a new piece of information will follow

4. The author mentions "millions of trees" in paragraph 2 in order to show
   - Ⓐ how many trees the rocks knocked over
   - Ⓑ how green the area around Lituya Bay was
   - Ⓒ how big the mountains around Lituya Bay were
   - Ⓓ how much damage resulted from the wave

PASSAGE TWO *(Questions 5–8)*

Paragraph   **Cats**

▶1   It is not known for sure when cats first moved out of the wild and began to live with people, but cats probably became domesticated (or tamed) around 5,000 years ago. Cats were certainly domesticated much later than dogs; dogs were domesticated around 50,000 years ago.

▶2   In addition, it is also not known for sure where cats first became domesticated. They were probably domesticated in different parts of the world. Domestic cats definitely existed in parts of North America, Europe, Asia, and Africa several thousand years ago.

▶3   Cats had a very important role in ancient Egypt. Cats came to be seen as deities, or gods and goddesses, in Egypt. If a cat died, this was more serious than the death of a family member. In addition, it was worse to kill a cat than to kill a human being. Someone who killed a cat could be executed, or put to death.

5. The author mentions "dogs" in paragraph 1 in a passage on cats in order to show

   Ⓐ that cats were domesticated relatively recently in comparison to dogs
   Ⓑ that cats became wild relatively recently in comparison to dogs
   Ⓒ that cats were domesticated relatively longer ago in comparison to dogs
   Ⓓ that cats became wild relatively longer ago in comparison to dogs

6. Why does the author begin paragraph 2 with the expression "In addition"?

   Ⓐ To show that there is more information about when cats were domesticated
   Ⓑ To show that it is also true that cats were domesticated in North America
   Ⓒ To show that there is something else that is not known with certainty
   Ⓓ To show that the place where cats were domesticated is also known

7. The author mentions "North America, Europe, Asia, and Africa" in paragraph 2 in order to show the many different places where cats

   Ⓐ ran wild
   Ⓑ exist today
   Ⓒ had a position of honor
   Ⓓ were domesticated

8. The author includes the fact that "Someone who killed a cat could be executed" in paragraph 3 in order to show that

   Ⓐ cats were not very important
   Ⓑ the society was violent
   Ⓒ people were more important than cats
   Ⓓ cats were extremely important

PASSAGE THREE (Questions 9–12)

The Amazon River System

Paragraph

1▶ The Amazon River is, in reality, a river system rather than a single river. There are more than 1,000 rivers in the Amazon River system, and some of them are very long. Seventeen of the more than 1,000 rivers in the system are each more than 1,000 miles in length.

2▶ The Amazon River system is in South America, and it is enormous. Imagine, this huge system drains water from half of the area of South America. It starts in the mountain tops high in the Andes Mountains in the west. It then flows through South America to the river mouth near the equator on the Atlantic coast of South America.

3▶ Because of the large number of rivers and the size of the river system, the Amazon River system carries an unbelievably large volume of water. Americans think that the Mississippi River is large. In comparison, however, the Amazon River system carries six times the volume of the Mississippi River system every day.

9. The author mentions "1,000 rivers" in paragraph 1 in order to show

  Ⓐ how many rivers there are in the world

  Ⓑ how big the Amazon River system is

  Ⓒ that the Amazon River system is actually one river

  Ⓓ why the Amazon River is actually not very long

10. Why does the author use the word "Imagine" in paragraph 2?

  Ⓐ Because something untrue follows

  Ⓑ Because a fictional story follows

  Ⓒ Because an almost unbelievable fact follows

  Ⓓ Because something that came before was untrue

11. Why does the author begin paragraph 3 with the phrase "Because of the large number of rivers and the size of the river system"?

  Ⓐ To add new details

  Ⓑ To introduce the ideas of the coming paragraph

  Ⓒ To give supporting details for a previous idea

  Ⓓ To summarize the ideas in the previous paragraphs

12. The author mentions the "Mississippi River" in paragraph 3 in order to

  Ⓐ compare the volume of water in the Amazon with that in the Mississippi

  Ⓑ show that the Amazon does not carry as much water as the Mississippi

  Ⓒ show that the Mississippi is six times as long as the Amazon

  Ⓓ compare the location of the Amazon with that of the Mississippi

READING EXERCISE (Skills 7–8): Read the passage.

Paragraph

The Pacific Ocean

1   The Pacific Ocean is a body of water of immense size and power. Its name, however, does not reflect the incredible size and force of this huge body of water.

2   In size, the Pacific Ocean is unequaled. The ocean covers an area of 64 million miles and is by far the largest of the world's oceans. It covers a third of the surface of the Earth, it is double the size of the Atlantic, and it contains more water than all of the world's other oceans combined.

3   As a force of nature, the Pacific Ocean can be very powerful indeed. The westerly winds produce areas of stormy precipitation in some parts of the ocean. Tropical cyclones, with winds that can be as high as 200 miles, or 300 kilometers, per hour, produce much of the rainfall in the Pacific and can cause an extreme amount of damage.

4   In view of the extreme size and power of the Pacific, the name that it carries is unexpected. The Pacific Ocean was given its name by Portuguese explorer Ferdinand Magellan, who sailed around the world in the early sixteenth century. The word "pacific" actually means "peaceful." Magellan named this giant of an ocean the Pacific because he found its waters to be so much more peaceful than the rough and stormy waters of the southern Atlantic that he had crossed earlier in his voyage.

Refer to this version of the passage to answer the questions that follow.

Paragraph

The Pacific Ocean

1   The Pacific Ocean is a body of water of immense size and power. Its name, however, does not reflect the incredible size and force of this huge body of water.

2   In size, the Pacific Ocean is unequaled. The ocean covers an area of 64 million miles and is by far the largest of the world's oceans. It covers a third of the surface of the Earth, it is double the size of the Atlantic, and it contains more water than all of the world's other oceans combined.

3   As a force of nature, the Pacific Ocean can be very powerful indeed. The westerly winds produce areas of stormy precipitation in some parts of the ocean. Tropical cyclones, with winds that can be as high as 200 miles, or 300 kilometers, per hour, produce much of the rainfall in the Pacific and can cause an extreme amount of damage.

4   In view of the extreme size and power of the Pacific, the name that it carries is unexpected. The Pacific Ocean was given its name by Portuguese explorer Ferdinand Magellan, who sailed around the world in the early sixteenth century. The word "pacific" actually means "peaceful." Magellan named this giant of an ocean the Pacific because he found its waters to be so much more peaceful than the rough and stormy waters of the southern Atlantic that he had crossed earlier in his voyage.

1. The author uses the word "however" in paragraph 1 in order to show
   Ⓐ a contrast between the name and reality of the Pacific Ocean
   Ⓑ a contrast between the size and power of the Pacific Ocean
   Ⓒ a positive relationship between the name and reality of the Pacific Ocean
   Ⓓ a positive relationship between the size and power of the Pacific Ocean

2. It can be inferred from paragraph 2 that the Indian Ocean and the Arctic Ocean combined are
   Ⓐ equal in size to the Pacific Ocean
   Ⓑ double the size of the Atlantic Ocean
   Ⓒ larger in size than the Pacific Ocean
   Ⓓ smaller in size than the Pacific Ocean

3. The author uses the word "indeed" in paragraph 3 in order to show
   Ⓐ surprise
   Ⓑ disbelief
   Ⓒ emphasis
   Ⓓ acceptance

4. A tropical cyclone would probably NOT have winds at
   Ⓐ 200 mph
   Ⓑ 220 mph
   Ⓒ 280 kph
   Ⓓ 300 kph

5. Why does the author use "the extreme size and power of the Pacific" near the beginning of paragraph 4?
   Ⓐ To summarize the ideas in the preceding paragraphs
   Ⓑ To introduce new ideas into the passage
   Ⓒ To announce new ideas to be discussed
   Ⓓ To give the answer to a question

6. Based on the information in the passage, which of the following would most likely be the dates of Magellan's voyage around the world?
   Ⓐ 1489–1492
   Ⓑ 1519–1522
   Ⓒ 1589–1592
   Ⓓ 1619–1622

7. It is implied in the passage that Magellan
   Ⓐ did not understand the true nature of the Pacific
   Ⓑ never actually crossed the Atlantic
   Ⓒ really thought the Atlantic was quite calm and peaceful
   Ⓓ never actually sailed on the Pacific

READING REVIEW EXERCISE (Skills 1–8): Read the passage.

Paragraph
Charles Dow

1▶ Charles Dow, an American journalist in the nineteenth century, was a pioneer in the reporting of up-to-date finance and investment news. His efforts to bring timely information to brokers and investors had effects that are still recognized today.

2▶ In his early career, Dow worked on a number of small newspapers before heading to New York City. He took a position as a reporter on the *Daily Republican* in Springfield, Massachusetts, in his twenties and later moved on to a job at the *Journal* in Providence, Rhode Island. In 1880, at the age of twenty-nine, he moved to New York City.

3▶ Only two years after arriving in New York, Dow founded Dow Jones & Co. with two friends, Edward Jones and Charles Bergstresser. The purpose of this company was to gather and distribute up-to-date financial information throughout the business day. The Dow Jones average of today is an average of selected stocks traded on the New York Stock Exchange; it still bears the name of the company that Dow and his friends started.

4▶ In 1889, the first issue of the *Wall Street Journal* appeared, with Charles Dow as its leader. The *Wall Street Journal* began simply, as a daily collection of brief news bulletins related to business. The *Wall Street Journal* of today is a major newspaper that provides business news on a global basis.

Refer to this version of the passage to answer the questions that follow.

Paragraph
Charles Dow

1▶ Charles Dow, an American journalist in the nineteenth century, was a pioneer in the reporting of up-to-date finance and investment news. His efforts to bring timely information to brokers and investors had effects that are still recognized today.

2▶ In his early career, Dow worked on a number of small newspapers before heading to New York City. He took a position as a reporter on the *Daily Republican* in Springfield, Massachusetts, in his twenties and later moved on to a job at the *Journal* in Providence, Rhode Island. In 1880, at the age of twenty-nine, he moved to New York City.

3▶ Only two years after arriving in New York, Dow founded Dow Jones & Co. with two friends, Edward Jones and Charles Bergstresser. The purpose of this company was to gather and distribute up-to-date financial information throughout the business day. The Dow Jones average of today is an average of selected stocks traded on the New York Stock Exchange; it still bears the name of the company that Dow and his friends started.

4▶ **10A** In 1889, the first issue of the *Wall Street Journal* appeared, with Charles Dow as its leader. **10B** The *Wall Street Journal* began simply, as a daily collection of brief news bulletins related to business. **10C** The *Wall Street Journal* of today is a major newspaper that provides business news on a global basis. **10D**

1. It is NOT mentioned in the passage
   Ⓐ where Dow was born
   Ⓑ what job Dow held in his twenties
   Ⓒ where Dow lived in his twenties
   Ⓓ when Dow went to New York

2. Which of the sentences below best expresses the essential information in the highlighted sentence in paragraph 1?
   Ⓐ Dow's efforts in bringing information to brokers and investors was very important in its day.
   Ⓑ Today, people still recognize Dow's work in giving brokers and investors up-to-date information.
   Ⓒ Brokers and investors had an effect on Dow with their timely information.
   Ⓓ Dow's information about brokers and investors is still important today.

3. The word "position" in paragraph 2 could best be replaced by
   Ⓐ location
   Ⓑ situation
   Ⓒ spot
   Ⓓ job

4. It can be inferred from the passage that Dow founded Dow Jones & Co.
   Ⓐ in 1878
   Ⓑ in 1880
   Ⓒ in 1882
   Ⓓ in 1889

5. According to the passage, the purpose of Dow Jones & Co. was
   Ⓐ to provide current news about finances
   Ⓑ to purchase an average number of stocks
   Ⓒ to establish the New York Stock Exchange
   Ⓓ to oppose the New York Stock Exchange

6. It can be inferred from the passage that the *Wall Street Journal*
   Ⓐ first appeared in the 1890s
   Ⓑ employed Dow as a reporter
   Ⓒ has been in existence for more than a century
   Ⓓ was initially composed of lengthy articles

7. The word "it" in paragraph 3 refers to
   Ⓐ the business day
   Ⓑ the Dow Jones average
   Ⓒ the New York Stock Exchange
   Ⓓ the name

8. The author discusses "The *Wall Street Journal* of today" in paragraph 4 to show that
   Ⓐ Charles Dow is still working there
   Ⓑ it has changed since Dow's time
   Ⓒ something that Dow started is still successful today
   Ⓓ it is still a young newspaper

9. Look at the word "global" in paragraph 4. This word is closest in meaning to
   Ⓐ circular
   Ⓑ short
   Ⓒ rapid
   Ⓓ worldwide

10. Look at the four squares [■] that indicate where the following sentence could be added to paragraph 4.

    Dow was both its editor and its publisher.

    Where would the sentence best fit? Click on a square [■] to add the sentence to the paragraph.

READING TO LEARN

Reading Skill 9: SELECT SUMMARY INFORMATION

In the Reading section of the TOEFL *iBT*, you may have to complete a summary chart. In this summary chart, the overall topic is given, and you must choose the major supporting ideas. This kind of question has three correct answers and is worth 2 points. You will receive 2 points for 3 correct answers, 1 point for 2 correct answers, and 0 points for either 1 or 0 correct answers.

Look at an example of a question that asks you to select summary information.

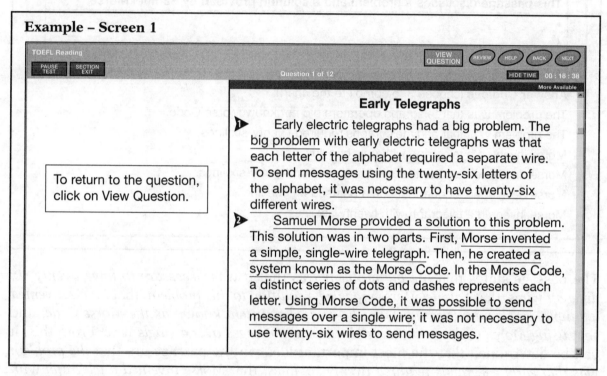

The passage is on one screen, and the question is on a different screen. You can click back and forth between the question and the passage while you are answering this type of question.

Example – Screen 2

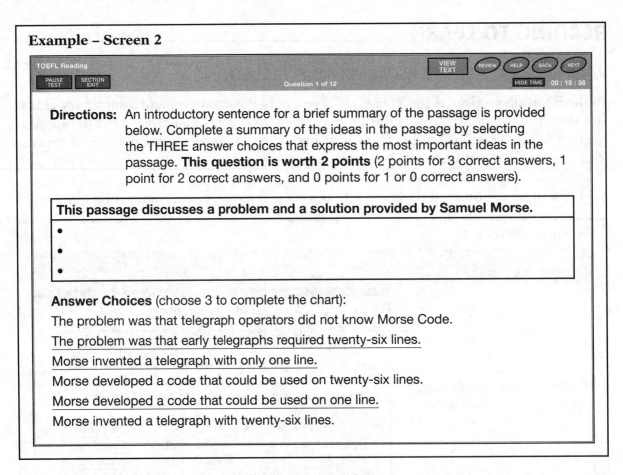

Directions: An introductory sentence for a brief summary of the passage is provided below. Complete a summary of the ideas in the passage by selecting the THREE answer choices that express the most important ideas in the passage. **This question is worth 2 points** (2 points for 3 correct answers, 1 point for 2 correct answers, and 0 points for 1 or 0 correct answers).

This passage discusses a problem and a solution provided by Samuel Morse.

-
-
-

Answer Choices (choose 3 to complete the chart):

The problem was that telegraph operators did not know Morse Code.

The problem was that early telegraphs required twenty-six lines.

Morse invented a telegraph with only one line.

Morse developed a code that could be used on twenty-six lines.

Morse developed a code that could be used on one line.

Morse invented a telegraph with twenty-six lines.

The passage states that *the big problem* was that *it was necessary to have twenty-six different wires,* that *Samuel Morse provided a solution to this problem,* that *Morse invented a simple, single-wire telegraph,* that *he created a system known as the Morse Code,* and that *using Morse Code, it was possible to send messages over a single wire.* From this, it can be determined that the most important ideas in the passage are that *the problem was that early telegraphs required twenty-six lines,* that *Morse invented a telegraph with only one line,* and that *Morse developed a code that could be used on one line.*

The following chart outlines the key information that you should remember about answering summary information questions.

QUESTIONS ABOUT SELECTING SUMMARY INFORMATION	
HOW TO IDENTIFY THE QUESTION	A summary chart is given.
WHERE TO FIND THE ANSWER	To answer this question, you must understand the major points and supporting details. This information is found throughout the passage.
HOW TO ANSWER THE QUESTION	1. Read the topic stated in the summary chart. 2. Read the passage. Focus on the key ideas as they relate to the topic stated in the summary chart. 3. Read each answer choice. Decide whether it is *true* information according to the passage, *false* information according to the passage, or *not discussed* in the passage. 4. Eliminate answers that are *false* or *not discussed*. 5. For each statement that is *true*, decide whether it is a *key idea* or a *minor detail*. 6. Select the answers that are *true* and that are *major factors*. 7. The answers that you select may be in any order. 8. You may receive partial credit if you correctly choose some but not all of the correct answers.
HOW TO SCORE THE RESPONSE	A summary question has 3 correct answers and is worth 2 points. 1. You get 2 points for 3 correct answers. 2. You get 1 point for 2 correct answers. 3. You get 0 points for 1 or 0 correct answers. The answers may be in any order in the chart to be correct.

READING EXERCISE 9: An introductory sentence for a brief summary of each passage is provided. Complete the summary by selecting the answer choices that express the most important ideas in the passage.

PASSAGE ONE *(Question 1)*

Paragraph   **Stress**

1 ▶   In humans, stress may be *biological* or *psychological.* It may also be a combination of the two.

2 ▶   If stress is biological, this means that it comes from the body itself. Biological stress can come from a variety of physical problems. It can come, for example, from disease or physical handicaps. It can also come from situations where there is not enough food or water or sleep or from situations where there is too much cold or heat or noise.

3 ▶   If stress is psychological, this means that it comes from the mind. Psychological stress can come from negative feelings such as feelings of fear, sadness, grief, panic, guilt, or failure.

4 ▶   Some situations can cause both biological and psychological stress. Wars, natural disasters like earthquakes and hurricanes, and serious illness can result in both biological and psychological stress. They can have serious negative effects on both the body and the mind.

Directions: An introductory sentence for a brief summary of the passage is provided below. Complete the summary by selecting the THREE answer choices that express the most important ideas in the passage. **This question is worth 2 points** (2 points for 3 correct answers, 1 point for 2 correct answers, and 0 points for 1 or 0 correct answers).

This passage discusses various kinds of stress.

-
-
-

Answer Choices (choose 3 to complete the chart):

(1) Stress can come from family and friends.

(2) Stress can come from negative feelings.

(3) Stress can come from a job.

(4) Stress can come from physical problems.

(5) Stress can come from a combination of positive and negative feelings.

(6) Stress can come from a combination of physical problems and negative feelings.

PASSAGE TWO *(Question 2)*

Paragraph

Robin Hood

1   Robin Hood is a well-known folk hero. In folk stories, Robin Hood is a kind outlaw who steals from rich people to take care of poor people. Was Robin Hood a real person, or was he only a character in stories? Experts in English history do not agree on the answer to this question. Various groups of authorities have different theories.

2   One theory is that Robin Hood was an actual well-known person. Some people believe that the Earl of Huntingdon was actually Robin Hood.

3   A second theory is that Robin Hood was an actual person but was someone who was not well known, as the Earl of Huntingdon was. Perhaps there was a real man named Robin who did some good deeds. Then folk stories grew up about his good deeds.

4   A third theory is that Robin Hood was not a real person. At the time, perhaps a number of men were taking action to help poor people. Maybe a folk story with a fictional hero, a hero who was not a real person, came to be. And maybe this fictional hero in the story was doing the kinds of things that many real men were doing at the time.

Directions: An introductory sentence for a brief summary of the passage is provided below. Complete the summary by selecting the THREE answer choices that express the most important ideas in the passage. **This question is worth 2 points** (2 points for 3 correct answers, 1 point for 2 correct answers, and 0 points for 1 or 0 correct answers).
Various theories exist about who Robin Hood was.
•   •   •

Answer Choices (choose 3 to complete the chart):

(1) One theory is that Robin Hood was someone who robbed from the poor.

(2) One theory is that Robin Hood was a real person who was well known.

(3) One theory is that Robin Hood was someone who wrote stories.

(4) One theory is that Robin Hood was a fictional person.

(5) One theory is that Robin Hood was a real person who was not well known.

(6) One theory is that Robin Hood was an expert in English history.

PASSAGE THREE *(Question 3)*

Paragraph

The Pocket Veto

1▶ When the U.S. Congress sends a bill, a proposed law, to the president of the United States, then the president has choices. The president can choose to do one of three things with the bill.

2▶ One thing that the president can choose to do is to sign the bill. If the president signs the bill, then the bill becomes an actual law.

3▶ A second way that the president can handle a bill that has been sent by the U.S. Congress is to veto the bill. If the president vetoes the bill, this means that he says "no" to it, or rejects it. A president would veto a bill that he did not want to become law. If the president vetoes a bill, the bill can still become a law. If the president vetoes a bill, the bill is sent back to the Congress; the Congress needs a two-thirds vote to pass a bill and make it a law if the president has vetoed it.

4▶ A third way that a president can handle a bill that Congress sends to the president is simply to do nothing with it. If the bill sits on the president's desk and the session of Congress ends, then the bill is dead. If the bill dies on the president's desk and the president has not either signed or vetoed the bill, this is called a pocket veto.

Directions: An introductory sentence for a brief summary of the passage is provided below. Complete the summary by selecting the THREE answer choices that express the most important ideas in the passage. **This question is worth 2 points** (2 points for 3 correct answers, 1 point for 2 correct answers, and 0 points for 1 or 0 correct answers).

This passage discusses the president's choices when a bill comes from Congress.

-
-
-

Answer Choices (choose 3 to complete the chart):

(1) The president can leave the bill unsigned.

(2) The president can veto the bill.

(3) The president can vote on the bill.

(4) The president can rewrite the bill.

(5) The president can send the bill to Congress.

(6) The president can sign the bill.

Reading Skill 10: COMPLETE SCHEMATIC TABLES

In the Reading section of the TOEFL *iBT*, you may have to complete a schematic table. A schematic table is a table that outlines the key information from a passage. This kind of question may have 5 or 7 correct answers. A question that has 5 correct answers is worth 3 points; in this type of question you will receive 3 points for 5 correct answers, 2 points for 4 correct answers, 1 point for 3 correct answers, and 0 points for either 2, 1, or 0 correct answers. A question that has 7 correct answers is worth 4 points; in this type of question, you will receive 4 points for 7 correct answers, 3 points for 6 correct answers, 2 points for 5 correct answers, 1 point for 4 correct answers, and 0 points for 3, 2, 1, or 0 correct answers.

Look at an example of a question that asks you to complete a schematic table.

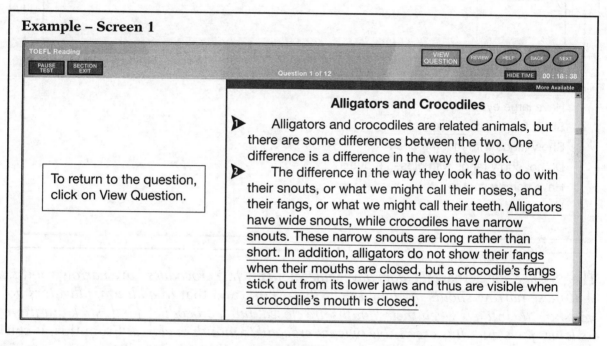

The passage is on one screen, and the question is on a different screen. You can click back and forth between the question and the passage while you are answering this type of question.

Example – Screen 2

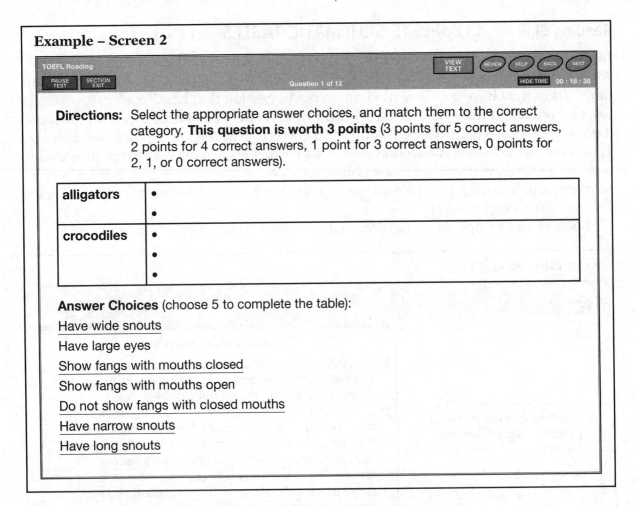

Directions: Select the appropriate answer choices, and match them to the correct category. **This question is worth 3 points** (3 points for 5 correct answers, 2 points for 4 correct answers, 1 point for 3 correct answers, 0 points for 2, 1, or 0 correct answers).

| **alligators** | •
 • |
| **crocodiles** | •
 •
 • |

Answer Choices (choose 5 to complete the table):

Have wide snouts

Have large eyes

Show fangs with mouths closed

Show fangs with mouths open

Do not show fangs with closed mouths

Have narrow snouts

Have long snouts

The passage states that *alligators have wide snouts, while crocodiles have narrow snouts,* that *these narrow snouts are long rather than short,* and that *in addition, alligators do not show their fangs when their mouths are closed, but a crocodile's fangs stick out from its lower jaws and thus are visible when a crocodile's mouth is closed.* From this, it can be determined that the best answers to complete the table are that alligators *have wide snouts* and *do not show fangs with closed mouths* and that crocodiles *have narrow snouts, show fangs with mouths closed,* and *have long snouts.*

The following chart outlines the key information that you should remember about completing schematic tables.

QUESTIONS ABOUT SCHEMATIC TABLES	
HOW TO IDENTIFY THE QUESTION	A schematic table is given.
WHERE TO FIND THE ANSWER	To answer this question, you must understand the major points and supporting details. This information is found throughout the passage.
HOW TO ANSWER THE QUESTION	1. Look at the information that is provided in the schematic table. 2. Read the passage. Focus on the key ideas as they relate to the topic stated in the schematic table. 3. Read each answer choice. Decide whether it is *true* information according to the passage, *false* information according to the passage, or *not discussed* in the passage. 4. Eliminate answers that are *false* or *not discussed*. 5. Match *true* answer choices with the correct category in the schematic table. 6. The answers that you select may be in any order. 7. You may receive partial credit if you correctly choose some but not all of the correct answers.
HOW TO SCORE THE RESPONSE	A schematic table question may have 5 or 7 correct answers. A question with 5 correct answers is worth 3 points. 1. You get 3 points for 5 correct answers. 2. You get 2 points for 4 correct answers. 3. You get 1 point for 3 correct answers. 4. You get 0 points for 2, 1, or 0 correct answers. A question with 7 correct answers is worth 4 points. 1. You get 4 points for 7 correct answers. 2. You get 3 points for 6 correct answers. 3. You get 2 points for 5 correct answers. 4. You get 1 point for 4 correct answers. 5. You get 0 points for 3, 2, 1, or 0 correct answers. The answers may be in any order in the correct box to be correct.

READING EXERCISE 10: Study each passage, and complete the schematic table that follows by matching the answer choice to its appropriate position in the table.

PASSAGE ONE *(Question 1)*

Paragraph

The Mile

1   In America and Great Britain, distances are measured in *miles*. A mile cannot be broken down into simple numbers. Instead, a mile is equal to a very messy 5,280 feet. You may wonder how this came to be.

2   It started with the Romans. The Romans had a rather simple way of measuring distances. The Romans used a measurement called the *mille passuum,* or mile. *Mille passuum* means "a thousand paces." A Roman mile was equal to a thousand paces, and one pace was equal to five feet. Thus, a Roman mile was equal to 5,000 feet, which is a nice, simple number. Unfortunately, the mile did not remain equal to the nice, simple 5,000 feet.

3   The English were the ones who were responsible for changing the mile from 5,000 feet to 5,280 feet. English farmers used a measurement called the furlong, which was equal to 660 feet. Furlongs were used to measure the size of farmers' fields. The English wanted to have a clear relationship between a 660-foot furlong and a 5,000-foot mile. The English decided to keep the furlong at 660 feet and change the mile to eight times the length of a furlong, or 5,280 feet. This is why the mile today is the rather messy 5,280 feet instead of the easier-to-use 5,000 feet.

Directions:	Select the appropriate phrases from the answer choices, and match them to the appropriate group. **This question is worth 3 points** (3 points for 5 correct answers, 2 points for 4 correct answers, 1 point for 3 correct answers, and 0 points for 2, 1, or 0 correct answers).
Romans	• • •
English	• •

Answer Choices (choose 5 to complete the table):

(1) Used a mile of 6 furlongs of 60 feet each

(2) Used a mile of 8 furlongs of 660 feet each

(3) Used a mile of 5,660 feet

(4) Used 1,000 paces of 5 feet each

(5) Used a mile of 5,280 feet

(6) Used a mile of 1,000 paces

(7) Used a mile of 5,000 feet

PASSAGE TWO *(Question 2)*

Paragraph   **Virginia Colony**

1   In the 1580s, the English wanted to create a colony on the mid-Atlantic coast of North America. They wanted to name this colony Virginia. Their efforts were not immediately successful. It took several attempts and a number of years for the English to establish a successful colony in Virginia.

2   The English sent their first group of colonists to Virginia in 1584. This group of colonists was not able to set up a working community. The colonists from this group soon returned to England.

3   Another group of colonists went to Roanoke Island in the Virginia colony in 1587. This group began working to set up a community on Roanoke Island. However, something mysterious happened. All of the colonists simply disappeared from Roanoke Island. Even today, no one is sure what happened to the Virginia colonists on Roanoke Island.

4   A third group of colonists tried again in 1606. This group of colonists settled in Jamestown in the Virginia colony. It was a very difficult task for the colonists at Jamestown to set up a working community, but they did succeed. By the 1620s, the Virginia colony at Jamestown was established.

Directions: Select the appropriate phrases from the answer choices, and match them to the appropriate group of colonists. **This question is worth 4 points** (4 points for 7 correct answers, 3 points for 6 correct answers, 2 points for 5 correct answers, 1 point for 4 correct answers, and 0 points for 3, 2, 1, or 0 correct answers).	
the first group of Virginia colonists	• •
the second group of Virginia colonists	• •
the third group of Virginia colonists	• • •

Answer Choices (choose 7 to complete the table):

(1) Returned to England

(2) Succeeded in establishing a colony

(3) Went to Virginia in 1600

(4) Went to Virginia in 1584

(5) Mysteriously disappeared

(6) Went to Virginia in 1606

(7) Settled a successful colony at Roanoke

(8) Went to Virginia in 1587

(9) Settled in Jamestown

PASSAGE THREE *(Question 3)*

Paragraph

Venus and Earth

▶**1** In the past, people thought that the planets Venus and Earth were very similar. Venus and Earth were called sister planets. Certainly, Venus and Earth are almost the same size: Venus is slightly smaller than Earth. However, there are many differences that make Venus and Earth look like they are not related. For example, Venus is surrounded by thick clouds, while Earth is not. In addition, the average temperature on Venus (480 degrees Centigrade, or 900 degrees Fahrenheit) is far higher than the average temperature on Earth of 60 degrees Fahrenheit. Earth and Venus really should not be called sister planets.

▶**2** In addition to these ways that Venus and Earth differ, they also differ in the direction of their rotation. Venus rotates in a clockwise direction, while Earth rotates in the opposite direction. While on Earth the Sun rises in the east and sets in the west, the opposite happens on Venus.

▶**3** Another difference between Venus and Earth is the length of a day. The length of a day on a planet is the amount of time it takes for the planet to spin on its axis. On Earth, a day is twenty-four hours. On Venus, a day is equal to 243 Earth days. Venus rotates really slowly on its axis.

▶**4** A final difference between Venus and Earth is the length of a year. A year is the amount of time it takes for a planet to move around the Sun. On Earth, a year is about 365 days, while on Venus a year is shorter. On Venus, a year is around 225 Earth days. It is interesting to note, and perhaps hard to understand, that a day on Venus (243 Earth days) is longer than a year on Venus (225 Earth days).

Directions:	Select the appropriate phrases from the answer choices, and match them to the appropriate planet. **This question is worth 4 points** (4 points for 7 correct answers, 3 points for 6 correct answers, 2 points for 5 correct answers, 1 point for 4 correct answers, and 0 points for 3, 2, 1, or 0 correct answers).
Venus	<ul><li></li><li></li><li></li><li></li></ul>
Earth	<ul><li></li><li></li><li></li></ul>

Answer Choices (choose 7 to complete the table):

(1) Has an average temperature of 480 degrees Centigrade

(2) Has a year of 225 Earth days

(3) Rotates in a counterclockwise direction

(4) Has an average temperature of 60 degrees Centigrade

(5) Is not surrounded by thick clouds

(6) Has a day of 243 hours

(7) Has an average temperature of 60 degrees Fahrenheit

(8) Has a day of 243 Earth days

(9) Rotates in a clockwise direction

READING EXERCISE (Skills 9–10): Study the passage, and choose the best answers to the questions that follow.

The Manned Space Program

➊ The U.S. manned space flight program of the 1960s and 1970s consisted of three distinct phases: Mercury, Gemini, and Apollo. Each of these distinct phases of the space flight program served a very different purpose.

➋ Mercury was the first phase of the manned space flight program. Its purpose was to get a person into orbital flight. The tiny Mercury capsule carried only a single astronaut. Alan B. Shepherd and Virgil Grissom piloted the first two Mercury flights, which were suborbital flights, in 1961. John Glenn, in the next Mercury flight, orbited the Earth in 1962. Three more Mercury flights followed.

➌ The next phase of the manned space flight program was Gemini; the name "Gemini" was taken from the name of the constellation, which means "twins." The purpose of the ten crewed Gemini flights in 1965 and 1966 was to conduct training tests necessary for longer space flights. Gemini, for example, carried out training in orbital docking techniques and tests of the effects of long-term weightlessness on astronauts. Unlike Mercury capsules, which held only one astronaut, the Gemini capsules were designed to carry two astronauts.

➍ The Apollo flights followed the Gemini flights with the goal of landing astronauts on the Moon. The Apollo spacecraft consisted of three modules. The command module carried three astronauts to and from the Moon, the service module housed the propulsion and environmental systems, and the lunar module separated from the command module to land two astronauts on the Moon. There were seventeen total Apollo flights, of which the first six carried no crew. The seventh through tenth Apollo flights (1968–1969) circumnavigated the Moon without landing and then returned to Earth. The next seven Apollo flights (1969–1972) were intended to land on the Moon. All of them did, except *Apollo 13,* which developed serious problems and had to abort the intended landing but still managed to return safely to Earth.

1.

Directions:	An introductory sentence for a brief summary of the passage is provided below. Complete the summary by selecting the THREE answer choices that express the most important ideas in the passage. **This question is worth 2 points** (2 points for 3 correct answers, 1 point for 2 correct answers, and 0 points for 1 or 0 correct answers).
This passage describes three phases in the U.S. manned space program.	
• • •	

Answer Choices (choose 3 to complete the chart):

(1) One phase sent a single person into suborbital and orbital flight.

(2) One phase sent a spaceship without an astronaut.

(3) One phase sent three astronauts together to the Moon.

(4) One phase sent a single person into suborbital flight only.

(5) One phase sent three astronauts together into orbital flight.

(6) One phase sent two astronauts together to conduct tests.

2.

Directions:	Select the appropriate phrases from the answer choices, and match them to the correct flights. **This question is worth 3 points** (3 points for 5 correct answers, 2 points for 4 correct answers, 1 point for 3 correct answers, and 0 points for 2, 1, or 0 correct answers).
Mercury flights	• •
Gemini flights	• •
Apollo flights	•

Answer Choices (choose 5 to complete the table):

(1) Had no astronauts

(2) Consisted of training tests to prepare for flights to the Moon

(3) Consisted of flights to the Moon

(4) Had one astronaut

(5) Consisted of flights beyond the Moon

(6) Had two astronauts

(7) Consisted of orbital and suborbital flights

3.

Directions: An introductory sentence for a brief summary of the passage is provided below. Complete the summary by selecting the THREE answer choices that express the most important ideas in the passage. **This question is worth 2 points** (2 points for 3 correct answers, 1 point for 2 correct answers, and 0 points for 1 or 0 correct answers).

The Mercury flights had these characteristics.

-
-
-

Answer Choices (choose 3 to complete the chart):

(1) They were U.S. space flights.

(2) They were part of the second phase of the space program.

(3) They were all suborbital flights.

(4) They carried one astronaut each.

(5) They consisted of a total of six flights.

(6) They started in 1961 and ended in 1962.

4.

Directions: An introductory sentence for a brief summary of the passage is provided below. Complete the summary by selecting the THREE answer choices that express the most important ideas in the passage. **This question is worth 2 points** (2 points for 3 correct answers, 1 point for 2 correct answers, and 0 points for 1 or 0 correct answers).

The Gemini flights had these characteristics.

-
-
-

Answer Choices (choose 3 to complete the chart):

(1) They were conducted in 1961–1962.

(2) They carried two astronauts each.

(3) They took place over a five-year period.

(4) They orbited the Moon.

(5) They consisted of a total of ten flights.

(6) They conducted training tests.

5.

Directions:	Select the appropriate phrases from the answer choices, and match them to the correct module. **This question is worth 3 points** (3 points for 5 correct answers, 2 points for 4 correct answers, 1 point for 3 correct answers, and 0 points for 2, 1, or 0 correct answers).
command module in the spacecraft	• •
service module in the spacecraft	• •
lunar module in the spacecraft	•

Answer Choices (choose 5 to complete the table):

(1) Carried astronauts between the spacecraft and the Moon

(2) Carried astronauts to the service module

(3) Carried astronauts from Earth to the Moon

(4) Carried systems to maintain the environment of the spacecraft

(5) Carried astronauts during training missions

(6) Carried systems to propel the spacecraft

(7) Carried astronauts from the Moon to the Earth

READING REVIEW EXERCISE (Skills 1–10): Read the passage.

Roald Dahl

1 ⮞ Roald Dahl (1916–1990) was the well-known author of more than a dozen children's books, including *James and the Giant Peach* (1961), *Charlie and the Chocolate Factory* (1967), and *George's Marvelous Medicine* (1981). Dahl began his writing career after serving in World War II, but not by writing stories for children. For many years at the onset of his career, he wrote short stories for adults. Many of these stories for adults were published, but Dahl did not achieve the same success with his stories for adults that he was to achieve with his stories for children.

2 ⮞ With the 1961 publication of *James and the Giant Peach,* his first book for children, Roald Dahl began building a huge audience for his writings, and he eventually became one of the world's most read and most popular authors of children's stories. In his books, the world is a wondrous and inventive place where children are able to triumph over evil. In *James and the Giant Peach,* James takes off on a fantastic adventure by burrowing into a large peach. The uncaring adults in his life, his parents and aunts Spicer and Sponge, are dealt with quite harshly. In *Charlie and the Chocolate Factory,* Charlie and his grandfather take a fantastic voyage through Willy Wonka's Chocolate Factory, an establishment equipped with amazing machinery that gives out punishment for bad behavior. In *George's Marvelous Medicine,* George provides his horrible grandmother with a kind of medicine that does incredibly imaginative things to her in retaliation for her misdeeds.

3 ⮞ As can be seen from these sketches of his work, Dahl did not write the saccharine-sweet stories of goodness often associated with children's literature. The combination in his work of fantasy and harshness in response to evil, nonetheless, has inspired quite an enthusiastic following.

Refer to this version of the passage to answer the questions that follow.

Paragraph

Roald Dahl

▶ 1   Roald Dahl (1916–1990) was the well-known author of more than a dozen children's books, including *James and the Giant Peach* (1961), *Charlie and the Chocolate Factory* (1967), and *George's Marvelous Medicine* (1981). Dahl began his writing career after serving in World War II, but not by writing stories for children. For many years at the onset of his career, he wrote short stories for adults. Many of these stories for adults were published, but Dahl did not achieve the same success with his stories for adults that he was to achieve with his stories for children.

▶ 2   With the 1961 publication of *James and the Giant Peach,* his first book for children, Roald Dahl began building a huge audience for his writings, and he eventually became one of the world's most read and most popular authors of children's stories. In his books, the world is a wondrous and inventive place where children are able to triumph over evil. In *James and the Giant Peach,* James takes off on a fantastic adventure by burrowing into a large peach. The uncaring adults in his life, his parents and aunts Spicer and Sponge, are dealt with quite harshly. In *Charlie and the Chocolate Factory,* Charlie and his grandfather take a fantastic voyage through Willy Wonka's Chocolate Factory, an establishment equipped with amazing machinery that gives out punishment for bad behavior. In *George's Marvelous Medicine,* George provides his horrible grandmother with a kind of medicine that does incredibly imaginative things to her in retaliation for her misdeeds.

▶ 3   **10A** As can be seen from these sketches of his work, Dahl did not write the saccharine-sweet stories of goodness often associated with children's literature. **10B** The combination in his work of fantasy and harshness in response to evil, nonetheless, has inspired quite an enthusiastic following. **10C**

1. Which of the following is NOT mentioned in the passage about Roald Dahl?
    (A) The years he lived
    (B) The number of children's books he wrote
    (C) When he wrote *James and the Giant Peach*
    (D) The names of all of his children's books

2. It can be inferred from the passage that, early in his adult life, Dahl was
    (A) in the military
    (B) in an orchestra
    (C) a factory employee
    (D) a medical doctor

3. The word "onset" in paragraph 1 is closest in meaning to
    (A) sunset
    (B) end
    (C) placement
    (D) start

4. Why does the author mention "short stories for adults" in a passage about children's stories?
    (A) To show the kind of material that Dahl really wanted to write
    (B) To show the kind of material that Dahl wrote for most of his life
    (C) To show that Dahl had not always written stories for children
    (D) To show that Dahl was an adult and not a child

5. What is stated in paragraph 1 about the stories that Dahl wrote for adults?
    (A) They were never published.
    (B) They were less successful than his children's stories.
    (C) They were as successful as his children's stories.
    (D) They were more successful than his children's stories.

6. Which of the sentences below best expresses the essential information in the highlighted sentence in paragraph 2?
    (A) Roald Dahl started writing children's books with *James and the Giant Peach*, and after some time many people began reading and enjoying his books.
    (B) Roald Dahl had already built a huge audience with children before he started writing *James and the Giant Peach*.
    (C) Roald Dahl really liked writing children's stories like *James and the Giant Peach*, but he never became successful writing children's stories.
    (D) Roald Dahl wrote many children's books before *James and the Giant Peach*, but that book is the one that made him really famous.

7.

Directions:	Select the appropriate phrases from the answer choices, and match them to the appropriate story. **This question is worth 4 points** (4 points for 7 correct answers, 3 points for 6 correct answers, 2 points for 5 correct answers, 1 point for 4 correct answers, and 0 points for 3, 2, 1, or 0 correct answers).

James and the Giant Peach	• • •
Charlie and the Chocolate Factory	• •
George's Marvelous Medicine	• •

Answer Choices (choose 7 to complete the table):

(1) Includes a grandfather

(2) Includes horrible brothers and sisters

(3) Is about a trip into a piece of fruit

(4) Includes a terrible grandparent

(5) Includes aunts who are not nice

(6) Takes place in a plant where sweets are made

(7) Is about a fantastic medication

(8) Includes a father named Willy Wonka

(9) Includes an uncaring mother and father

8. The word "her" in paragraph 2 refers to

Ⓐ aunts Spicer and Sponge

Ⓑ grandmother

Ⓒ George

Ⓓ Dahl

9. The word "misdeeds" in paragraph 2 is closest in meaning to

Ⓐ bad behavior

Ⓑ good will

Ⓒ incorrect answers

Ⓓ nice sayings

10. Look at the three squares [■] that indicate where the following sentence could be added to paragraph 3.

Quite the opposite, his stories are often filled with horrid images.

Where would the sentence best fit? Click on a square [■] to add the sentence to the paragraph.

11.

Directions: An introductory sentence for a brief summary of the passage is provided below. Complete the summary by selecting the THREE answer choices that express the most important ideas in the passage. **This question is worth 2 points** (2 points for 3 correct answers, 1 point for 2 correct answers, and 0 points for 1 or 0 correct answers).

Roald Dahl's stories for children have certain unique characteristics.

-
-
-

Answer Choices (choose 3 to complete the chart):

(1) Life is always sweet.

(2) Adults can be bad.

(3) The world can be a fantastic place.

(4) Family members are always kind to children.

(5) Fruit is in every story.

(6) Children can triumph over evil.

READING POST-TEST

30 minutes

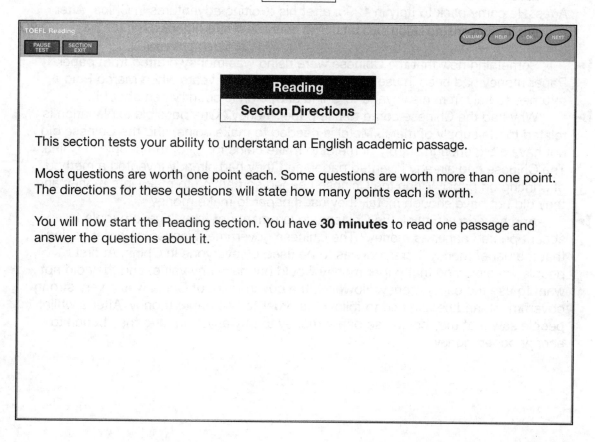

PAUSE TEST | SECTION EXIT

VOLUME | HELP | OK | NEXT

Reading
Section Directions

This section tests your ability to understand an English academic passage.

Most questions are worth one point each. Some questions are worth more than one point. The directions for these questions will state how many points each is worth.

You will now start the Reading section. You have **30 minutes** to read one passage and answer the questions about it.

Read the passage.

A New Idea

1   Italian adventurer Marco Polo traveled to China near the end of the Middle Ages. He came back to Italy in 1295, after his exciting adventures in China. After his return, he told the Italians about some really new and different things the Chinese were doing.

2   Something new that the Chinese were using was money crafted from paper. Paper money had been in use in China for hundreds of years when Marco Polo returned to Italy from his voyage to China and told his countrymen about it.

3   Why had the Chinese come to use paper money? One possible explanation is related to the supply of metal. Metal is needed to make coins, and the Chinese did not have a big enough supply of metal to make coins for all of the people in China. The Chinese had already invented paper, and they had already invented a method of printing on paper. When the Chinese needed something to make into money and they did not have enough metal, they used paper to make money.

4   And how do you think the Chinese government got the Chinese people to accept printed paper as money? The Chinese government issued an order saying that the paper money it created was to be used by everyone in China. At first, people were worried that paper money would not have any value, and they did not want to use the paper money. However, the government of China was a very strong government, and people had to follow the order to use paper money. After a while, people saw that they could use paper money to buy anything, and they began to accept paper money.

Refer to this version of the passage to answer the questions that follow.

Paragraph   **A New Idea**

▶❶   **3A** Italian adventurer Marco Polo traveled to China near the end of the Middle Ages. **3B** He came back to Italy in 1295, after his exciting adventures in China. **3C** After his return, he told the Italians about some really new and different things the Chinese were doing. **3D**

▶❷   Something new that the Chinese were using was money crafted from paper. Paper money had been in use in China for hundreds of years when Marco Polo returned to Italy from his voyage to China and told his countrymen about it.

▶❸   Why had the Chinese come to use paper money? One possible explanation is related to the supply of metal. Metal is needed to make coins, and the Chinese did not have a big enough supply of metal to make coins for all of the people in China. The Chinese had already invented paper, and they had already invented a method of printing on paper. When the Chinese needed something to make into money and they did not have enough metal, they used paper to make money.

▶❹   And how do you think the Chinese government got the Chinese people to accept printed paper as money? **15A** The Chinese government issued an order saying that the paper money it created was to be used by everyone in China. At first, people were worried that paper money would not have any value, and they did not want to use the paper money. **15B** However, the government of China was a very strong government, and people had to follow the order to use paper money. **15C** After a while, people saw that they could use paper money to buy anything, and they began to accept paper money. **15D**

1. According to paragraph 1, when did Marco Polo return to Italy from his trip to China?

Ⓐ At the start of the twelfth century
Ⓑ At the end of the twelfth century
Ⓒ At the start of the thirteenth century
Ⓓ At the end of the thirteenth century

2. According to paragraph 1, Marco Polo did all of the following EXCEPT

Ⓐ travel outside of Italy
Ⓑ visit China
Ⓒ live in China throughout his life
Ⓓ return to Italy after his travels

3. Look at the four squares [■] that indicate where the following sentence could be added to paragraph 1.

It was a trip that lasted twenty-four years.

Where would the sentence best fit? Click on a square [■] to add the sentence to the paragraph.

4. The word "crafted" in paragraph 2 could best be replaced by

Ⓐ shipped
Ⓑ made
Ⓒ brought
Ⓓ chosen

5. It can be inferred from the passage that the Chinese might have begun using paper money

Ⓐ in the ninth or tenth century
Ⓑ in the twelfth or thirteenth century
Ⓒ in the fourteenth or fifteenth century
Ⓓ in the sixteenth or seventeenth century

6. The word "voyage" in paragraph 2 is closest in meaning to

Ⓐ flight
Ⓑ image
Ⓒ dream
Ⓓ trip

7. The word "it" in paragraph 2 refers to

Ⓐ paper money
Ⓑ use
Ⓒ China
Ⓓ Italy

8. It is NOT mentioned in paragraph 3 that the Chinese

Ⓐ invented paper
Ⓑ created a way of printing
Ⓒ mined for metals
Ⓓ created paper money

9. The author begins paragraph 3 with the question "Why had the Chinese come to use paper money" in order to show that

Ⓐ the answer is unknown to the author
Ⓑ the passage is written in a casual style
Ⓒ the answer is a really easy one
Ⓓ the question is answered in the rest of the paragraph

10. Which of the sentences below best expresses the essential information in the second highlighted sentence in paragraph 3?

Ⓐ The Chinese were not able to make metal coins because they did not have enough metal.
Ⓑ The Chinese had so much metal that it was too valuable to be used in coins.
Ⓒ The Chinese did not want to use metal in coins.
Ⓓ The Chinese did not have enough of a supply of money to make metal.

11. It is implied in paragraph 3 that

Ⓐ a method of printing was invented before paper was created
Ⓑ a method of printing was invented before paper money was created
Ⓒ printing was used only to create paper money
Ⓓ paper was invented in order to make paper money

12. The word "it" in paragraph 4 refers to

Ⓐ printed paper

Ⓑ the Chinese government

Ⓒ an order

Ⓓ paper money

13. Which of the sentences below best expresses the essential information in the highlighted sentence in paragraph 4?

Ⓐ At first, people used paper money, but then it lost its value.

Ⓑ People never used paper money from the beginning because it was too valuable.

Ⓒ From the beginning, people were afraid of using paper money because it might be worthless.

Ⓓ People were worried in the beginning that they would not have enough money.

14. The author uses the word "However" in paragraph 4 in order to show that

Ⓐ the opposite of what people wanted happened

Ⓑ the government of China was not very strong

Ⓒ the people really wanted to use paper money

Ⓓ it was expected that the people would use paper money

15. Look at the four squares [■] that indicate where the following sentence could be added to paragraph 4.

Everyone had to use it even if they did not want to.

Where would the sentence best fit? Click on a square [■] to add the sentence to the paragraph.

16. According to paragraph 4, what happened after a while?

Ⓐ People could not use paper money.

Ⓑ People refused to follow the order to use paper money.

Ⓒ Paper money went away because people would not use it.

Ⓓ People began to think that paper money was all right.

17.

Marco Polo learned about a certain new idea in China.

-
-
-

Answer Choices (choose 3 to complete the chart):

(1) The government of China got the people to use paper money by ordering it.

(2) Paper was used for money in China because it was lighter than metal.

(3) The new idea was the use of paper for money.

(4) The government of China got people to use paper money by suggesting it.

(5) The new idea was the invention of paper.

(6) Paper was used for money in China because there was not enough metal.

18.

Directions:	Select the appropriate answer choices about the new idea from the passage, and match them to the correct category. **This question is worth 3 points** (3 points for 5 correct answers, 2 points for 4 correct answers, 1 point for 3 correct answers, 0 points for 2, 1, or 0 correct answers).
what it was	•
why it happened	• •
how it happened	• •

Answer Choices (choose 5 to complete the table):

(1) Eventual acceptance by the people

(2) Money made from paper

(3) A request from Marco Polo

(4) An order from the Chinese government

(5) An inadequate supply of paper

(6) An ability to print on paper

(7) An inadequate supply of metal

Turn to pages 448–450 to *diagnose* your errors and *record* your results.

SECTION TWO

LISTENING

LISTENING DIAGNOSTIC PRE-TEST

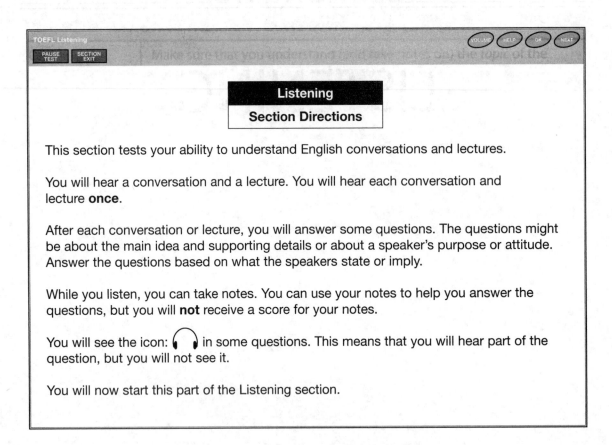

TOEFL Listening

PAUSE TEST | SECTION EXIT

VOLUME | HELP | OK | NEXT

Listening
Section Directions

This section tests your ability to understand English conversations and lectures.

You will hear a conversation and a lecture. You will hear each conversation and lecture **once**.

After each conversation or lecture, you will answer some questions. The questions might be about the main idea and supporting details or about a speaker's purpose or attitude. Answer the questions based on what the speakers state or imply.

While you listen, you can take notes. You can use your notes to help you answer the questions, but you will **not** receive a score for your notes.

You will see the icon: 🎧 in some questions. This means that you will hear part of the question, but you will not see it.

You will now start this part of the Listening section.

Questions 1–6

Listen as two students have a conversation.
The conversation is on an economics class.

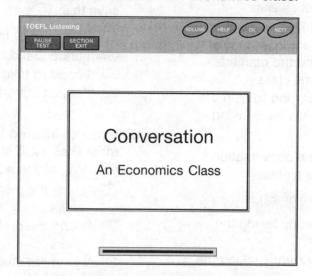

1. Why is the woman talking with the man?
   - (A) Because she is having a problem with one of her classes
   - (B) Because she enjoys economics class more than the man does
   - (C) Because she and the man are taking the same class
   - (D) Because she is trying to help the man with a class he is taking

2. What is stated in the conversation about the economics class?

   Click on 2 answers.

   - [A] The man is currently taking the course.
   - [B] The woman is currently taking the course.
   - [C] The man thinks it is an enjoyable class.
   - [D] The woman thinks it is an enjoyable class.

3. How does the woman seem to feel about the economics class?
   - (A) She seems to think that the professor asks too many questions in class.
   - (B) She seems to think that she understands less than the other students.
   - (C) She seems to think that the professor is not really likeable.
   - (D) She seems to think that none of the students understands the professor.

4. Listen again to part of the passage. Then answer the question.

   What does the man mean when he says this:
   - (A) "I'm afraid of that."
   - (B) "I understand that."
   - (C) "I need to take more time on that."
   - (D) "I'm just not sure about that."

5. It can be inferred that the man would most likely NOT suggest which of the following to the woman?
   - (A) Asking the professor questions in class
   - (B) Asking the professor questions after class
   - (C) Asking the students questions during class
   - (D) Asking the students questions after class

6. Is each of these discussed in the passage? **This question is worth 2 points** (2 points for 4 correct answers, 1 point for 3 correct answers, and 0 points for 2, 1, or 0 correct answers).

   For each answer, click in the YES or NO column.

	YES	NO
A problem the man is having		
A problem the woman is having		
A solution offered by the man		
A solution offered by the woman		

Questions 7–12

Listen to a discussion in a geography class.
The discussion is on Antarctica.

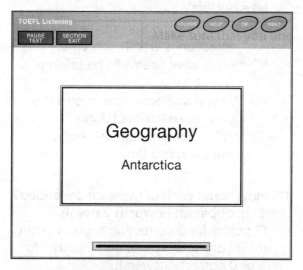

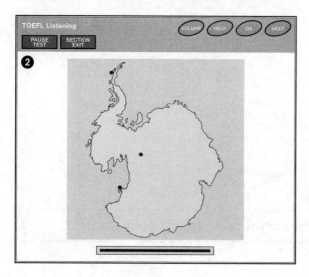

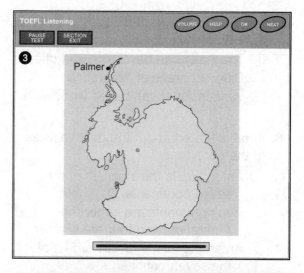

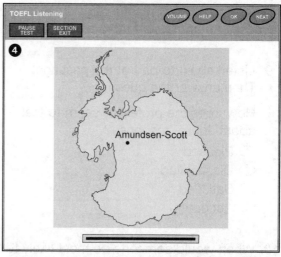

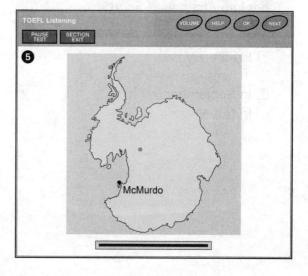

7. What is the lecture mainly about?

Ⓐ The relative size of Antarctica

Ⓑ The American bases on Antarctica

Ⓒ Different areas of Antarctica

Ⓓ Various American bases worldwide

8. What is stated about the relative sizes of the continents?

Ⓐ Antarctica is the smallest of the seven continents.

Ⓑ Two continents are larger than Antarctica, and four are smaller.

Ⓒ Antarctica is the fourth largest of the seven continents.

Ⓓ Four continents are larger than Antarctica, and two are smaller.

9. Listen again to part of the passage. Then answer the question. 🎧

How does the professor seem to feel about John's response?

Ⓐ Pleased

Ⓑ Dissatisfied

Ⓒ Satisfied

Ⓓ Accepting

10. When would someone be most likely to get into Amundsen-Scott?

Click on 2 answers.

Ⓐ In January

Ⓑ In June

Ⓒ In September

Ⓓ In November

11. Listen again to part of the passage. Then answer the question. 🎧

What does the professor mean when he says this?

Ⓐ "I'm sure John can answer the question correctly this time."

Ⓑ "Pat always seems to be talking about John."

Ⓒ "Maybe someone else knows the answer better than John."

Ⓓ "I think John should ask Pat a question this time."

12. How could each of these be described? **This question is worth 2 points** (2 points for 3 correct answers, 1 point for 2 correct answers, and 0 points for 1 or 0 correct answers).

Click on a phrase. Then drag it to the space where it belongs. Each answer will be used one time only.

Is nearest the South Pole	Is used mainly for wildlife studies	Is the biggest American base

Palmer	Amundsen-Scott	McMurdo

Turn to pages 451-453 to *diagnose* your errors and *record* your results.

LISTENING OVERVIEW

The second section on the TOEFL *iBT* is the Listening section. This section consists of six passages, each followed by five or six questions. You may take notes as you listen to the passages and use your notes as you answer the questions.

- The **passages** are set in an academic environment. Each listening section has two conversations that take place outside of the classroom and four lectures or discussions that take place inside the classroom. The shorter conversations are each followed by five questions, while the longer lectures or discussions are each followed by six questions.

- The **questions** may ask about main ideas and details, the speaker's function or stance, the organization of ideas, and inferences based on the passage.

The following strategies can help you in the Listening section.

STRATEGIES FOR LISTENING

1. **Be familiar with the directions.** The directions on every test are the same, so it is not necessary to spend time reading the directions carefully when you take the test. You should be completely familiar with the directions before the day of the test.

2. **Dismiss the directions as soon as they come up.** The time starts when the directions come up. You should already be familiar with the directions, so you can click on Continue as soon as it appears and save all of your time for the passages and questions.

3. **Do not worry if a listening passage is on a topic that is not familiar to you.** All of the information that you need to answer the questions is included in the passage. You do not need any background knowledge to answer the questions.

4. **Listen carefully to the passage.** You will hear the passage one time only. You may not repeat the passage during the test.

5. **Use the visuals to help you to understand the passage.** Each passage begins with a photograph showing the setting (such as a classroom or a campus office) and the person or people who are speaking. There may be other visuals (such as a diagram, a drawing, or a chalkboard with important terminology) to help you to understand the content of the passage.

6. **Take careful notes as you listen to the spoken material.** You should focus on the main points and key supporting material. Do not try to write down everything you hear. Do not write down too many unnecessary details.

---

7. **Look at each question to determine what type of question it is.** The type of question tells you how to proceed to answer the question.

- For *gist questions,* listen carefully to the beginning of the passage to develop an initial idea about the gist of the passage. Then, as you listen to the rest of the passage, adjust your idea about the gist of the passage as you listen to what the speakers are saying.

- For *detail questions,* listen carefully to the details in the passage. Then look for an answer that restates the information from the passage.

- For *function questions,* listen carefully to what the speaker says in the part of the passage that is repeated. Then draw a conclusion about why the speaker says it.

- For *stance questions,* listen carefully to what the speaker says in the part of the passage that is repeated. Then draw a conclusion about what the speaker feels.

- For *organization questions,* listen carefully to each of the points in the passage, and consider how these points are organized. Then look for an answer that shows the organization of the points.

- For *relationship questions,* listen carefully to each of the points in the passage, and consider how these points might be related. Then look for an answer that shows how the points are related.

8. **Choose the best answer to each question.** You may be certain of a particular answer, or you may eliminate any definitely incorrect answers and choose from among the remaining answers.

9. **Think carefully about a question before you answer it.** You may not return to a question later in the test. You have only one opportunity to answer a given question.

10. **Do not spend too much time on a question you are unsure of.** If you truly do not know the answer to a question, simply guess and go on.

11. **Monitor the time carefully on the title bar of the computer screen.** The title bar indicates the time remaining in the section, the total number of questions in the section, and the number of the question that you are working on.

12. **Guess to complete the section before time is up.** It can only increase your score to guess the answers to questions that you do not have time to complete. (Points are not subtracted for incorrect answers.)

LISTENING SKILLS

The following skills will help you to implement these strategies in the Listening section of the TOEFL *iBT*.

BASIC COMPREHENSION

Basic comprehension questions are related to what is stated in the passage. These questions may ask about the **gist** (the main idea or overall topic), or they may ask about specific **details** in the passage.

Listening Skill 1: UNDERSTAND THE GIST

Gist questions are questions that ask about the overall ideas of a passage as a whole. They may ask about the *subject, topic,* or *main idea* of the passage. The gist of a passage may be directly stated in the beginning of the passage. It may also be necessary to bring together information from different parts of the passage to understand the gist. Look at an example of part of a listening passage.

Example

You see on the computer screen:

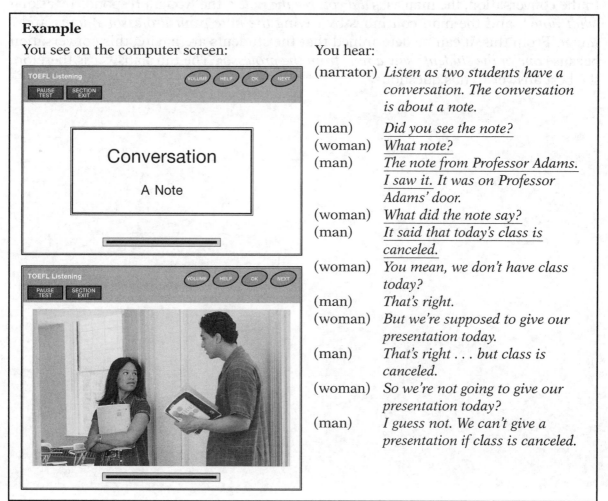

You hear:

(narrator) *Listen as two students have a conversation. The conversation is about a note.*

(man) *Did you see the note?*
(woman) *What note?*
(man) *The note from Professor Adams. I saw it. It was on Professor Adams' door.*
(woman) *What did the note say?*
(man) *It said that today's class is canceled.*
(woman) *You mean, we don't have class today?*
(man) *That's right.*
(woman) *But we're supposed to give our presentation today.*
(man) *That's right . . . but class is canceled.*
(woman) *So we're not going to give our presentation today?*
(man) *I guess not. We can't give a presentation if class is canceled.*

After you listen to the conversation, the question and answer choices appear on the computer screen as the narrator states the question. This is a gist question that asks about the topic of the passage.

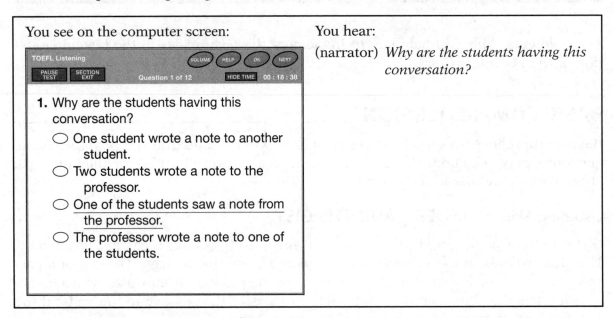

You see on the computer screen:

You hear:

(narrator) *Why are the students having this conversation?*

In the conversation, the man asks *did you see the note?*, the woman responds by asking *what note?*, and the man continues by saying *the note from Professor Adams* and *I saw it*. From this, it can be determined that the students are having this conversation because *one of the students saw a note from the professor*. The third answer is therefore the best answer to this question.

Now look at an example of another type of gist question. This question asks about the overall topic of the passage.

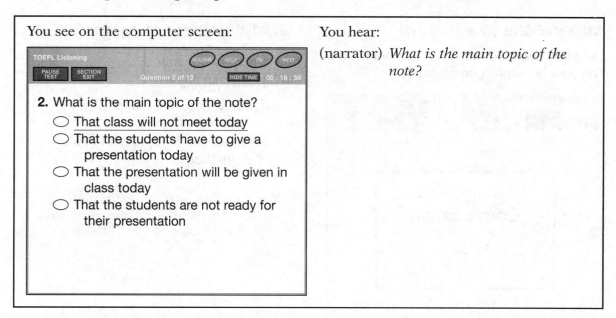

In the conversation, the woman asks *what did the note say?*, and the man replies that *it said that today's class is canceled*. From this, it can be determined that the main topic of the note is *that class will not meet today*. The first answer is therefore the best answer to this question.

The following chart outlines the key points that you should remember about gist questions.

QUESTIONS ABOUT THE GIST OF A PASSAGE	
HOW TO IDENTIFY THE QUESTION	What is the **subject** of the passage? What is the **topic** of the passage? What is the **main idea** of the passage? What is the **purpose** of the passage? **Why** . . . in the passage?
WHERE TO FIND THE ANSWER	Information to help you understand the gist may be directly stated at the *beginning* of the passage. It may also be necessary to bring together information from *different parts* of the passage to understand the gist.
HOW TO ANSWER THE QUESTION	1. Listen carefully to the *beginning* of the passage to develop an initial idea about the gist of the passage. 2. Then, as you listen to the *rest of the passage,* adjust your idea of the gist as you focus on the main points of the passage.

LISTENING EXERCISE 1: Listen to each passage and the questions that follow. Then choose the best answers to the questions.

PASSAGE ONE *(Questions 1–2)*

Listen as two students have a conversation. The conversation is on an exam.

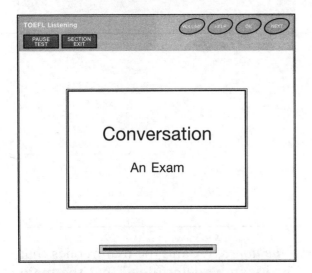

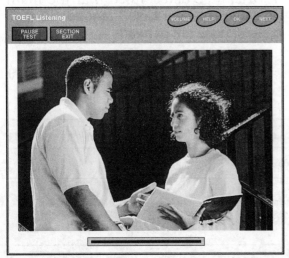

1. Why does the woman want to talk with the man?
- Ⓐ To find out what is on the English exam
- Ⓑ To find out about an exam they took
- Ⓒ To find out when the English exam will be given
- Ⓓ To find out what is on the math exam

2. What is covered on the exam?
- Ⓐ Only Chapter 9 in the textbook
- Ⓑ Only Chapters 10 and 11 in the textbook
- Ⓒ Only Chapters 9 and 10 in the textbook
- Ⓓ Chapters 9, 10, and 11 in the textbook

PASSAGE TWO (Questions 3–4)

Listen as a student consults with a professor. The conversation is about a reading assignment.

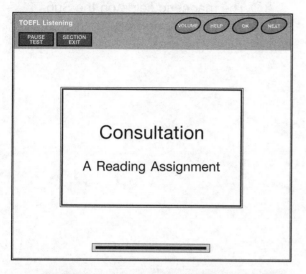

3. Why does the student go to see the professor?
   Ⓐ To turn in an assignment
   Ⓑ To get an answer to a question
   Ⓒ To answer the professor's question
   Ⓓ To get a copy of an article

4. What is the student mainly confused about?
   Ⓐ Which articles to read
   Ⓑ How many articles to read
   Ⓒ When to finish reading the articles
   Ⓓ Where the names of the articles were written

PASSAGE THREE *(Questions 5–6)*

Listen to a lecture in an astronomy class. The lecture is on sunspots.

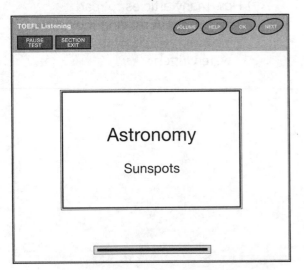

5. Why is the professor discussing this material?

 Ⓐ Because it is going to be included on a test

 Ⓑ Because a student asked a question about it

 Ⓒ Because it is covered in the textbook

 Ⓓ Because the students must complete an assignment on it

6. What is the talk mainly about?

 Ⓐ The high temperatures on the Sun

 Ⓑ Some important characteristics of sunspots

 Ⓒ The magnetic fields on the Sun

 Ⓓ The irregular number of sunspots

Listening Skill 2: UNDERSTAND THE DETAILS

Detail questions ask you about specific pieces of information that are stated in a passage. As you listen to each passage, you should focus on the details from the passage because questions about details are quite common. Multiple-choice questions are used to test details, and these multiple-choice questions may have one correct answer or two correct answers. Look at an example of part of a listening passage.

Example

You see on the computer screen:

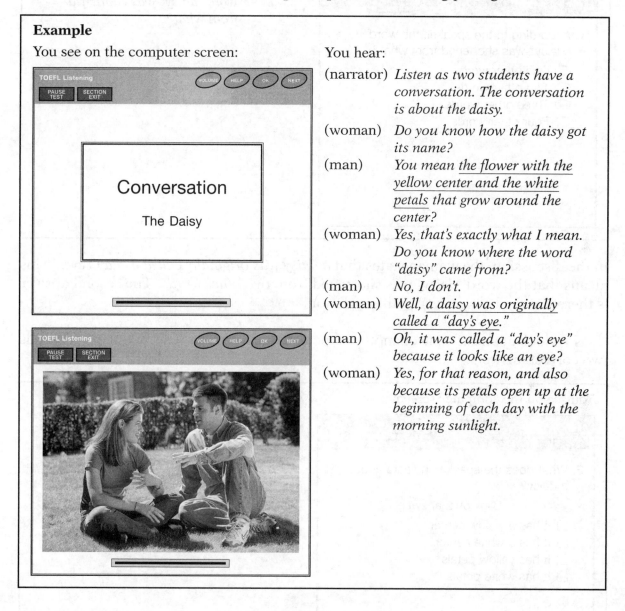

You hear:

(narrator) *Listen as two students have a conversation. The conversation is about the daisy.*

(woman) *Do you know how the daisy got its name?*

(man) *You mean the flower with the yellow center and the white petals that grow around the center?*

(woman) *Yes, that's exactly what I mean. Do you know where the word "daisy" came from?*

(man) *No, I don't.*

(woman) *Well, a daisy was originally called a "day's eye."*

(man) *Oh, it was called a "day's eye" because it looks like an eye?*

(woman) *Yes, for that reason, and also because its petals open up at the beginning of each day with the morning sunlight.*

After you listen to the conversation, the first question and answer choices appear on the computer screen as the narrator states the question. This is a detail question with one correct answer.

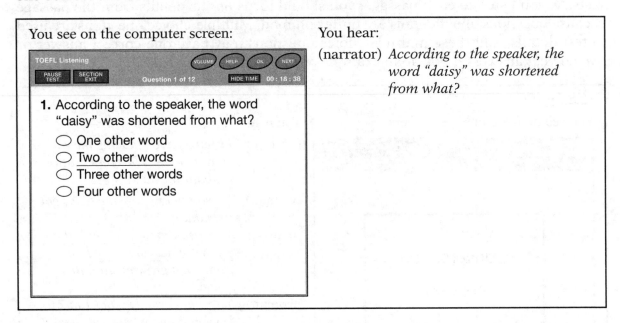

You see on the computer screen:	You hear:
	(narrator) *According to the speaker, the word "daisy" was shortened from what?*

1. According to the speaker, the word "daisy" was shortened from what?
- One other word
- Two other words
- Three other words
- Four other words

In the discussion, the woman states that *a daisy was originally called a "day's eye."* This means that the word *"daisy"* was shortened from *two other words*. The second answer is therefore the best answer to this question.

Now look at an example of another type of detail question. This detail question has two correct answers.

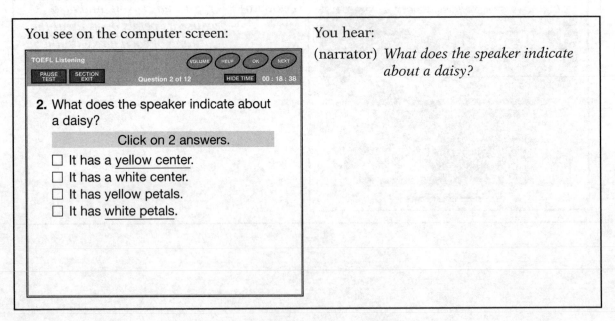

You see on the computer screen:	You hear:
	(narrator) *What does the speaker indicate about a daisy?*

2. What does the speaker indicate about a daisy?

Click on 2 answers.
- ☐ It has a yellow center.
- ☐ It has a white center.
- ☐ It has yellow petals.
- ☐ It has white petals.

In the discussion, the man mentions *the flower with the yellow center and the white petals.* This means that a daisy has a *yellow center* and *white petals*. The first and last answers are therefore the best answers to this question.

The following chart outlines the key points that you should remember about detail questions.

QUESTIONS ABOUT THE DETAILS IN A PASSAGE	
HOW TO IDENTIFY THE QUESTION	What is **stated** in the passage? What is **indicated** in the passage? **According to** the speaker, . . . ?
WHERE TO FIND THE ANSWER	Information needed to answer detail questions is *directly stated* in the passage. The answers to detail questions are generally found in order in the passage.
HOW TO ANSWER THE QUESTION	1. Listen carefully to the *details* in the passage. 2. Look for an answer that *restates* the information from the passage. 3. Choose the best answer or answers.

LISTENING EXERCISE 2: Listen to each passage and the questions that follow. Then choose the best answers to the questions.

PASSAGE ONE (Questions 1–4)

Listen as two students have a conversation. The conversation is about a recital.

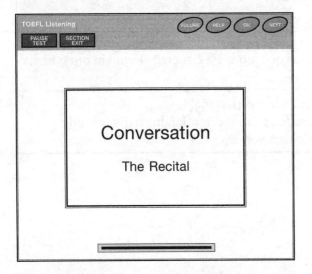

1. What is the man doing during the conversation?

  Ⓐ Working in the Music Building
  Ⓑ Holding a musical instrument
  Ⓒ Practicing a song
  Ⓓ Studying some music

2. Why is the man going to the Music Building?

  Ⓐ To get a tuba
  Ⓑ To practice his tuba
  Ⓒ To see a play
  Ⓓ To take part in a recital

3. What does the man state about the recital?

> Click on 2 answers.

  Ⓐ It starts in a half hour.
  Ⓑ It starts in an hour and a half.
  Ⓒ It lasts for a half hour.
  Ⓓ It lasts for an hour and a half.

4. What is the woman going to do?

  Ⓐ Study now and go to the recital later
  Ⓑ Study and not go to the recital
  Ⓒ Go to the recital now and study later
  Ⓓ Go to the recital now and not study

PASSAGE TWO (Questions 5–10)

Listen to a lecture in a geography class. The lecture is on the Carlsbad Caverns.

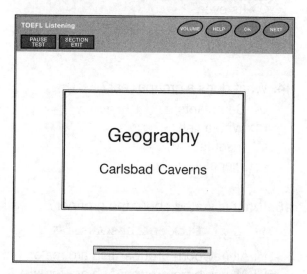

5. In which state is Carlsbad Caverns located?

Ⓐ In New York
Ⓑ In New Mexico
Ⓒ In New Jersey
Ⓓ In New Hampshire

6. In which part of the state is Carlsbad Caverns located?

Ⓐ In the northwestern part
Ⓑ In the southeastern part
Ⓒ In the southwestern part
Ⓓ In the northeastern part

7. How long ago was Carlsbad Caverns formed?

Ⓐ 200,000 years ago
Ⓑ 2,000,000 years ago
Ⓒ 200,000,000 years ago
Ⓓ 2,000,000,000 years ago

8. What is true about the number of caves in Carlsbad Caverns?

Click on 2 answers.

Ⓐ There are not very many caves.
Ⓑ The caves have all been counted.
Ⓒ There is a huge number of caves.
Ⓓ The caves have not all been counted.

9. What is the name of the largest cave?

Ⓐ The Big Cave
Ⓑ The Big Room
Ⓒ The Huge Cave
Ⓓ The Huge Room

10. What is stated about the largest cave?

Click on 2 answers.

Ⓐ It is the length of ten football fields.
Ⓑ It is the length of twenty football fields.
Ⓒ It is the height of a ten-story building.
Ⓓ It is the height of a twenty-story building.

PASSAGE THREE (Questions 11–16)

Listen to a discussion in a zoology class. The discussion is on the grouper.

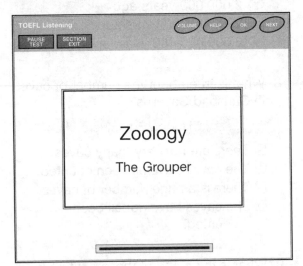

11. What is a grouper?
- Ⓐ A type of bird
- Ⓑ A type of boat
- Ⓒ A type of mammal
- Ⓓ A type of fish

12. Where do groupers live?

> Click on 2 answers.

- Ⓐ In lakes
- Ⓑ In oceans
- Ⓒ Near the shore
- Ⓓ Far from the shore

13. What part of the grouper is larger in relation to the rest of the body?
- Ⓐ Its mouth
- Ⓑ Its eyes
- Ⓒ Its fins
- Ⓓ Its tail

14. What does a grouper eat?
- Ⓐ Sea plants
- Ⓑ Whole fish
- Ⓒ Insects
- Ⓓ Pieces of fish

15. What is stated about the grouper?

> Click on 2 answers.

- Ⓐ All newborn grouper fish are male.
- Ⓑ All newborn grouper fish are female.
- Ⓒ All older grouper fish are male.
- Ⓓ All older grouper fish are female.

16. What are the students going to do next?
- Ⓐ Watch a comedy
- Ⓑ Watch a love story
- Ⓒ Watch a musical
- Ⓓ Watch a documentary

LISTENING REVIEW EXERCISE (Skills 1–2): Listen to the passage and the questions that follow. Then choose the best answers to the questions.

Questions 1–9

Listen to a lecture in an architecture class. The professor is talking about the London Bridge.

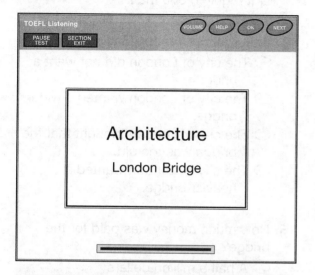

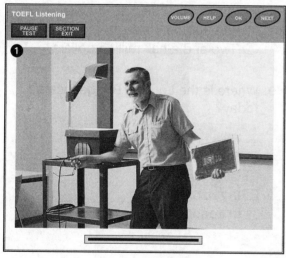

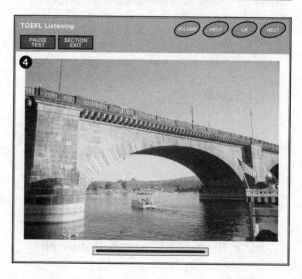

1. What is the topic of the lecture?
   - Ⓐ A bridge that is still in London
   - Ⓑ A bridge that was originally built in Arizona
   - Ⓒ A bridge that moved from Arizona to London
   - Ⓓ A bridge that moved from London to Arizona

2. What does the professor mainly discuss about the bridge?
   - Ⓐ What it took to build it, move it, and rebuild it
   - Ⓑ Why it was moved twice
   - Ⓒ When it was built and then later rebuilt
   - Ⓓ Who bought it and moved it from its original location

3. Why does the professor discuss this topic?
   - Ⓐ He is preparing the students for an exam.
   - Ⓑ He is reviewing something from the textbook.
   - Ⓒ He is reviewing an assignment he gave the students.
   - Ⓓ He is discussing something that is not in the textbook.

4. How many arches does the London Bridge have?
   - Ⓐ One
   - Ⓑ Three
   - Ⓒ Five
   - Ⓓ Seven

5. When was the London Bridge originally built?
   - Ⓐ In the first half of the eighteenth century
   - Ⓑ In the last half of the eighteenth century
   - Ⓒ In the first half of the nineteenth century
   - Ⓓ In the last half of the nineteenth century

6. What is true about the building of the original London Bridge?

Click on 2 answers.
   - Ⓐ It took seven years.
   - Ⓑ It took eight years.
   - Ⓒ It required 700 men.
   - Ⓓ It required 800 men.

7. Why was the London Bridge replaced?
   - Ⓐ The city of London did not want a bridge.
   - Ⓑ The city of London wanted a wider bridge.
   - Ⓒ The city of London thought that the bridge was too old.
   - Ⓓ The city of London wanted a heavier bridge.

8. How much money was paid for the bridge?
   - Ⓐ A half a million dollars
   - Ⓑ One and a half million dollars
   - Ⓒ Two million dollars
   - Ⓓ Two and a half million dollars

9. Where is the London Bridge located today?

Click on 2 answers.
   - Ⓐ On a lake
   - Ⓑ Over a river
   - Ⓒ In Arizona
   - Ⓓ In London

PRAGMATIC UNDERSTANDING

Pragmatic understanding questions may ask about the speaker's **function**, or purpose, in saying something. They may also ask about the speaker's **stance**, or attitude, toward something.

Listening Skill 3: UNDERSTAND THE FUNCTION

In the Listening part of the test, you may be asked about the speaker's function, or purpose, in saying something. This type of question asks you to understand *why* the speaker says something. To answer this kind of question, you must listen to what the speaker says and draw a conclusion about the speaker's purpose in saying it. Look at an example of part of a listening passage.

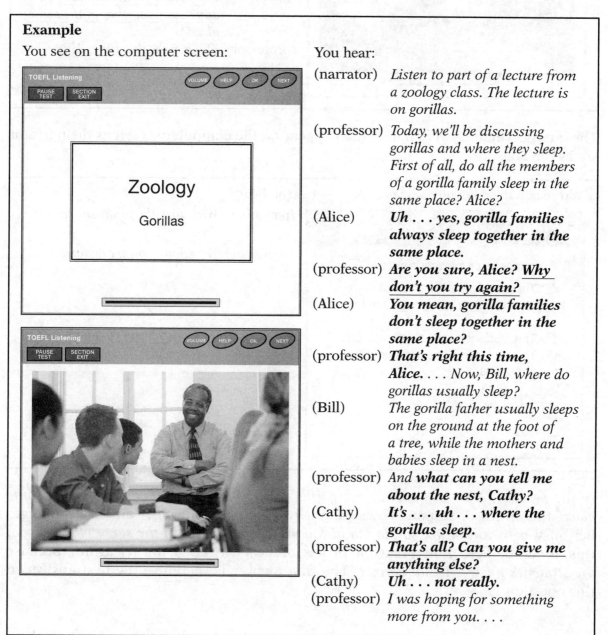

Example

You see on the computer screen:

You hear:

(narrator) *Listen to part of a lecture from a zoology class. The lecture is on gorillas.*

(professor) *Today, we'll be discussing gorillas and where they sleep. First of all, do all the members of a gorilla family sleep in the same place? Alice?*

(Alice) ***Uh . . . yes, gorilla families always sleep together in the same place.***

(professor) ***Are you sure, Alice? Why don't you try again?***

(Alice) ***You mean, gorilla families don't sleep together in the same place?***

(professor) ***That's right this time, Alice.*** *. . . Now, Bill, where do gorillas usually sleep?*

(Bill) *The gorilla father usually sleeps on the ground at the foot of a tree, while the mothers and babies sleep in a nest.*

(professor) *And **what can you tell me about the nest, Cathy?***

(Cathy) ***It's . . . uh . . . where the gorillas sleep.***

(professor) ***That's all? Can you give me anything else?***

(Cathy) ***Uh . . . not really.***

(professor) *I was hoping for something more from you. . . .*

After you listen to the lecture, a function question asks about the speaker's purpose in saying something. To start this question, a part of the conversation is replayed.

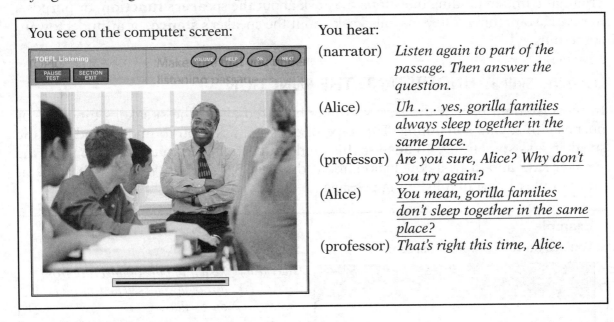

You see on the computer screen:

You hear:

(narrator) *Listen again to part of the passage. Then answer the question.*

(Alice) *Uh . . . yes, gorilla families always sleep together in the same place.*

(professor) *Are you sure, Alice? Why don't you try again?*

(Alice) *You mean, gorilla families don't sleep together in the same place?*

(professor) *That's right this time, Alice.*

The question and answer choices then appear on the computer screen as the narrator states the question.

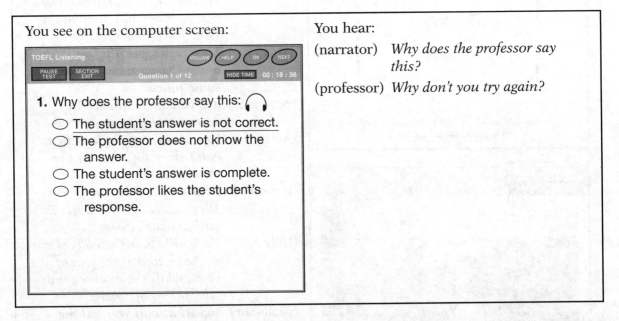

You see on the computer screen:

1. Why does the professor say this:
   ○ The student's answer is not correct.
   ○ The professor does not know the answer.
   ○ The student's answer is complete.
   ○ The professor likes the student's response.

You hear:

(narrator) *Why does the professor say this?*

(professor) *Why don't you try again?*

In the passage, Alice says *uh . . . yes, gorilla families always sleep together in the same place,* the professor responds by saying *why don't you try again?,* and Alice changes her answer to *you mean, gorilla families don't sleep together in the same place?* From this, it can be determined that the professor says *why don't you try again?* because *the student's answer is not correct.* The first answer is therefore the best answer to this question.

Now look at an example that asks about a different type of function. To start this question, a part of the passage is replayed.

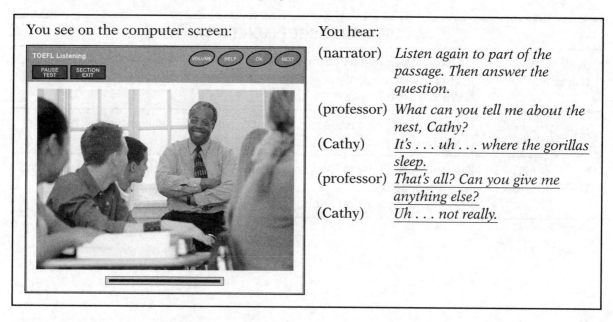

You see on the computer screen:

You hear:

(narrator) *Listen again to part of the passage. Then answer the question.*

(professor) *What can you tell me about the nest, Cathy?*

(Cathy) *It's . . . uh . . . where the gorillas sleep.*

(professor) *That's all? Can you give me anything else?*

(Cathy) *Uh . . . not really.*

The question and answer choices then appear on the computer screen as the narrator states the question.

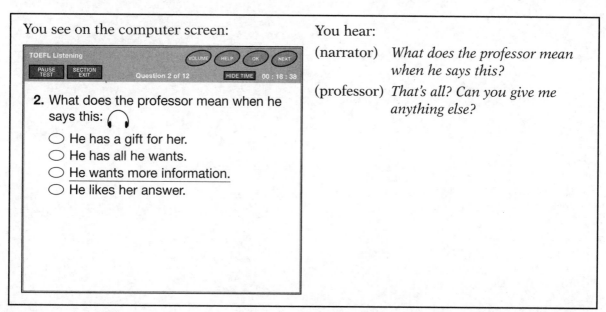

You see on the computer screen:

You hear:

(narrator) *What does the professor mean when he says this?*

(professor) *That's all? Can you give me anything else?*

2. What does the professor mean when he says this:
- ◯ He has a gift for her.
- ◯ He has all he wants.
- ◯ He wants more information.
- ◯ He likes her answer.

In the passage, the student says *it's . . . uh . . . where the gorillas sleep,* the professor responds by asking the questions *that's all?* and *can you give me anything else?*, and the student replies *uh . . . not really.* From this context, it can be determined that the professor says *that's all?* and *can you give me anything else?* because *he wants more information.* The third answer is therefore the best answer to this question.

The following chart outlines the key points that you should remember about function questions.

QUESTIONS ABOUT FUNCTION	
HOW TO IDENTIFY THE QUESTION	**Listen again** to part of the passage. **Why** does the speaker say this? **What** does the speaker **mean** ...?
WHERE TO FIND THE ANSWER	The part of the passage that indicates what the speaker says will be *replayed* for you.
HOW TO ANSWER THE QUESTION	1. Listen carefully to *what* the speaker says in the part of the passage that is repeated. 2. Draw a conclusion about *why* the speaker says it.

LISTENING EXERCISE 3: Listen to each passage and the questions that follow. Then choose the best answers to the questions.

PASSAGE ONE *(Questions 1–2)*

Listen as two students have a conversation. The conversation is about a professor's grading.

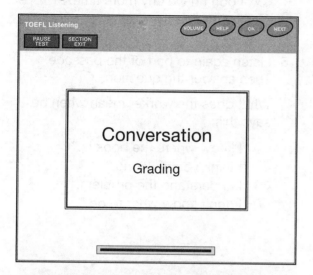

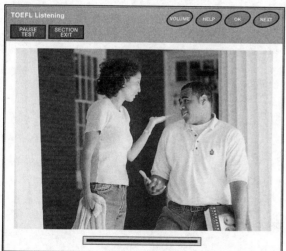

1. Listen again to part of the passage. Then answer the question. 🎧

Why does the man say this: 🎧

  Ⓐ To show that he agrees with the woman

  Ⓑ To show that the woman's ideas are clear

  Ⓒ To show that he does not understand

  Ⓓ To show that the woman's words were not nice

2. Listen again to part of the passage. Then answer the question. 🎧

What does the woman mean when she says this: 🎧

  Ⓐ "Could you say that again?"

  Ⓑ "I disagree with you."

  Ⓒ "You should say it."

  Ⓓ "How important is that?"

PASSAGE TWO *(Questions 3–5)*

Listen as a student consults with a bookstore clerk. The conversation is about finding a book.

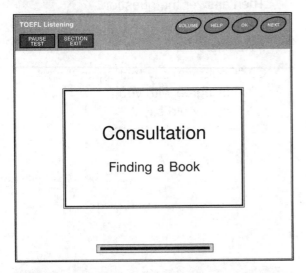

Consultation

Finding a Book

3. Listen again to part of the passage. Then answer the question.

Why does the student say this?

Ⓐ To ask how the worker spends his free time

Ⓑ To find out from the worker what time it is

Ⓒ To show that she does not have very much time

Ⓓ To ask the worker if he is able to help her

4. Listen again to part of the passage. Then answer the question.

What does the student mean when she says this:

Ⓐ "I can't find the book."

Ⓑ "The shelf is too long."

Ⓒ "I don't have any more time."

Ⓓ "I can't find the shelf."

5. Listen again to part of the passage. Then answer the question.

What does the worker mean when he says this:

Ⓐ "I know where the book is."

Ⓑ "I think you're wrong."

Ⓒ "I understand the problem."

Ⓓ "I don't know what to do."

PASSAGE THREE *(Questions 6–8)*

Listen to a discussion from a geography class. The discussion is about rivers.

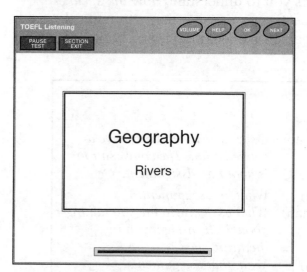

6. Listen again to part of the passage. Then answer the question. 🎧

   What does the professor mean when she says this: 🎧

   Ⓐ "Could you repeat that, please?"
   Ⓑ "That was a good effort."
   Ⓒ "You should change your response."
   Ⓓ "Please speak louder."

7. Listen again to part of the passage. Then answer the question. 🎧

   Why does the professor say this: 🎧

   Ⓐ To tell the students that Steve would like to help them
   Ⓑ To indicate that Steve does not seem to know the answer
   Ⓒ To show the other students that Steve is a friendly person
   Ⓓ To make it clear that Steve will have more time to respond

8. Listen again to part of the passage. Then answer the question. 🎧

   What does the professor mean when she says this?

   Ⓐ "You did a good job."
   Ⓑ "You need to understand me."
   Ⓒ "This material is rather easy."
   Ⓓ "Some other students helped you."

Listening Skill 4: UNDERSTAND THE SPEAKER'S STANCE

In the Listening part of the test, you may be asked about the speaker's stance, or attitude, toward something. This type of question asks you to understand *how the speaker feels* about something. To answer this kind of question, you must listen to what the speaker says and draw a conclusion about the speaker's stance in saying it. Look at an example of part of a listening passage.

Example

You see on the computer screen:

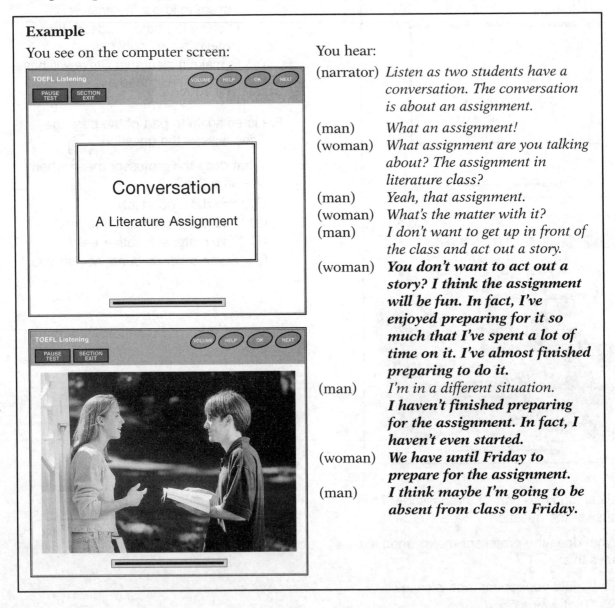

You hear:

(narrator) *Listen as two students have a conversation. The conversation is about an assignment.*

(man) *What an assignment!*

(woman) *What assignment are you talking about? The assignment in literature class?*

(man) *Yeah, that assignment.*

(woman) *What's the matter with it?*

(man) *I don't want to get up in front of the class and act out a story.*

(woman) ***You don't want to act out a story? I think the assignment will be fun. In fact, I've enjoyed preparing for it so much that I've spent a lot of time on it. I've almost finished preparing to do it.***

(man) *I'm in a different situation.* ***I haven't finished preparing for the assignment. In fact, I haven't even started.***

(woman) ***We have until Friday to prepare for the assignment.***

(man) ***I think maybe I'm going to be absent from class on Friday.***

After you listen to the conversation, the question and answer choices appear on the computer screen as the narrator states the question. This is a stance question that asks about the speaker's attitude toward something. To start this question, a part of the conversation is replayed.

You see on the computer screen:	You hear:
	(narrator) *Listen again to part of the conversation. Then answer the question.*
	(woman) *You don't want to act out a story? I think the assignment will be fun. In fact, I've enjoyed preparing for it so much that I've spent a lot of time on it. I've almost finished preparing to do it.*

The question and answer choices then appear on the computer screen as the narrator states the question.

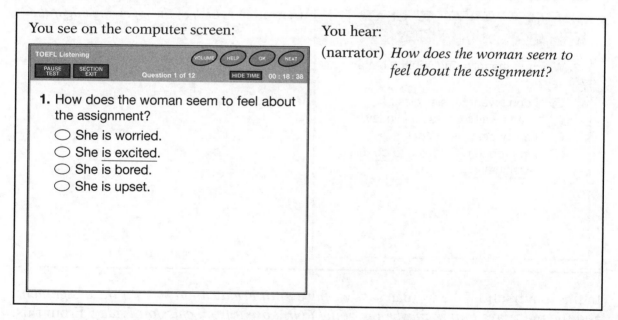

You see on the computer screen:	You hear:
	(narrator) *How does the woman seem to feel about the assignment?*

In the conversation, the woman says *I think the assignment will be fun* and *I've enjoyed preparing for it so much that I've spent a lot of time on it.* From this context, it can be determined that the woman *is excited* about the assignment. The second answer is therefore the best answer to this question.

Now look at an example of a different type of question that asks about the speaker's attitude.

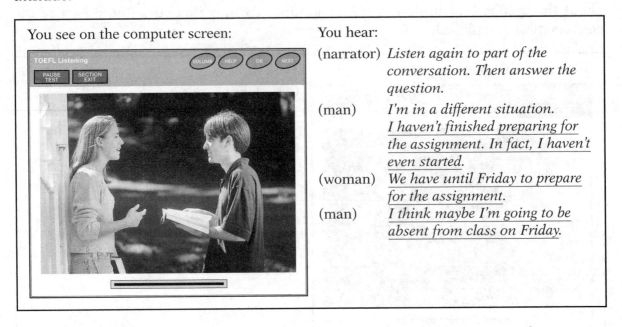

You see on the computer screen:	You hear:
	(narrator) *Listen again to part of the conversation. Then answer the question.*
	(man) *I'm in a different situation. I haven't finished preparing for the assignment. In fact, I haven't even started.*
	(woman) *We have until Friday to prepare for the assignment.*
	(man) *I think maybe I'm going to be absent from class on Friday.*

The question and answer choices then appear on the computer screen as the narrator states the question.

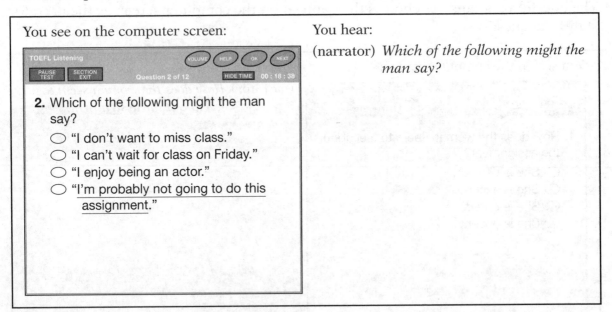

You hear:

(narrator) *Which of the following might the man say?*

In the conversation, the woman says *we have until Friday to prepare for the assignment,* and the man says *I think maybe I'm going to be absent from class on Friday.* From this, it can be determined that the man might say *I'm probably not going to do this assignment.* The last answer is therefore the best answer to this question.

The following chart outlines the key points that you should remember about questions on the speaker's stance.

QUESTIONS ABOUT THE SPEAKER'S STANCE	
HOW TO IDENTIFY THE QUESTION	**Listen again** to part of the passage. Select the sentence that best expresses how the speaker **feels**. Which of the following might the speaker **say**?
WHERE TO FIND THE ANSWER	The part of the passage that indicates what the speaker says will be *replayed* for you.
HOW TO ANSWER THE QUESTION	1. Listen carefully to *what* the speaker says in the part of the passage that is repeated. 2. Draw a conclusion about *how the speaker feels*.

LISTENING EXERCISE 4: Listen to each passage and the questions that follow. Then choose the best answers to the questions.

PASSAGE ONE *(Questions 1–2)*

Listen as two students have a conversation. The conversation is about a meeting.

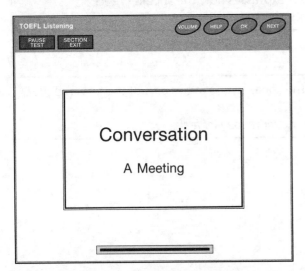

1. Listen again to part of the passage. Then answer the question.

Which of the following might the man say about the meeting?

Ⓐ "The meeting isn't very important."

Ⓑ "I'm not sure where the meeting is."

Ⓒ "You really shouldn't miss this meeting."

Ⓓ "I don't know which meeting this is."

2. Listen again to part of the passage. Then answer the question.

How does the woman seem to feel about the meeting?

Ⓐ Uninterested

Ⓑ Excited

Ⓒ Afraid

Ⓓ Pleased

PASSAGE TWO (Questions 3–5)

Listen as a student consults with a professor. The conversation is about turning in a late paper.

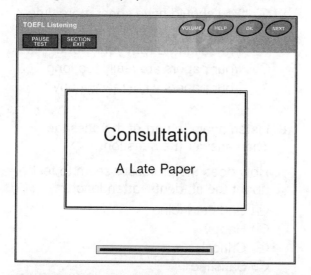

3. Listen again to part of the passage. Then answer the question. 🎧

How does the professor seem to feel about the student's situation?

Ⓐ He wants to hear the student's excuse.

Ⓑ He does not want to listen to explanations.

Ⓒ He will not accept her assignment.

Ⓓ He understands her reasons.

4. Listen again to part of the passage. Then answer the question. 🎧

How does the student seem to feel about the professor's offer?

Ⓐ Bothered

Ⓑ Doubtful

Ⓒ Worried

Ⓓ Appreciative

5. Listen again to part of the passage. Then answer the question. 🎧

Which of the following might the professor say?

Ⓐ "I won't be so generous next time."

Ⓑ "I'm giving you a failing grade this time."

Ⓒ "I'm absolutely not going to help you this time."

Ⓓ "Take your time doing any assignments."

PASSAGE THREE *(Questions 6–8)*

Listen as a professor begins a lecture. The professor is making some announcements.

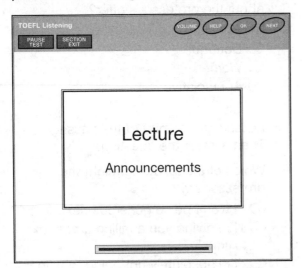

6. Listen again to part of the passage. Then answer the question. 🎧

   How does the professor seem to feel about not returning the papers?

   Ⓐ Angry
   Ⓑ Insincere
   Ⓒ Pleased
   Ⓓ Apologetic

7. Listen again to part of the passage. Then answer the question. 🎧

   Which of the following might the professor say about the term papers?

   Ⓐ "You should have spent more time on your papers."
   Ⓑ "I'm delighted with your work."
   Ⓒ "Your papers are really too long."
   Ⓓ "Your papers were really funny."

8. Listen again to part of the passage. Then answer the question. 🎧

   How does the professor seem to feel about the students' attendance?

   Ⓐ Understanding
   Ⓑ Happy
   Ⓒ Critical
   Ⓓ Satisfied

LISTENING EXERCISE (Skills 3–4): Listen to the passage and the questions that follow. Then choose the best answers to the questions.

Questions 1–5

Listen as a student consults with her advisor. The conversation is about a music class.

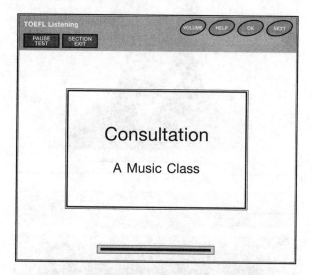

1. Listen again to part of the passage. Then answer the question.

What does the advisor mean when he says this:

Ⓐ "I strongly disagree with you."
Ⓑ "What you're saying isn't correct."
Ⓒ "What do you mean?"
Ⓓ "I certainly agree with you."

2. Listen again to part of the passage. Then answer the question.

How does the student seem to feel about the music requirement in this part of the passage?

Ⓐ Happy
Ⓑ Worried
Ⓒ Satisfied
Ⓓ Unconcerned

3. Listen again to part of the passage. Then answer the question.

What does the student mean when she says this:

Ⓐ "I thought I had to do this."
Ⓑ "I don't like what you're saying."
Ⓒ "I really want to do this."
Ⓓ "I'm not surprised by your response."

4. Listen again to part of the passage. Then answer the question.

What does the advisor mean when he says this:

Ⓐ "Could you repeat that, please?"
Ⓑ "I couldn't hear what you said."
Ⓒ "That's not very important."
Ⓓ "I completely agree with you."

5. Listen again to part of the passage. Then answer the question.

What might the student say about the music requirement at the end of the conversation?

Ⓐ "I'm not looking forward to this."
Ⓑ "This might be rather interesting."
Ⓒ "I'm so glad there's no music requirement."
Ⓓ "I think this is going to be just awful."

LISTENING REVIEW EXERCISE (Skills 1–4): Listen to the passage and the questions that follow. Then choose the best answers to the questions.

Questions 1–8

Listen to a lecture in a literature class. The professor is talking about James Fenimore Cooper.

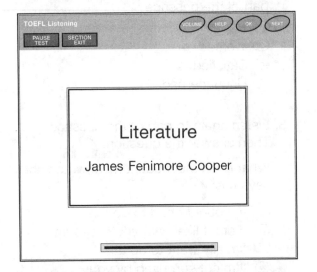

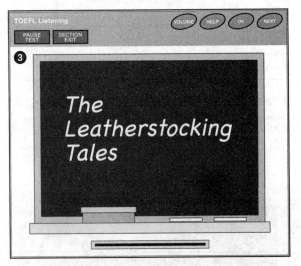

1. What is the main topic of this talk?

   Ⓐ All of James Fenimore Cooper's novels

   Ⓑ The character called Hawkeye

   Ⓒ James Fenimore Cooper's *Leatherstocking Tales*

   Ⓓ The life of James Fenimore Cooper

2. Approximately how many novels did James Fenimore Cooper write?

   Ⓐ five

   Ⓑ ten

   Ⓒ twenty

   Ⓓ thirty

3. What was true about the Leatherstocking novels?

   Ⓐ They had the same main character.

   Ⓑ They were the only novels that Cooper wrote.

   Ⓒ They had the same characters as his other novels.

   Ⓓ They had completely different main characters.

4. By what other names was Leatherstocking known?

> **Click on 2 answers.**

   Ⓐ The Last of the Mohicans

   Ⓑ Natty Bumpo

   Ⓒ James Fenimore Cooper

   Ⓓ Hawkeye

5. Listen again to part of the passage. Then answer the question. 🎧

What does the professor mean when she says this: 🎧

   Ⓐ "I'd like to know your answer."

   Ⓑ "I want to know who is paying attention."

   Ⓒ "I'd like to know who is present."

   Ⓓ "I want you to ask me questions."

6. What is true about how Cooper wrote *The Leatherstocking Tales*?

   Ⓐ He wrote them in chronological order.

   Ⓑ He wrote them all in the same year.

   Ⓒ He wrote them in the first half of the eighteenth century.

   Ⓓ He wrote them out of order.

7. Listen again to part of the passage. Then answer the question. 🎧

Why does the professor say this?

   Ⓐ She wants to introduce a new topic.

   Ⓑ She wants to wake the students up.

   Ⓒ She wants to bring the lecture to an end.

   Ⓓ She wants to provide additional details.

8. Listen again to part of the passage. Then answer the question. 🎧

How does the professor seem to feel about the assignment?

   Ⓐ She thinks it is very easy.

   Ⓑ She thinks it will take a lot of time and effort.

   Ⓒ She thinks the students will enjoy it.

   Ⓓ She thinks it is impossible to finish.

CONNECTING INFORMATION

Questions about connecting information involve a number of ideas rather than a single idea. These questions may ask about the **organization** of the ideas or about the **relationships** between or among ideas.

Listening Skill 5: UNDERSTAND THE ORGANIZATION

Organization questions are questions that ask about how the ideas in the passage are organized. They may ask specifically about how information is organized, or they may ask you to fill out a chart that shows the organization. Look at an example of part of a listening passage.

Example

You see on the computer screen:

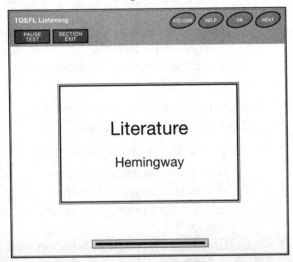

You hear:

(narrator) *Listen to part of a lecture in a literature class. The lecture is on Hemingway.*

(professor) *For the quiz tomorrow, you need to be prepared to answer questions about three of the novels of Ernest Hemingway, novels that he wrote in different parts of his career.*

One of the novels is The Sun Also Rises, *which Hemingway wrote in 1926, in the early part of his career. It is about a group of Americans in the aftermath of World War I who were disillusioned with the war. He had served as an ambulance driver in World War I and lived in Europe after the war, during the 1920s. He based characters from the novel on himself and on friends from that period.*

The next novel is For Whom the Bell Tolls, *which he wrote in the middle part of his career. He wrote* For Whom the Bell Tolls *in 1940. It is about an American taking part in the Spanish Civil War. He worked as a newspaper reporter during the Civil War in Spain in 1937. He based his characters in this novel on people he met during this period.*

> *The third novel is* The Old Man and the Sea, *which Hemingway wrote later in his career. He wrote* The Old Man and the Sea *twelve years after he wrote* For Whom the Bell Tolls. The Old Man and the Sea *is about a fisherman and his struggle to catch a giant marlin. He wrote this novel while he was living in Cuba. He lived in Cuba in the 1940s and 1950s and spent a lot of time sailing and fishing there.*

After you listen to the passage, the first question and answer choices appear on the computer screen as the narrator states the question. This is a multiple-choice question that asks about the organization of the information in the passage.

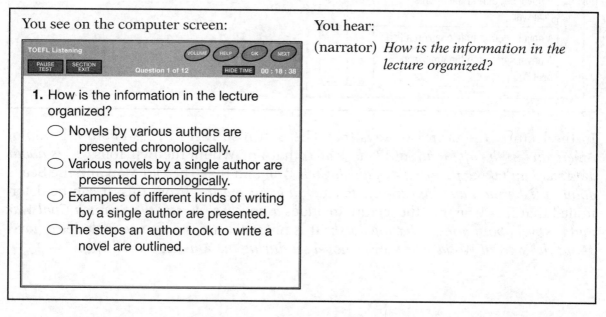

You see on the computer screen:

TOEFL Listening
VOLUME HELP OK NEXT
PAUSE TEST   SECTION EXIT   Question 1 of 12   HIDE TIME   00 : 18 : 38

1. How is the information in the lecture organized?
○ Novels by various authors are presented chronologically.
○ <u>Various novels by a single author are presented chronologically.</u>
○ Examples of different kinds of writing by a single author are presented.
○ The steps an author took to write a novel are outlined.

You hear:

(narrator) *How is the information in the lecture organized?*

In the lecture, the professor discusses The Sun Also Rises, *which Hemingway wrote in 1926, in the early part of his career,* For Whom the Bell Tolls, *which he wrote in the middle part of his career,* and The Old Man and the Sea, *which Hemingway wrote later in his career.* From this, it can be determined that the organization of the information in the passage is that *various novels by a single author are presented chronologically.* The second answer is therefore the best answer to this question.

Now look at an example of an organization question that asks what is included in the passage. To answer this question, you must click in the correct column for each term.

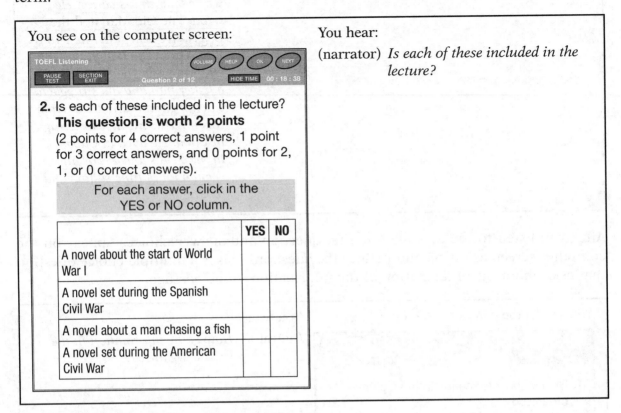

You see on the computer screen:

TOEFL Listening   VOLUME HELP OK NEXT
PAUSE TEST   SECTION EXIT   Question 2 of 12   HIDE TIME 00 : 18 : 38

2. Is each of these included in the lecture?
This question is worth 2 points
(2 points for 4 correct answers, 1 point for 3 correct answers, and 0 points for 2, 1, or 0 correct answers).

For each answer, click in the YES or NO column.

	YES	NO
A novel about the start of World War I		
A novel set during the Spanish Civil War		
A novel about a man chasing a fish		
A novel set during the American Civil War		

You hear:

(narrator) *Is each of these included in the lecture?*

In the lecture, the professor says that The Sun Also Rises . . . *is about a group of Americans in the aftermath of World War I,* that For Whom the Bell Tolls . . . *is about an American taking part in the Spanish Civil War,* and that The Old Man and the Sea *is about a fisherman and his struggle to catch a giant marlin.* From this, it can be determined that it is true that the lecture includes *a novel set during the Spanish Civil War* and *a novel about a man chasing a fish.* It is not true that the lecture includes *a novel about the start of World War I* and *a novel set during the American Civil War.*

Now look at an example of an organization question that asks about the year that each novel was written. To answer this question, you must click in the correct column for each novel.

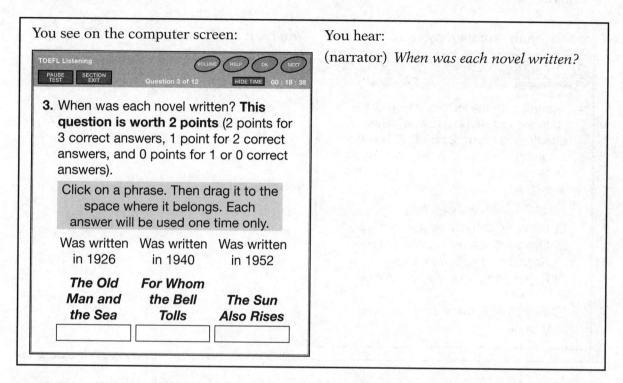

You see on the computer screen:	You hear:
	(narrator) *When was each novel written?*

In the lecture, the professor mentions The Sun Also Rises, *which Hemingway wrote in 1926,* and states that Hemingway *wrote* For Whom the Bell Tolls *in 1940* and *wrote* The Old Man and the Sea *twelve years after he wrote* For Whom the Bell Tolls. From this, it can be determined that *The Old Man and the Sea* was written in 1952, that *For Whom the Bell Tolls* was written in 1940, and that *The Sun Also Rises* was written in 1926.

Next, look at an example of an organization question that asks you to choose three things that Hemingway did. To answer this question, you must click on the three correct answers.

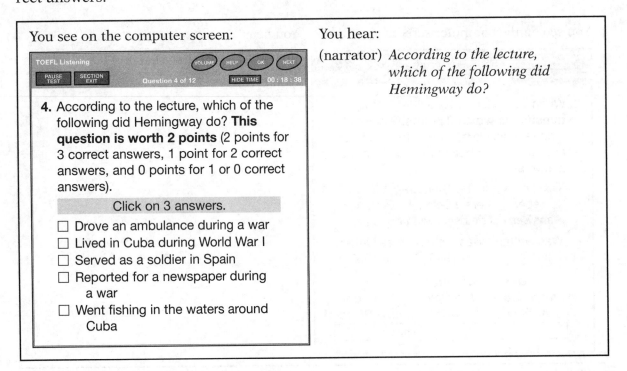

You see on the computer screen:

TOEFL Listening

PAUSE TEST   SECTION EXIT   Question 4 of 12   HIDE TIME   00 : 18 : 36

VOLUME   HELP   OK   NEXT

4. According to the lecture, which of the following did Hemingway do? **This question is worth 2 points** (2 points for 3 correct answers, 1 point for 2 correct answers, and 0 points for 1 or 0 correct answers).

Click on 3 answers.

☐ Drove an ambulance during a war
☐ Lived in Cuba during World War I
☐ Served as a soldier in Spain
☐ Reported for a newspaper during a war
☐ Went fishing in the waters around Cuba

You hear:

(narrator) *According to the lecture, which of the following did Hemingway do?*

In the lecture, the professor mentions Hemingway and states that *he had served as an ambulance driver in World War I,* that *he worked as a newspaper reporter during the Civil War in Spain,* and that *he lived in Cuba in the 1940s and 1950s and spent a lot of time sailing and fishing there.* From this, it can be determined that Hemingway *drove an ambulance during a war, reported for a newspaper during a war,* and *went fishing in the waters around Cuba.* You should therefore click on the first, fourth, and fifth answers to this question.

Finally, look at an example of an organization question that asks you to put four events in Hemingway's life in the order that they occurred. To answer this question, you should click on each answer and then drag it to the correct space for that answer.

You see on the computer screen:

TOEFL Listening

VOLUME   HELP   OK   NEXT

PAUSE   SECTION
TEST   EXIT   Question 5 of 12   HIDE TIME   00 : 18 : 38

5. In the lecture, the professor discusses events in Hemingway's life. Put these events in the correct order. **This question is worth 2 points** (2 points for 4 correct answers, 1 point for 3 or 2 correct answers, and 0 points for 1 or 0 correct answers).

> Click on a phrase. Then drag it to the space where it belongs.
> Use each phrase only once.

Lived in Cuba
Drove an ambulance
Reported during the Spanish Civil War
Lived in Europe following World War I

1. _____
2. _____
3. _____
4. _____

You hear:

(narrator) *In the lecture, the professor discusses events in Hemingway's life. Put these events in the correct order.*

In the lecture, the professor states that *he had served as an ambulance driver in World War I and lived in Europe after the war, during the 1920s,* that *he worked as a newspaper reporter during the Civil War in Spain in 1937,* and that *he lived in Cuba in the 1940s and 1950s.* From this, it can be determined that you should click on *Drove an ambulance* and drag it to the first space, that you should click on *Lived in Europe following World War I* and drag it to the second space, that you should click on *Reported during the Spanish Civil War* and drag it to the third space, and that you should click on *Lived in Cuba* and drag it to the fourth space.

The following chart outlines the key points that you should remember about organization questions.

QUESTIONS ABOUT THE ORGANIZATION	
HOW TO IDENTIFY THE QUESTION	How is the information in the passage **organized**? Click in the correct **column** … Click in the correct **box** … Click on **3 answers**. Click in the **Yes** or **No** column.
WHERE TO FIND THE ANSWER	Information to answer organization questions is *not directly stated* in a single point in the passage. It is necessary to understand the main points and *draw a conclusion* based on the main points to answer the question.
HOW TO ANSWER THE QUESTION	1. Listen carefully to each of the *main points* in the passage. 2. Consider how these main points are *organized*. 3. Look for an answer that shows the *organization* of the points. 4. Choose the best answer.

LISTENING EXERCISE 5: Listen to each passage and the questions that follow. Then choose the best answers to the questions.

PASSAGE ONE (Questions 1–3)

Listen to a discussion about a history class. The discussion is on the city of Chicago.

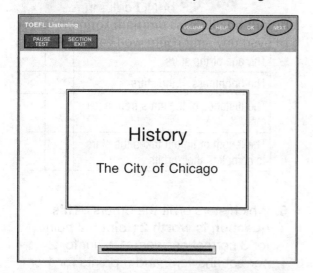

1. How is the information in the passage organized?

   Ⓐ In order of importance from least to most

   Ⓑ In order of importance from most to least

   Ⓒ In chronological order from earliest to latest

   Ⓓ In chronological order from latest to earliest

2. In the lecture, the professor discusses events in the history of Chicago. Put these events in the order that they occurred. **This question is worth 2 points** (2 points for 4 correct answers, 1 point for 3 or 2 correct answers, and 0 points for 1 or 0 correct answers).

> Click on a sentence. Then drag it to the space where it belongs. Use each sentence only once.

Fort Dearborn was built.
Chicago hosted a world's fair.
A fire destroyed much of Chicago.
Chicago became a town.

1. _____
2. _____
3. _____
4. _____

3. Which of these are discussed in the lecture? **This question is worth 2 points** (2 points for 3 correct answers, 1 point for 2 correct answers, and 0 points for 1 or 0 correct answers).

> Click on 3 answers.

Ⓐ An army fort
Ⓑ A war
Ⓒ A financial problem
Ⓓ A giant fire
Ⓔ A world's fair

PASSAGE TWO *(Questions 4–6)*

Listen to a lecture in an astronomy class. The lecture is on Alpha Centauri.

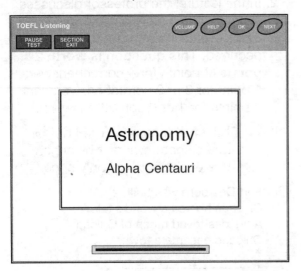

4. How is the information in the passage organized?

    Ⓐ Three different star systems near our Sun are classified.

    Ⓑ Three stars near our Sun are contrasted.

    Ⓒ The development of a star system is presented in chronological order.

    Ⓓ Three different stars in a star system are described.

5. Is each of these mentioned in the passage? **This question is worth 2 points** (2 points for 4 correct answers, 1 point for 3 correct answers, and 0 points for 2, 1, or 0 correct answers).

> For each answer, click in the YES or NO column.

	YES	NO
The age of the stars		
The brightness of the stars		
The distance of the stars from each other		
The length of time it takes the stars to complete their orbits		

6. Which stars orbit the others? **This question is worth 2 points** (2 points for 3 correct answers, 1 point for 2 correct answers, and 0 points for 1 or 0 correct answers).

> Click on a phrase. Then drag it to the space where it belongs. Each answer will be used one time only.

Orbits around one of the other stars	Has two stars orbiting around it	Orbits around the two other stars
Alpha Centauri A	**Alpha Centauri B**	**Proxima Centauri**

PASSAGE THREE (Questions 7–10)

Listen to a discussion about a political science course. The discussion is on the course syllabus.

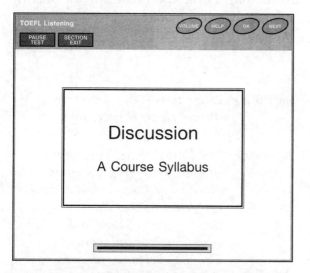

7. How is the information in the discussion organized?

Ⓐ Various kinds of legislatures are outlined.

Ⓑ Various kinds of executives are contrasted.

Ⓒ Various kinds of governments are contrasted.

Ⓓ Various branches of government are described.

8. Is each of these covered in the discussion? **This question is worth 2 points** (2 points for 4 correct answers, 1 point for 3 correct answers, and 0 points for 2, 1, or 0 correct answers).

For each answer, click in the YES or NO column.		
	YES	NO
Information from a syllabus		
Topics on a syllabus		
Length of time spent on each topic		
Kind of exam on each topic		

9. What will be the topic of each of these parts of the course? **This question is worth 2 points** (2 points for 3 correct answers, 1 point for 2 correct answers, and 0 points for 1 or 0 correct answers).

Click on a phrase. Then drag it to the space where it belongs. Each answer will be used one time only.

Is covered in weeks 1–4	Is covered in weeks 5–8	Is covered in weeks 9–12
The executive branch	**The legislative branch**	**The judicial branch**

10. What are the three main branches of the U.S. government? **This question is worth 2 points** (2 points for 3 correct answers, 1 point for 2 correct answers, and 0 points for 1 or 0 correct answers).

Click on 3 answers.

Ⓐ The branch that covers the courts

Ⓑ The branch that covers the military

Ⓒ The branch that covers the congress

Ⓓ The branch that covers the economy

Ⓔ The branch that covers the president

Listening Skill 6: UNDERSTAND RELATIONSHIPS

Relationship questions ask you to understand how different ideas or pieces of information in the passage are related. As you listen to a passage, you should listen to the different ideas and focus on how the ideas are related. Look at an example of part of a listening passage.

Example

You see on the computer screen:

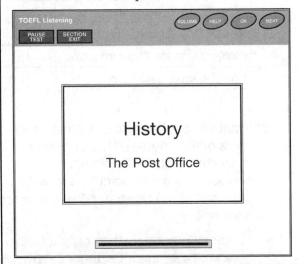

You hear:

(narrator) *Listen to part of a lecture in a history class. The lecture is on the Post Office.*

(professor) *The United States Post Office in California faced a serious problem in 1849. The serious problem was that there were just too many letters and not enough postal workers. This was because gold was discovered in California in 1849.*

The population of California increased suddenly. Huge numbers of people came into the state very quickly. With the sudden increase in population, there was also a huge increase in the number of letters arriving in the state. There were thousands and thousands more letters than there had been the year before. To make the problem worse, there weren't enough workers to deal with the increase in letters. Workers weren't interested in working for the Post Office when they believed they had better opportunities somewhere else.

After you listen to the passage, a question and answer choices appear on the screen as the narrator states the question. This is a relationship question with one correct answer.

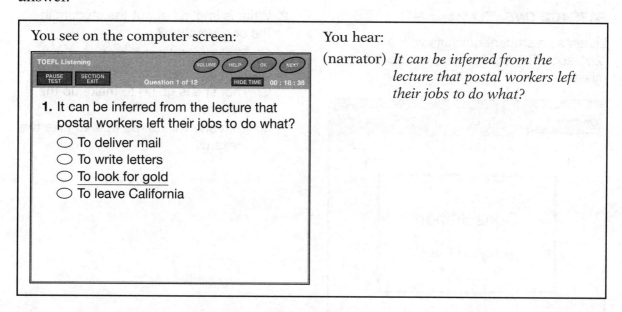

You see on the computer screen:	You hear:
TOEFL Listening PAUSE TEST · SECTION EXIT · Question 1 of 12 · HIDE TIME 00 : 18 : 38 VOLUME HELP OK NEXT **1.** It can be inferred from the lecture that postal workers left their jobs to do what? ○ To deliver mail ○ To write letters ○ To look for gold ○ To leave California	(narrator) *It can be inferred from the lecture that postal workers left their jobs to do what?*

In the lecture, the professor states that *gold was discovered in California in 1849* and that *workers weren't interested in working for the Post Office when they believed they had better opportunities somewhere else.* From this, it can be determined that postal workers most likely left their jobs *to look for gold.* The third answer is therefore the best answer to this question.

The following chart outlines the key points that you should remember about relationship questions.

QUESTIONS ABOUT RELATIONSHIPS	
HOW TO IDENTIFY THE QUESTION	What is most **likely** ...? What is **probably** ...? What is **implied** ...? What can be **inferred** ...?
WHERE TO FIND THE ANSWER	Information needed to answer relationship questions is *not directly stated* in the passage. It is necessary to understand the main points and *draw a conclusion* based on the main points to answer the question.
HOW TO ANSWER THE QUESTION	1. Listen carefully to each of the *main points* in the passage. 2. Consider how these points may be *related*. 3. Look for an answer that shows how the points are *related*. 4. Choose the best answer.

LISTENING EXERCISE 6: Listen to each passage and the questions that follow. Then choose the best answers to the questions.

PASSAGE ONE (Questions 1–2)

Listen as a student consults with a professor. The conversation is about a missed exam.

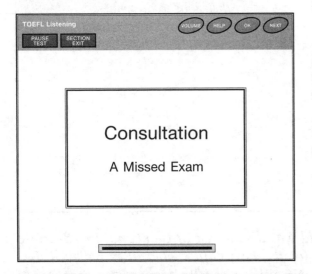

1. What can be inferred from the conversation?
   - Ⓐ That the student did not have a good reason to miss the exam
   - Ⓑ That the student was not actually able to go skiing
   - Ⓒ That the student was really sick
   - Ⓓ That the student did not really intend to miss the exam

2. What is implied about the student in the conversation?
   - Ⓐ That she did not miss the exam
   - Ⓑ That she was sick last week
   - Ⓒ That she is going to make up the exam
   - Ⓓ That she will not be able to take the exam

PASSAGE TWO *(Questions 3–4)*

Listen to a lecture from a zoology class. The lecture is on the robin.

3. When would a robin most likely sing?

Ⓐ When it wants to relax

Ⓑ When it wants to entertain other birds

Ⓒ When it thinks people can hear it

Ⓓ When it thinks other birds are too close

4. In what situation would a robin most probably begin to sing?

Ⓐ When it wakes up in the morning

Ⓑ When it feels happy

Ⓒ When it notices an unknown bird

Ⓓ When it is far from home

PASSAGE THREE (Questions 5–7)

Listen to a discussion from an astronomy class. The discussion is on auroras.

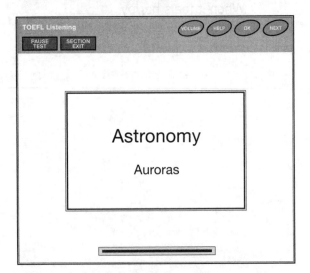

5. When would an aurora most probably occur?

- Ⓐ At 1:00 A.M.
- Ⓑ At 7:00 A.M.
- Ⓒ At 1:00 P.M.
- Ⓓ At 5:00 P.M.

6. Where would an aurora most likely be visible?

Click on 2 answers.

- Ⓐ In the northern part of the Southern Hemisphere
- Ⓑ In the northern part of the Northern Hemisphere
- Ⓒ In the southern part of the Southern Hemisphere
- Ⓓ In the southern part of the Northern Hemisphere

7. It is implied that which of the following is quite unusual?

Click on 2 answers.

- Ⓐ Eight auroras during the spring
- Ⓑ Eight auroras during the summer
- Ⓒ A single aurora during the fall
- Ⓓ A single aurora during the winter

LISTENING EXERCISE (Skills 5–6): Listen to the passage and the questions that follow. Then choose the best answers to the questions.

Questions 1–5

Listen to a discussion about a business class. The discussion is on the Harley-Davidson Company.

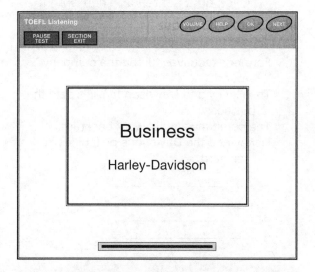

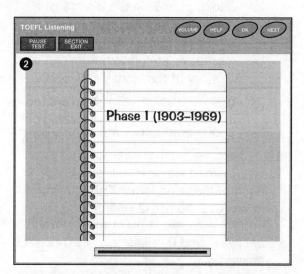

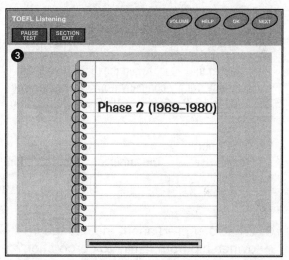

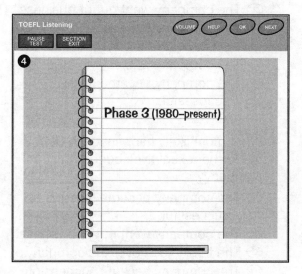

1. How is the information in the passage organized?

  Ⓐ Various phases in the history of a company are outlined.

  Ⓑ Various products produced by a company are classified.

  Ⓒ A history of the Harley-Davidson Company is presented chronologically.

  Ⓓ Various companies are contrasted.

2. Who owned Harley-Davidson during each of these periods? **This question is worth 2 points** (2 points for 3 correct answers, 1 point for 2 correct answers, and 0 points for 1 or 0 correct answers).

> Click on a phrase. Then drag it to the space where it belongs. Each answer will be used one time only.

Owned the company from 1903 to 1969	Owned the company from 1969 to 1980	Owned the company from 1980 to the present

Former executives	**The families**	**A corporation**

3. What is implied about the change in ownership from family to corporation?

  Ⓐ The company went out of business.

  Ⓑ The company became less successful.

  Ⓒ The company was sold to a bank.

  Ⓓ The company became more successful.

4. What most likely happened when the former executives bought the company?

  Ⓐ The company became less successful.

  Ⓑ The company went out of business.

  Ⓒ The family took over the company.

  Ⓓ The company became successful again.

5. In the lecture, the professor discusses events in the history of Harley-Davidson. Put these events in the correct order. **This question is worth 2 points** (2 points for 4 correct answers, 1 point for 3 or 2 correct answers, and 0 points for 1 or 0 correct answers).

> Click on a sentence. Then drag it to the space where it belongs. Use each sentence only once.

Former executives turned the company around.

The Harley and Davidson families sold the business.

The company almost went bankrupt.

Harley and the Davidsons built bikes in their yard.

1. _____
2. _____
3. _____
4. _____

LISTENING REVIEW EXERCISE (Skills 1–6): Listen to the passage and the questions that follow. Then choose the best answers to the questions.

Questions 1–7

Listen to a lecture in an oceanography class. The professor is talking about the Mid-Atlantic Ridge.

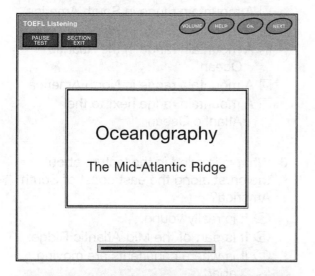

1. What does the professor mainly discuss in the lecture?

    Ⓐ Various mountain ranges
    Ⓑ Undersea mountain ranges
    Ⓒ Older crust material in the Atlantic Ocean
    Ⓓ The world's longest mountain range

2. Listen again to part of the passage. Then answer the question. 🎧

How does the professor seem to feel the students will respond to this question: 🎧

> Click on 2 answers.

    Ⓐ With a correct response
    Ⓑ With an incorrect response
    Ⓒ With an answer about the Mid-Atlantic Ridge
    Ⓓ With an answer about the Himalayas

3. What is stated about the Mid-Atlantic Ridge?

> Click on 2 answers.

    Ⓐ It reaches the Arctic Circle in the north.
    Ⓑ It does not extend north of the equator.
    Ⓒ It does not extend south of the equator.
    Ⓓ It reaches Antarctica in the south.

4. Listen again to part of the passage. Then answer the question. 🎧

Why does the professor say this?

    Ⓐ To emphasize an important point
    Ⓑ To ask the students a question
    Ⓒ To introduce a new point to the lecture
    Ⓓ To respond to a question by a student

5. Which mountain ranges are discussed in the lecture? **This question is worth 2 points** (2 points for 3 correct answers, 1 point for 2 correct answers, and 0 points for 1 or 0 correct answers).

> Click on 3 answers.

    Ⓐ A mountain range in South America
    Ⓑ A mountain range in Asia
    Ⓒ A mountain range in the Atlantic Ocean
    Ⓓ A mountain range in North America
    Ⓔ A mountain range next to the Atlantic Ocean

6. What is implied in the lecture about the crust along the east coast of South America?

    Ⓐ It is really young.
    Ⓑ It is part of the Mid-Atlantic Ridge.
    Ⓒ It is where continents are moving apart.
    Ⓓ It is made of old crust material.

7. In the lecture, the professor discusses events in the creation of the Mid-Atlantic Ridge. Put these events in the correct order. **This question is worth 2 points** (2 points for 4 correct answers, 1 point for 3 or 2 correct answers, and 0 points for 1 or 0 correct answers).

> Click on a sentence. Then drag it to the space where it belongs. Use each sentence only once.

Older crust moved toward the continents.
Newer crust pushed up along the Mid-Atlantic Ridge.
No Atlantic Ocean existed.
The continents started separating.

1. _____
2. _____
3. _____
4. _____

LISTENING POST-TEST

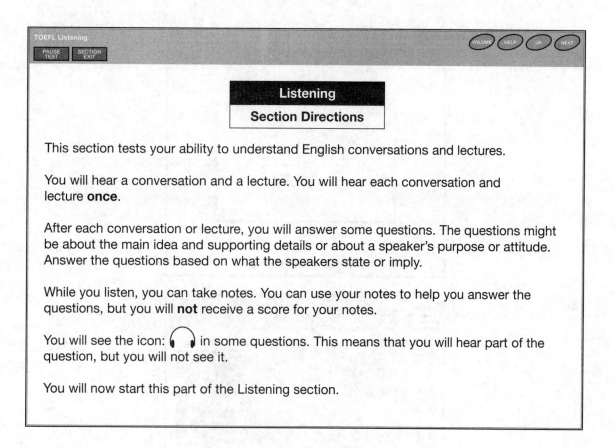

Listening
Section Directions

This section tests your ability to understand English conversations and lectures.

You will hear a conversation and a lecture. You will hear each conversation and lecture **once**.

After each conversation or lecture, you will answer some questions. The questions might be about the main idea and supporting details or about a speaker's purpose or attitude. Answer the questions based on what the speakers state or imply.

While you listen, you can take notes. You can use your notes to help you answer the questions, but you will **not** receive a score for your notes.

You will see the icon: 🎧 in some questions. This means that you will hear part of the question, but you will not see it.

You will now start this part of the Listening section.

Questions 1–6

Listen as a student consults with her professor. The conversation is about an exam.

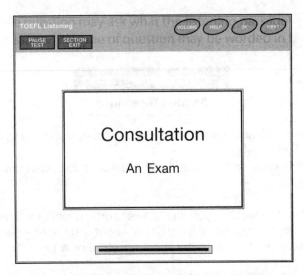

1. Why does the student go to see the professor?

    Ⓐ To find out what her grade is on an exam

    Ⓑ To retake an exam to get a higher score

    Ⓒ To get the lecture notes from class

    Ⓓ To find out why her exam grade was not very good

2. Listen again to part of the passage. Then answer the question. 🎧

   How does the professor seem to feel about the exam grade?

    Ⓐ He seems to think it was not as good as it could be.

    Ⓑ He seems to think it was pretty good.

    Ⓒ He seems to think it was better than it should have been.

    Ⓓ He seems to think it was as high as it could be.

3. Listen again to part of the passage. Then answer the question. 🎧

   What does the student mean when she says this: 🎧

    Ⓐ "Oh, that's very clear to me."

    Ⓑ "What are you talking about?"

    Ⓒ "You can say that again."

    Ⓓ "That's no surprise to me."

4. What problem did the student have on the exam?

    Ⓐ She did not study the textbook chapters.

    Ⓑ She did not attend lectures.

    Ⓒ She did not understand that the exam covered the textbook.

    Ⓓ She did not understand that the lecture covered more than the textbook.

5. What can be inferred from the conversation?

    Ⓐ That the student actually did quite well on the exam

    Ⓑ That the exams cover the lectures more than they cover the textbook

    Ⓒ That the lectures cover different material from the textbook

    Ⓓ That the student needs to spend more time studying the textbook chapters

6. Is each of these true based on the conversation? **This question is worth 2 points** (2 points for 4 correct answers, 1 point for 3 correct answers, and 0 points for 2, 1, or 0 correct answers).

For each answer, click in the YES or NO column.		
	YES	NO
The student did well on the exam.		
The student studied the textbook thoroughly.		
The student took good notes during the lectures.		
The exam covered only the lectures.		

Questions 7–12

Listen to a group of students discussing information from a history class. The discussion is on the Roosevelts.

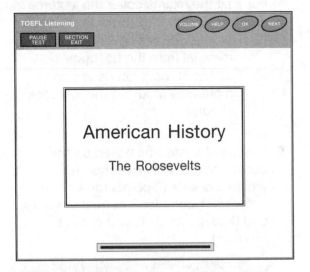

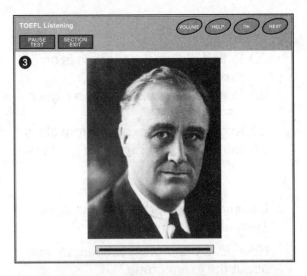

7. Why are these students discussing the Roosevelts?

   Ⓐ The final exam is in a few days.
   Ⓑ They are discussing a quiz they just took.
   Ⓒ They will be tested on the topic soon.
   Ⓓ They are preparing for a talk on the Roosevelts.

8. Listen again to part of the passage. Then answer the question. 🎧

What does the woman mean when she says this: 🎧

   Ⓐ "That's a different topic."
   Ⓑ "I don't understand."
   Ⓒ "You should repeat that."
   Ⓓ "That's not quite correct."

9. How were the Roosevelts related?

> Click on 2 answers.

   Ⓐ Eleanor was married to Franklin.
   Ⓑ Eleanor was Teddy's niece.
   Ⓒ Franklin was Teddy's brother.
   Ⓓ Teddy was Eleanor's father.

10. Which Roosevelt accomplished the following? **This question is worth 2 points** (2 points for 3 correct answers, 1 point for 2 correct answers, and 0 points for 1 or 0 correct answers).

> Click on a phrase. Then drag it to the space where it belongs. Each answer will be used one time only.

Was married to a president	Was president during the Depression	Was president early in the 20th century
Teddy	**Franklin**	**Eleanor**

11. What is implied in the discussion about Teddy, Franklin, and Eleanor Roosevelt?

   Ⓐ They were not related.
   Ⓑ They all served as president of the United States.
   Ⓒ They were all not very healthy.
   Ⓓ They were all involved in public activities.

12. How do the students seem to feel about the material?

   Ⓐ More confused by the end of the discussion
   Ⓑ Completely confident about the material from the start
   Ⓒ Less confused by the end of the discussion
   Ⓓ Completely confused about the material from start to finish

> Turn to pages 451–453 to *diagnose* your errors and *record* your results.

SECTION THREE

SPEAKING

SPEAKING DIAGNOSTIC PRE-TEST

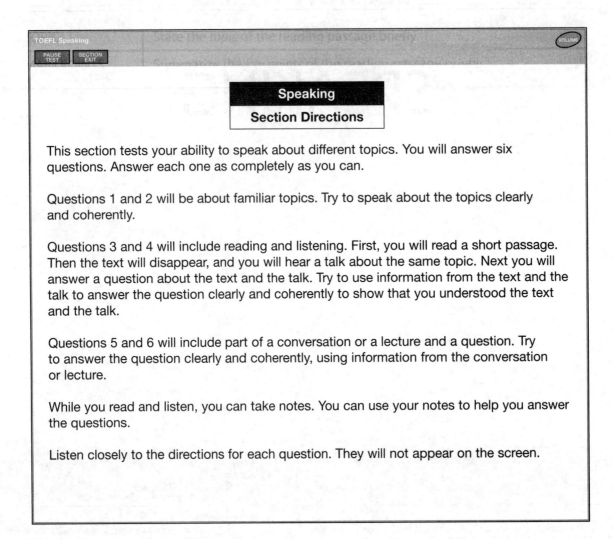

PAUSE TEST SECTION EXIT

VOLUME

Speaking
Section Directions

This section tests your ability to speak about different topics. You will answer six questions. Answer each one as completely as you can.

Questions 1 and 2 will be about familiar topics. Try to speak about the topics clearly and coherently.

Questions 3 and 4 will include reading and listening. First, you will read a short passage. Then the text will disappear, and you will hear a talk about the same topic. Next you will answer a question about the text and the talk. Try to use information from the text and the talk to answer the question clearly and coherently to show that you understood the text and the talk.

Questions 5 and 6 will include part of a conversation or a lecture and a question. Try to answer the question clearly and coherently, using information from the conversation or lecture.

While you read and listen, you can take notes. You can use your notes to help you answer the questions.

Listen closely to the directions for each question. They will not appear on the screen.

Questions 1–6

Question 1

Read the question. Take notes on the main points of a response. Then respond to the question.

> Preparation Time: 15 seconds
> Response Time: 45 seconds

What kind of material do you read most often? Use reasons in your response.

INTRODUCTION:

SUPPORTING IDEA 1:

SUPPORTING IDEA 2:

CONCLUSION:

Question 2

Read the question. Take notes on the main points of a response. Then respond to the question.

> Preparation Time: 15 seconds
> Response Time: 45 seconds

Is it better to live in the mountains or by the ocean? Use reasons in your response.

INTRODUCTION:

SUPPORTING IDEA 1:

SUPPORTING IDEA 2:

CONCLUSION:

Question 3

Read the passage. Take notes on the main points of the reading passage.

Reading Time: 45 seconds

Announcement posted in the campus dormitory

The dormitory will close for the summer at 5:00 P.M. on June 4. All students must move all of their belongings out of the dormitory by exactly 5:00 on that date. No one may stay any later, for any reason. We are sorry if this causes any problems for any students. We look forward to seeing you again on September 3, when the dormitory reopens for the fall semester.

TOPIC OF READING PASSAGE:

main points about the topic:

•

•

Listen to the passage. Take notes on the main points of the listening passage.

TOPIC OF LISTENING PASSAGE:

main points about the topic:

-

-

-

Now answer the following question:

How is the information in the listening passage related to the information in the reading passage?

| Preparation Time: 30 seconds |
| Response Time: 60 seconds |

Question 4

Read the passage. Take notes on the main points of the reading passage.

Reading Time: 45 seconds

Tornado Alley

Tornado Alley is the name given to an area of the United States where many of the world's tornadoes occur. More tornadoes occur in the United States than in any other country of the world; the average number of tornadoes that occur in the United States is between 800 and 900 a year. Most, but not all, of these 800 to 900 tornadoes occur in the area named Tornado Alley. This is a flat area in the middle of the country, the country's central plains.

TOPIC OF READING PASSAGE:

main points about the topic:

-

-

-

Listen to the passage. Take notes on the main points of the listening passage.

TOPIC OF LISTENING PASSAGE:

main points about the topic:

-

-

-

Now answer the following question:

How is the information in the listening passage related to the information in the reading passage?

Preparation Time: 30 seconds
Response Time: 60 seconds

Question 5

Listen to the passage. Take notes on the main points of the listening passage.

TOPIC OF LISTENING PASSAGE:

main points about the topic:

-

-

-

Now answer the following question:

What are the students discussing?

| Preparation Time: 20 seconds |
| Response Time: 60 seconds |

Question 6

Listen to the passage. Take notes on the main points of the listening passage.

TOPIC OF LISTENING PASSAGE:

main points about the topic:

•

•

•

Now answer the following question:

What does the professor say about clams?

> Preparation Time: 20 seconds
> Response Time: 60 seconds

Turn to pages 455–465 to *assess* the skills used in the test, *score* the test
using the Speaking Scoring Criteria, and *record* your results.

SPEAKING OVERVIEW

The third section on the TOEFL *iBT* is the Speaking section. This section consists of six tasks: two independent tasks and four integrated tasks. Two of the integrated tasks combine reading and listening with speaking, and the other two integrated tasks combine listening with speaking. To complete these tasks, you will speak into a microphone, and your responses will be recorded on the computer.

- The two **independent** tasks each consist of a question to be answered. The ideas in your responses come from your personal experience rather than from material that is given to you.

- The two **reading, listening, and speaking integrated** tasks each consist of a reading passage, a listening passage, and a question that asks how the ideas in the two passages are related.

- The two **listening and speaking integrated** tasks each consist of a longer listening passage and a question that asks you to summarize key points of the passage.

Because these kinds of tasks are different, there are different strategies for each kind. The following strategies can help you on the independent tasks in the Speaking section.

STRATEGIES FOR AN INDEPENDENT SPEAKING TASK

1. **Be familiar with the directions.** The directions on every test are the same, so it is not necessary to spend time reading the directions carefully when you take the test. You should be completely familiar with the directions before the day of the test.

2. **Dismiss the directions as soon as they come up.** The time starts when the directions come up. You should already be familiar with the directions, so you can click on Continue as soon as it appears and save all of your time for the passages and questions.

3. **Read the question carefully, and answer the question exactly as it is asked.** You will be given some time at the beginning of the task to be sure that you understand the question and what the question is asking you to do.

4. **Organize your response very clearly.** You should have an introduction, supporting details, and perhaps a conclusion.

5. **Stick to vocabulary, sentence structures, and grammatical points that you know.** This is not the best time to try out new words, structures, or grammar points.

---

6. **Speak slowly and distinctly.** It is better to speak clearly so that you can be understood than to race through your response so that you will be able to say more.

7. **Monitor the time carefully on the title bar of the computer screen.** The title bar indicates how much time you have to complete your response.

The following strategies can help you on the reading, listening, and speaking integrated tasks in the Speaking section.

STRATEGIES FOR AN INTEGRATED SPEAKING TASK
(Reading, Listening, and Speaking)

1. **Be familiar with the directions.** The directions on every test are the same, so it is not necessary to spend time reading the directions carefully when you take the test. You should be completely familiar with the directions before the day of the test.

2. **Dismiss the directions as soon as they come up.** The time starts when the directions come up. You should already be familiar with the directions, so you can click on Continue as soon as it appears and save all of your time for the passages and questions.

3. **Do not worry if the material in the integrated task is on a topic that is not familiar to you.** All of the information that you need to make your response is included in the passages. You do not need any background knowledge to answer the questions.

4. **Read the reading passage carefully.** You will have only a limited time to read the passage.

5. **Take careful notes as you read the passage.** You should focus on the main points and key supporting material. Do not try to write down everything you read. Do not write down too many unnecessary details.

6. **Listen carefully to the passage.** You will hear the passage one time only. You may not hear the passage again.

7. **Take careful notes as you listen to the spoken material.** You should focus on the main points and key supporting material. Do not try to write down everything you hear. Do not write down too many unnecessary details.

8. **Organize your response very clearly.** You should have an overall topic statement that shows the relationship between the reading passage and the listening passage. You should also discuss the reading passage and the listening passage.

9. **Stick to vocabulary, sentence structures, and grammatical points that you know.** This is not the best time to try out new words, structures, or grammar points.

10. **Speak slowly and distinctly.** It is better to speak clearly so that you can be understood than to race through your response so that you can say more.

11. **Monitor the time carefully on the title bar of the computer screen.** The title bar indicates how much time you have to complete your response.

The following strategies can help you on the listening and speaking integrated tasks in the Speaking section.

STRATEGIES FOR AN INTEGRATED SPEAKING TASK
(Listening and Speaking)

1. **Be familiar with the directions.** The directions on every test are the same, so it is not necessary to spend time reading the directions carefully when you take the test. You should be completely familiar with the directions before the day of the test.

2. **Dismiss the directions as soon as they come up.** The time starts when the directions come up. You should already be familiar with the directions, so you can click on Continue as soon as it appears and save all of your time for the passages and questions.

3. **Do not worry if the material in the integrated task is on a topic that is not familiar to you.** All of the information that you need to make your response is included in the passage. You do not need any background knowledge to answer the questions.

4. **Listen carefully to the passage.** You will hear the passage one time only. You may not hear the passage again.

5. **Take careful notes as you listen to the spoken material.** You should focus on the main points and key supporting material. Do not try to write down everything you hear. Do not write down too many unnecessary details.

6. **Organize your response very clearly.** You should have an overall topic statement that states the main point of the response and details that support the main point.

7. **Stick to vocabulary, sentence structures, and grammatical points that you know.** This is not the best time to try out new words, structures, or grammar points.

8. **Speak slowly and distinctly.** It is better to speak clearly so that you can be understood than to race through your response so that you can say more.

9. **Monitor the time carefully on the title bar of the computer screen.** The title bar indicates how much time you have to complete your response.

SPEAKING SKILLS

The following skills will help you to implement these strategies in the Speaking section of the TOEFL *iBT*.

INDEPENDENT TASKS

There are two independent speaking tasks. These two independent speaking tasks are a free-choice response and a paired-choice response.

Speaking Skill 1: PLAN THE FREE-CHOICE RESPONSE

The first and most important step in the independent free-choice task in the Speaking section of the TOEFL *iBT* is to decode the question to determine what the intended outline is. Independent free-choice questions generally give clear clues about how your response should be constructed. It is important to follow the clues that are given in the question when you are planning your answer. Study the following question.

> **Question**
>
> What do you need to improve most about your English? Use reasons in your response.

As you read this topic, you should determine that you should clearly state *what you need to improve most about your English* and give *reasons* that explain why. Study the following plan for the response to this question.

INTRODUCTION:	need to improve speaking
SUPPORTING IDEA 1:	first reason
	• have studied a lot of grammar (but not speaking)
SUPPORTING IDEA 2:	second reason
	• have studied a lot of vocabulary (but not speaking)
CONCLUSION:	the reasons for needing to improve speaking

In this plan, there is an introduction about needing to improve speaking and supporting details giving reasons. There is also a conclusion that reinforces the reasons for the need to improve speaking.

The following chart outlines the key information that you should remember about planning the response.

PLANNING THE RESPONSE	
QUESTION	Each question in the independent free-choice task shows you *what* you should discuss and *how* you should organize your response. You must decode the question to determine how to organize your response.
INTRODUCTION	Begin your response with an introduction.
SUPPORTING IDEAS	Support your introduction with the kinds of ideas that the question asks for (such as reasons, details, or examples).
CONCLUSION	If you have time, end with a conclusion that restates the main point in your introduction.

SPEAKING EXERCISE 1: For each of the following questions, prepare a plan that shows the type of information you will include in your response.

1.
What do you do when you are feeling sad? Use details in your response.

INTRODUCTION:

SUPPORTING IDEA 1:

SUPPORTING IDEA 2:

CONCLUSION:

2. What is your favorite month of the year? Use reasons in your response.

INTRODUCTION:

SUPPORTING IDEA 1:

SUPPORTING IDEA 2:

CONCLUSION:

3. What do you like most about the other students in your class? Use examples in your response.

INTRODUCTION:

SUPPORTING IDEA 1:

SUPPORTING IDEA 2:

CONCLUSION:

Speaking Skill 2: MAKE THE FREE-CHOICE RESPONSE

After you have planned your response, you need to make your response. As you make your response, you should think about the following two things: (1) you should start with an introduction and (2) you should support the introduction.

Look at the plan for a response to the independent speaking task on the need to improve speaking.

INTRODUCTION:	need to improve speaking
SUPPORTING IDEA 1:	first reason
	• have studied a lot of grammar (but not speaking)
SUPPORTING IDEA 2:	second reason
	• have studied a lot of vocabulary (but not speaking)
CONCLUSION:	the reasons for needing to improve speaking

> I am studying English because I need to learn a lot of things. But maybe the most important thing that I need to improve in my English is my speaking.
>
> I have studied a lot of English grammar. However, when I have studied English grammar, I have not learned how to speak well.
>
> I have also studied a lot of English vocabulary. However, when I have studied English vocabulary, I have also not learned to speak well.
>
> I know a lot of English grammar and a lot of English vocabulary. Now, I need to learn to speak English better.

You should notice that this response includes an introduction about the need to improve speaking. This introduction is supported by two reasons. The response ends with a conclusion that restates the reasons for the need to improve speaking.

The following chart outlines the key information that you should remember about making the response.

MAKING THE RESPONSE	
INTRODUCTION	Start your response with an introduction that states the topic and your main point about the topic.
SUPPORT	Include details to support the introduction.
CONCLUSION	End your response with a conclusion that restates the main point.

SPEAKING EXERCISE 2: Create responses for the independent speaking tasks that you have been working on in Speaking Skills 1–2.

Speaking Skill 3: PLAN THE PAIRED-CHOICE RESPONSE

The first and most important step in the independent paired-choice task in the Speaking section of the TOEFL *iBT* is to decode the question to determine what the intended outline is. Independent paired-choice questions generally give clear clues about how your response should be constructed. It is important to follow the clues that are given in the question when you are planning your answer. Study the following question.

Question
You must choose to study either history or math. Which one do you choose? Use reasons in your response.

As you read this topic, you should determine that you should clearly state whether you would *choose to study either history or math* and use *reasons* to explain why. Study the following plan for the response to this question.

INTRODUCTION:	choose math instead of history
SUPPORTING IDEA 1:	first reason • I am very good at math
SUPPORTING IDEA 2:	second reason • math has many uses
CONCLUSION:	reasons for choosing math instead of history

In this plan, there is an introduction about choosing math instead of history and reasons for the choice. There is also a conclusion that restates the main point.

The following chart outlines the key information that you should remember about planning the response.

PLANNING THE RESPONSE	
QUESTION	Each question in the independent paired-choice task shows you *what* you should discuss and *how* you should organize your response. You must decode the question to determine how to organize your response.
INTRODUCTION	Begin your response with an introduction.
SUPPORTING IDEAS	Support your introduction with the kinds of ideas that the question asks for (such as reasons, details, or examples).
CONCLUSION	If you have time, end with a conclusion that restates the main point in the introduction.

SPEAKING EXERCISE 3: For each of the following questions, prepare a plan that shows the type of information you will include in your response.

1.
> If you can be an astronaut or a famous musician, which one will you choose? Use reasons in your response.

INTRODUCTION:

SUPPORTING IDEA 1:

SUPPORTING IDEA 2:

CONCLUSION:

2.
> Do you get work done early in the day or wait until the last possible moment? Use examples in your response.

INTRODUCTION:

SUPPORTING IDEA 1:

SUPPORTING IDEA 2:

CONCLUSION:

3.
> Is it better to have love or money? Use reasons in your response.

INTRODUCTION:

SUPPORTING IDEA 1:

SUPPORTING IDEA 2:

CONCLUSION:

Speaking Skill 4: MAKE THE PAIRED-CHOICE RESPONSE

After you have planned your response, you need to make your response. As you make your response, you should think about the following two things: (1) you should start with an introduction and (2) you should support the introduction.

Look at the plan for a response to the independent speaking task on a choice between math and history.

INTRODUCTION: choose math instead of history

SUPPORTING IDEA 1:   first reason
                    • I am very good at math

SUPPORTING IDEA 2:   second reason
                    • math has many uses

CONCLUSION: reasons for choosing math instead
                    of history

If I have to make a choice between history and math, I am pretty sure that I will choose math instead of history. I have two reasons for thinking this.

The first reason that I will choose math instead of history is that I am good with numbers. It is easy for me to do calculations in math.

The second reason that I will choose math instead of history is that math has many uses. If I study math, I will be able to use it in my life. I will also be able to find a good job.

These are the reasons why I will choose math instead of history if I have to make this choice.

You should notice that this response includes an introduction about choosing math instead of history. This introduction is supported by two reasons. The response ends with a conclusion that restates the decision to choose math instead of history.

The following chart outlines the key information that you should remember about making the response.

MAKING THE RESPONSE	
INTRODUCTION	Start your response with an introduction that states the topic and your main point about the topic.
SUPPORT	Include details to support the introduction.
CONCLUSION	End your response with a conclusion that restates the main point.

SPEAKING EXERCISE 4: Create responses for the independent speaking tasks that you have been working on in Speaking Skills 3–4.

SPEAKING REVIEW EXERCISE (Skills 1–4): Read each question. Take notes on the main points of a response. Then respond to the question.

1. | What kinds of activities do people enjoy most in your hometown? Use details in your response. |

INTRODUCTION:

SUPPORTING IDEA 1:

SUPPORTING IDEA 2:

CONCLUSION:

2. | Do you prefer lecture classes or discussion classes? Use reasons in your response. |

INTRODUCTION:

SUPPORTING IDEA 1:

SUPPORTING IDEA 2:

CONCLUSION:

INTEGRATED TASKS (Reading and Listening) _____

There are two integrated tasks that integrate speaking with reading and listening. These two integrated speaking tasks are on a campus topic and on an academic topic.

Speaking Skill 5: NOTE THE MAIN POINTS AS YOU READ

In the first reading, listening, and speaking integrated task in the Speaking section of the TOEFL *iBT*, you will have to read a passage from a campus setting as part of the task. Look at the following example of a reading passage that is part of this integrated speaking task.

Reading Passage

An article in a school newspaper

Congratulations to the school's basketball team. The team won its game last night. Now it will play in the championship game next Wednesday evening at 7:30 in the school gymnasium. Get your tickets early, or there will not be any left for you.

As you read the passage, you should take notes on the topic and main points of the reading passage. Look at these notes on the topic and main points of the reading passage.

TOPIC OF READING PASSAGE: article in school newspaper on school's basketball team

main points about the topic:
• team won game
• team will play in championship game
• it is important to get tickets early

These notes show that the topic of the reading passage is an *article in the school newspaper*. The main points about the topic are that the *team won the game*, the *team will play in a championship game*, and *it is important to get tickets early* for the game.

The following chart outlines the key information you should remember about dealing with the reading passage in the reading, listening, and speaking integrated speaking task.

NOTING THE MAIN POINTS IN THE READING PASSAGE	
TOPIC	Make sure that you understand (and take notes on) the *topic* of the reading passage.
MAIN POINTS	Then focus on (and take notes on) the *main points* that are used to support the topic of the reading passage.

SPEAKING EXERCISE 5: Read each of the following passages, and note the *topic* and the *main points* that are used to support the topic.

1. Read the passage. Take notes on the main points of the reading passage.

A note on the door of a professor's classroom

Professor Jones will not be in his classes on Thursday, November 8 and Friday, November 9. He will be absent from his classes because he is suffering from an illness. All of his classes are canceled on those days. Professor Jones expects to return to his classes on Monday, November 12.

TOPIC OF READING PASSAGE:

main points about the topic:

-

-

2. Read the passage. Take notes on the main points of the reading passage.

A memo from the Literature Department, May 1

All students in the department must fill out a schedule form and turn it in to the Literature Department. Schedule forms must be turned in no later than April 30. Do not be late in turning schedule forms in to the Literature Department. Schedule forms will not be accepted after April 30.

TOPIC OF READING PASSAGE:

main points about the topic:

-
-
-

3. Read the passage. Take notes on the main points of the reading passage.

A notice posted in the library

Part-time jobs are available in the university library. These jobs are available for full-time students only, and they are available during evening and weekend hours. If you are a full-time student who is available evenings during the week or on weekends and you are looking for a part-time job, this may be a good job for you. Contact the head librarian in the library office between 9:00 A.M. and 5:00 P.M. if you are interested in having one of these jobs.

TOPIC OF READING PASSAGE:

main points about the topic:

-
-
-

Speaking Skill 6: NOTE THE MAIN POINTS AS YOU LISTEN

In the first reading, listening, and speaking integrated task in the Speaking section of the TOEFL *iBT*, you will have to listen to a passage from a campus setting as part of the task. Look at the following example of a listening passage that is part of this integrated speaking task.

Listening Passage

(woman)   *I'm so happy about the basketball team.*

(man)   *I'm happy for the team, but I'm not happy for myself.*

(woman)   *Why not?*

(man)   *I can't go to the game.*

(woman)   *You can't? Why not?*

(man)   *I've got a class on Wednesday evenings, and it's a class I just can't miss.*

(woman)   *That's too bad. I'm going for sure. I'm on my way to get a ticket right now.*

(man)   *Unfortunately, I'm going to have to miss the game.*

As you listen to the passage, you should take notes on the topic and main points of the listening passage. Look at these notes on the topic and main points of the listening passage.

TOPIC OF LISTENING PASSAGE: student discussion about basketball team

main points about the topic:
- woman is happy about basketball team's win
- woman will go to championship game
- man is happy about basketball team's win
- man can't go to championship game because of a class

These notes show that the topic of the listening passage is a *student discussion about a basketball team*. The main points of the discussion are that the *woman is happy about the basketball team's win*, and she *will go to the championship game*. The *man is happy about the win*, but he *can't go to the championship game because* he has to attend *a class*.

The following chart outlines the key information you should remember about dealing with the listening passage in the integrated speaking task.

NOTING THE MAIN POINTS IN THE LISTENING PASSAGE	
TOPIC	Make sure that you understand (and take notes on) the *topic* of the listening passage.
MAIN POINTS	Then focus on (and take notes on) the *main points* that are used to support the topic of the listening passage.

SPEAKING EXERCISE 6: Listen to each of the following passages, and note the *topic* and the *main points* that are used to support the topic.

1. Listen to the passage. Take notes on the main points of the listening passage.

TOPIC OF LISTENING PASSAGE:

main points about the topic:

-

-

2. Listen to the passage. Take notes on the main points of the listening passage.

TOPIC OF LISTENING PASSAGE:

main points about the topic:

-

-

3. Listen to the passage. Take notes on the main points of the listening passage.

TOPIC OF LISTENING PASSAGE:

main points about the topic:

-

-

Speaking Skill 7: PLAN BEFORE YOU SPEAK

After you have noted the main points of the reading passage and the main points of the listening passage in the campus integrated reading, listening, and speaking task, you need to read the question and plan your response.

The question will most likely be about how the main points of the reading passage and the main points of the listening passage are related. Look at the following example of a question in an integrated speaking task on the article in a school newspaper.

Question

How is the information in the listening passage related to the information in the reading passage?

You can see that the question is asking you to show how the main points of the two passages are related.

To prepare a plan for your response, you should look at the notes you have taken on the reading passage and the notes you have taken on the listening passage. You should then think about how the ideas in the two passages are related. Look at a plan for the response on the school basketball team.

Reading Passage = *newspaper article on basketball team*

TOPIC OF READING PASSAGE: article in school newspaper on school's basketball team

main points about the topic:
- team won game
- team will play in championship game
- it is important to get tickets for game early

Listening Passage = *discussion about basketball team*

TOPIC OF LISTENING PASSAGE: student discussion about basketball team

main points about the topic:
- woman is happy about basketball team's win
- woman will go to championship game
- man is happy about basketball team's win
- man can't go to championship game because of a class

From this plan, you can see that the ideas in the reading passage and the ideas in the listening passage are related. The plan shows that the reading passage describes a *newspaper article on* the *basketball team* and the listening passage is a *discussion about the basketball team.*

The following chart outlines the key information you should remember about planning before you speak in a reading, listening, and speaking integrated task.

PLANNING BEFORE YOU SPEAK	
QUESTION	Study the *question* to determine what is being asked. Expect that the question is asking how the ideas in the reading passage and the listening passage are related.
RELATIONSHIP	Look at the notes you have taken on the reading passage and the listening passage. Focus on the main points or topics of each passage. Then describe how the ideas in the two passages are *related*.

SPEAKING EXERCISE 7: Look at the notes that you prepared for the reading passages in Speaking Exercise 5 and the listening passages in Speaking Exercise 6. Read the question for each task. Then prepare a plan for your response. Be sure to note the relationship between the reading passage and the listening passage.

1. How is the information in the listening passage related to the information in the reading passage?

2. How is the information in the listening passage related to the information in the reading passage?

3. How is the information in the listening passage related to the information in the reading passage?

Speaking Skill 8: MAKE THE RESPONSE

After you have planned your response, you need to make your response. As you make your response, you should think about the following two things: (1) you should start with a topic statement and (2) you should support the topic statement.

Look at the plan for a response in the integrated speaking task on the newspaper article on the school's basketball team.

Reading Passage = *newspaper article on basketball team*

TOPIC OF READING PASSAGE: article in school newspaper on school's basketball team

main points about the topic:
- team won game
- team will play in championship game
- it is important to get tickets for game early

Listening Passage = *discussion about basketball team*

TOPIC OF LISTENING PASSAGE: student discussion about basketball team

main points about the topic:
- woman is happy about basketball team's win
- woman will go to championship game
- man is happy about basketball team's win
- man can't go to championship game because of a class

In this set of materials, the reading passage is an article in a school newspaper on the basketball team. Two students discuss the basketball team in the listening passage.

The article in the school newspaper is on the school's basketball team. The team won an important game and will play in a championship game soon. It is important for students to get tickets for the game early if they want to go to the game.

In the listening passage, the students discuss the basketball team. The woman is really happy about the basketball team's win, and she absolutely will go to the championship game. The man is happy about the basketball team's win, but he's really unhappy because he can't go to the championship game. He can't go to the game because he has to go to a class.

You should notice that this response begins with a topic statement showing the relationship between the information in the reading passage and the listening passage. Two supporting paragraphs follow the topic statement. They describe the main points of the reading passage and the main points of the listening passage.

The following chart outlines the key information you should remember about making the response.

MAKING THE RESPONSE	
TOPIC	Start your response with a *topic statement* that shows how the ideas in the reading passage and the ideas in the listening passage are related.
SUPPORT	Include the *key points* of the reading passage and the listening passage in your response.

SPEAKING EXERCISE 8: Create responses for the integrated reading, listening, and speaking tasks that you have been working on in Speaking Skills 5–8.

SPEAKING REVIEW EXERCISE (Skills 5–8):
Read the passage. Take notes on the main points of the reading passage.

An assignment in a business class

Your assignment for Friday is to write about the strengths and weaknesses of a leader. You must choose one of the leaders who is discussed in Chapter 6 on leadership in the textbook. First, choose three strengths of this leader, and write one paragraph about each of the strengths. Then, choose three weaknesses of the leader, and write one paragraph about each of the weaknesses.

TOPIC OF READING PASSAGE:

main points about the topic:

•

•

•

Listen to the passage. Take notes on the main points of the listening passage.

TOPIC OF LISTENING PASSAGE:

main points about the topic:

-

-

-

-

-

Now answer the following question:

How is the information in the listening passage related to the information in the reading passage?

Speaking Skill 9: NOTE THE MAIN POINTS AS YOU READ

In the second reading, listening, and speaking integrated task in the Speaking section of the TOEFL *iBT*, you will have to read an academic passage as part of the task. Look at the following example of a reading passage that is part of this integrated speaking task.

Reading Passage

A Blizzard

A blizzard is a type of storm, a really severe kind of storm. It is a storm that occurs during winter, and it combines heavy snowfall, very cold temperatures, and strong winds.

As you read the passage, you should take notes on the topic and main points of the reading passage. Look at these notes on the topic and main points of the reading passage.

TOPIC OF READING PASSAGE: blizzard

main points about the topic:
- is severe storm
- occurs during winter
- has snowfall, cold temperatures, strong winds

These notes show that the topic of the reading passage is blizzards. The main points about the topic are that a blizzard is a *severe storm* that *occurs during winter* and that it *has snowfall, cold temperatures,* and *strong winds.*

The following chart outlines the key information you should remember about dealing with the reading passage in the reading, listening, and speaking integrated speaking task.

NOTING THE MAIN POINTS IN THE READING PASSAGE	
TOPIC	Make sure that you understand (and take notes on) the *topic* of the reading passage.
MAIN POINTS	Then focus on (and take notes on) the *main points* that are used to support the topic of the reading passage.

SPEAKING EXERCISE 9: Read each of the following passages, and note the *topic* and the *main points* that are used to support the topic.

1. Read the passage. Take notes on the main points of the reading passage.

Venus

The planet Venus is the second planet from the Sun in our solar system. An amazing fact about the planet Venus is that its surface is at an extremely high temperature. The surface temperature on Venus is 890 degrees Fahrenheit, or 470 degrees centigrade. This is far warmer than the surface temperature on Earth, and it is even warmer than the surface temperature of the planet Mercury. This might seem surprising because Mercury is even closer to our Sun than Venus is.

TOPIC OF READING PASSAGE:

main points about the topic:

•

•

•

2. Read the passage. Take notes on the main points of the reading passage.

Mountains and Snow

Let's talk a little bit about mountains and snow. If I ask you which mountains have permanent snow on them, what's your response? Is your response about the height of the mountains? Is your response that taller mountains have permanent snow on them, while shorter mountains don't? If this is your response, then you're not completely correct. The response that the height of mountains determines whether or not there is permanent snow on them is only partially true.

There is another factor, in addition to the height of mountains, that determines whether or not mountains have permanent snow on them. This second factor is the distance from the equator.

TOPIC OF READING PASSAGE:

main points about the topic:

-

-

3. Read the passage. Take notes on the main points of the reading passage.

Honeybees

Honeybees are those buzzing animals that produce honey. Honeybees live in colonies of up to 60,000 members. A colony contains a queen bee, a few hundred male drone bees, and thousands of female worker bees.

Honeybees are known for their painful sting. Honeybees sting people or animals to protect their colony. The sting can be very painful, and it has even been known to kill a human on occasion.

TOPIC OF READING PASSAGE:

main points about the topic:

-

-

-

Speaking Skill 10: NOTE THE MAIN POINTS AS YOU LISTEN

In the second reading, listening, and speaking integrated task in the Speaking section of the TOEFL *iBT*, you will have to listen to an academic passage as part of the task. Look at the following example of a listening passage that is part of this integrated speaking task.

Listening Passage

(professor) *Now I'd like to talk about one particular blizzard so that you can see just how severe a blizzard can be. A huge blizzard occurred in the eastern United States in 1888. It lasted for four days in March of that year. During this four-day blizzard, there was a huge amount of snow. There was so much snow that the snow completely covered single-story buildings and reached up to the windows on the second level of buildings with more than one level.*

As you listen to the passage, you should take notes on the topic and main points of the listening passage. Look at these notes on the topic and main points of the listening passage.

TOPIC OF LISTENING PASSAGE: example of one blizzard

main points about the topic:
- it occurred in 1888
- it lasted four days
- snow reached windows on second floor of buildings

These notes show that the topic of the listening passage is an *example of one blizzard*. The main points about the topic are that the blizzard *occurred in 1888* and *lasted for four days. Snow reached the windows on the second floor of buildings* in the area.

The following chart outlines the key information you should remember about dealing with the listening passage in the integrated speaking task.

NOTING THE MAIN POINTS IN THE LISTENING PASSAGE	
TOPIC	Make sure that you understand (and take notes on) the *topic* of the listening passage.
MAIN POINTS	Then focus on (and take notes on) the *main points* that are used to support the topic of the listening passage.

SPEAKING EXERCISE 10: Listen to each of the following passages, and note the *topic* and the *main points* that are used to support the topic.

1. Listen to the passage. Take notes on the main points of the listening passage.

TOPIC OF LISTENING PASSAGE:

main points about the topic:

•

•

2. Listen to the passage. Take notes on the main points of the listening passage.

TOPIC OF LISTENING PASSAGE:

main points about the topic:

-

-

-

3. Listen to the passage. Take notes on the main points of the listening passage.

TOPIC OF LISTENING PASSAGE:

main points about the topic:

-

-

Speaking Skill 11: PLAN BEFORE YOU SPEAK

After you have noted the main points of the reading passage and the main points of the listening passage in the academic integrated reading, listening, and speaking task, you need to read the question and plan your response.

The question will most likely be about how the main points of the reading passage and the main points of the listening passage are related. Look at the following example of a question in an integrated speaking task on blizzards.

> **Question**
>
> How is the information in the listening passage related to the information in the reading passage?

You can see that the question is asking you to show how the main points of the two passages are related.

To prepare a plan for your response, you should look at the notes you have taken on the reading passage and the notes you have taken on the listening passage. You should then think about how the ideas in the two passages are related. Look at a plan for the response on blizzards.

Reading Passage = *kind of storm*

TOPIC OF READING PASSAGE: blizzard

main points about the topic:
- is severe storm
- occurs during winter
- has snowfall, cold temperatures, strong winds

Listening Passage = *example of kind of storm*

TOPIC OF LISTENING PASSAGE: example of one blizzard

main points about the topic:
- it occurred in 1888
- it lasted four days
- snow reached windows on second floor of buildings

From this plan, you can see that the ideas in the reading passage and the ideas in the listening passage are related. The plan shows that the reading passage describes a *kind of storm* and the listening passage gives an *example of that kind of storm*.

The following chart outlines the key information you should remember about planning before you speak in a reading, listening, and speaking integrated task.

PLANNING BEFORE YOU SPEAK	
QUESTION	Study the *question* to determine what is being asked. Expect that the question is asking how the ideas in the reading passage and the listening passage are related.
RELATIONSHIP	Look at the notes you have taken on the reading passage and the listening passage. Focus on the main points or topics of each passage. Then describe how the ideas in the two passages are *related*.

SPEAKING EXERCISE 11: Look at the notes that you prepared for the reading passages in Speaking Exercise 9 and the listening passages in Speaking Exercise 10. Read the question for each task. Then prepare a plan for your response. Be sure to note the relationship between the reading passage and the listening passage.

1. How is the information in the listening passage related to the information in the reading passage?

2. How is the information in the listening passage related to the information in the reading passage?

3. How is the information in the listening passage related to the information in the reading passage?

Speaking Skill 12: MAKE THE RESPONSE

After you have planned your response, you need to make your response. As you make your response, you should think about the following two things: (1) you should start with a topic statement and (2) you should support the topic statement.

Look at the plan for a response in the integrated speaking task on blizzards.

Reading Passage = *kind of storm*

TOPIC OF READING PASSAGE: blizzard

main points about the topic:
- is severe storm
- occurs during winter
- has snowfall, cold temperatures, strong winds

Listening Passage = *example of kind of storm*

TOPIC OF LISTENING PASSAGE: example of one blizzard

main points about the topic:
- it occurred in 1888
- it lasted four days
- snow reached windows on second floor of buildings

The reading passage discusses a kind of storm. The listening passage provides an example of that kind of storm.

The reading passage gives information about blizzards. Blizzards are severe storms that occur during the winter months. During blizzards, there is a lot of snowfall, cold temperatures, and strong winds.

The listening passage gives an example of one particularly strong blizzard. This blizzard occurred in 1888, and it lasted for four days. There was so much snow during the storm that snow reached the windows on the second floor of buildings.

You should notice that this response begins with a topic statement showing the relationship between the information in the reading passage and the listening passage. Two supporting paragraphs follow the topic statement. They describe the main points of the reading passage and the main points of the listening passage.

The following chart outlines the key information you should remember about making the response.

MAKING THE RESPONSE	
TOPIC	Start your response with a *topic statement* that shows how the ideas in the reading passage and the ideas in the listening passage are related.
SUPPORT	Include the *key points* of the reading passage and the listening passage in your response.

SPEAKING EXERCISE 12: Create responses for the integrated reading, listening, and speaking tasks that you have been working on in Speaking Skills 9–12.

SPEAKING REVIEW EXERCISE (Skills 9–12):
Read the passage. Take notes on the main points of the reading passage.

Mercantilism

Early in the seventeenth century, the rulers of Europe came to understand that it was important to have colonies. It was a good idea to have colonies because colonies would make the mother country richer and more powerful. This idea that it was good for business for a country to have colonies was called mercantilism.

TOPIC OF READING PASSAGE:

main points about the topic:

•

•

•

Listen to the passage. Take notes on the main points of the listening passage.

TOPIC OF LISTENING PASSAGE:

main points about the topic:

-

-

-

Now answer the following question:

How is the information in the listening passage related to the information in the reading passage?

INTEGRATED TASKS (Listening)

There are two integrated speaking tasks that integrate speaking with listening. These two integrated speaking tasks are on a campus topic and on an academic topic.

Speaking Skill 13: NOTE THE MAIN POINTS AS YOU LISTEN

In the first listening and speaking integrated task in the Speaking section of the TOEFL *iBT*, you will have to listen to a passage from a campus setting as part of the task. Look at the following example of a listening passage that is part of this integrated speaking task.

Listening Passage

(man) *We have a really long assignment, don't we?*

(woman) *We do? The assignment doesn't seem that long to me.*

(man) *But it's a really long assignment. Usually we have to write about one page, but this time we have to write five pages.*

(woman) *Five pages? . . . But that's not the assignment.*

(man) *It's not?*

(woman) *No. The assignment is to write five paragraphs.*

(man) *Five paragraphs, and not five pages?*

(woman) *That's right. So the five paragraphs will be about one page long.*

(man) *And that's a very normal assignment.*

(woman) *Yes, it is. Usually we write about one page, and this time we have to write five paragraphs, and that's about one page. We really don't have to write five pages. I think you were confused about the assignment.*

(man) *I'm so happy to learn that I was confused . . . and so happy that I didn't write five pages by mistake.*

As you listen to the passage, you should take notes on the topic and main points of the listening passage. Look at these notes on the topic and main points of the listening passage.

TOPIC OF LISTENING PASSAGE: student discussion about a writing assignment

main points about the topic:
- man thinks assignment is long (five pages)
- woman knows assignment is not long (five paragraphs)
- woman says man is confused
- man is happy about shorter writing assignment

These notes show that the topic of the reading passage is a *student discussion about a writing assignment*. The main points about the topic are that the *man thinks the assignment is* to write a *long*, five-page paper, and the *woman knows* that the *assignment is not long* because it is only five paragraphs. The *woman says* the *man is confused*, and the *man is happy about* the *shorter assignment*.

The following chart outlines the key information you should remember about dealing with the listening passage in the integrated speaking task.

NOTING THE MAIN POINTS IN THE LISTENING PASSAGE	
TOPIC	Make sure that you understand (and take notes on) the *topic* of the listening passage.
MAIN POINTS	Then focus on (and take notes on) the *main points* that are used to support the topic of the listening passage.

SPEAKING EXERCISE 13: Listen to each of the following passages, and note the *topic* and the *main points* that are used to support the topic.

1. Listen to the passage. Take notes on the main points of the listening passage.

TOPIC OF LISTENING PASSAGE:

main points about the topic:

•

•

•

2. Listen to the passage. Take notes on the main points of the listening passage.

TOPIC OF LISTENING PASSAGE:

main points about the topic:

-

-

-

3. Listen to the passage. Take notes on the main points of the listening passage.

TOPIC OF LISTENING PASSAGE:

main points about the topic:

-

-

-

-

Speaking Skill 14: PLAN BEFORE YOU SPEAK

After you have noted the main points of the listening passage in the campus integrated listening and speaking task, you need to read the question and plan your response.

The question will most likely be about the main points of the listening passage. Look at the following example of a question in an integrated speaking task on a writing assignment.

Question

What do the students say about the assignment?

You can see that the question is asking you what the students say about the assignment.

To prepare a plan for your response, you should focus on the notes you have taken on the listening passage. Look at a plan for the response on the writing assignment.

Listening Passage = *man's confusion about assignment and woman's clarification of it*

TOPIC OF LISTENING PASSAGE: student discussion about a writing assignment

main points about the topic:
- man thinks assignment is long (five pages)
- woman knows assignment is not long (five paragraphs)
- woman says man is confused
- man is happy about shorter writing assignment

From this plan, you can see that the passage is about the man's confusion about the assignment and the woman's clarification of it.

The following chart outlines the key information you should remember about planning the response in a reading, listening, and speaking integrated task.

PLANNING BEFORE YOU SPEAK	
QUESTION	Study the *question* to determine what is being asked. Expect that the question is about the main points of the listening passage.
FOCUS	Look at the notes you have taken on the listening passage. Focus on the *main points* of the passage. Then describe the main points of the listening passage.

SPEAKING EXERCISE 14: Look at the notes you prepared for the listening passages in Speaking Exercise 13. Read the question for each task. Then prepare a plan for each response including a topic statement.

1. What are the two students discussing?

2. What are the students saying about the notes?

3. What are the students saying about the economics class?

Speaking Skill 15: MAKE THE RESPONSE

After you have planned your response, you need to make your response. As you make your response, you should think about the following two things: (1) you should start with a topic statement and (2) you should support the topic statement.

Look at the plan for a response in the integrated speaking task on a writing assignment.

Listening Passage = *man's confusion about assignment and woman's clarification of it*

TOPIC OF LISTENING PASSAGE: student discussion about a writing assignment

main points about the topic:
- man thinks assignment is long (five pages)
- woman knows assignment is not long (five paragraphs)
- woman says man is confused
- man is happy about shorter writing assignment

   In this listening passage, two students are having a discussion about a writing assignment. The man is confused about the assignment, and the woman clarifies the assignment for him.

   The man thinks that the writing assignment is very long. He thinks that the assignment is to write five pages.

   The woman clarifies the assignment for the man. She knows that the assignment is not long, and she also thinks that the man is confused.

   The woman tells the man that the assignment is to write only five paragraphs and not five pages.

   When the man hears this, he is very happy. He is happy he was wrong and happy that the assignment is much shorter than he thought.

You should notice that this response includes a topic statement. The topic statement is followed by a number of supporting ideas.

The following chart outlines the key information you should remember about making the response.

MAKING THE RESPONSE	
TOPIC	Start your response with a *topic statement* that states the main point of the response.
SUPPORT	Include *details* to support the topic statement.

SPEAKING EXERCISE 15: Create responses for the independent speaking tasks that you have been working on in Speaking Skills 13–15.

SPEAKING REVIEW EXERCISE (Skills 13–15):

Listen to the passage. Take notes on the main points of the listening passage.

TOPIC OF LISTENING PASSAGE:

main points about the topic:

-

-

-

Now answer the following question:

What do the students have to say about preparing for the exam?

Speaking Skill 16: NOTE THE MAIN POINTS AS YOU LISTEN

In the second listening and speaking integrated task in the Speaking section of the TOEFL *iBT*, you will have to listen to an academic passage as part of the task. Look at the following example of a listening passage that is part of this integrated speaking task.

Listening Passage

(professor) *What color do you think blood is? A lot of people think that blood is always red, but this isn't completely true.*

Blood is sometimes red and sometimes blue; it depends on whether or not there is oxygen in the blood. Blood that is combined with oxygen is red. Blood that isn't combined with oxygen is blue.

In the body, when blood is traveling to the heart, it's blue in color. It's blue in color because it doesn't have oxygen in it. The opposite is true when blood is traveling from the heart. When blood is traveling from the heart, it's red in color because it's oxygenated in the heart.

Outside the body, blood is always red. This is because blood combines with oxygen when it's outside the body.

As you listen to the passage, you should take notes on the topic and main points of the listening passage. Look at these notes on the topic and main points of the listening passage.

TOPIC OF LISTENING PASSAGE: color of blood

main points about the topic:
- blood with oxygen is red
- blood without oxygen is blue
- blood traveling from heart is red (has oxygen)
- blood traveling to heart is blue (doesn't have oxygen)
- blood outside the body is red (has oxygen)

These notes show that the topic of the reading passage is the *color of blood*. The main points about the topic are that *blood with oxygen is red*, while *blood without oxygen is blue*. *Blood traveling from the heart is red* because it *has oxygen*, while *blood traveling to the heart is blue* because it *does not have oxygen*. *Blood outside the body is red* because it *has oxygen*.

The following chart outlines the key information you should remember about dealing with the listening passage in the integrated speaking task.

NOTING THE MAIN POINTS IN THE LISTENING PASSAGE	
TOPIC	Make sure that you understand (and take notes on) the *topic* of the listening passage.
MAIN POINTS	Then focus on (and take notes on) the *main points* that are used to support the topic of the listening passage.

SPEAKING EXERCISE 16: Listen to each of the passages, and note the *topic* and the *main points* about the topic.

1. Listen to the passage. Take notes on the main points of the listening passage.

TOPIC OF LISTENING PASSAGE:

main points about the topic:

-

-

-

-

-

-

2. Listen to the passage. Take notes on the main points of the listening passage.

TOPIC OF LISTENING PASSAGE:

main points about the topic:

*

*

3. Listen to the passage. Take notes on the main points of the listening passage.

TOPIC OF LISTENING PASSAGE:

main points about the topic:

-

-

-

-

-

Speaking Skill 17: PLAN BEFORE YOU SPEAK

After you have noted the main points of the listening passage in the academic integrated listening and speaking task, you need to read the question and plan your response.

The question will most likely be about the main points of the listening passage. Look at the following example of a question in an integrated speaking task on the color of blood.

> **Question**
>
> What points does the professor make about the color of blood?

You can see that the question is asking you about the key points of the passage.

To prepare a plan for your response, you should focus on the notes you have taken on the listening passage. Look at a plan for the response on the color of blood.

> **Listening Passage** = *key points on the color of blood*
>
> TOPIC OF LISTENING PASSAGE: *color of blood*
>
> main points about the topic:
> - blood with oxygen is red
> - blood without oxygen is blue
> - blood traveling from heart is red (has oxygen)
> - blood traveling to heart is blue (doesn't have oxygen)
> - blood outside the body is red (has oxygen)

From this plan, you can see that the listening passage is about *key points on the color of blood.*

The following chart outlines the key information you should remember about planning the response in a listening and speaking integrated task.

PLANNING BEFORE YOU SPEAK	
QUESTION	Study the *question* to determine what is being asked. Expect that the question is about the main points of the listening passage.
FOCUS	Look at the notes you have taken on the listening passage. Focus on the *main points* of the passage. Then describe the main points of the listening passage.

SPEAKING EXERCISE 17: Look at the notes that you prepared for the listening passages in Speaking Exercise 16. Read the question for each task. Then prepare a plan for your response including a topic statement.

1. What does the professor say about the bald eagle?

2. What does the professor have to say about hot-air balloons?

3. What points does the professor make about the "dark days"?

Speaking Skill 18: MAKE THE RESPONSE

After you have planned your response, you need to make your response. As you make your response, you should think about the following two things: (1) you should start with a topic statement and (2) you should support the topic statement.

Look at the plan for a response in the integrated speaking task on blood.

Listening Passage = *key points on the color of blood*

TOPIC OF LISTENING PASSAGE: color of blood

<u>main points about the topic:</u>
- blood with oxygen is red
- blood without oxygen is blue
- blood traveling from heart is red (has oxygen)
- blood traveling to heart is blue (doesn't have oxygen)
- blood outside the body is red (has oxygen)

In this listening passage, the professor discusses key points about the color of blood. Blood combined with oxygen is red, and blood without oxygen is blue. Inside the body, blood traveling from the heart is red because it has oxygen in it; blood traveling to the heart is blue because it doesn't have oxygen in it. Outside the body, blood is red because it has oxygen in it.

You should notice that this response includes a topic statement. The topic statement is followed by a number of supporting details.

The following chart outlines the key information you should remember about making the response.

MAKING THE RESPONSE	
TOPIC	Start your response with a *topic statement* that states the main point of the response.
SUPPORT	Include *details* to support the topic statement.

SPEAKING EXERCISE 18: Create responses for the integrated tasks that you have been working on in Speaking Skills 16–18.

SPEAKING REVIEW EXERCISE (Skills 16–18):
Listen to the passage. Take notes on the main points of the listening passage.

TOPIC OF LISTENING PASSAGE:

main points about the topic:

-

-

-

Now answer the following question:

What point does the professor make about the human brain?

SPEAKING POST-TEST

Speaking
Section Directions

This section tests your ability to speak about different topics. You will answer six questions. Answer each one as completely as you can.

Questions 1 and 2 will be about familiar topics. Try to speak about the topics clearly and coherently.

Questions 3 and 4 will include reading and listening. First, you will read a short passage. Then the text will disappear, and you will hear a talk about the same topic. Next you will answer a question about the text and the talk. Try to use information from the text and the talk to answer the question clearly and coherently to show that you understood the text and the talk.

Questions 5 and 6 will include part of a conversation or a lecture and a question. Try to answer the question clearly and coherently, using information from the conversation or lecture.

While you read and listen, you can take notes. You can use your notes to help you answer the questions.

Listen closely to the directions for each question. They will not appear on the screen.

Questions 1–6

Question 1

Read the question. Take notes on the main points of a response. Then respond to the question.

> Preparation Time: 15 seconds
> Response Time: 45 seconds

What is your dream job? Use reasons in your response.

INTRODUCTION:

SUPPORTING IDEA 1:

SUPPORTING IDEA 2:

CONCLUSION:

Question 2

Read the question. Take notes on the main points of a response. Then respond to the question.

> Preparation Time: 15 seconds
> Response Time: 45 seconds

Are you forgetful, or do you always remember important things?
Use examples in your response.

INTRODUCTION:

SUPPORTING IDEA 1:

SUPPORTING IDEA 2:

CONCLUSION:

Question 3

Read the passage. Take notes on the main points of the reading passage.

Reading Time: 45 seconds

A notice posted in the dormitory

The dormitory has a policy against pets. This means that absolutely no pets will be allowed in the dormitory, <u>ever</u>. Any student who breaks this rule and brings any pets into the dormitory will be asked to move out of the dormitory immediately and find a new place to live.

TOPIC OF READING PASSAGE:

main points about the topic:

-

-

Listen to the passage. Take notes on the main points of the listening passage.

TOPIC OF LISTENING PASSAGE:

main points about the topic:

-

-

-

Now answer the following question:

How does the information in the listening passage add to the ideas in the reading passage?

| Preparation Time: 30 seconds |
| Response Time: 60 seconds |

Question 4

Read the passage. Take notes on the main points of the reading passage.

Reading Time: 45 seconds

The City of Los Angeles

Today, the city of Los Angeles is a huge city in the state of California. It is a huge city that covers over 450 square miles. When Los Angeles was founded by the Spanish in 1781, it was just a small town. It remained a small town for more than a century. Then, rather suddenly, Los Angeles grew into a city in the 1880s.

TOPIC OF READING PASSAGE:

main points about the topic:

•

•

•

Listen to the passage. Take notes on the main points of the listening passage.

TOPIC OF LISTENING PASSAGE:

main points about the topic:

•

•

Now answer the following question:

How is the information in the listening passage related to the information in the reading passage?

Preparation Time: 30 seconds
Response Time: 60 seconds

Question 5

Listen to the passage. Take notes on the main points of the listening passage.

TOPIC OF LISTENING PASSAGE:

main points about the topic:

-

-

-

Now answer the following question:

What are the two students discussing?

| Preparation Time: 20 seconds |
| Response Time: 60 seconds |

Question 6

Listen to the passage. Take notes on the main points of the listening passage.

TOPIC OF LISTENING PASSAGE:

main points about the topic:

-

-

-

-

Now answer the following question:

What does the professor say about the period 65 million years ago?

Preparation Time: 20 seconds
Response Time: 60 seconds

Turn to pages 455–465 to *assess* the skills used in the test, *score* the test using the Speaking Scoring Criteria, and *record* your results.

WRITING

WRITING DIAGNOSTIC PRE-TEST

Writing
Section Directions

This section tests your ability to communicate in writing in an academic environment. There are two writing tasks.

In the first writing task, you will read a passage and listen to a lecture. Then you will answer a question using information from the passage and the lecture. In the second task, you will answer a question using your own background knowledge.

Integrated Writing Directions

For this task, you will read a passage about an academic topic. You have **3 minutes** to read the passage, and then the passage will disappear. Then you will hear a lecture about the same topic. You can take notes while you read and listen.

You will then write an answer to a question about the relationship between the reading passage and the lecture. Try to use information from the passage and the lecture to answer the question. You will **not** be asked for your personal opinion. You can see the reading passage again when you are ready to write. You can use your notes to help you. You have **20 minutes** to write your response.

A successful answer will usually be around 150 to 225 words. Try to show that you can write well and give complete, accurate information.

Remember that you can see the passage again when you write your response. As soon as the reading time ends, the lecture will begin.

Independent Writing Directions

In this task, you will write an essay that states, explains, and supports your opinion about an issue. You have **30 minutes** to plan, write, and revise your essay.

A successful essay will usually be at least 300 words. Try to show that you can write well by developing your ideas, organizing your essay, and using language accurately to express your ideas.

Question 1

Read the passage. Take notes on the main points of the reading passage.

Reading Time: 3 minutes

Old World monkeys are monkeys that live in Africa or Asia. Other kinds of monkeys live in other parts of the world, but the monkeys that live in Africa or Asia are Old World monkeys.

Old World monkeys are easy to identify from their nostrils, or noses. Old World monkeys have very thin, or narrow, nostrils. These thin nostrils easily identify a monkey as an Old World monkey.

Old World monkeys are omnivores. This means that they eat insects and animals as well as plants; they eat both meat and vegetables.

Old World monkeys do not have prehensile tails, as other kinds of monkeys do. Prehensile tails are tails that are used to hold onto tree branches. Because Old World monkeys generally do not spend most of their time in trees, they do not need prehensile tails.

TOPIC OF READING PASSAGE:

main points about the topic:

-

-

-

Listen to the passage. Take notes on the main points of the listening passage.

TOPIC OF LISTENING PASSAGE:

main points about the topic:

-

-

-

Now answer the following question:

> How does the information in the listening passage add to the
> ideas in the reading passage?

| Preparation Time: 1 minute |
| Response Time: 20 minutes |

Question 2

Read the question. Take notes on the main points of a response. Then write your response.

What is your favorite season of the year? Why?

Response Time: 30 minutes

TOPIC: _____ is my favorite season of the year

why:

•

•

Turn to pages 467–472 to *assess* the skills used in the test, *score* the test
using the Writing Scoring criteria, and *record* your results.

WRITING OVERVIEW

The last section on the TOEFL *iBT* is the Writing section. This section consists of two tasks: one integrated task and one independent task. You write your responses to these two tasks on the computer.

- The **integrated** task consists of a reading passage and a lecture on the same academic topic. The information in the reading passage and the information in the listening passage are related, but the listening passage does not simply repeat what is in the reading passage. You take notes on the information in each of the passages, and then you must write a response about how the information in the two passages is related.

- The **independent** task consists of an essay topic. You must write an essay on the topic that is given. The ideas in your essay come from your personal experience rather than from material that is given to you.

Because these tasks are different, there are different strategies for each task. The following strategies can help you on the integrated task in the Writing section.

STRATEGIES FOR THE INTEGRATED WRITING TASK

1. **Be familiar with the directions.** The directions on every test are the same, so it is not necessary to spend time reading the directions carefully when you take the test. You should be completely familiar with the directions before the day of the test.

2. **Dismiss the directions as soon as they come up.** The time starts when the directions come up. You should already be familiar with the directions, so you can click on Continue as soon as it appears and save all of your time for the passages and questions.

3. **Do not worry if the material in the integrated task is on a topic that is not familiar to you.** All of the information that you need to write your response is included in the passages. You do not need any background knowledge to answer the questions.

4. **Read the reading passage carefully.** You will have only a limited amount of time to read the passage.

5. **Take careful notes as you read the passage.** You should focus on the main points and key supporting material. Do not try to write down everything you read. Do not write down too many unnecessary details.

6. **Listen carefully to the passage.** You will hear the passage one time only. You may not hear the passage again.

7. **Take careful notes as you listen to the spoken material.** You should focus on the main points and key supporting material. Do not try to write down everything you hear. Do not write down too many unnecessary details.

---

8. **Organize your response very clearly.** You should have an overall topic statement that shows the relationship between the reading passage and the listening passage. You should also have a paragraph about the reading passage and a paragraph about the listening passage that incorporates the ideas of the reading passage.

9. **Stick to vocabulary, sentence structures, and grammatical points that you know.** This is not the best time to try out new words, structures, or grammar points.

10. **Monitor the time carefully on the title bar of the computer screen.** The title bar indicates how much time you have to complete your response.

11. **Finish writing your response a few minutes early so that you have time to edit what you wrote.** You should spend the last three to five minutes checking your response for problems in sentence structure and grammatical errors.

The following strategies can help you on the independent task in the Writing section.

STRATEGIES FOR THE INDEPENDENT WRITING TASK

1. **Be familiar with the directions.** The directions on every test are the same, so it is not necessary to spend time reading the directions carefully when you take the test. You should be completely familiar with the directions before the day of the test.

2. **Dismiss the directions as soon as they come up.** The time starts when the directions come up. You should already be familiar with the directions, so you can click on Continue as soon as it appears and save all of your time for the passages and questions.

3. **Read the question carefully, and answer the question exactly as it is asked.** Take some time at the beginning of the task to be sure that you understand the question and what the question is asking you to do.

4. **Organize your response very clearly.** You should think of having an introduction, body paragraphs that develop the introduction, and a conclusion to end your essay.

5. **Whenever you make a general statement, be sure to support that statement.** You can use examples, reasons, facts, or personal information to support any general statement.

6. **Stick to vocabulary, sentence structures, and grammatical points that you know.** This is not the best time to try out new words, structures, or grammar points.

7. **Monitor the time carefully on the title bar of the computer screen.** The title bar indicates how much time you have to complete your essay.

8. **Finish writing your essay a few minutes early so that you have time to edit what you wrote.** You should spend the last three to five minutes checking your essay for problems in sentence structure and grammatical errors.

WRITING SKILLS

The following skills will help you to implement these strategies in the Writing section of the TOEFL *iBT*.

INTEGRATED TASK

Writing Skill 1: NOTE THE MAIN POINTS AS YOU READ

In the integrated task in the Writing section of the TOEFL *iBT*, you will have to read an academic passage as part of the task. Look at an example of a reading passage that is part of an integrated writing task on earthquake swarms.

Reading Passage 1

Have you ever heard of earthquake swarms? A swarm is a bunch, a group, a large number together. A swarm of bees, for example, is a large group of bees together. However, it is not just bees that swarm; earthquakes can also come in swarms. There can be a large number of earthquakes that occur within a limited period of time, and this is called a swarm of earthquakes.

There may not be any large earthquakes in a swarm; there may be a really large number of rather small earthquakes in a swarm. It is not the power of the earthquakes but instead the large number of them that creates a swarm.

As you read the passage, you should take notes on the topic and main points of the reading passage. Look at these notes on the topic and main points of the reading passage.

TOPIC OF READING PASSAGE: earthquake swarms (large groups of earthquakes that take place within a short period of time)

main points about the topic:
- earthquakes in swarm may be large or small
- number of earthquakes makes an earthquake swarm
- power of earthquakes does not make an earthquake swarm

These notes show that the topic of the reading passage is *earthquake swarms*, which are *large groups of earthquakes that take place within a short period of time*. The main points about the topic are that the *earthquakes in* a *swarm may be large or small*, that it is the *number of earthquakes* that *makes an earthquake swarm*, and that it is *not the power of the earthquakes* that *makes an earthquake swarm*.

Now look at another example of a reading passage that is part of an integrated writing task on overachievement.

Reading Passage 2

    Student overachievers are students who do a lot of extra work. They do much more work than their teachers expect them to do. People tend to believe that the causes of overachievement are positive. They generally believe that students enjoy hard work. They also believe that parents and teachers have positive ways to encourage overachievement. They believe that parents work hard to encourage their children to enjoy school and that teachers encourage their students to enjoy learning. They believe that this enjoyment of school and learning causes students who are properly encouraged to overachieve.

As you read the passage, you should take notes on the topic and main points of the reading passage. Look at these notes on the topic and main points of the reading passage.

TOPIC OF READING PASSAGE: positive causes of overachievement by students

main points about the topic:
- students enjoy hard work
- parents encourage their children to enjoy school
- teachers encourage their students to enjoy learning

These notes show that the topic of the reading passage is the *positive causes of overachievement by students.* The main points about the topic are that students may overachieve because they *enjoy hard work,* that students may overachieve because their *parents encourage* them *to enjoy school,* and that students may overachieve because their *teachers encourage* them *to enjoy learning.*

The following chart outlines the key information you should remember about dealing with the reading passage in the integrated writing task.

NOTING THE MAIN POINTS IN THE READING PASSAGE	
TOPIC	Make sure that you understand (and take notes on) the *topic* of the reading passage.
MAIN POINTS	Then focus on (and take notes on) the *main points* that are used to support the topic of the reading passage.

WRITING EXERCISE 1: Read each of the passages, and note the *topic* and the *main points* that are used to support each topic.

1. Read the passage. Take notes on the main points of the passage.

> In 1900, agriculture in the United States was very different from agriculture of today. In 1900, 40 percent of the labor force of the country was working in agriculture. Farms were generally family-owned, and four out of ten farmers lived on family farms and supported themselves through agriculture.
>
> Farmers in the 1900s were not able to be as productive as farmers of today. A typical farmer in 1900 managed to grow food for an average of five people. Farmers were able to produce only this amount of food because farm chores had to be completed mostly by means of manual labor by the farmer and his family, with some assistance from horse-drawn plows.

TOPIC OF READING PASSAGE:

main points about the topic:

-

-

-

-

2. Read the passage. Take notes on the main points of the passage.

Many people believe that dolphins are extraordinarily intelligent beings. People believe this for certain reasons. One thing that causes people to believe that dolphins are intelligent is the size of a dolphin's brain. A dolphin's brain is actually larger than a human's brain.

Another thing that causes people to believe that dolphins are intelligent is that dolphins seem to show behaviors that indicate that they are reaching out to humans. Dolphins have been known, for example, to save humans that are drowning by supporting them so that their heads are out of the water.

A third thing that causes people to believe that dolphins are intelligent is the ability of some dolphins to learn commands and follow the commands. Some dolphins have demonstrated that they understand dozens of different commands.

TOPIC OF READING PASSAGE:

main points about the topic:

•

•

•

3. Read the passage. Take notes on the main points of the passage.

From the time he was a child, Leonardo da Vinci dreamed about flight. He wanted to learn everything he could about flying, so he started by watching birds fly. He then wrote down in notebooks everything he learned about the flight of birds.

Leonardo learned many things about the flight of birds. He saw how birds moved their heads to maintain their balance. He saw how birds used their tails to change direction. He saw how birds spread their tail feathers to reduce their speed before they landed.

From all of his studies of birds, Leonardo came to some conclusions about what it would take for man to fly. One conclusion was about the wings needed to support a man in flight. Leonardo concluded that a man would need wings of a certain size to support him in flight. Another of Leonardo's conclusions was about the power needed to raise a man and his wings into the air. Leonardo concluded that a man's legs were powerful enough to push a man into flight.

TOPIC OF READING PASSAGE:

main points about the topic:

-

-

Writing Skill 2: NOTE THE MAIN POINTS AS YOU LISTEN

In the integrated task in the Writing section of the TOEFL *iBT,* you will have to listen to an academic passage as part of the task. Look at the following example of a listening passage that is part of the integrated writing task on earthquake swarms.

Listening Passage 1

(professor) *So you read about earthquake swarms? And you understood that an earthquake swarm is when a large number of earthquakes occur over a limited period of time? Now, let me give you an example of a time when there was a really amazing swarm of earthquakes. Well, this really amazing earthquake swarm occurred in Japan over a two-year period from 1965 to 1967. In that two-year period, there were hundreds of thousands of earthquakes in Japan, a few large ones and many, many small ones. Not hundreds and not thousands, hundreds of thousands, in a two-year period. Almost all of these earthquakes were not very strong, but this was still a huge number within a relatively short period of time.*

As you listen to the passage, you should take notes on the topic and main points of the listening passage. Look at these notes on the topic and main points of the listening passage.

TOPIC OF LISTENING PASSAGE: an example of an earthquake swarm (occurred in Japan from 1965 through 1967)

main points about the topic:
- hundreds of thousands of earthquakes occurred
- a few were large
- most were very weak

These notes show that the topic of the listening passage is *an example of an earthquake swarm* that *occurred in Japan from 1965 through 1967.* The main points about the topic are that *hundreds of thousands of earthquakes occurred,* that *a few were large,* and that *most were very weak.*

Now look at another example of a listening passage that is part of the integrated writing task on overachievement.

Listening Passage 2

(professor) *Unfortunately, many of the beliefs in the reading passage are just not true. A certain study shows that students most often become overachievers for negative reasons.*

Often, students do extra work because they're afraid of failure. It's not pleasure, or enjoyment of hard work, that motivates them. Instead, it's a fear of failure that causes them to overachieve, and not enjoyment.

The study also shows that parents can cause their children to overachieve in a negative way. Parents can cause their children to overachieve when they put a lot of emphasis on success instead of enjoyment of school. When parents put too much emphasis on success, this can cause their children to overachieve.

Finally, the study shows that teachers can play a negative role in encouraging their students to overachieve. Teachers can cause their students to overachieve when they put a lot of emphasis on high test scores and grades rather than on the enjoyment of learning. When teachers put too much emphasis on high test scores and grades, this can cause their students to overachieve.

As you listen to the passage, you should take notes on the topic and main points of the listening passage. Look at these notes on the topic and main points of the listening passage.

TOPIC OF LISTENING PASSAGE: negative causes of overachievement by students

main points about the topic:
- students want to avoid failure
- parents really stress the need for success
- teachers really stress high test scores and grades

These notes show that the topic of the listening passage is *negative causes of overachievement by students.* The main points about the topic are that *students* may overachieve because they *want to avoid failure,* that students may overachieve because their *parents stress the need for success,* and that students may overachieve because their *teachers really stress* the need for *high test scores and grades.*

The following chart outlines the key information you should remember about dealing with the listening passage in the integrated writing task.

NOTING THE MAIN POINTS IN THE LISTENING PASSAGE	
TOPIC	Make sure that you understand (and take notes on) the *topic* of the listening passage.
MAIN POINTS	Then focus on (and take notes on) the *main points* that are used to support the topic of the listening passage.

WRITING EXERCISE 2: Listen to each of the following passages, and note the *topic* and the *main points* that are used to support the topic.

1. Listen to the passage. Take notes on the main points of the listening passage.

TOPIC OF LISTENING PASSAGE:

main points about the topic:

•

•

•

•

2. Listen to the passage. Take notes on the main points of the listening passage.

TOPIC OF LISTENING PASSAGE:

main points about the topic:

-

-

-

3. Listen to the passage. Take notes on the main points of the listening passage.

TOPIC OF LISTENING PASSAGE:

main points about the topic:

-

-

Writing Skill 3: PLAN BEFORE YOU WRITE

After you have noted the main points of the reading passage and the main points of the listening passage in the integrated writing task, you need to read the question and plan your response.

The question will be about the relationship between the main points of the reading passage and the main points of the listening passage. The question will most likely ask how the information in the listening passage either *adds to (supports)* or *casts doubt on (challenges)* the information in the reading passage. A listening passage may add to the reading passage by providing examples, or reasons, or causes. A listening passage may cast doubt on the reading passage by providing information that shows that the information in the reading passage is not correct.

Look at the following example of a question in an integrated writing task on earthquake swarms. In this example, the information in the listening passage adds to the information in the reading passage.

Question

How does the information in the listening passage support the information in the reading passage?

You can see that the question is asking you to show how the information in the listening passage supports the information in the reading passage.

To prepare a plan for your response, you should look at the notes you have taken on the reading passage and the notes you have taken on the listening passage. You should then think about how the ideas in the two passages are related. Look at a plan for the response on earthquake swarms.

Reading Passage = *a concept*

TOPIC OF READING PASSAGE: earthquake swarms (large groups of earthquakes that take place within a short period of time)

main points about the topic:
- earthquakes in swarm may be large or small
- number of earthquakes makes an earthquake swarm
- power of earthquakes does not make an earthquake swarm

Listening Passage = *an example*

TOPIC OF LISTENING PASSAGE: an example of an earthquake swarm (occurred in Japan from 1965 through 1967)

main points about the topic:
- hundreds of thousands of earthquakes occurred
- a few were large
- most were very weak

From this plan, you can see that the ideas in the reading passage and the ideas in the listening passage are related. The plan shows that the reading passage describes *a concept* and the listening passage *supports* the concept by adding *an example* of the concept.

Now look at another example of a question in an integrated writing task on over-achievement. In this example, the information in the listening passage casts doubt on the information in the reading passage.

Question

How does the information in the listening passage cast doubt on the information in the reading passage?

You can see that the question is asking you to show how the information in the listening passage helps to show that the information in the reading passage is not accurate.

To prepare a plan for your response, you should look at the notes you took on the reading passage and the notes you took on the listening passage. You should then look at how the ideas in the two passages are related. Look at a plan for the response on overachievement.

Reading Passage = *positive causes*

TOPIC OF READING PASSAGE: *positive causes of overachievement by students*

main points about the topic:
- *students enjoy hard work*
- *parents encourage their children to enjoy school*
- *teachers encourage their students to enjoy learning*

Listening Passage = *negative causes*

TOPIC OF LISTENING PASSAGE: *negative causes of overachievement by students*

main points about the topic:
- *students want to avoid failure*
- *parents really stress the need for success*
- *teachers really stress high test scores and grades*

From this plan, you can see that the ideas in the reading passage and the ideas in the listening passage are related. The plan shows that the reading passage describes positive causes and the listening passage describes negative causes. The listening passage *casts doubt* on the reading passage by showing that the positive causes listed in the reading passage may not be accurate.

The following chart outlines the key information you should remember about planning before you write in an integrated writing task.

PLANNING BEFORE YOU WRITE	
ADDING TO THE READING PASSAGE	The question may ask what the listening passage *adds* to the reading passage. This type of question may be worded in the following way: How do the ideas in the listening passage **add to** … How do the ideas in the listening passage **support** …
CASTING DOUBT ON THE READING PASSAGE	The question may ask how the listening passage shows that the reading passage *may not be accurate*. This type of question may be worded in the following way: How do the ideas in the listening passage **cast doubt on** … How do the ideas in the listening passage **challenge** …

WRITING EXERCISE 3: Look at the notes that you prepared for the reading passages in Writing Exercise 1 and the listening passages in Writing Exercise 2. Read the question for each task. Then prepare a plan for your response.

1. How does the information in the listening passage add to the information in the reading passage?

2. How does the information in the listening passage cast doubt on the information in the reading passage?

3. How does the information in the listening passage support and challenge the information in the reading passage?

Writing Skill 4: WRITE A TOPIC STATEMENT

After you plan your response, you should begin writing your response with an overall topic statement. Your topic statement should show how the information in the reading passage and the information in the listening passage are related. It should also include the terminology *adds to, supports, casts doubt on,* or *challenges* from the question. Look at this information from the integrated writing task on earthquake swarms.

Reading Passage = *a concept*

TOPIC OF READING PASSAGE: earthquake swarms (large groups of earthquakes that take place within a short period of time)

Listening Passage = *an example*

TOPIC OF LISTENING PASSAGE: an example of an earthquake swarm (occurred in Japan from 1965 through 1967)

As you study this information, you should think about writing an overall topic statement that includes information about the topics of each of the passages and about how the two passages are related. Look at a possible topic statement for the integrated writing task on earthquake swarms.

Topic Statement

In this set of materials, the reading passage describes a concept. The listening passage supports the information in the reading passage by giving an example of this concept.

You should notice that this topic statement does not include all the details about the topic and instead simply gives the overall idea. It also includes the terminology *supports* from the question.

Now look at this information from the integrated writing task on overachievement.

Reading Passage = *causes that are positive*

TOPIC OF READING PASSAGE: positive causes of overachievement by students

Listening Passage = *causes that are negative*

TOPIC OF LISTENING PASSAGE: negative causes of overachievement by students

---

As you study this information, you should think about writing an overall topic statement that includes information about the topics of each of the passages and about how the two passages are related. Look at a possible topic statement for the integrated writing task on overachievement.

Topic Statement

In this set of materials, the reading passage gives positive causes of a certain behavior. The listening passage casts doubt on the information in the reading passage by showing that the causes of this behavior may be negative.

You should notice again that this topic statement does not include all the details about the topic and instead simply gives the overall idea. It also includes the terminology *cast doubt on* from the question.

The following chart outlines the key information you should remember about planning before you write in an integrated writing task.

WRITING A TOPIC STATEMENT	
RELATIONSHIP	The topic statement comes at the beginning of your response. This topic statement should show how the topic of the reading passage and the topic of the listening passage are related.
TERMINOLOGY	Be sure to include the terminology *adds to, supports, casts doubt on,* or *challenges* from the question in the topic statement.

WRITING EXERCISE 4: Look at the plans that you prepared for the integrated writing tasks in Writing Exercise 3. Then write a topic statement for each task.

1. In this set of materials, the reading passage _____

_____

The listening passage _____

_____

2. In this set of materials, the reading passage _____

_____

The listening passage _____

_____

3. In this set of materials, the reading passage _____

_____

The listening passage _____

_____

Writing Skill 5: WRITE SUPPORTING PARAGRAPHS ON READING PASSAGES

A supporting paragraph on the ideas in the reading passage should be very short. It should state the topic and the main points of the reading passage as briefly as possible. Look at the notes on the reading passage on earthquake swarms and the supporting paragraph that is based on the notes.

TOPIC OF READING PASSAGE: earthquake swarms (large groups of earthquakes that take place within a short period of time)

main points about the topic:
- earthquakes in swarm may be large or small
- number of earthquakes makes an earthquake swarm
- power of earthquakes does not make an earthquake swarm

  The reading passage describes earthquake swarms, which are large groups of earthquakes that take place within a short period of time. The earthquakes in a swarm may be small or large. The number of earthquakes, and not the power of the earthquakes, makes an earthquake swarm.

As you read the supporting paragraph on the reading passage, you should note that it covers the topic and the main points of the reading passage very briefly.

Now look at the notes on the reading passage on overachievement and the supporting paragraph that is based on the notes.

TOPIC OF READING PASSAGE: positive causes of overachievement by students

main points about the topic:
- students enjoy hard work
- parents encourage their children to enjoy school
- teachers encourage their students to enjoy learning

  The reading passage shows that the causes of overachievement may be positive. Overachievement can occur because students enjoy hard work, because parents encourage their children to enjoy school, and because teachers encourage their students to enjoy learning.

As you read the supporting paragraph on the reading passage, you should again note that it covers the topic and the main points of the reading passage very briefly.

The following chart outlines the key information you should remember about writing supporting paragraphs on reading passages.

WRITING SUPPORTING PARAGRAPHS ON READING PASSAGES	
TOPIC	State the *topic* of the reading passage briefly.
MAIN POINTS	Summarize the *key points* of the reading passage briefly.

WRITING EXERCISE 5: Write supporting paragraphs on the reading passages for the integrated writing tasks that you worked on in Writing Exercises 1–4.

1. supporting paragraph on reading:

2. supporting paragraph on reading:

3. supporting paragraph on reading:

Writing Skill 6: WRITE SUPPORTING PARAGRAPHS ON LISTENING PASSAGES

A supporting paragraph on the ideas in the listening passage should be more complicated than the supporting paragraph on the ideas in the reading passage. It should indicate the topic and the main points of the listening passage, and it should also relate the ideas in the listening passage to the ideas in the reading passage. Look at the notes on the listening passage on earthquake swarms and the supporting paragraph that is based on the notes.

TOPIC OF LISTENING PASSAGE: an example of an earthquake swarm (occurred in Japan from 1965 through 1967)

main points about the topic:
- hundreds of thousands of earthquakes occurred
- a few were large
- most were very weak

   The listening passage gives an example of an earthquake swarm. This was an earthquake swarm because of the large number of earthquakes that occurred and not because of the power of the earthquakes. The earthquake swarm in the example occurred in Japan from 1965 through 1967. Hundreds of thousands of earthquakes occurred during this two-year period of time, and they were mostly small and mostly weak. Because there were hundreds of thousands of earthquakes, this was an earthquake swarm.

As you read the supporting paragraph on the listening passage, you should note that it contains the topic and the main points of the listening passage and also refers to the main points of the reading passage. The information about earthquake swarms in general comes from the reading passage. The information about the specific example of an earthquake swarm in Japan comes from the listening passage.

Now look at the notes on the listening passage on overachievement and the supporting paragraph that is based on the notes.

> TOPIC OF LISTENING PASSAGE: negative causes of overachievement by students
>
> main points about the topic:
> • students want to avoid failure
> • parents really stress the need for success
> • teachers really stress high test scores and grades
>
> ---
>
> According to the listening passage, the ideas in the reading passage may not be true. The causes of overachievement may be negative. Overachievement may occur because students want to avoid failure and not because they enjoy hard work. In addition, overachievement may occur because parents really stress the need for success instead of encouraging their children to enjoy school. Finally, overachievement may occur because teachers really stress high test scores and grades instead of encouraging their students to enjoy learning.

As you read the supporting paragraph on the listening passage, you should again note that it contains the topic and the main points of the listening passage and also refers to the main points of the reading passage. The information about positive causes of overachievement comes from the reading passage. The information about negative causes of overachievement comes from the listening passage.

The following chart outlines the key information you should remember about writing supporting paragraphs on listening passages.

WRITING SUPPORTING PARAGRAPHS ON LISTENING PASSAGES	
TOPIC	State the *topic* of the listening passage.
MAIN POINTS	Summarize the *key points* of the listening passage.
RELATIONSHIPS	*Relate* the key points of the listening passage to the key points of the reading passage.

WRITING EXERCISE 6: Write supporting paragraphs on the listening passages for the integrated writing tasks that you worked on in Writing Exercises 1–5.

1. supporting paragraph on listening:

2. supporting paragraph on listening:

3. supporting paragraph on listening:

Writing Skill 7: REVIEW SENTENCE STRUCTURE

After you have written your response, it is important for you to review the sentence structure in your response. You should check the sentence structure of simple sentences, compound sentences, and complex sentences.

> NOTE: For a review of sentence structure, see APPENDIX A.

Look at the following sentences from a response about a journal article.

> Because the <u>students</u> <u>read</u> the journal article.

> The <u>students</u> <u>read</u> the article, <u>they</u> <u>enjoyed</u> it.

The structure of each of the sentences is not correct. The first sentence is an incorrect simple sentence. In this sentence, the subordinate connector *Because* in front of the subject and verb *students read* makes the sentence incomplete. The second sentence is an incorrect compound sentence. In this sentence, the main clauses *students read* and *they enjoyed* are connected with a comma (,), and a comma cannot be used to connect two main clauses.

The following chart outlines the key information you should remember about reviewing sentence structure.

REVIEWING SENTENCE STRUCTURE	
SENTENCE STRUCTURE	Check for errors in sentence structure in your response. Be sure to check for errors in simple sentences, compound sentences, and complex sentences.

WRITING EXERCISE 7: Correct the errors in sentence structure in the following passage. (The number in parentheses at the end of each paragraph indicates the number of errors in the paragraph.)

Paragraph

1   In this set of materials, the reading passage presents a traditional story, the listening passage discusses this traditional story. The traditional story it is not generally accepted today. (2)

2   The reading passage describing a traditional story about the origin of the word "news." According to this traditional story, the word "news" came from the first letters of compass directions. Compass directions are north, east, west, and south, the first letters of each of these compass directions make up the word "news." Since news seems to come from all directions at the same time. A traditional story arose. According to this story, the word "news" was created because represents the idea of the four directions, north, east, west, and south. (4)

3   According to the listening passage, this traditional story about the origin of the word "news" not true. Though it makes a nice and interesting story the actual origin of the word it is not so exotic. As you might be able to guess, the word "news" actually developed from the Latin word that means "new." The news, indeed, a description of new events just after have occurred. (5)

Writing Skill 8: REVIEW GRAMMAR

After you have written your response, it is important for you to review the grammar in your response. You should check for errors in nouns and pronouns, verbs, adjectives and adverbs, and agreement.

> NOTE: For a review of grammar, see APPENDIX B.

Look at the following sentence from a response on a research paper.

The research paper *must includes* an introduction,

three body paragraph, and a conclusion.

This sentence contains two grammar errors. The main verb *includes* should be the base form *include* because it follows the helping verb *must*. The singular noun *paragraph* should be the plural *paragraphs* because it follows the plural quantifier *three*.

The following chart outlines the key information you should remember about reviewing grammar.

REVIEWING GRAMMAR	
GRAMMAR	Check for errors in grammar in your response. Be sure to check for errors in nouns and pronouns, verbs, adjectives and adverbs, and agreement.

WRITING EXERCISE 8: Correct the errors in grammar in the following passages. (The number in parentheses at the end of each paragraph indicates the number of errors in the paragraph.)

Paragraph

▶1   In this set of materials, the reading passage discusses a concept. The listening passage gives an example of the concept. (0)

▶2   The reading passage discusses the "halo effect." A halo is a large number of band of light around the head of an angel, and the "halo effect" is something that can occurring when a business manager is hire someone to work in a company. The "halo effect" occurs when an applicant for a position has one quality that is true outstanding and a manager hires that person because of this one outstanding quality. Because the manager sees only this one quality, he or her does not see the applicant's other qualities, and each of these other qualities are not guaranteed to be good. (6)

▶3   An example of the concept of the "halo effect" are provided in the listening passage. This example concerns a young woman named Ms. Owen. Ms. Owen had good test scores when he completed her university studies; in fact, all of her test scores was extremely good. When she applied for her first job after finishing hers studies, the manager who interviewed her thought that she seemed perfectly for the job because of her test scores. In fact, because he was so impressed with her test scores, he did not ask about anything else. He did not learn that Ms. Owen is someone who rare gets work done on time. Because the manager saw only one of Ms. Owen's good qualities and did not find out about much of her other qualities, he made a carelessly and quick hiring decision. Since she was hired, Ms. Owen has have a lot of problems on the job. The problems she had were not only her fault but also were the fault of the manager. The manager had not done a good job in hiring Ms. Owen because of the halo effect. (10)

WRITING REVIEW EXERCISE (Skills 1–8): Read the passage. Take notes on the main points of the reading passage.

▶ 1   Company X must choose between centralized decision-making and decentralized decision-making. If a company uses centralized decision-making, then all decisions are made by one high-level manager. If a company uses decentralized decision-making, then decisions are made by lower-level managers.

▶ 2   Company X has its headquarters, or main office, in the state of Texas. It has local offices in five other U.S. states: California, Maine, Michigan, Washington, and Alabama. These offices are in very different areas with different conditions around the offices, so decisions need to be made at the local level. Each of the local offices is headed by an intelligent and talented manager because the company pays high salaries to its local managers and is able to attract good managers.

▶ 3   Based upon these characteristics of Company X, the company decides to use centralized decision-making.

TOPIC OF READING PASSAGE:

main points about the topic:

•

•

•

Listen to the passage. Take notes on the main points of the listening passage.

TOPIC OF LISTENING PASSAGE:

main points about the topic:

-

-

-

Now answer the following question.

How does the information in the listening passage cast doubt on the decision in the reading passage?

INDEPENDENT TASK

Writing Skill 9: PLAN BEFORE YOU WRITE

The first and most important step in the independent task in the Writing section of the TOEFL *iBT* is to decode the question to determine what the intended outline is. Writing questions generally give clear clues about how your response should be constructed. It is important to follow the clues that are given in the question when you are planning your answer. Study the following question.

Question
How do you react when you are angry or upset? What steps do you take?

As you read this topic, you should determine that you should clearly state the steps that you take when you are angry or upset. Study the following plan for the response to this question.

INTRODUCTION:	steps I take when I am angry or upset
SUPPORTING PARAGRAPH 1:	first step • spend time alone
SUPPORTING PARAGRAPH 2:	second step • eat something delicious
CONCLUSION:	these steps work for me

In this plan, there is an introduction about steps I take when I am angry or upset, supporting paragraphs about the two steps I take, and a conclusion showing that these two steps work for me.

The following chart outlines the key information that you should remember about planning the response.

PLANNING BEFORE YOU WRITE	
QUESTION	Each question in the independent task shows you *what* you should discuss and *how* you should organize your response. You must decode the question to determine how to organize your response.
INTRODUCTION	Begin your response with an *introduction*.
SUPPORTING IDEAS	*Support* your topic statement with the kinds of ideas that the question asks for (such as reasons, details, or examples).
CONCLUSION	End your response with a *conclusion*.

WRITING EXERCISE 9: For each of the following writing topics, prepare a plan that shows the type of information you will include in each paragraph of the essay.

1. What do you like most about the English class you are taking? Why?

INTRODUCTION:

SUPPORTING PARAGRAPH 1:

SUPPORTING PARAGRAPH 2:

CONCLUSION:

2. The teacher assigns a paper and says that you can either write the paper by yourself or with other students. Do you prefer to write the paper alone or with others? Why?

INTRODUCTION:

SUPPORTING PARAGRAPH 1:

SUPPORTING PARAGRAPH 2:

CONCLUSION:

3. Imagine that you won a million dollars in the lottery. What three things are you going to do with it?

INTRODUCTION:

SUPPORTING PARAGRAPH 1:

SUPPORTING PARAGRAPH 2:

SUPPORTING PARAGRAPH 3:

CONCLUSION:

Writing Skill 10: WRITE THE INTRODUCTION

The purpose of the introduction is to explain clearly to the reader what you are going to discuss and how you are going to organize the discussion. Study the following essay question.

Question

How do you react when you are angry or upset? What steps do you take?

The following example shows one possible introduction to an essay that answers this question.

INTRODUCTION

Sometimes I get angry or upset. In this case, I know that it is not a good idea to yell at the people around me or say bad things to them. I have a way of dealing with my anger, without yelling or saying bad things. This way of dealing with anger has two steps.

In this introduction, the writer shows that the topic is a way of dealing with anger and that the discussion will be organized in two steps.

The following chart outlines the key information that you should remember about writing an introduction.

WRITING THE INTRODUCTION	
TOPIC	You should state the *topic* directly in the middle of the introduction.
ORGANIZATION	You should end the introduction with a statement that shows the *organization* of the discussion of the topic.

WRITING EXERCISE 10: For each of the writing topics, write introductions that state the *topic* and show the *organization* of the discussion of the topic.

1. What do you like most about the English class you are taking? Why?

2. The teacher assigns a paper and says that you can either write the paper by yourself or with other students. Do you prefer to write the paper alone or with others? Why?

3. Imagine that you won a million dollars in the lottery. What three things are you going to do with it?

Writing Skill 11: WRITE SUPPORTING PARAGRAPHS

A good way to begin writing supporting paragraphs in an independent writing task is to study your notes carefully before you begin to write. Then, as you write, you should think about introducing the main idea of each paragraph and about supporting the main idea with details. Look at the notes on the first supporting paragraph of the essay and the supporting paragraph that is based on the notes.

SUPPORTING PARAGRAPH 1: <u>first step I take</u>
      • spend time alone

      The first step in dealing with anger is to spend time alone. The first reason I spend time alone is that it is good for me to get away from other people when I am angry because I do not want to say bad things to them or yell at them. In addition, when I am alone, I can spend time thinking quietly.

As you read the first supporting paragraph in the essay, you should see that the first sentence is a topic sentence and the remaining two sentences give details about this topic.

Look at the notes on the second supporting paragraph of the essay and the supporting paragraph that is based on the notes.

SUPPORTING PARAGRAPH 2: <u>second step I take</u>
      • eat something delicious

      I have a second step that I follow when I am angry or upset. It is not enough just to spend time alone. I also must have something delicious to eat. I like to have something delicious and sweet, something like ice cream. It is impossible to feel angry and upset when I am eating ice cream.

As you read the second supporting paragraph in the essay, you should see that the first sentence is a topic sentence and the remaining four sentences give details about this topic.

The following chart outlines the key information that you should remember about writing supporting paragraphs.

WRITING SUPPORTING PARAGRAPHS	
MAIN IDEA	Begin each supporting paragraph with a topic sentence showing the *main idea*.
DETAILS	Add *details* to support the main idea.

WRITING EXERCISE 11: Write supporting paragraphs for the independent writing tasks that you worked on in Writing Exercise 9.

1. first supporting paragraph:

second supporting paragraph:

2. first supporting paragraph:

second supporting paragraph:

3. first supporting paragraph:

second supporting paragraph:

third supporting paragraph:

Writing Skill 12: WRITE THE CONCLUSION

The purpose of the conclusion is to close your essay. In a clear conclusion, you should make sure that your *overall idea* is clear, and you should summarize the *main points* that you used to arrive at this overall idea.

Question

How do you react when you are angry or upset? What steps do you take?

The following example shows one possible conclusion to an essay that answers this question.

CONCLUSION

These are the two steps that I take when I am feeling angry or upset. I take some ice cream, and I go someplace where I can be alone. I enjoy that ice cream and think. Very quickly I feel good again.

Here the writer refers to the overall idea of the *steps that I take when I am feeling angry or upset* and summarizes the two points of having *some ice cream* and going *someplace where I can be alone*.

The following chart outlines the key information that you should remember about writing a conclusion.

WRITING THE CONCLUSION	
OVERALL IDEA	You should make sure that your *overall idea* is clear.
MAIN POINTS	You should summarize the *main points* that you used to arrive at this overall idea.

WRITING EXERCISE 12: For each of the writing topics, write conclusions that *restate the main idea* and *summarize the main points*.

1.
> What do you like most about the English class you are taking? Why?

2.
> The teacher assigns a paper and says that you can either write the paper by yourself or with other students. Do you prefer to write the paper alone or with others? Why?

3.
> Imagine that you won a million dollars in the lottery. What three things are you going to do with it?

Writing Skill 13: REVIEW SENTENCE STRUCTURE

After you have written your response, it is important for you to review the sentence structure in your response. You should check the sentence structure of simple sentences, compound sentences, and complex sentences.

> NOTE: For a review of sentence structure, see APPENDIX A.

Look at the following sentences from a response about an exam.

> If the exam is given on Friday.

> The exam is on Friday, it will be very difficult.

The structure of each of the sentences is not correct. The first sentence is an incorrect simple sentence. In this sentence, the subordinate connector *If* in front of the subject and verb *exam is given* makes the sentence incomplete. The second sentence is an incorrect compound sentence. In this sentence, the main clauses *exam is* and *it will be* are connected with a comma (,), and a comma cannot be used to connect two main clauses.

The following chart outlines the key information you should remember about reviewing sentence structure.

REVIEWING SENTENCE STRUCTURE	
SENTENCE STRUCTURE	Check for errors in sentence structure in your response. Be sure to check for errors in simple sentences, compound sentences, and complex sentences.

WRITING EXERCISE 13: Correct the errors in sentence structure in the following passage. (The number in parentheses at the end of each paragraph indicates the number of errors in the paragraph.)

Paragraph

▶ **1**   There is no question about it. I a really messy person, you just need to look in the kitchen sink, on the floor of my bedroom, or on my desk to know that this is true. (2)

▶ **2**   Whenever use dishes, I put the dirty dishes in the kitchen sink and leave them there for two or three weeks. I wash them only I really need to use a dish and there are not any clean dishes. Is one way that shows how messy I am. (3)

▶ **3**   You can also see how messy I am by the dirty clothes all over the floor of my bedroom. Whenever I take clothes off I just drop them on the floor of my bedroom. The dirty clothes staying on the floor for a long time. There piles of clothes on the floor of my bedroom. (3)

▶ **4**   Can also see how messy I am by looking at the papers all over my desk. Whenever I write something on a piece of paper or print something from my computer. I put the papers on my desk. Right now, my desk it is covered with so many piles of paper. I cannot sit down at my desk to work, because there are so many papers on my desk. (4)

▶ **5**   From these examples, you can see my point, I am not a very neat person. The dirty dishes in the sink, the dirty clothes all over the bedroom floor, and the piles of papers all over my desk they clearly prove this point. (2)

Writing Skill 14: REVIEW GRAMMAR

After you have written your response, it is important for you to review the grammar in your response. You should check for errors in nouns and pronouns, verbs, adjectives and adverbs, and agreement.

NOTE: For a review of grammar, see APPENDIX B.

Look at the following sentence from a response on an assignment.

> The assignment for tomorrow *are* to write a *briefly* composition
>
> and to turn *them* in at the beginning of class.

This sentence contains three grammar errors. The plural verb *are* should be changed to the singular verb *is* because it should agree with the singular subject *assignment*. The adverb *briefly* should be changed to the adjective *brief* because it describes the noun *composition*. The plural pronoun *them* should be changed to the singular pronoun *it* because it refers to the singular noun *composition*.

The following chart outlines the key information you should remember about reviewing grammar.

REVIEWING GRAMMAR	
GRAMMAR	Check for errors in grammar in your response. Be sure to check for errors in nouns and pronouns, verbs, adjectives and adverbs, and agreement.

WRITING EXERCISE 14: Correct the errors in grammar in the following passage. (The number in parentheses at the end of each paragraph indicates the number of errors in the paragraph.)

Paragraph

1   There are many possible ways to spend free time, and every person have different ways of doing this. I spend my free time in two different ways. Both of the way that I spend my free time involve both moving a lot or not moving at all. (3)

2   One way that I spend my free time is to move a lot. I enjoy tennis, volleyball, swimming, running, bicycling, and hiking in the hills. I have always enjoy these sports and others. Whenever I am not work and I have some free time, I sometimes like to be very actively. Either I will get involved in one of those activities with a little of my friends, or maybe my friends and me will get involved in more than one of it. (6)

3   I do not spend all of mine free time moving a lot, however. Another way that I spend my free time is by not moving at all. In some of my free time, I like to sit quietly and not think very much. Maybe I sit quietly and listening to music, or maybe I sit quietly and watch a television program. When I am sitting quietly and not thinking, I can relaxed complete. (4)

4   I spend my free time in two very difference ways. One of the ways involve a lot of movement, and the other way does not. These two ways of spending my free time is necessary for me to have a good life. (3)

WRITING REVIEW EXERCISE (Skills 9–14): Read the question. Take notes on the main points of a response. Then write your response.

Do you prefer to go to bed early and get up early or to go to bed late and get up late? Why?

INTRODUCTION:

SUPPORTING PARAGRAPH 1:

SUPPORTING PARAGRAPH 2:

CONCLUSION:

WRITING POST-TEST

Writing
Section Directions

This section tests your ability to communicate in writing in an academic environment. There are two writing tasks.

In the first writing task, you will read a passage and listen to a lecture. Then you will answer a question using information from the passage and the lecture. In the second task, you will answer a question using your own background knowledge.

Integrated Writing Directions

For this task, you will read a passage about an academic topic. You have **3 minutes** to read the passage, and then the passage will disappear. Then you will hear a lecture about the same topic. You can take notes while you read and listen.

You will then write an answer to a question about the relationship between the reading passage and the lecture. Try to use information from the passage and the lecture to answer the question. You will **not** be asked for your personal opinion. You can see the reading passage again when you are ready to write. You can use your notes to help you. You have **20 minutes** to write your response.

A successful answer will usually be around 150 to 225 words. Try to show that you can write well and give complete, accurate information.

Remember that you can see the passage again when you write your response. As soon as the reading time ends, the lecture will begin.

Independent Writing Directions

In this task, you will write an essay that states, explains, and supports your opinion about an issue. You have **30 minutes** to plan, write, and revise your essay.

A successful essay will usually be at least 300 words. Try to show that you can write well by developing your ideas, organizing your essay, and using language accurately to express your ideas.

Question 1

Read the passage. Take notes on the main points of the reading passage.

Reading Time: 3 minutes

A proposal has been made to change the Elm County Elementary School District from a nine-month school year to a twelve-month school year. This means that the current school year runs from September through May, with summer vacation from June through August. This would be changed to a school year that runs from September through August, with four shorter vacations throughout the year. Each plan has 180 school days per year.

The school district has offered several reasons for this change in the school year. One reason that the school district gives is that students will remember more material without a long break in the summer. The school district believes that students forget a lot over the summer, and the students have to learn the material over again the next year. Another reason that the school district gives for the change is that there will be a savings in cost. The school district can save money because it cannot offer summer school under the new plan. A final reason that the school district gives for the change is that families will have more opportunities to take vacations. There will be four vacation periods under the new plan, so families will have four opportunities to take vacations under the new plan.

TOPIC OF READING PASSAGE:

main points about the topic:

•

•

•

Listen to the passage. Take notes on the main points of the listening passage.

TOPIC OF LISTENING PASSAGE:

main points about the topic:

-

-

-

Now answer the following question:

How does the information in the listening passage challenge the proposal in the reading passage?

| Preparation Time: 1 minute |
| Response Time: 20 minutes |

Question 2

Read the question. Take notes on the main points of a response. Then write your response.

You see a classmate cheating on an exam. What will you do?

| Response Time: 30 minutes |

TOPIC:

<u>what</u>:

-
-
-

Turn to pages 467–472 to *assess* the skills used in the test, *score* the test
using the Writing Scoring criteria, and *record* your results.

MINI-TEST 1

READING

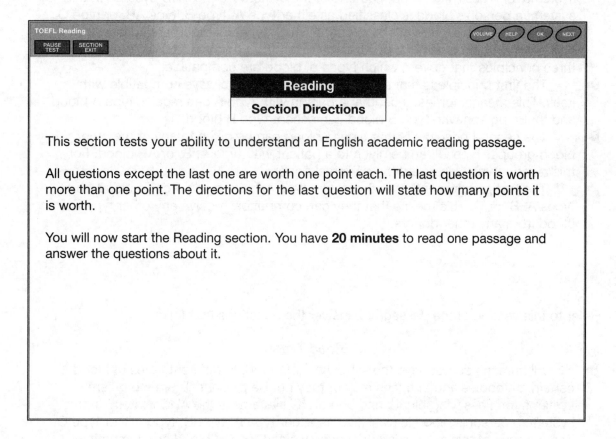

TOEFL Reading

PAUSE TEST | SECTION EXIT

VOLUME | HELP | OK | NEXT

Reading
Section Directions

This section tests your ability to understand an English academic reading passage.

All questions except the last one are worth one point each. The last question is worth more than one point. The directions for the last question will state how many points it is worth.

You will now start the Reading section. You have **20 minutes** to read one passage and answer the questions about it.

Read the passage.

Paragraph
Blood Types

1▶ All humans do not have the same type of blood. In different types of blood, certain antibodies and antigens may or may not be present. There are different systems for classifying blood, and one of the systems is the ABO system. In this system, a person's blood is classified as either type A, type B, type AB, or type O. The purpose of this system is to describe which types of blood are compatible. This means which types of blood can be taken from or given to a person. There are three principles that govern which types of blood are compatible.

2▶ The first principle is that a particular blood type is always compatible with itself. This means, for instance, that a person with type A can receive type A blood and that a person with type B blood can accept type B blood.

3▶ The second principle is that type O blood can be given to any of the other blood groups. Type O can be given to a patient with type A, B, or AB blood. For this reason, type O is called the universal donor.

4▶ The last principle is that patients with type AB blood can receive blood from types A, B, or O. This means that they can compatibly receive any other types of blood from any other donors.

Refer to this version of the passage to answer the questions that follow.

Paragraph
Blood Types

1▶ All humans do not have the same type of blood. In different types of blood, certain antibodies and antigens may or may not be present. There are different systems for classifying blood, and one of the systems is the ABO system. In this system, a person's blood is classified as either type A, type B, type AB, or type O. The purpose of this system is to describe which types of blood are compatible. This means which types of blood can be taken from or given to a person. There are three principles that govern which types of blood are compatible.

2▶ **8A** The first principle is that a particular blood type is always compatible with itself. **8B** This means, for instance, that a person with type A can receive type A blood and that a person with type B blood can accept type B blood. **8C**

3▶ The second principle is that type O blood can be given to any of the other blood groups. Type O can be given to a patient with type A, B, or AB blood. For this reason, type O is called the universal donor.

4▶ The last principle is that patients with type AB blood can receive blood from types A, B, or O. This means that they can compatibly receive any other types of blood from any other donors.

1. The word "type" in paragraph 1 is closest in meaning to
   Ⓐ manner
   Ⓑ kind
   Ⓒ style
   Ⓓ method

2. It is stated in paragraph 1 that certain antibodies and antigens in the blood
   Ⓐ are omitted from the ABO system
   Ⓑ have not been classified
   Ⓒ are universal donors
   Ⓓ may not be in all blood

3. Which of the sentences below best expresses the essential information in the highlighted sentence in paragraph 1?
   Ⓐ The ABO system is the only system for classifying blood.
   Ⓑ All of the systems for classifying blood are based on the ABO system.
   Ⓒ The ABO system is one of the systems for classifying blood.
   Ⓓ One of the many ABO systems is used to classify blood.

4. What is NOT true about the ABO system, according to the passage?
   Ⓐ It classifies blood as one of four types.
   Ⓑ It describes which types of blood can work together.
   Ⓒ It shows which types of blood can be taken from one person for another.
   Ⓓ It does not show which kind of blood can be given to a person.

5. The word "principles" in paragraph 1 is most likely
   Ⓐ leaders
   Ⓑ effects
   Ⓒ rules
   Ⓓ trials

6. The author uses the phrase "for instance" in paragraph 2 to show that
   Ⓐ an example will follow
   Ⓑ a contrasting idea will follow
   Ⓒ a result will follow
   Ⓓ an explanation will follow

7. The word "receive" in paragraph 2 is closest in meaning to
   Ⓐ send
   Ⓑ offer
   Ⓒ deny
   Ⓓ accept

8. Look at the three squares [■] that indicate where the following sentence could be added to paragraph 2.

   It also means that a person with type AB blood can receive type AB blood and that a person with type O blood can receive type O blood.

   Where would the sentence best fit? Click on a square [■] to add the sentence to the paragraph.

9. It can be inferred from the passage that type A blood can
   Ⓐ accept types A or O blood
   Ⓑ accept types O or AB blood
   Ⓒ accept types A or AB blood
   Ⓓ accept types A or B blood

10. The word "donor" in paragraph 3 is most likely someone who
    Ⓐ receives
    Ⓑ gives
    Ⓒ shows
    Ⓓ takes

11. The word "they" in paragraph 4 refers to
    Ⓐ patients with type AB blood
    Ⓑ types A, B, or O
    Ⓒ types of blood
    Ⓓ donors

12. It can be inferred from the passage that type AB blood can be donated to

Ⓐ types A, B, O, or AB blood

Ⓑ types A or AB blood only

Ⓒ type AB blood only

Ⓓ type ABO blood only

13.

Directions: An introductory sentence for a brief summary of the passage is provided below. Complete a summary of the ideas in the passage by selecting the THREE answer choices that express the most important ideas in the passage. **This question is worth 2 points** (2 points for 3 correct answers, 1 point for 2 correct answers, and 0 points for 1 or 0 correct answers).

Principles that govern the compatibility of blood.

-
-
-

Answer Choices (choose 3 to complete the chart):

(1) Compatibility of type AB with A, B, or O

(2) Compatibility of any blood type with itself

(3) Compatibility of type B with any type of blood

(4) Compatibility of type O with any type of blood

(5) Ability of type A to accept AB

(6) Ability of AB to accept A, B, or O

Turn to pages 448–450 to *diagnose* your errors and *record* your results.

MINI-TEST 1

LISTENING

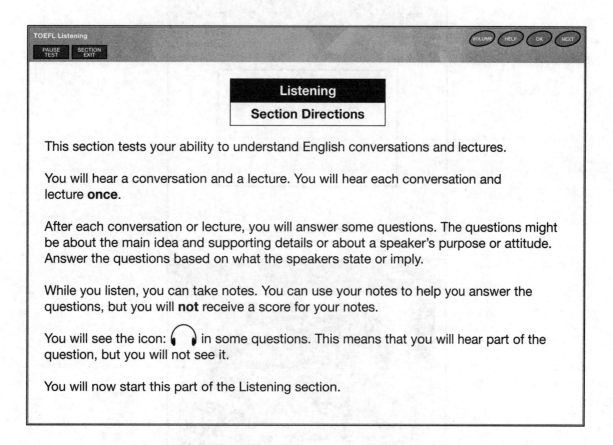

Questions 1–5

Listen as a student consults with his professor. The conversation is about the professor's attendance policy.

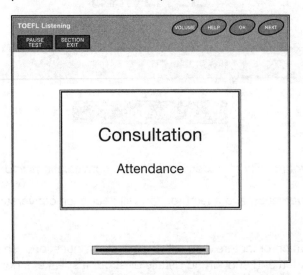

1. Why does the student go to see the professor?

    Ⓐ To explain why he has missed a class

    Ⓑ To get the notes from a class he missed

    Ⓒ To ask about the penalty for missing a class

    Ⓓ To ask what was covered in a class he missed

2. What happens if a student misses one class?

    Ⓐ The student will have to get the notes from another student.

    Ⓑ The student will have to attend an extra class.

    Ⓒ The student will receive a lowered grade.

    Ⓓ The student will meet with the professor in the professor's office.

3. What happens if a student misses more than two classes?

    Ⓐ The student will fail the class.

    Ⓑ The student will receive a lowered grade.

    Ⓒ The student will have to attend an extra class.

    Ⓓ The student will meet with the professor in the professor's office.

4. Listen again to part of the passage. Then answer the question.

What does the professor mean when she says this:

    Ⓐ "You need to look for something!"

    Ⓑ "You need to study harder!"

    Ⓒ "You need to pay attention to me!"

    Ⓓ "You need to be careful!"

5. How does the student seem to feel by the end of the conversation?

    Ⓐ Unhappy

    Ⓑ Satisfied

    Ⓒ Afraid

    Ⓓ Surprised

Questions 6–11

Listen to a lecture in a geography class.
The professor is talking about waterfalls.

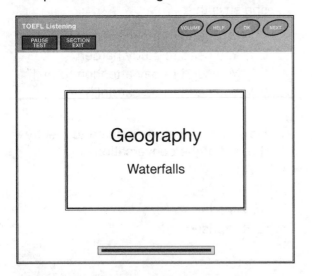

6. Which waterfalls are discussed in the lecture? **This question is worth 2 points** (2 points for 3 correct answers, 1 point for 2 correct answers, and 0 points for 1 or 0 correct answers).

Click on 3 answers.

Ⓐ A waterfall in North America
Ⓑ A waterfall in South America
Ⓒ A waterfall in Africa
Ⓓ A waterfall in Asia
Ⓔ A waterfall in Europe

7. What is stated about Victoria Falls?

Ⓐ It is more than a mile wide at the top.
Ⓑ It is much wider at the bottom than at the top.
Ⓒ It is in South America.
Ⓓ It is as wide as Niagara Falls.

8. Why is Niagara Falls so impressive?

Click on 2 answers.

Ⓐ Because it has an upper falls and a lower falls
Ⓑ Because so much water passes over it
Ⓒ Because it is so high
Ⓓ Because it is so wide

9. How tall is each of these falls? **This question is worth 2 points** (2 points for 3 correct answers, 1 point for 2 correct answers, and 0 points for 1 or 0 correct answers).

Click on a phrase. Then drag it to the space where it belongs. Each answer will be used one time only.

Is 167 feet tall	Is 355 feet tall	Is 3,000 feet tall

Angel Falls	**Victoria Falls**	**Niagara Falls**

10. What can be inferred from the lecture?

Ⓐ Angel Falls is not as tall as Niagara Falls.
Ⓑ Victoria Falls is not as tall as Angel Falls.
Ⓒ Niagara Falls is not as wide as Angel Falls.
Ⓓ Niagara Falls is not as wide as Victoria Falls.

11. Listen again to part of the passage. Then answer the question. 🎧

What does the professor mean when he says this: 🎧

Ⓐ "This is really important."
Ⓑ "This is all clear."
Ⓒ "We are finished."
Ⓓ "We have more to cover."

Turn to pages 451–453 to *diagnose* your errors and *record* your results.

MINI-TEST 1

SPEAKING

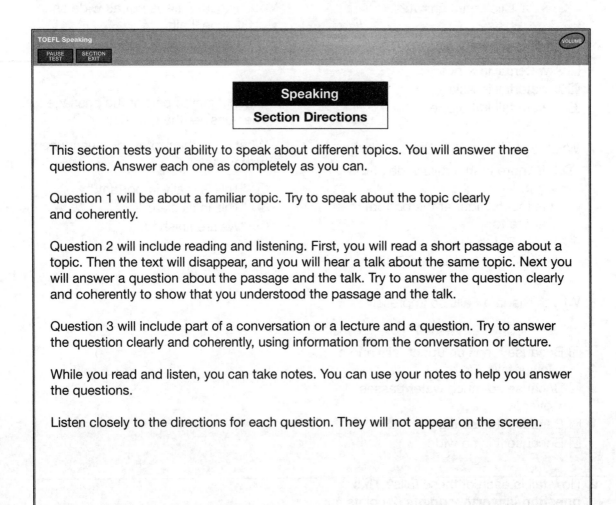

TOEFL Speaking

PAUSE TEST | SECTION EXIT

VOLUME

Speaking
Section Directions

This section tests your ability to speak about different topics. You will answer three questions. Answer each one as completely as you can.

Question 1 will be about a familiar topic. Try to speak about the topic clearly and coherently.

Question 2 will include reading and listening. First, you will read a short passage about a topic. Then the text will disappear, and you will hear a talk about the same topic. Next you will answer a question about the passage and the talk. Try to answer the question clearly and coherently to show that you understood the passage and the talk.

Question 3 will include part of a conversation or a lecture and a question. Try to answer the question clearly and coherently, using information from the conversation or lecture.

While you read and listen, you can take notes. You can use your notes to help you answer the questions.

Listen closely to the directions for each question. They will not appear on the screen.

Questions 1–3

Question 1

Read the question. Take notes on the main points of a response. Then respond to the question.

What is your favorite sport? Use reasons in your response.

> Preparation Time: 15 seconds
> Response Time: 45 seconds

INTRODUCTION:

SUPPORTING IDEA 1:

SUPPORTING IDEA 2:

CONCLUSION:

Question 2

Read the passage. Take notes on the main points of the reading passage.

Reading Time: 45 seconds

A notice on the door of the library

The library is closed at this moment. We regret if this causes any problems for professors or students. We sincerely hope that the library will be open soon. Please return later today or tomorrow to see if the library is open then. Once again, we apologize for this problem.

TOPIC OF READING PASSAGE:

main points about the topic:

●

●

Listen to the passage. Take notes on the main points of the listening passage.

TOPIC OF LISTENING PASSAGE:

main points about the topic:

•

•

•

Now answer the following question:

How does the information in the listening passage add to the ideas in the reading passage?

> Preparation Time: 30 seconds
> Response Time: 60 seconds

Question 3

Listen to the passage. Take notes on the main points of the listening passage.

TOPIC OF LISTENING PASSAGE:

<u>main points about the topic:</u>

-

-

-

-

Now answer the following question:

What points does the professor make about Catlin?

> Preparation Time: 20 seconds
> Response Time: 60 seconds

> Turn to pages 454–465 to *assess* the skills used in the test, *score* the test using the Speaking Scoring Criteria, and *record* your results.

MINI-TEST 1

WRITING

Writing
Section Directions

This section tests your ability to communicate in writing in an academic environment. There is one writing task.

In this writing task, you will read a passage and listen to a lecture. Then you will answer a question using information from the passage and the lecture.

Integrated Writing Directions

For this task, you will read a passage about an academic topic. You have **3 minutes** to read the passage, and then the passage will disappear. Then you will hear a lecture about the same topic. You can take notes while you read and listen.

You will then write an answer to a question about the relationship between the reading passage and the lecture. Try to use information from the passage and the lecture to answer the question. You will **not** be asked for your personal opinion. You can see the reading passage again when you are ready to write. You can use your notes to help you. You have **20 minutes** to write your response.

A successful answer will usually be around 150 to 225 words. Try to show that you can write well and give complete, accurate information.

Now you will read the passage. Remember that you can see it again when you write your response. As soon as the reading time ends, the lecture will begin.

Read the passage. Take notes on the main points of the reading passage.

> Reading Time: 3 minutes

Assateague Island is a well-known island with some interesting inhabitants. The island is a small island with a long, thin shape. It is 35 miles long and under a mile wide. It is located just off the eastern coast of the United States. It is called a barrier island because it runs along the eastern coast of the country and it protects the coast from bad weather coming from the ocean.

The island's interesting inhabitants are wild ponies. There are many wild ponies living freely on the island. The island is a national park that offers protection to the wild ponies there.

TOPIC OF READING PASSAGE:

main points about the topic:

•

•

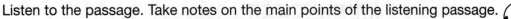Listen to the passage. Take notes on the main points of the listening passage.

TOPIC OF LISTENING PASSAGE:

main points about the topic:

-

-

-

Now answer the following question:

How does the information in the listening passage add to the information in the reading passage?

| Preparation Time: 1 minute |
| Response Time: 20 minutes |

Turn to pages 466–472 to *assess* the skills used in the test, *score* the test using the Writing Scoring Criteria, and *record* your results.

MINI-TEST 2

READING

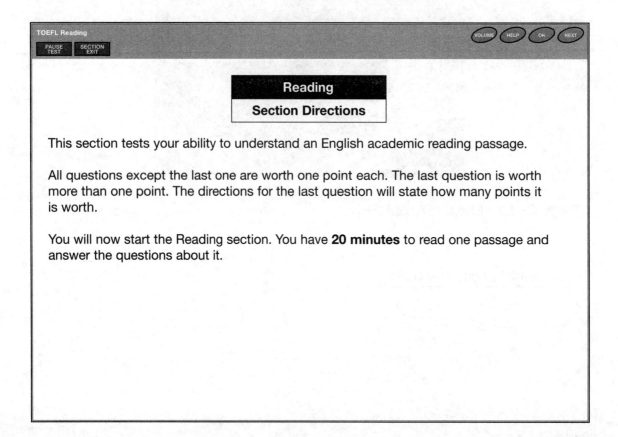

TOEFL Reading

PAUSE TEST   SECTION EXIT

VOLUME   HELP   OK   NEXT

Reading
Section Directions

This section tests your ability to understand an English academic reading passage.

All questions except the last one are worth one point each. The last question is worth more than one point. The directions for the last question will state how many points it is worth.

You will now start the Reading section. You have **20 minutes** to read one passage and answer the questions about it.

Read the passage.

The French Quarter

▶ 1   The French Quarter is the oldest section of the city of New Orleans. The influences from a number of different cultures can be spotted in it.

▶ 2   The city of New Orleans was first colonized by the French in 1718. The French planned and laid out what is today called the French Quarter as a walled town. The plan of the French Quarter was created by the French in the eighteenth century. It shows the formal organization that was popular in France at the time. Though very few buildings that are purely French in design remain, the overall design of the area is completely French.

▶ 3   Spain took possession of New Orleans from France in 1762. During the period that Spain was in control of New Orleans, there were Spanish influences in the architecture of the French Quarter. Spanish-style courtyards, which were full of plants and flowers, were added to houses, and wrought iron was used to decorate the houses in the Spanish style of the time.

▶ 4   Another influence on the architecture of New Orleans came from the West Indies. Wealthy planters from the West Indies began opening houses in the French Quarter of New Orleans in the latter part of the eighteenth century. The weather in the West Indies is very hot, and houses in the West Indies were built in ways that would help keep them cool. Planters who came to the French Quarter from the West Indies influenced the architecture of the French Quarter by making their houses there more able to keep the people living in them cool. Two ways that planters from the West Indies influenced houses in the French Quarter to make them cooler in the heat was to build ground floors out of stone and to add wide verandas, or covered porches, on second stories.

Refer to this version of the passage to answer the questions that follow.

Paragraph

The French Quarter

▶ The French Quarter is the oldest section of the city of New Orleans. The influences from a number of different cultures can be spotted in it.

▶ The city of New Orleans was first colonized by the French in 1718. The French planned and laid out what is today called the French Quarter as a walled town. The plan of the French Quarter was created by the French in the eighteenth century. It shows the formal organization that was popular in France at the time. Though very few buildings that are purely French in design remain, the overall design of the area is completely French.

▶ Spain took possession of New Orleans from France in 1762. During the period that Spain was in control of New Orleans, there were Spanish influences in the architecture of the French Quarter. Spanish-style courtyards, which were full of plants and flowers, were added to houses, and wrought iron was used to decorate the houses in the Spanish style of the time.

▶ Another influence on the architecture of New Orleans came from the West Indies. **11A** Wealthy planters from the West Indies began opening houses in the French Quarter of New Orleans in the latter part of the eighteenth century. **11B** The weather in the West Indies is very hot, and houses in the West Indies were built in ways that would help keep them cool. **11C** Planters who came to the French Quarter from the West Indies influenced the architecture of the French Quarter by making their houses there more able to keep the people living in them cool. **11D** Two ways that planters from the West Indies influenced houses in the French Quarter to make them cooler in the heat was to build ground floors out of stone and to add wide verandas, or covered porches, on second stories.

1. It can be inferred from paragraph 1 that the French Quarter

   Ⓐ is located outside of New Orleans
   Ⓑ is not built in a single style
   Ⓒ was built only recently
   Ⓓ has a single strong culture

2. The word "spotted" in paragraph 1 can best be replaced by

   Ⓐ seen
   Ⓑ circled
   Ⓒ taken
   Ⓓ interested

3. According to paragraph 2, it is NOT true that

   Ⓐ New Orleans was first colonized in the eighteenth century
   Ⓑ the French planned the area called the French Quarter
   Ⓒ the French Quarter was originally a walled town
   Ⓓ many buildings in the French Quarter today are French in design

4. The word "purely" in paragraph 2 could best be replaced by

   Ⓐ simply
   Ⓑ completely
   Ⓒ clearly
   Ⓓ cleanly

5. It is stated in paragraph 3 that Spain

   Ⓐ gave New Orleans to France in 1762
   Ⓑ took possession of France in the eighteenth century
   Ⓒ gave France to New Orleans in 1762
   Ⓓ got New Orleans from France in the eighteenth century

6. The phrase "was in control of" in paragraph 3 could best be replaced by

   Ⓐ had a desire for
   Ⓑ was located in
   Ⓒ had authority over
   Ⓓ was looking for

7. A home in Spain in the late eighteenth century would most likely

   Ⓐ have French-style architecture
   Ⓑ be located in a courtyard
   Ⓒ be made of wrought iron
   Ⓓ have a courtyard full of flowers

8. Why does the author say that "The weather in the West Indies is very hot" in a passage on the French Quarter?

   Ⓐ Because most of the people living in the French Quarter had to move to the West Indies
   Ⓑ Because the style of houses built for the weather of the West Indies was used in the French Quarter
   Ⓒ Because the weather in the West Indies is very different from the weather in the French Quarter
   Ⓓ Because the French Quarter is located in the West Indies

9. The word "built" in paragraph 4 is closest in meaning to

   Ⓐ viewed
   Ⓑ located
   Ⓒ constructed
   Ⓓ transported

10. The word "them" in paragraph 4 refers to

    Ⓐ planters
    Ⓑ West Indies
    Ⓒ houses
    Ⓓ people

11. Look at the four squares [■] that indicate where the following sentence could be added to paragraph 4.

    This was necessary because the weather in New Orleans could be extremely hot.

    Where would the sentence best fit? Click on a square [■] to add the sentence to the paragraph.

12. Which of the sentences below best expresses the essential information in the last highlighted sentence in paragraph 4?

Ⓐ French Quarter houses were built in the style of the West Indies with stone ground floors and verandas.

Ⓑ Planters from the West Indies used two ways to keep their plantations cooler.

Ⓒ Planters from the West Indies did not like wide verandas because they did not stay cooler.

Ⓓ West Indian planters built two different kinds of houses in New Orleans.

13.

Directions: Select the appropriate answer choices about influences on the French Quarter, and match them to the correct category. **This question is worth 3 points** (3 points for 5 correct answers, 2 points for 4 correct answers, 1 point for 3 correct answers, 0 points for 2, 1, or 0 correct answers).

from France	•
from Spain	• •
from the West Indies	• •

Answer Choices (choose 5 to complete the table):

(1) Wide covered porches

(2) Formal organization

(3) Stone walls

(4) Wrought iron decorations

(5) Buildings painted with flowers

(6) Stone ground floors

(7) Courtyards full of plant life

Turn to pages 448–450 to *diagnose* your errors and *record* your results.

MINI-TEST 2

LISTENING

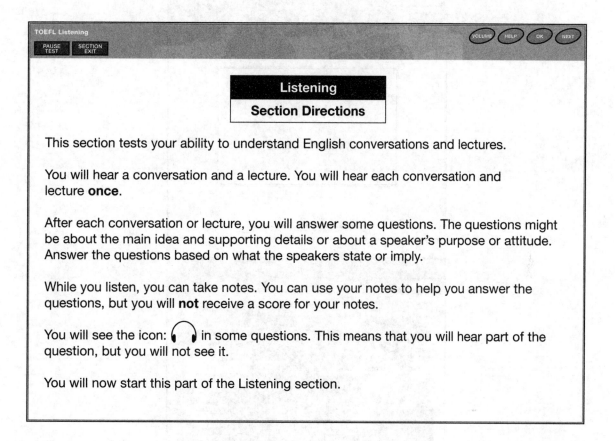

TOEFL Listening

PAUSE TEST | SECTION EXIT

VOLUME | HELP | OK | NEXT

Listening
Section Directions

This section tests your ability to understand English conversations and lectures.

You will hear a conversation and a lecture. You will hear each conversation and lecture **once**.

After each conversation or lecture, you will answer some questions. The questions might be about the main idea and supporting details or about a speaker's purpose or attitude. Answer the questions based on what the speakers state or imply.

While you listen, you can take notes. You can use your notes to help you answer the questions, but you will **not** receive a score for your notes.

You will see the icon: 🎧 in some questions. This means that you will hear part of the question, but you will not see it.

You will now start this part of the Listening section.

Questions 1–5

Listen as a student consults with his advisor. The conversation is about a math class.

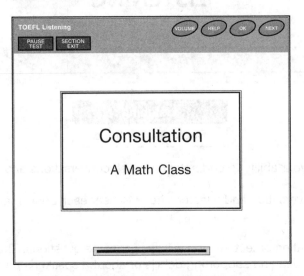

1. Why does the student go to see the advisor?

   Ⓐ To discuss a class he wants to add
   Ⓑ To discuss a class the advisor is going to teach
   Ⓒ To discuss a class he wants to get out of
   Ⓓ To find out when classes start

2. How does the student seem to feel about his math class?

   Ⓐ He thinks it is rather easy.
   Ⓑ He thinks the class is quite interesting.
   Ⓒ He thinks it is a great class.
   Ⓓ He thinks the class is too difficult.

3. Is each of these something the advisor says in response to the student's request? **This question is worth 2 points** (2 points for 4 correct answers, 1 point for 3 correct answers, and 0 points for 2, 1, or 0 correct answers).

For each statement, click in the YES or NO column.		
	YES	NO
It is correct that you need a signature from your advisor.		
It is incorrect that you need a signature from your advisor.		
It is correct that you can drop your math class.		
It is incorrect that you can drop your math class.		

4. Listen again to part of the passage. Then answer the question. 🎧

   How does the student seem to feel?
   Ⓐ Very unhappy
   Ⓑ Not so surprised
   Ⓒ Rather pleased
   Ⓓ Quite amused

5. Listen again to part of the passage. Then answer the question. 🎧

   What does the advisor mean when she says this: 🎧

   Ⓐ "I don't have any response."
   Ⓑ "There isn't any time."
   Ⓒ "It's absolutely impossible."
   Ⓓ "You shouldn't go this way."

Questions 6–11

Listen to a discussion from a history class.
The discussion is on Stone Mountain.

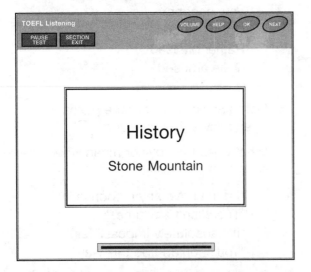

6. What is the professor mainly discussing?

    Ⓐ A location that has historical importance

    Ⓑ A place where a Civil War battle was fought

    Ⓒ An event that caused the Civil War

    Ⓓ A place where certain war leaders met

7. Where is Stone Mountain located?

    Ⓐ In the southwestern part of the United States

    Ⓑ In the northeastern part of the United States

    Ⓒ In the southeastern part of the United States

    Ⓓ In the northwestern part of the United States

8. When was the Civil War?

    Ⓐ In the first half of the eighteenth century

    Ⓑ In the second half of the eighteenth century

    Ⓒ In the first half of the nineteenth century

    Ⓓ In the second half of the nineteenth century

9. Who are these people? **This question is worth 2 points** (2 points for 3 correct answers, 1 point for 2 correct answers, and 0 points for 1 or 0 correct answers).

> Click on a phrase. Then drag it to the space where it belongs. Each answer will be used one time only.

Was President of the Confederacy	Was general in chief	Was a general under the chief

Robert E. Lee	Jefferson Davis	Stonewall Jackson

10. Listen again to part of the passage. Then answer the question. 🎧

How does the professor seem to feel about the student's response?

    Ⓐ Pleasantly surprised

    Ⓑ Decidedly unhappy

    Ⓒ Completely matter-of-fact

    Ⓓ Unbelievably upset

11. What is Traveller?

    Ⓐ A rock

    Ⓑ An animal

    Ⓒ A general

    Ⓓ A battle

Turn to pages 451–453 to *diagnose* your errors and *record* your results.

MINI-TEST 2

SPEAKING

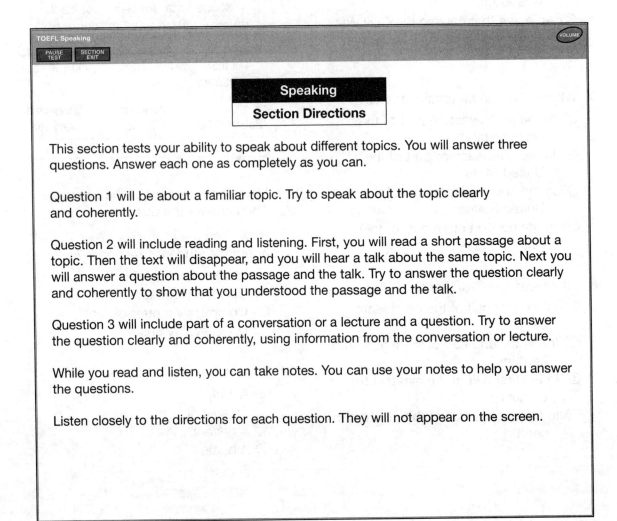

> **TOEFL Speaking**
>
> [PAUSE TEST] [SECTION EXIT]   (VOLUME)
>
> ### Speaking
> ### Section Directions
>
> This section tests your ability to speak about different topics. You will answer three questions. Answer each one as completely as you can.
>
> Question 1 will be about a familiar topic. Try to speak about the topic clearly and coherently.
>
> Question 2 will include reading and listening. First, you will read a short passage about a topic. Then the text will disappear, and you will hear a talk about the same topic. Next you will answer a question about the passage and the talk. Try to answer the question clearly and coherently to show that you understood the passage and the talk.
>
> Question 3 will include part of a conversation or a lecture and a question. Try to answer the question clearly and coherently, using information from the conversation or lecture.
>
> While you read and listen, you can take notes. You can use your notes to help you answer the questions.
>
> Listen closely to the directions for each question. They will not appear on the screen.

Questions 1–3

Question 1

Read the question. Take notes on the main points of a response. Then respond to the question.

Is it always better to tell the truth, or is it sometimes better to lie?
Use reasons in your response.

Preparation Time: 15 seconds
Response Time: 45 seconds

INTRODUCTION:

SUPPORTING IDEA 1:

SUPPORTING IDEA 2:

CONCLUSION:

Question 2

Read the passage. Take notes on the main points of the reading passage.

| Reading Time: 45 seconds |

Earthquakes

In the period of time before a major earthquake happens, there can be several smaller earthquakes. These smaller earthquakes before a major earthquake are called foreshocks. Foreshocks can occur when one of the tectonic plates in the Earth's crust first begins to move. Then, when a plate makes a big and sudden movement, a major earthquake occurs.

TOPIC OF READING PASSAGE:

main points about the topic:

●

●

Listen to the passage. Take notes on the main points of the listening passage.

TOPIC OF LISTENING PASSAGE:

main points about the topic:

•

•

Now answer the following question:

How does the information in the listening passage add to the
ideas in the reading passage?

Preparation Time: 30 seconds
Response Time: 60 seconds

Question 3

Listen to the passage. Take notes on the main points of the listening passage.

TOPIC OF LISTENING PASSAGE:

main points about the topic:

-

-

-

Now answer the following question:

What do the students have to say about the exam?

Preparation Time: 20 seconds
Response Time: 60 seconds

Turn to pages 454–465 to *assess* the skills used in the test, *score* the test using the Speaking Scoring Criteria, and *record* your results.

MINI-TEST 2

WRITING

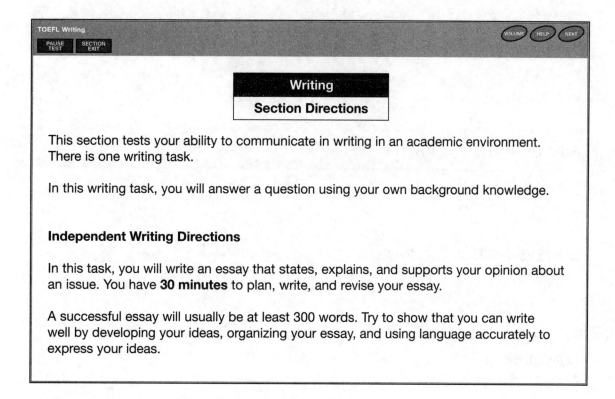

Read the question. Take notes on the main points of a response. Then write your response.

Do you prefer to take a vacation in a big city or in a natural spot? Why?

Response Time: 30 minutes

INTRODUCTION:

SUPPORTING PARAGRAPH 1:

SUPPORTING PARAGRAPH 2:

CONCLUSION:

Turn to pages 466–472 to *assess* the skills used in the test, *score* the test using the Writing Scoring Criteria, and *record* your results.

MINI-TEST 3

READING

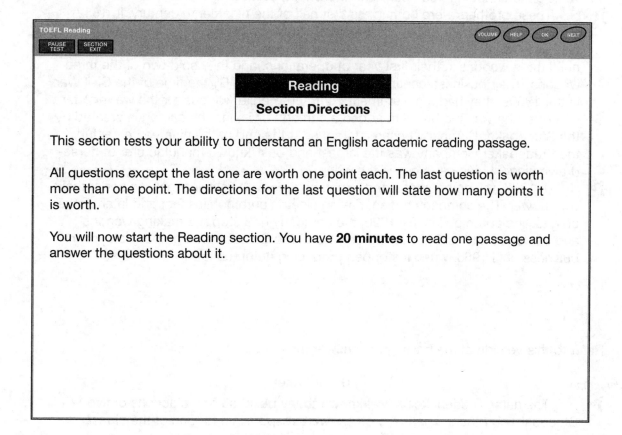

Reading
Section Directions

This section tests your ability to understand an English academic reading passage.

All questions except the last one are worth one point each. The last question is worth more than one point. The directions for the last question will state how many points it is worth.

You will now start the Reading section. You have **20 minutes** to read one passage and answer the questions about it.

Read the passage.

Studebaker

1 ▶ The name Studebaker is well known today because of the actions of five Studebaker brothers. The five brothers were responsible for one of the oldest vehicle manufacturing companies in the United States.

2 ▶ These brothers were born in the first half of the nineteenth century. In 1852, two of the Studebaker brothers opened a wagon-building shop. Their entire resources were some tools for building wagons and 68 dollars. They managed to build three wagons in their first year of operations, and they sold two of the three wagons. Their business continued to increase steadily. By the time of the Civil War in the 1860s, they had a government contract to build wagons for the war effort.

3 ▶ After the war, the brothers added a carriage division. The carriages created by the Studebaker Company became famous. At the end of the nineteenth century, the Studebaker Company was the largest and best-known manufacturer of horse-drawn wagons and carriages in the world.

4 ▶ In 1897, the company started experimenting with vehicles that ran under their own power. The company began making electric automobiles first and later worked on gasoline automobiles. By 1920, the company had stopped making wagons and carriages and was producing only cars. The Studebaker Company stayed in business until 1966, when it stopped producing automobiles.

Refer to this version of the passage to answer the questions that follow.

Paragraph

Studebaker

1 ▶ The name Studebaker is well known today because of the actions of five Studebaker brothers. The five brothers were responsible for one of the oldest vehicle manufacturing companies in the United States.

2 ▶ These brothers were born in the first half of the nineteenth century. In 1852, two of the Studebaker brothers opened a wagon-building shop. Their entire resources were some tools for building wagons and 68 dollars. They managed to build three wagons in their first year of operations, and they sold two of the three wagons. Their business continued to increase steadily. By the time of the Civil War in the 1860s, they had a government contract to build wagons for the war effort.

3 ▶ After the war, the brothers added a carriage division. The carriages created by the Studebaker Company became famous. At the end of the nineteenth century, the Studebaker Company was the largest and best-known manufacturer of horse-drawn wagons and carriages in the world.

4 ▶ In 1897, the company started experimenting with vehicles that ran under their own power. **10A** The company began making electric automobiles first and later worked on gasoline automobiles. **10B** By 1920, the company had stopped making wagons and carriages and was producing only cars. **10C** The Studebaker Company stayed in business until 1966, when it stopped producing automobiles. **10D**

1. Which of the following is NOT mentioned about the Studebaker brothers?
   Ⓐ The number of brothers
   Ⓑ The kind of manufacturing company they started
   Ⓒ When they opened their first company
   Ⓓ The number of children they had

2. The word "entire" in paragraph 2 is closest in meaning to
   Ⓐ total
   Ⓑ earned
   Ⓒ finished
   Ⓓ partial

3. It is indicated in paragraph 2 that, when the Studebaker brothers started their first company, they had
   Ⓐ a number of wagons
   Ⓑ a government contract to build wagons
   Ⓒ some tools for working on cars
   Ⓓ only a small amount of money

4. The word "they" in paragraph 2 refers to
   Ⓐ two of the Studebaker brothers
   Ⓑ their entire resources
   Ⓒ their wagons
   Ⓓ operations

5. Why does the author mention the "Civil War" in paragraph 2?
   Ⓐ Because it caused their business to end
   Ⓑ Because it was fought over their wagons
   Ⓒ Because it increased demand for their product
   Ⓓ Because their business closed after it

6. It can be inferred from the passage that, right after the Civil War, the Studebaker brothers
   Ⓐ continued building wagons
   Ⓑ stopped producing carriages
   Ⓒ started producing automobiles
   Ⓓ stopped building wagons

7. Which of the sentences below best expresses the essential information in the highlighted sentence in paragraph 3?
   Ⓐ By 1900, the Studebaker brothers were the best-known manufacturers in the world.
   Ⓑ By 1900, the Studebaker Company was the world's number one manufacturer of carriages and wagons.
   Ⓒ By the end of the nineteenth century, the Studebaker Company was manufacturing both wagons and carriages.
   Ⓓ In the nineteenth century, the Studebaker Company added production of carriages to production of wagons.

8. According to the passage, the Studebaker brothers
   Ⓐ developed gasoline cars before electric cars
   Ⓑ stopped producing wagons in 1897
   Ⓒ developed electric cars before gasoline cars
   Ⓓ began making cars in 1920

9. Look at the word "stayed" in paragraph 4. This word is closest in meaning to
   Ⓐ remained
   Ⓑ held
   Ⓒ left
   Ⓓ managed

10. Look at the four squares [■] that indicate where the following sentence could be added to paragraph 4.

For the next forty-six years, the company concentrated on the manufacture of automobiles.

Where would the sentence best fit? Click on a square [■] to add the sentence to the paragraph.

11. Which of the following was NOT mentioned as something the Studebaker brothers produced?

Ⓐ Wagons
Ⓑ Carriages
Ⓒ Cars
Ⓓ Airplanes

12. The word "producing" in paragraph 4 is closest in meaning to

Ⓐ manufacturing
Ⓑ designing
Ⓒ considering
Ⓓ drawing

13.

Directions: An introductory sentence for a brief summary of the passage is provided below. Complete the summary by selecting the THREE answer choices that express the most important ideas in the passage. **This question is worth 2 points** (2 points for 3 correct answers, 1 point for 2 correct answers, and 0 points for 1 or 0 correct answers).
The Studebakers built various products at different points in their history.
•   •   •

Answer Choices (choose 3 to complete the chart):

(1) Before the Civil War, they built only wagons.

(2) From the Civil War to 1920, they built only wagons and carriages.

(3) From 1920 to 1966, they built wagons, carriages, and cars.

(4) Before the Civil War, the Studebakers built wagons and carriages.

(5) From 1920 to 1966, they built only cars.

(6) From the Civil War to 1920, they built wagons and carriages and eventually added cars.

Turn to pages 448–450 to *diagnose* your errors and *record* your results.

MINI-TEST 3

LISTENING

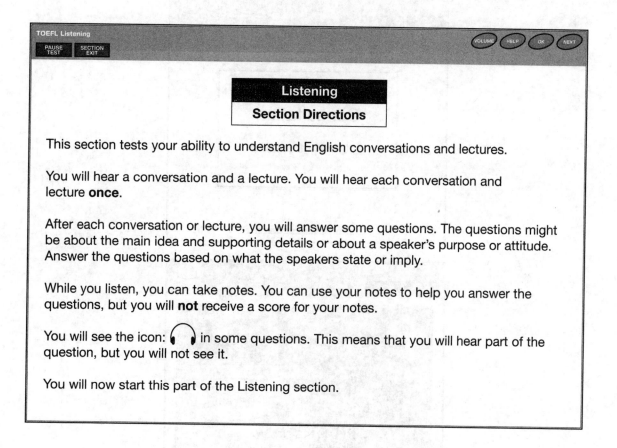

Listening
Section Directions

This section tests your ability to understand English conversations and lectures.

You will hear a conversation and a lecture. You will hear each conversation and lecture **once**.

After each conversation or lecture, you will answer some questions. The questions might be about the main idea and supporting details or about a speaker's purpose or attitude. Answer the questions based on what the speakers state or imply.

While you listen, you can take notes. You can use your notes to help you answer the questions, but you will **not** receive a score for your notes.

You will see the icon: 🎧 in some questions. This means that you will hear part of the question, but you will not see it.

You will now start this part of the Listening section.

Questions 1–5

Listen as a student consults with a librarian. The conversation is about some library books.

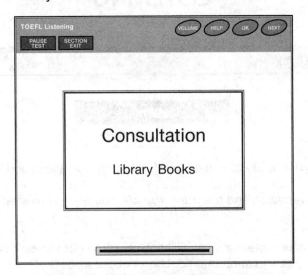

1. Why does the student go to see the librarian?
   - Ⓐ To check some books out of the library
   - Ⓑ To find out about some reference books
   - Ⓒ To ask what "R" on a book means
   - Ⓓ To ask about the call numbers on some books

2. Listen again to part of the passage. Then answer the question. 🎧

   What does the student mean when she says this: 🎧
   - Ⓐ "I'm sorry for interrupting."
   - Ⓑ "I'm not sure I understand."
   - Ⓒ "I apologize for asking this."
   - Ⓓ "I agree with what you said."

3. What does the librarian say about the reference books?
   - Ⓐ There are no reference books in the library.
   - Ⓑ The reference books are not on the first floor.
   - Ⓒ The reference books can all be checked out.
   - Ⓓ The reference books must be used in the library.

4. Is each of these true about call numbers? **This question is worth 2 points** (2 points for 4 correct answers, 1 point for 3 correct answers, and 0 points for 2, 1, or 0 correct answers).

For each statement, click in the YES or NO column.		
	YES	NO
They are identification numbers.		
They are only on books that cannot be checked out.		
They are on the cover of each book.		
They are used only on reference books.		

5. How can someone know which books are reference books?
   - Ⓐ The word "reference" is on them.
   - Ⓑ They are identified with the letter "R."
   - Ⓒ They do not have a call number.
   - Ⓓ They are marked with "first floor."

Questions 6–11

Listen to a lecture in an American history class. The professor is talking about Leland Stanford.

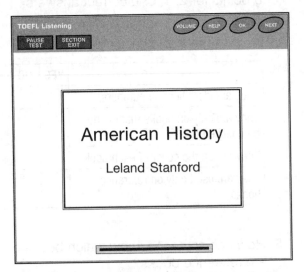

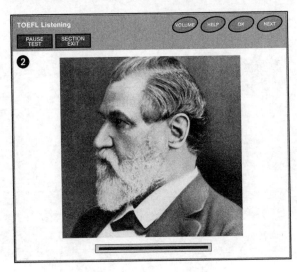

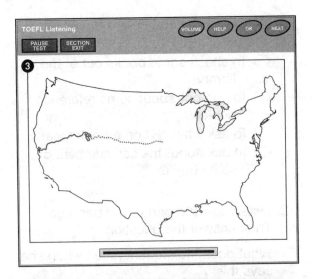

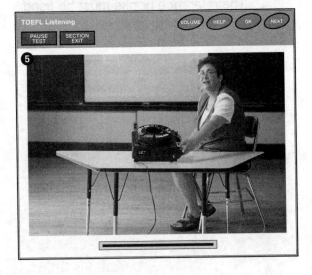

6. What is the topic of the lecture?
   - Ⓐ The political work of Leland Stanford
   - Ⓑ One man's contribution to Stanford University
   - Ⓒ The history of the Central Pacific Railroad
   - Ⓓ The varied accomplishments of one man

7. How is the information in the passage organized?
   - Ⓐ The history of the Central Pacific Railroad is presented chronologically.
   - Ⓑ The important people in Leland Stanford's life are each described.
   - Ⓒ The various kinds of work that Leland Stanford did in his life are classified.
   - Ⓓ Leland Stanford's successes in politics and business are compared and contrasted.

8. What was stated about the Central Pacific Railroad?

   Click on 2 answers.

   - Ⓐ Leland Stanford served as its president.
   - Ⓑ It was part of the first transcontinental railroad.
   - Ⓒ It was in the eastern part of the country.
   - Ⓓ It lost a lot of money.

9. Listen again to part of the passage. Then answer the question. ⌒

   Why does the professor say this: ⌒
   - Ⓐ To introduce those ideas to the passage
   - Ⓑ To provide examples of a concept
   - Ⓒ To make the lecture more interesting
   - Ⓓ To refer to previously discussed ideas

10. In the lecture, the professor discusses a series of events in Leland Stanford's life. Put these events in the correct order. **This question is worth 2 points** (2 points for 4 correct answers, 1 point for 3 or 2 correct answers, and 0 points for 1 or 0 correct answers).

    Click on a sentence. Then drag it to the space where it belongs. Use each sentence only once.

    Stanford started a university.
    Stanford's son died.
    Stanford made millions.
    Stanford started a railroad.

    1. _____
    2. _____
    3. _____
    4. _____

11. Based on the lecture, what is most likely true?
    - Ⓐ That Stanford's work on the railroad was part of his philanthropic work
    - Ⓑ That Stanford created a university as part of his railroad empire
    - Ⓒ That Stanford's work as a philanthropist started after his work as a businessman
    - Ⓓ That Stanford was very successful in politics because of his philanthropy

Turn to pages 451–453 to *diagnose* your errors and *record* your results.

MINI-TEST 3

SPEAKING

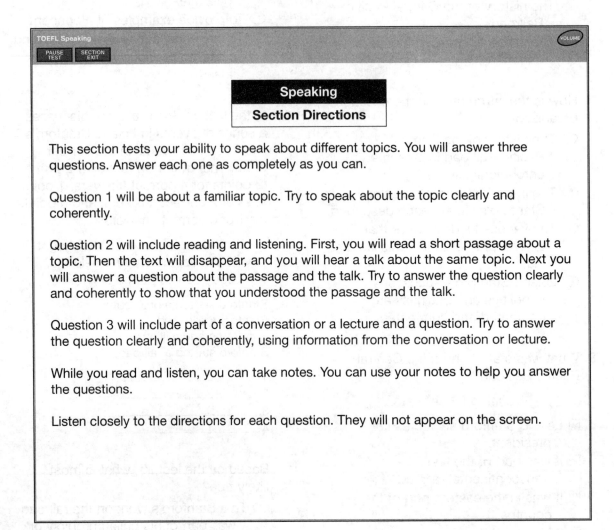

Questions 1–3

Question 1

Read the question. Take notes on the main points of a response. Then respond to the question.

> What things do you do with your friends when you go out? Use reasons in your response.

> Preparation Time: 15 seconds
> Response Time: 45 seconds

INTRODUCTION:

SUPPORTING IDEA 1:

SUPPORTING IDEA 2:

SUPPORTING IDEA 3:

CONCLUSION:

Question 2

Read the passage. Take notes on the main points of the reading passage.

Reading Time: 45 seconds

A notice posted on the door of a professor's office

Your lab reports were due by 3:00. Because it is now past 3:00, lab reports will no longer be accepted. Any lab reports that have not yet been turned in will receive a failing grade.

TOPIC OF READING PASSAGE:

main points about the topic:

-

-

-

Listen to the passage. Take notes on the main points of the listening passage.

TOPIC OF LISTENING PASSAGE:

main points about the topic:

-

-

-

-

-

Now answer the following question:

> How does the information in the listening passage add to the ideas in the reading passage?

| Preparation Time: 30 seconds |
| Response Time: 60 seconds |

Question 3

Listen to the passage. Take notes on the main points of the listening passage.

TOPIC OF LISTENING PASSAGE:

<u>main points about the topic:</u>

•

•

•

Now answer the following question:

What does the professor have to say about injuries?

| Preparation Time: 20 seconds |
| Response Time: 60 seconds |

Turn to pages 454–465 to *assess* the skills used in the test, *score* the test using the Speaking Scoring Criteria, and *record* your results.

MINI-TEST 3

WRITING

Writing
Section Directions

This section tests your ability to communicate in writing in an academic environment. There is one writing task.

In this writing task, you will read a passage and listen to a lecture. Then you will answer a question using information from the passage and the lecture.

Integrated Writing Directions

For this task, you will read a passage about an academic topic. You have **3 minutes** to read the passage, and then the passage will disappear. Then you will hear a lecture about the same topic. You can take notes while you read and listen.

You will then write an answer to a question about the relationship between the reading passage and the lecture. Try to use information from the passage and the lecture to answer the question. You will **not** be asked for your personal opinion. You can see the reading passage again when you are ready to write. You can use your notes to help you. You have **20 minutes** to write your response.

A successful answer will usually be around 150 to 225 words. Try to show that you can write well and give complete, accurate information.

Now you will read the passage. Remember that you can see it again when you write your response. As soon as the reading time ends, the lecture will begin.

Read the passage. Take notes on the main points of the reading passage.

Reading Time: 3 minutes

Until a few decades ago, until 1977, scientists were not sure what was at the bottom of the ocean. They were not sure because they had never seen the bottom of the ocean.

At that time, scientists believed that there were no living beings at the bottom of the ocean. They believed there was no life at the bottom of the ocean, and they believed that there was no life at the bottom of the ocean because there was no light at the bottom of the ocean. They believed that light was necessary for life. They believed that, if there was no light at the bottom of the ocean, then there could not be any life there.

TOPIC OF READING PASSAGE:

main points about the topic:

-

-

-

Listen to the passage. Take notes on the main points of the listening passage.

TOPIC OF LISTENING PASSAGE:

main points about the topic:

-

-

-

Now answer the following question:

How does the information in the listening passage challenge the information in the reading passage?

| Preparation Time: 1 minute |
| Response Time: 20 minutes |

Turn to pages 466–472 to *assess* the skills used in the test, *score* the test using the Writing Scoring Criteria, and *record* your results.

MINI-TEST 4

READING

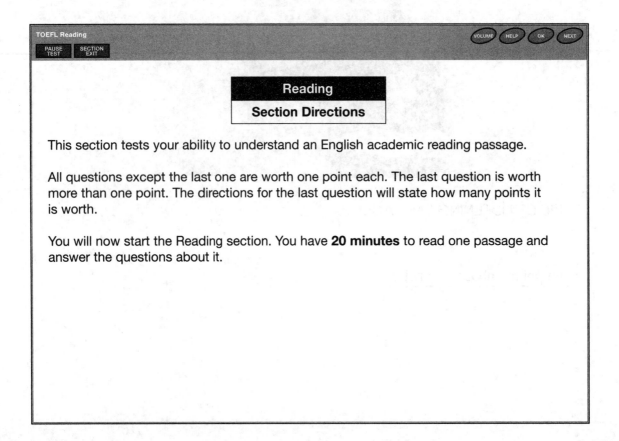

PAUSE TEST | SECTION EXIT

VOLUME | HELP | OK | NEXT

Reading
Section Directions

This section tests your ability to understand an English academic reading passage.

All questions except the last one are worth one point each. The last question is worth more than one point. The directions for the last question will state how many points it is worth.

You will now start the Reading section. You have **20 minutes** to read one passage and answer the questions about it.

Read the passage.

Songs of the Humpback Whale

▶1 One amazing characteristic of the humpback whale is its ability to sing. A male humpback whale may sing individually, or it may sing in concert with other nearby male humpback whales. One song can last as long as 15 minutes, and it can be made up of as many as seven themes that are used repeatedly throughout the song. The song consists of low moaning sounds, blasts that sound like horns, and high squeals.

▶2 There is a lot that scientists know about the songs of the humpback whale. However, some of the things are not known with certainty. They are how the humpback whales produce their songs, why they are singing the songs, and when and where the humpback whales sing.

▶3 It is unclear how humpback whales are able to produce sounds while they are singing. This is unclear because humpback whales do not have vocal cords. It is also unclear because their mouths are not moving while they are singing.

▶4 Something else that is not clear is the reason why humpback whales sing. When a male humpback whale begins singing, other male humpback whales respond. It is not female whales that respond. Perhaps the males are joining together to sing because they want female whales that are far away to hear them.

▶5 In addition to not understanding how and why humpback whales sing, scientists also do not understand fully when and where they produce their songs. Humpback whales from Alaska travel to Hawaii for the winter months of November through May, and then they return to Alaska. The whales rarely sing when they are in Alaska, but sometimes they do. They sing a lot more and a lot more often when they are in the waters of Hawaii.

Refer to this version of the passage to answer the questions.

Paragraph

Songs of the Humpback Whale

▶ One amazing characteristic of the humpback whale is its ability to sing. A male humpback whale may sing individually, or it may sing in concert with other nearby male humpback whales. One song can last as long as 15 minutes, and it can be made up of as many as seven themes that are used repeatedly throughout the song. The song consists of low moaning sounds, blasts that sound like horns, and high squeals.

▶ There is a lot that scientists know about the songs of the humpback whale. However, some of the things are not known with certainty. They are how the humpback whales produce their songs, why they are singing the songs, and when and where the humpback whales sing.

▶ **7A** It is unclear how humpback whales are able to produce sounds while they are singing. **7B** This is unclear because humpback whales do not have vocal cords. **7C** It is also unclear because their mouths are not moving while they are singing. **7D**

▶ Something else that is not clear is the reason why humpback whales sing. When a male humpback whale begins singing, other male humpback whales respond. It is not female whales that respond. Perhaps the males are joining together to sing because they want female whales that are far away to hear them.

▶ In addition to not understanding how and why humpback whales sing, scientists also do not understand fully when and where they produce their songs. Humpback whales from Alaska travel to Hawaii for the winter months of November through May, and then they return to Alaska. The whales rarely sing when they are in Alaska, but sometimes they do. They sing a lot more and a lot more often when they are in the waters of Hawaii.

1. The word "amazing" in paragraph 1 is closest in meaning to
   Ⓐ common
   Ⓑ surprising
   Ⓒ average
   Ⓓ boring

2. Based on the information in paragraph 1, which of the following would be the least likely to occur?
   Ⓐ Two male whales singing for 15 minutes
   Ⓑ A single male whale repeating five different themes
   Ⓒ A male and a female whale repeating seven themes
   Ⓓ Two male whales joining another male whale for 10 minutes of singing

3. What kind of whale sound is NOT mentioned in paragraph 1?
   Ⓐ Moaning
   Ⓑ Blasting
   Ⓒ Squealing
   Ⓓ Clicking

4. The expression "with certainty" in paragraph 2 could best be replaced by
   Ⓐ for sure
   Ⓑ as a possibility
   Ⓒ at most
   Ⓓ by chance

5. Why does the author say "They are how the humpback whales produce their songs, why they are singing the songs, and when and where the humpback whales sing" in paragraph 2?
   Ⓐ To add new details about the humpback whale
   Ⓑ To announce the organization of the information that follows
   Ⓒ To summarize the key points that came before
   Ⓓ To give an example of an idea that has already been presented

6. What is indicated in paragraph 3 about how whales produce sounds?
   Ⓐ They use their vocal cords and move their mouths.
   Ⓑ They use their vocal cords but do not use their mouths.
   Ⓒ They do not use their vocal cords but do use their mouths.
   Ⓓ They do not use their vocal cords and do not use their mouths.

7. Look at the four squares [■] that indicate where the following sentence could be added to paragraph 3.

   This is different from human production of sounds, in which vocal cords are used and the mouth is moving.

   Where would the sentence best fit? Click on a square [■] to add the sentence to the paragraph.

8. Which of the sentences below best expresses the essential information in the highlighted sentence in paragraph 4?
   Ⓐ It is possible that male whales sing together to attract distant female whales.
   Ⓑ Perhaps male whales sing with female whales in order to sing really loudly.
   Ⓒ Maybe male whales sing only when they are together with female whales.
   Ⓓ It is possible that male whales sing because they want female whales to stay away.

9. The word "fully" in paragraph 5 could best be replaced by
   Ⓐ usually
   Ⓑ normally
   Ⓒ completely
   Ⓓ accurately

10. The word "they" in paragraph 5 refers to

    Ⓐ humpback whales

    Ⓑ scientists

    Ⓒ songs

    Ⓓ winter months

11. It can be inferred from paragraph 5 that humpback whales would most likely be in Alaska in

    Ⓐ January

    Ⓑ April

    Ⓒ September

    Ⓓ November

12. According to paragraph 5, when do humpback whales sing?

    Ⓐ They always sing when they are in Alaska.

    Ⓑ They never sing when they are in Alaska.

    Ⓒ They never sing when they are in Hawaii.

    Ⓓ They sing more often in Hawaii than they do in Alaska.

13.

Directions: An introductory sentence for a brief summary of the passage is provided below. Complete the summary by selecting the THREE answer choices that express the most important ideas in the passage. **This question is worth 2 points** (2 points for 3 correct answers, 1 point for 2 correct answers, and 0 points for 1 or 0 correct answers).
Certain things are not known about the songs of whales.
•   •   •

    Answer Choices (choose 3 to complete the chart):

    (1) The way that whales produce songs

    (2) The kinds of sounds that are used in whale songs

    (3) The kind of whales that sing

    (4) The time and place the whales sing

    (5) The purpose of the songs the whales sing

    (6) Whether or not whales have vocal cords

Turn to pages 448–450 to *diagnose* your errors and *record* your results.

MINI-TEST 4
LISTENING

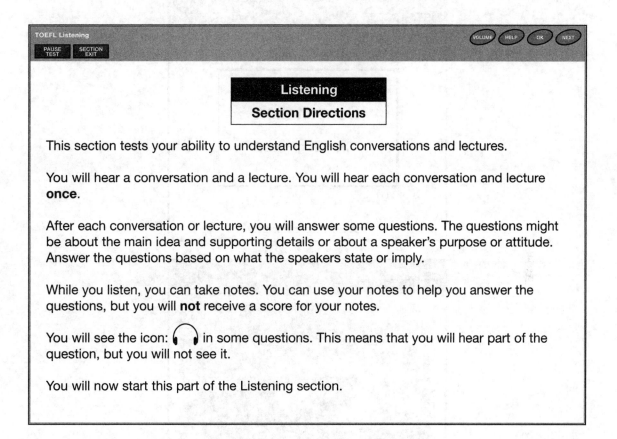

Questions 1–5

Listen as a student consults with her professor. The conversation is about an assignment.

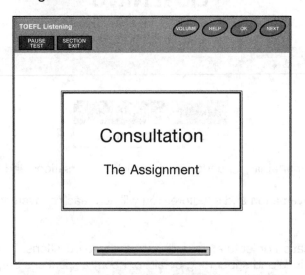

1. Why does the student go to see the professor?

    Ⓐ To ask about an assignment

    Ⓑ To ask about an article the professor wrote

    Ⓒ To ask the names of some articles

    Ⓓ To ask what will happen in the next class

2. Listen again to part of the passage. Then answer the question. 🎧

    How does the professor seem to feel?

    Ⓐ He does not seem to like the assignment the student wrote.

    Ⓑ He does not seem to know what the student is asking.

    Ⓒ He seems to think the student is in the wrong class.

    Ⓓ He seems to think the student did not do the writing assignment.

3. What does the student think the professor said in class?

    Ⓐ She thinks he told the students to write three articles.

    Ⓑ She thinks he told the students to read an article.

    Ⓒ She thinks he told the students to write an article.

    Ⓓ She thinks he told the students to read three articles.

4. What did the professor actually tell the students to do in class?

    Ⓐ To write an article

    Ⓑ To write three articles

    Ⓒ To read an article

    Ⓓ To read three articles

5. What did the professor write on the board?

    Ⓐ The name of an article the students were supposed to write

    Ⓑ The names of three articles the students were supposed to write

    Ⓒ The name of an article the students were supposed to read

    Ⓓ The names of three articles the students were supposed to read

Questions 6–11

Listen to a discussion from an astronomy class. The discussion is on the planet Neptune.

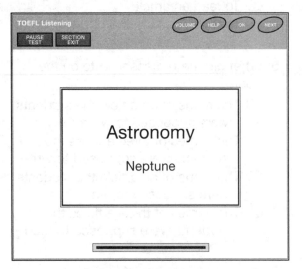

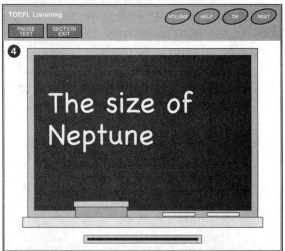

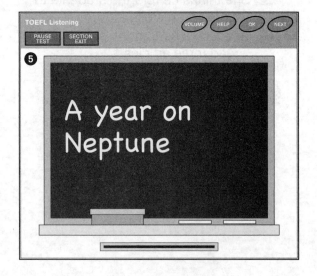

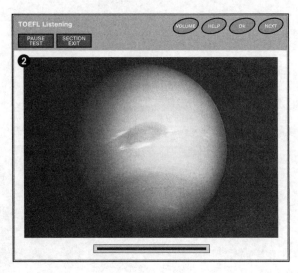

6. Which of these are true about the planet Neptune? **This question is worth 2 points** (2 points for 3 correct answers, 1 point for 2 correct answers, and 0 points for 1 or 0 correct answers).

Click on 3 answers.

- Ⓐ It is the eighth planet from the Sun.
- Ⓑ It is outside our solar system.
- Ⓒ It is visible from Earth with a telescope.
- Ⓓ It is gray in color.
- Ⓔ Its color is a mix of blue and green.

7. Listen again to part of the passage. Then answer the question.

What does the professor mean when she says this:

- Ⓐ "That was an easy question."
- Ⓑ "That's a good answer."
- Ⓒ "That answer is hard to understand."
- Ⓓ "That's a bad response."

8. What is Triton?

- Ⓐ Neptune's only moon
- Ⓑ Neptune's biggest moon
- Ⓒ Neptune's only mountain
- Ⓓ Neptune's biggest mountain

9. What are the relative sizes of Earth and Neptune?

- Ⓐ The diameter of Earth is one half that of Neptune.
- Ⓑ The diameter of Neptune is one quarter that of Earth.
- Ⓒ The diameter of Neptune is one half that of Earth.
- Ⓓ The diameter of Earth is one quarter that of Neptune.

10. Is each of these facts true about Neptune? **This question is worth 2 points** (2 points for 4 correct answers, 1 point for 3 correct answers, and 0 points for 2, 1, or 0 correct answers).

For each answer, click in the YES or NO column.

	YES	NO
Neptune has six moons.		
Neptune orbits the Sun in 165 Earth-years.		
A day on Neptune is longer than a day on Earth.		
Neptune rotates on its axis in 18 hours.		

11. What is implied in the discussion about the rotation of Neptune on its axis?

- Ⓐ Neptune does not rotate on its axis.
- Ⓑ Neptune rotates more slowly on its axis than Earth does.
- Ⓒ Neptune rotates on its axis at the same speed as Earth does.
- Ⓓ Neptune rotates more quickly on its axis than Earth does.

Turn to pages 451–453 to *diagnose* your errors and *record* your results.

MINI-TEST 4

SPEAKING

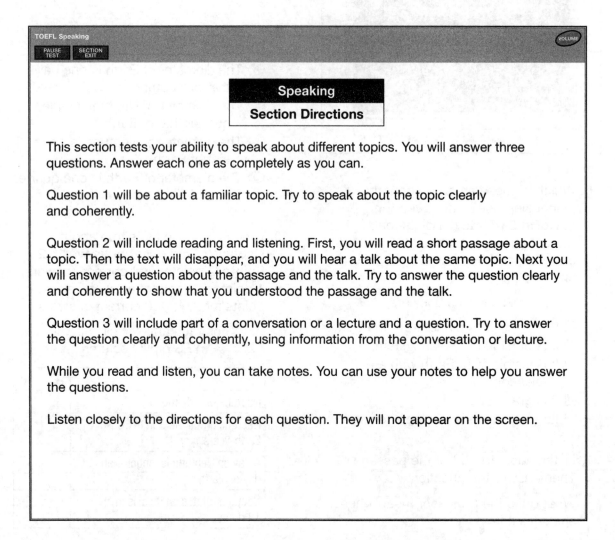

Question 1

Read the question. Take notes on the main points of a response. Then respond to the question.

Do you prefer to write a paper or give an oral presentation? Use reasons in your response.

Preparation Time: 15 seconds
Response Time: 45 seconds

INTRODUCTION:

SUPPORTING IDEA 1:

SUPPORTING IDEA 2:

CONCLUSION:

Question 2

Read the passage. Take notes on the main points of the reading passage.

Reading Time: 45 seconds

The Gettysburg Address

U.S. President Abraham Lincoln gave a very important speech on November 19, 1863. This famous speech was delivered at the height of the Civil War. It was known as the Gettysburg Address.

There are well-known stories about how the Gettysburg Address was prepared. It is said that Lincoln was not sure about what to say until the last moment, so he wrote the speech on the train as he was traveling to Gettysburg. It is also said that Lincoln did not have any paper with him on the train, so he wrote the speech on the back of an envelope.

TOPIC OF READING PASSAGE:

main points about the topic:

•

•

Listen to the passage. Take notes on the main points of the listening passage.

TOPIC OF LISTENING PASSAGE:

main points about the topic:

-

-

Now answer the following question:

How does the information in the listening passage challenge the information in the reading passage?

| Preparation Time: 30 seconds |
| Response Time: 60 seconds |

Question 3

Listen to the passage. Take notes on the main points of the listening passage.

TOPIC OF LISTENING PASSAGE:

main points about the topic:

•

•

•

Now answer the following question:

What are the students discussing?

| Preparation Time: 20 seconds |
| Response Time: 60 seconds |

Turn to pages 454–465 to *assess* the skills used in the test, *score* the test using the Speaking Scoring Criteria, and *record* your results.

MINI-TEST 4

WRITING

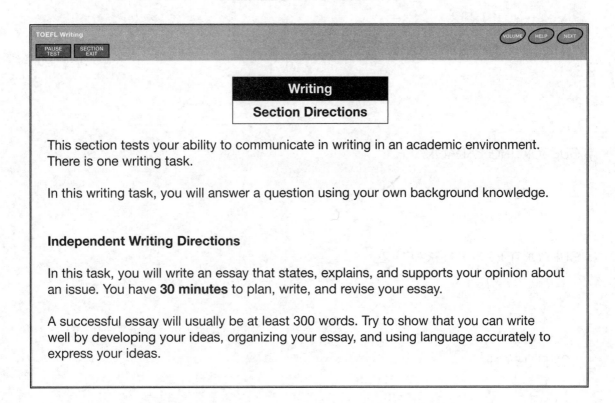

Read the question. Take notes on the main points of a response. Then write your response.

Describe the perfect boss. What are the most important characteristics of the perfect boss?

Response Time: 30 minutes

INTRODUCTION:

SUPPORTING PARAGRAPH 1:

SUPPORTING PARAGRAPH 2:

CONCLUSION:

Turn to pages 466–472 to *assess* the skills used in the test, *score* the test using the Writing Scoring Criteria, and *record* your results.

COMPLETE TEST

READING 1

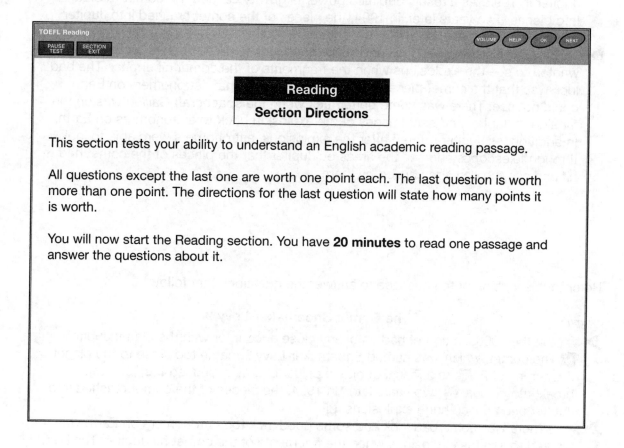

PAUSE TEST   SECTION EXIT

VOLUME   HELP   OK   NEXT

Reading
Section Directions

This section tests your ability to understand an English academic reading passage.

All questions except the last one are worth one point each. The last question is worth more than one point. The directions for the last question will state how many points it is worth.

You will now start the Reading section. You have **20 minutes** to read one passage and answer the questions about it.

Read the passage.

The Comet Shoemaker-Levy 9

Paragraph

1   In the 1990s, a comet had an overly close encounter with the planet Jupiter. The comet, which was named Shoemaker-Levy 9, came too close to the planet Jupiter in 1992. As a result, Jupiter's powerful gravity caused the comet to break into pieces. Two years later, in 1994, the pieces of the comet crashed into Jupiter and caused huge explosions.

2   There was some bad luck and some good luck for astronomers on Earth who wanted to see the explosions when the fragments of the comet hit Jupiter. The bad luck was that the comet pieces hit the side of Jupiter that astronomers on Earth could not see. There was some better luck when the spacecraft *Galileo* was on the far side of Jupiter and sent images of the explosion back to astronomers on Earth. In addition, as Jupiter rotated after the explosions, astronomers were able to look through telescopes and see the areas on Jupiter that the pieces of the comet had hit and see the damage caused by them.

Refer to this version of the passage to answer the questions that follow.

The Comet Shoemaker-Levy 9

Paragraph

1   In the 1990s, a comet had an overly close encounter with the planet Jupiter. **6A** The comet, which was named Shoemaker-Levy 9, came too close to the planet Jupiter in 1992. **6B** As a result, Jupiter's powerful gravity caused the comet to break into pieces. **6C** Two years later, in 1994, the pieces of the comet crashed into Jupiter and caused huge explosions. **6D**

2   There was some bad luck and some good luck for astronomers on Earth who wanted to see the explosions when the fragments of the comet hit Jupiter. The bad luck was that the comet pieces hit the side of Jupiter that astronomers on Earth could not see. There was some better luck when the spacecraft *Galileo* was on the far side of Jupiter and sent images of the explosion back to astronomers on Earth. In addition, as Jupiter rotated after the explosions, astronomers were able to look through telescopes and see the areas on Jupiter that the pieces of the comet had hit and see the damage caused by them.

1. The word "encounter" in paragraph 1 is closest in meaning to
   Ⓐ trip
   Ⓑ number
   Ⓒ friendship
   Ⓓ meeting

2. According to the passage, what was Shoemaker-Levy 9?
   Ⓐ A planet
   Ⓑ A comet
   Ⓒ A piece of a comet
   Ⓓ An explosion

3. Which of the sentences below best expresses the essential information in the highlighted sentence in paragraph 1?
   Ⓐ Therefore, the comet broke up because of Jupiter's strong gravity.
   Ⓑ The result of Jupiter's powerful gravity was that Jupiter broke apart.
   Ⓒ The comet's powerful gravity caused pieces of Jupiter to break off.
   Ⓓ When the comet came close, Jupiter's gravity became more powerful.

4. The passage states that, in 1994
   Ⓐ the comet flew past Jupiter
   Ⓑ parts of the comet hit Jupiter
   Ⓒ Jupiter crashed into the comet and exploded
   Ⓓ the comet exploded before it hit Jupiter

5. It can be inferred from paragraph 1 that
   Ⓐ the comet did not break up until it hit Jupiter
   Ⓑ huge explosions in Jupiter caused the comet to break up
   Ⓒ it took a lot of time for the pieces of the comet to hit Jupiter after the comet broke up
   Ⓓ the powerful gravity caused the pieces of the comet to hit Jupiter immediately after the comet broke up

6. Look at the four squares [■] that indicate where the following sentence could be added to paragraph 1.

   The number of pieces was actually 21.

   Where would the sentence best fit? Click on a square [■] to add the sentence to the paragraph.

7. The word "fragments" in paragraph 2 is closest in meaning to
   Ⓐ lights
   Ⓑ pieces
   Ⓒ causes
   Ⓓ strengths

8. It is indicated in paragraph 2 that the astronomers did NOT
   Ⓐ see the pieces of the comet hit Jupiter
   Ⓑ want to see the pieces of the comet hit Jupiter
   Ⓒ see the pictures of an explosion
   Ⓓ want to see the pictures of an explosion

9. The word "images" in paragraph 2 is closest in meaning to
   Ⓐ ideas
   Ⓑ pieces
   Ⓒ news
   Ⓓ pictures

10. The author uses the phrase "In addition" in paragraph 2 to show that
- Ⓐ there were more changes
- Ⓑ all of the luck was not good
- Ⓒ the damage resulted from the explosions
- Ⓓ there was more good luck

11. The word "rotated" in paragraph 2 is closest in meaning to
- Ⓐ shone
- Ⓑ turned
- Ⓒ brightened
- Ⓓ shrank

12. The word "them" in paragraph 2 refers to
- Ⓐ astronomers
- Ⓑ telescopes
- Ⓒ areas
- Ⓓ pieces

13.

Directions: An introductory sentence for a brief summary of the passage is provided below. Complete the summary by selecting the THREE answer choices that express the most important ideas in the passage. **This question is worth 2 points** (2 points for 3 correct answers, 1 point for 2 correct answers, and 0 points for 1 or 0 correct answers).
There was good and bad luck when a comet came close to Jupiter.
 • • •

Answer Choices (choose 3 to complete the chart):

(1) It was bad luck that *Galileo* was in the area of the explosion.

(2) It was good luck that astronomers saw the damage caused by the pieces of the comet hitting Jupiter.

(3) It was bad luck that the pieces of the comet hit a certain side of Jupiter.

(4) It was good luck that *Galileo* was in the area of the explosion.

(5) It was good luck that astronomers saw the pieces of the comet hitting Jupiter.

(6) It was good luck that the pieces of the comet hit a certain side of Jupiter.

READING 2

Read the passage.

Paragraph

The Age of Earth

1   There has been a lot of confusion about Earth's age throughout history. Until the nineteenth century, scientists held a really mistaken belief about the age of our planet. Prior to this time, they had thought that Earth was created around 4,000 or 5,000 B.C.

2   In the middle of the nineteenth century, British physicist Lord Kelvin, the person that the Kelvin temperature scale is named after, came up with a very different idea about Earth's age. His idea may have been well-reasoned, but it was, unfortunately, also incorrect. Lord Kelvin determined Earth's age based upon its temperature. Scientists at the time understood that Earth's center was very hot, much hotter than Earth's surface. Lord Kelvin determined Earth's age by calculating how long it would take the surface to cool down from the scorching temperatures inside. Based on these calculations, Lord Kelvin calculated that Earth was approximately 100 million years old.

3   Lord Kelvin's calculation of Earth's age was better than previous calculations, but it was still not an accurate estimate. It was not correct because Lord Kelvin did not understand the effect of radioactivity on the cooling of Earth's surface. Radioactivity occurs naturally on Earth, and radioactivity creates heat. The naturally occurring radioactivity on Earth has caused Earth to cool much less swiftly than Lord Kelvin had calculated. In the twentieth century, based on an understanding of the effect of radioactivity on the cooling of Earth's surface, scientists calculated that Earth is between 4 and 5 billion years old.

Refer to this version of the passage to answer the questions that follow.

The Age of Earth

Paragraph

1   There has been a lot of confusion about Earth's age throughout history. Until the nineteenth century, scientists held a really mistaken belief about the age of our planet. Prior to this time, they had thought that Earth was created around 4,000 or 5,000 B.C.

2   In the middle of the nineteenth century, British physicist Lord Kelvin, the person that the Kelvin temperature scale is named after, came up with a very different idea about Earth's age. **18A** His idea may have been well-reasoned, but it was, unfortunately, also incorrect. **18B** Lord Kelvin determined Earth's age based upon its temperature. Scientists at the time understood that Earth's center was very hot, much hotter than Earth's surface. **18C** Lord Kelvin determined Earth's age by calculating how long it would take the surface to cool down from the scorching temperatures inside. **18D** Based on these calculations, Lord Kelvin calculated that Earth was approximately 100 million years old.

3   Lord Kelvin's calculation of Earth's age was better than previous calculations, but it was still not an accurate estimate. It was not correct because Lord Kelvin did not understand the effect of radioactivity on the cooling of Earth's surface. Radioactivity occurs naturally on Earth, and radioactivity creates heat. The naturally occurring radioactivity on Earth has caused Earth to cool much less swiftly than Lord Kelvin had calculated. In the twentieth century, based on an understanding of the effect of radioactivity on the cooling of Earth's surface, scientists calculated that Earth is between 4 and 5 billion years old.

14. The word "confusion" in paragraph 1 is closest in meaning to
- Ⓐ surprise
- Ⓑ misunderstanding
- Ⓒ anger
- Ⓓ agreement

15. It can be inferred from paragraph 1 that early scientists believed that Earth was
- Ⓐ 2,000 to 3,000 years old
- Ⓑ 4,000 to 5,000 years old
- Ⓒ 6,000 to 7,000 years old
- Ⓓ 8,000 to 10,000 years old

16. Why does the author mention "the person that the Kelvin temperature scale is named after" in paragraph 2?
- Ⓐ Because the author thinks this information might help the reader to recognize the name
- Ⓑ Because the author thinks the reader does not know about the Kelvin temperature scale
- Ⓒ Because the author wants to make the paragraph more interesting
- Ⓓ Because the author wants to discuss the Kelvin temperature scale thoroughly

17. Which of the following best restates the highlighted sentence in paragraph 2?
- Ⓐ He had good reasons but, sadly, broke the law.
- Ⓑ Sadly, he knew that his idea was wrong.
- Ⓒ It was fortunate that his idea was reasonable.
- Ⓓ He thought clearly but, sadly, made a mistake.

18. Look at the four squares [■] that indicate where the following sentence could be added to paragraph 2.

They knew this from studies of active volcanoes at the time.

Where would the sentence best fit? Click on a square [■] to add the sentence to the paragraph.

19. The word "scorching" in paragraph 2 is closest in meaning to
- Ⓐ growing
- Ⓑ freezing
- Ⓒ burning
- Ⓓ aging

20. According to paragraph 2, Lord Kelvin
- Ⓐ was American
- Ⓑ wanted to determine Earth's age
- Ⓒ was a biologist
- Ⓓ determined Earth's age correctly

21. Which of the following could best replace the word "calculated" in paragraph 2?
- Ⓐ Determined
- Ⓑ Added
- Ⓒ Argued
- Ⓓ Taught

22. The author mentions "Lord Kelvin's calculation" at the beginning of paragraph 3 because
- Ⓐ this is an interesting new point
- Ⓑ this refers to a key point in paragraph 2
- Ⓒ Lord Kelvin did not really make the calculation
- Ⓓ this will be the topic of paragraph 3

23. The word "it" in paragraph 3 refers to
- Ⓐ calculation
- Ⓑ Earth
- Ⓒ age
- Ⓓ estimate

24. Which of the following is NOT true about radiation, according to paragraph 3?
- Ⓐ It causes heat to build.
- Ⓑ It affects the cooling of the Earth.
- Ⓒ It can occur without any help from humans.
- Ⓓ It was thoroughly understood by Lord Kelvin.

25. The expression "much less swiftly" in paragraph 3 could best be replaced by

Ⓐ much more rapidly
Ⓑ much less softly
Ⓒ much more slowly
Ⓓ much less evenly

26.

Directions: Select the appropriate phrases from the answer choices, and match them to the appropriate scientist category. **This question is worth 3 points** (3 points for 5 correct answers, 2 points for 4 correct answers, 1 point for 3 correct answers, and 0 points for 2, 1, or 0 correct answers).	
early scientists	•
Lord Kelvin	• •
twentieth-century scientists	• •

Answer Choices (choose 5 to complete the table):

(1) Believed Earth was 4,000 to 5,000 years old

(2) Believed Earth was 100 million years old

(3) Made calculations based on temperature and radioactivity

(4) Believed Earth was less than 7,000 years old

(5) Made calculations based on radioactivity but not temperature

(6) Believed Earth was 4 to 5 billion years old

(7) Made calculations based on temperature but not radioactivity

READING 3

Read the passage.

Paragraph

Elizabeth Cady Stanton

1   Elizabeth Cady Stanton lived from 1815 to 1902. She was important in obtaining the right to vote for American women.

2   Elizabeth was born into a wealthy family in 1815. She was the daughter of a judge. She had many opportunities in her childhood, and she was headed toward the normal life as the daughter in a wealthy family.

3   Her life changed considerably after she married. She married abolitionist Henry Stanton. He was against slavery, and he was working hard to end slavery. Elizabeth went with her husband to attend the World Anti-Slavery Convention. At the anti-slavery convention, Elizabeth and the other women who were attending the conference were not allowed to take part in the convention. The men who were running the conference forced all the women to sit behind curtains and did not allow them to participate in discussions during the convention. At this convention, Elizabeth and some of the other women decided to change their focus from fighting against slavery to fighting for rights for women.

4   In the period after the anti-slavery convention, Elizabeth wrote an article named "Declaration of Sentiments." She wrote this article in the style of the Declaration of Independence. In the Declaration of Independence, America declared its independence from England. In Elizabeth's "Declaration of Sentiments," women declared their independence from men.

5   A conference dedicated to rights for women was held in 1848 in Seneca Falls, New York. Seneca Falls was the hometown of Elizabeth and her husband. More than 200 women and 40 men attended this conference. At the conference, the people discussed Elizabeth's "Declaration of Sentiments." After a while, the conference agreed to all of the points in the documents. They even agreed to the demand for women to have the right to vote.

6   Elizabeth worked hard for the right to vote for American women for the rest of her life. By the time of Elizabeth's death in 1902, women had gotten the right to vote in only a few states in the United States. In 1920, eighteen years after Elizabeth's death, the U.S. Congress changed the Constitution and gave all American women the right to vote.

Refer to this version of the passage to answer the questions that follow.

Elizabeth Cady Stanton

Paragraph

1   Elizabeth Cady Stanton lived from 1815 to 1902. She was important in obtaining the right to vote for American women.

2   Elizabeth was born into a wealthy family in 1815. She was the daughter of a judge. She had many opportunities in her childhood, and she was headed toward the normal life as the daughter in a wealthy family.

3   Her life changed considerably after she married. She married abolitionist Henry Stanton. **32A** He was against slavery, and he was working hard to end slavery. **32B** Elizabeth went with her husband to attend the World Anti-Slavery Convention. **32C** At the anti-slavery convention, Elizabeth and the other women who were attending the conference were not allowed to take part in the convention. **32D** The men who were running the conference forced all the women to sit behind curtains and did not allow them to participate in discussions during the convention. At this convention, Elizabeth and some of the other women decided to change their focus from fighting against slavery to fighting for rights for women.

4   In the period after the anti-slavery convention, Elizabeth wrote an article named "Declaration of Sentiments." She wrote this article in the style of the Declaration of Independence. In the Declaration of Independence, America declared its independence from England. In Elizabeth's "Declaration of Sentiments," women declared their independence from men.

5   A conference dedicated to rights for women was held in 1848 in Seneca Falls, New York. Seneca Falls was the hometown of Elizabeth and her husband. More than 200 women and 40 men attended this conference. At the conference, the people discussed Elizabeth's "Declaration of Sentiments." After a while, the conference agreed to all of the points in the documents. They even agreed to the demand for women to have the right to vote.

6   Elizabeth worked hard for the right to vote for American women for the rest of her life. By the time of Elizabeth's death in 1902, women had gotten the right to vote in only a few states in the United States. In 1920, eighteen years after Elizabeth's death, the U.S. Congress changed the Constitution and gave all American women the right to vote.

27. The word "obtaining" in paragraph 1 is closest in meaning to

(A) getting

(B) giving

(C) losing

(D) buying

28. What is NOT true about Elizabeth Cady Stanton, according to paragraph 2?

(A) Her family was not poor.

(B) She was born in the early nineteenth century.

(C) Her father was a judge.

(D) She had very few opportunities.

29. According to paragraph 3, an abolitionist

(A) owns slaves

(B) likes to work hard

(C) wants to end slavery

(D) is a husband

30. The expression "take part in" in paragraph 3 could best be replaced by

(A) take hold of

(B) work on

(C) think about

(D) participate in

31. The word "them" in paragraph 3 refers to

(A) men

(B) women

(C) curtains

(D) discussions

32. Look at the four squares [■] that indicate where the following sentence could be added to paragraph 3.

This conference took place in London.

Where would the sentence best fit? Click on a square [■] to add the sentence to the paragraph.

33. It is implied in paragraph 3 that the actions of the men at the conference

(A) caused Elizabeth to decide to fight for women's rights

(B) pleased Elizabeth and the other women at the conference

(C) showed that the men believed in women's rights

(D) caused Elizabeth to decide to work against slavery

34. Why does the author mention the "Declaration of Independence" in paragraph 4?

(A) Because Elizabeth helped to write it

(B) Because Elizabeth believed in every part of it

(C) Because Elizabeth used it as a model for an article

(D) Because Elizabeth felt that it gave the right to vote to women

35. It is stated in paragraph 5 that the Seneca Falls conference

(A) had under 200 attendees

(B) created the "Declaration of Sentiments" article

(C) agreed to the points in the "Declaration of Sentiments"

(D) disagreed about the right of women to vote

36. The word "rest" in paragraph 6 could best be replaced by

(A) remainder

(B) sleep

(C) time

(D) interest

37. Which of the sentences below best expresses the essential information in the highlighted sentence in paragraph 6?

Ⓐ Women had the right to vote throughout the United States when Elizabeth died in 1902.

Ⓑ Elizabeth herself was able to vote before she died in 1902.

Ⓒ Elizabeth died trying to get the right to vote for American women, but she was not successful in any states.

Ⓓ When Elizabeth died in 1902, women were not able to vote in many places in the United States.

38. The author mentions "1920, eighteen years after Elizabeth's death" in paragraph 6 because that was when

Ⓐ Elizabeth's death was first celebrated

Ⓑ women first voted for Elizabeth

Ⓒ Elizabeth's goal was finally reached

Ⓓ the U.S. Congress was finally established

39.

Directions: An introductory sentence for a brief summary of the passage is provided below. Complete the summary by selecting the THREE answer choices that express the most important ideas in the passage. **This question is worth 2 points** (2 points for 3 correct answers, 1 point for 2 correct answers, and 0 points for 1 or 0 correct answers).
The passage describes key points in Elizabeth's life work.
•   •   •

Answer Choices (choose 3 to complete the chart):

(1) She had the normal life as the daughter of a wealthy family.

(2) She worked hard to end slavery.

(3) She took part in a conference dedicated to women's rights.

(4) She wrote an article declaring that women were independent.

(5) Her treatment at a conference convinced her to work for women's rights.

(6) She took part in writing the Declaration of Independence.

Turn to pages 448–450 to *diagnose* your errors and *record* your results.

LISTENING

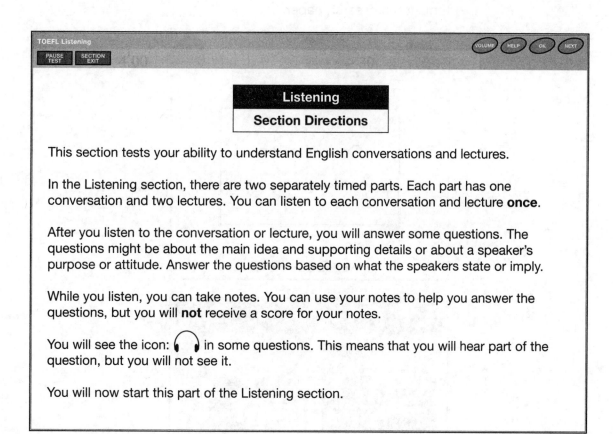

PAUSE TEST | SECTION EXIT

VOLUME | HELP | OK | NEXT

Listening

Section Directions

This section tests your ability to understand English conversations and lectures.

In the Listening section, there are two separately timed parts. Each part has one conversation and two lectures. You can listen to each conversation and lecture **once**.

After you listen to the conversation or lecture, you will answer some questions. The questions might be about the main idea and supporting details or about a speaker's purpose or attitude. Answer the questions based on what the speakers state or imply.

While you listen, you can take notes. You can use your notes to help you answer the questions, but you will **not** receive a score for your notes.

You will see the icon: 🎧 in some questions. This means that you will hear part of the question, but you will not see it.

You will now start this part of the Listening section.

Questions 1–5

Listen as a student consults with her professor. The conversation is about the topic for a research paper.

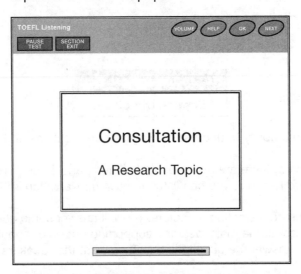

1. What does the student want to talk about?
   Ⓐ The due date for a paper
   Ⓑ What she will write about
   Ⓒ The topic of the next lecture
   Ⓓ A paper she wrote

2. Why is the professor unable to talk now?
   Ⓐ He has another meeting.
   Ⓑ He has an office hour.
   Ⓒ He has to prepare for class.
   Ⓓ He needs to go to class.

3. Listen again to part of the passage. Then answer the question. 🎧

   How does the professor seem to feel?
   Ⓐ Displeased
   Ⓑ Grateful
   Ⓒ Amused
   Ⓓ Eager

4. On which day does this conversation most likely take place?
   Ⓐ Monday
   Ⓑ Tuesday
   Ⓒ Wednesday
   Ⓓ Thursday

5. When are the student and professor scheduled to meet?
   Ⓐ Later that day
   Ⓑ The next morning
   Ⓒ The next afternoon
   Ⓓ During the next class

Questions 6–10

Listen as a student consults with his professor. The consultation is about an assignment.

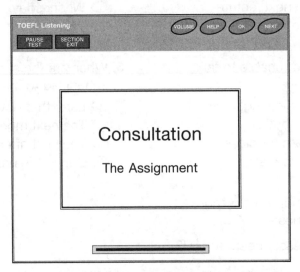

6. Why does the student go to see the professor?

    Ⓐ To find out when an assignment is due

    Ⓑ To find out what he should do to complete an assignment

    Ⓒ To find out why he did not do well on an assignment

    Ⓓ To find out how he can do better on the next exam

7. Listen again to part of the passage. Then answer the question.

    What does the professor mean when she says this:

    Ⓐ "I understand the problem."

    Ⓑ "I can see your paper."

    Ⓒ "I don't know what happened."

    Ⓓ "I don't see a problem."

8. How did the student seem to think he did on the assignment?

    Ⓐ He knew he wrote on the wrong topic.

    Ⓑ He thought he turned the assignment in late.

    Ⓒ He knew he received a high grade.

    Ⓓ He thought he wrote on the right topic.

9. What problem did the student have?

    Ⓐ He wrote about the causes of the Civil War.

    Ⓑ He did not turn the paper in on time.

    Ⓒ He did not write a paper on the Civil War.

    Ⓓ He did not write about the causes of the Civil War.

10. What message does the professor want the student to understand?

    Ⓐ That the professor's specific assignments should be followed exactly

    Ⓑ That it is always important to do assignments

    Ⓒ That the student should have a better understanding of the causes of the Civil War

    Ⓓ That assignments should always be completed on time

Questions 11–16

Listen to a lecture in a government class. The lecture is on the Pentagon.

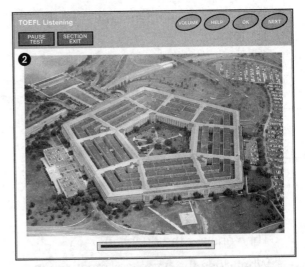

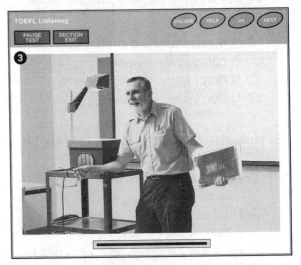

11. What does the professor mainly discuss?

Ⓐ The various uses of the Pentagon

Ⓑ The unusual location of the Pentagon

Ⓒ The reason the Pentagon has five sides

Ⓓ The structure and construction of the Pentagon

12. Which of these are true about the Pentagon? **This question is worth 2 points** (2 points for 3 correct answers, 1 point for 2 correct answers, and 0 points for 1 or 0 correct answers).

> Click on 3 answers.

Ⓐ It is a military fort.

Ⓑ It is a huge office building.

Ⓒ It has five sides and five stories.

Ⓓ It houses the Department of the Interior.

Ⓔ It was built in only about two years.

13. Approximately how many people work in the Pentagon?

Ⓐ 250

Ⓑ 2,500

Ⓒ 25,000

Ⓓ 250,000

14. Listen again to part of the passage. Then answer the question. 🎧

What does the professor mean when he says this: 🎧

Ⓐ "I'm sure you already know this."

Ⓑ "I know you won't like what I'm going to say."

Ⓒ "Maybe you're not sure of this."

Ⓓ "I don't like saying this."

15. What is a "pentad" most likely to be?

Ⓐ A period of five years

Ⓑ A type of apartment

Ⓒ A young fish

Ⓓ A recent advertisement

16. In which decade was the Pentagon constructed?

Ⓐ In the 1920s

Ⓑ In the 1930s

Ⓒ In the 1940s

Ⓓ In the 1950s

Questions 17–22

Listen to a lecture in a theater course. The lecture is on the musical *The Unsinkable Molly Brown*.

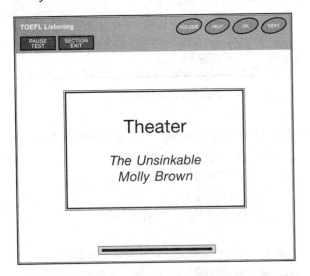

17. What is the topic of this talk?

- Ⓐ The story of a famous ship disaster
- Ⓑ The relationship between a real person and a play
- Ⓒ The relationship between a musical and a movie
- Ⓓ The history of a very famous event

18. What does the professor say about Molly Brown?

Click on 2 answers.

- Ⓐ She did not really exist.
- Ⓑ She is alive today.
- Ⓒ She really existed.
- Ⓓ She lived about 100 years ago.

19. What is implied in the lecture about Molly Brown?

- Ⓐ She never saw the musical about her life.
- Ⓑ She wrote the musical about her life.
- Ⓒ She never traveled on a ship.
- Ⓓ She acted in a musical about her life.

20. Listen again to part of the passage. Then answer the question. 🎧

What does the professor mean when she says this: 🎧

- Ⓐ "I don't think you know about the *Titanic*."
- Ⓑ "I'm sure all of you enjoy going to the movies."
- Ⓒ "I'm going to tell you now about a famous event."
- Ⓓ "I'm sure you already know about the *Titanic*."

21. In the lecture, the professor discusses events in Molly's life. Put these events in the correct order. **This question is worth 2 points** (2 points for 4 correct answers, 1 point for 3 or 2 correct answers, and 0 points for 1 or 0 correct answers).

> Click on a sentence. Then drag it to the space where it belongs. Use each sentence only once.

A musical about Molly was created.
Molly became rich.
Molly survived a ship disaster.
Molly traveled to Europe.

1. _____
2. _____
3. _____
4. _____

22. What happened in each of these places? **This question is worth 2 points** (2 points for 3 correct answers, 1 point for 2 correct answers, and 0 points for 1 or 0 correct answers).

> Click on a phrase. Then drag it to the space where it belongs. Each answer will be used one time only.

Was where Molly traveled	Was where a show about Molly was presented	Was where Molly lived
Denver	**Europe**	**New York**

Questions 23–28

Listen to a discussion in an astronomy class. The discussion is on Olympus Mons.

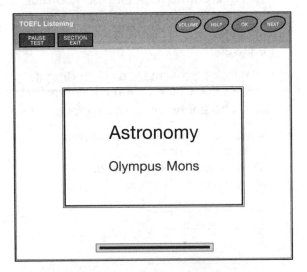

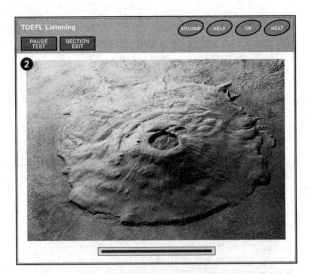

23. Where is Olympus Mons located?

ⓐ On Mount Olympus

ⓑ Near Mount Everest

ⓒ On the Moon

ⓓ On the planet Mars

24. Listen again to part of the passage. Then answer the question. 🎧

How does Judy seem to feel about her response?

ⓐ She thinks she is completely wrong.

ⓑ She is completely sure of her response.

ⓒ She is not quite sure of her response.

ⓓ She is making a wild guess.

25. What is stated about the caldera on Olympus Mons?

Click on 2 answers.

Ⓐ It is half as deep as the Grand Canyon.

Ⓑ It is twice as deep as the Grand Canyon.

Ⓒ It is 1 mile deep.

Ⓓ It is 2 miles deep.

26. Listen again to part of the passage. Then answer the question. 🎧

Why does the professor say this?

ⓐ To announce the start of a new topic

ⓑ To use up remaining class time

ⓒ To suggest that the students are not paying attention

ⓓ To show that a review of information is about to begin

27. Which of the following has a shield volcano?

ⓐ Mount Everest

ⓑ Mount St. Helens

ⓒ The Grand Canyon

ⓓ The Hawaiian Islands

28. Is each of these true according to the lecture? **This question is worth 2 points** (2 points for 4 correct answers, 1 point for 3 correct answers, and 0 points for 2, 1, or 0 correct answers).

For each answer, click in the YES or NO column.

	YES	NO
Olympus Mons is shorter than Mount Everest.		
Olympus Mons has a caldera.		
The Grand Canyon has a caldera.		
Olympus Mons is a shield volcano.		

Questions 29-34

Listen to a lecture in an engineering class. The professor is talking about dams.

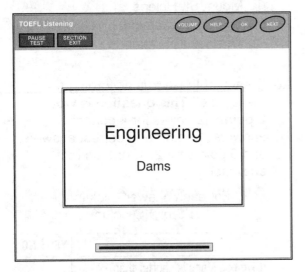

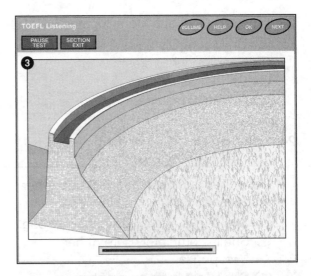

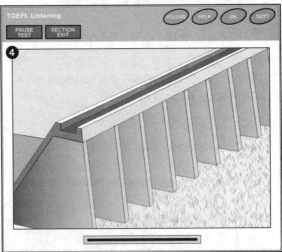

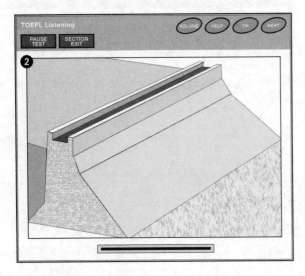

PAUSE TEST   SECTION EXIT

VOLUME   HELP   OK   NEXT

6

29. **Listen again to part of the passage. Then answer the question.**

What does the professor mean?

Ⓐ "We have a very special topic today."

Ⓑ "I hope you always pay attention."

Ⓒ "This is a really difficult topic."

Ⓓ "This topic is not going to be very interesting."

30. How is each type of dam described in the lecture? **This question is worth 2 points** (2 points for 3 correct answers, 1 point for 2 correct answers, and 0 points for 1 or 0 correct answers).

Click on a phrase. Then drag it to the space where it belongs. Each answer will be used one time only.

Is a straight dam without supports	Is a curved dam	Is a dam with supports
An arch dam	**A buttress dam**	**A gravity dam**

31. What is the purpose of the arch in an arch dam?

Ⓐ To give the dam a modern style rather than an older style

Ⓑ To transfer some of the weight of the water to the sides of the dam

Ⓒ To provide buttresses to support the dam wall

Ⓓ To help to force the water up against the dam wall

32. Which of these are true about Hoover Dam? **This question is worth 2 points** (2 points for 3 correct answers, 1 point for 2 correct answers, and 0 points for 1 or 0 correct answers).

Click on 3 answers.

Ⓐ It is a buttress dam.

Ⓑ It was a cause of the Great Depression.

Ⓒ It is an arch dam.

Ⓓ It is not in the state of Colorado.

Ⓔ It provided work during the Great Depression.

33. Why does the professor mention the Great Depression in a passage on dams?

Ⓐ To show why a certain dam was built

Ⓑ To introduce a new topic to the lecture

Ⓒ To show the result of building a certain dam

Ⓓ To make the lecture more interesting

34. What is stated about the name of the dam discussed in the lecture?

Click on 2 answers.

Ⓐ It was originally named Boulder Dam.

Ⓑ It was originally named Hoover Dam.

Ⓒ Its name was later changed to Boulder Dam.

Ⓓ Its name was later changed to Hoover Dam.

Turn to pages 451–453 to *diagnose* your errors and *record* your results.

SPEAKING

Speaking
Section Directions

This section tests your ability to speak about different topics. You will answer six questions. Answer each one as completely as you can.

Questions 1 and 2 will be about familiar topics. Try to speak about the topics clearly and coherently.

Questions 3 and 4 will include reading and listening. First, you will read a short passage. Then the text will disappear, and you will hear a talk about the same topic. Next you will answer a question about the text and the talk. Try to use information from the text and the talk to answer the question clearly and coherently to show that you understood the text and the talk.

Questions 5 and 6 will include part of a conversation or a lecture and a question. Try to answer the question clearly and coherently, using information from the conversation or lecture.

While you read and listen, you can take notes. You can use your notes to help you answer the questions.

Listen closely to the directions for each question. They will not appear on the screen.

Questions 1–6

Question 1

Read the question. Take notes on the main points of a response. Then respond to the question.

> What gift would you like to receive most? Use reasons in your response.

> Preparation Time: 15 seconds
> Response Time: 45 seconds

INTRODUCTION:

SUPPORTING IDEA 1:

SUPPORTING IDEA 2:

CONCLUSION:

Question 2

Read the question. Take notes on the main points of a response. Then respond to the question.

> If someone says something mean to you, is it better for you to say something or to say nothing? Use reasons in your response.

> Preparation Time: 15 seconds
> Response Time: 45 seconds

INTRODUCTION:

SUPPORTING IDEA 1:

SUPPORTING IDEA 2:

CONCLUSION:

Question 3

Read the passage. Take notes on the main points of the reading passage.

Reading Time: 45 seconds

Part of a syllabus from a math class

There is a lot of work in this class, so you should take this class only if you are ready to work very hard. There are quizzes every Monday and Wednesday, and homework assignments are due every Tuesday and Thursday. An exam will be given every Friday. You should think about all of this very carefully, and then you should decide if you want to stay in this class or move to a different class.

TOPIC OF READING PASSAGE:

main points about the topic:

-

-

-

Listen to the passage. Take notes on the main points of the listening passage.

TOPIC OF LISTENING PASSAGE:

main points about the topic:

-

-

Now answer the following question:

How does the information in the listening passage add to the ideas in the reading passage?

| Preparation Time: 30 seconds |
| Response Time: 60 seconds |

Question 4

Read the passage. Take notes on the main points of the reading passage.

Reading Time: 45 seconds

New Amsterdam

In 1612, Dutch explorers from the Netherlands traveled to an island in the Hudson River. This island was the island of Manhattan, the island where New York City is located today. The Dutch landed on the island and created a settlement there. They named the settlement New Amsterdam after a city in their homeland. The settlement by the Dutch on Manhattan was rather small. The Dutch settlement was on only one part of the island, the eastern tip of the island.

TOPIC OF READING PASSAGE:

main points about the topic:

-
-
-

Listen to the passage. Take notes on the main points of the listening passage.

TOPIC OF LISTENING PASSAGE:

main points about the topic:

•

•

•

Now answer the following question:

How does the information in the listening passage add to the ideas in the reading passage?

Preparation Time: 30 seconds
Response Time: 60 seconds

Question 5

Listen to the passage. Take notes on the main points of the listening passage.

TOPIC OF LISTENING PASSAGE:

<u>main points about the topic:</u>

-

-

-

-

Now answer the following question:

What are the students saying about their math books?

Preparation Time: 20 seconds
Response Time: 60 seconds

Question 6

Listen to the passage. Take notes on the main points of the listening passage.

TOPIC OF LISTENING PASSAGE:

main points about the topic:

•

•

•

Now answer the following question:

> What does the professor have to say about the
> Continental Divide?

> Preparation Time: 20 seconds
> Response Time: 60 seconds

Turn to pages 454–465 to *assess* the skills used in the test, *score* the test
using the Speaking Scoring Criteria, and *record* your results.

WRITING

Writing
Section Directions

This section tests your ability to communicate in writing in an academic environment. There are two writing tasks.

In the first writing task, you will read a passage and listen to a lecture. Then you will answer a question using information from the passage and the lecture. In the second task, you will answer a question using your own background knowledge.

Integrated Writing Directions

For this task, you will read a passage about an academic topic. You have **3 minutes** to read the passage, and then the passage will disappear. Then you will hear a lecture about the same topic. You can take notes while you read and listen.

You will then write an answer to a question about the relationship between the reading passage and the lecture. Try to use information from the passage and the lecture to answer the question. You will **not** be asked for your personal opinion. You can see the reading passage again when you are ready to write. You can use your notes to help you. You have **20 minutes** to write your response.

A successful answer will usually be around 150 to 225 words. Try to show that you can write well and give complete, accurate information.

Remember that you can see the passage again when you write your response. As soon as the reading time ends, the lecture will begin.

Independent Writing Directions

In this task, you will write an essay that states, explains, and supports your opinion about an issue. You have **30 minutes** to plan, write, and revise your essay.

A successful essay will usually be at least 300 words. Try to show that you can write well by developing your ideas, organizing your essay, and using language accurately to express your ideas.

Question 1

Read the passage. Take notes on the main points of the reading passage.

Reading Time: 3 minutes

Today, some businesses are allowing their workers to telecommute. When workers telecommute, they work from home and communicate with their offices by computer or telephone.

Last year, Sylvia Martin decided to telecommute. She thought it would be so much better to work at home than to work in the office. She thought about the possible advantages of telecommuting. She thought, first of all, that she would have much more time for work by telecommuting. After all, she would not have to spend any time traveling to and from the office. In addition, she thought telecommuting would be better than working in the office because her co-workers would not be able to disturb her. When she is working in the office now, her co-workers come into her office a lot and interrupt her work. She also thought that telecommuting would be better than working in the office because of her boss. When she is working in the office now, her boss checks on her work often throughout the day, perhaps as many as five times a day. She thinks that her boss will not be able to check her work so much if she telecommutes, and she is happy about that.

TOPIC OF READING PASSAGE:

main points about the topic:

-

-

-

Listen to the passage. Take notes on the main points of the listening passage.

TOPIC OF LISTENING PASSAGE:

main points about the topic:

-

-

-

Now answer the following question:

How does the information in the listening passage challenge the information in the reading passage?

| Preparation Time: 1 minute |
| Response Time: 20 minutes |

Question 2

Read the question. Take notes on the main points of a response. Then write your response.

Do you prefer to go out in the evening or to stay home with friends? Why?

Response Time: 30 minutes

INTRODUCTION:

SUPPORTING PARAGRAPH 1:

SUPPORTING PARAGRAPH 2:

CONCLUSION:

Turn to pages 466–472 to *assess* the skills used in the test, *score* the test using the Writing Scoring Criteria, and *record* your results.

TOEFL-LEVEL TEST

READING

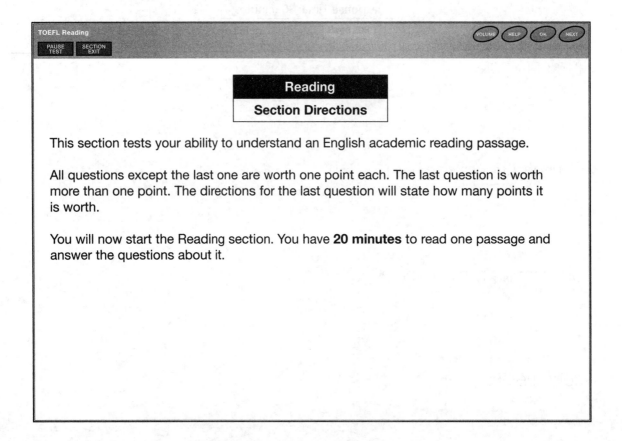

Read the passage.

Paragraph

Pepper

▶1 The spice pepper, which is obtained from the vine *Piper nigrum,* has had a long and interesting history, one that dates back three or four thousand years. Pepper originated in the monsoonal areas of southwest India and from there was brought to the Mediterranean by Arab traders, where it was a much-sought-after commodity.

▶2 The Greeks valued the medical benefits of pepper. As early as 400 B.C., the Greek physician Hippocrates was prescribing pepper to deal with various medical complaints, and a century later pepper was listed in a medical text as an antidote to poisoning. During this period, it was quite difficult to get hold of pepper because the Arab traders who dealt with the spice did not want their Mediterranean customers to know where it came from. The Greeks were willing to pay the exorbitant prices necessary to obtain pepper because it was considered so valuable, but they also put a great deal of effort into determining how to set up trade routes of their own to get pepper. The Greeks eventually managed to do so.

▶3 Just as the Greeks had held pepper in high regard, the Romans also placed a high value on pepper. However, unlike the Greeks, who had valued pepper for its medicinal properties, the Romans looked at pepper as a highly prized flavoring for food. The value that the Romans placed on pepper can be seen in the prominence of the *Via Piperatica,* or "Pepper Street," in Rome's spice market. Pepper's value can also be seen in the actions of the Visigoths as they laid siege to Rome while the Roman Empire was in a state of decline. In addition to asking the Romans for huge quantities of their gold, silver, and silk to lift the siege, the Visigoths also demanded huge quantities of the Romans' pepper. The Romans paid what the Visigoths asked to be free from the siege.

▶4 During the Middle Ages, pepper retained its position as a valuable commodity. During this era, pepper was used alongside gold as a medium of exchange; in addition, it was possible to pay rents and taxes with pepper or to create dowries for blushing brides with the same. It was a lust for pepper that was, at least in part, responsible for prodding fifteenth-century explorers to head to the East.

▶5 One of the goals of the European explorers at the end of the fifteenth century was the acquisition of pepper. When Christopher Columbus made his voyage to the New World, one of his many goals was to bring spices back to Europe from the East. Upon his arrival in the New World, Columbus was unable to find any *Piper nigrum* plants to take back to Europe; he found another spicy plant, the chili, and named it pepper and took it back to Europe along with the claim that he had found a new kind of pepper. Then, only a few years after Columbus started his explorations, Portuguese explorer Vasco de Gama managed to travel around the Horn of Africa to reach India and the *Piper nigrum* plants there.

▶6 Pepper added an interesting footnote to history in the seventeenth century. In 1672, a young man from New England named Elihu Yale traveled to India to work as a clerk, a low-paying position, at the British East India Company. At the time, the British East India Company was in control of a huge part of the pepper trade between Asia and the West. Over the years that Elihu Yale worked at the British East India Company, he became remarkably wealthy, a rather suspicious result from someone who was working as a clerk and a result that most likely came about because of some rather nefarious dealings on Yale's part. When Yale donated some of his ill-gotten wealth to a small college in Connecticut, the college demonstrated how thankful it was for this donation by changing its name to Yale. Today, Yale is one of the top U.S. universities, in very small part because of pepper.

Refer to this version of the passage to answer the questions that follow.

Paragraph

Pepper

▶1   The spice pepper, which is obtained from the vine *Piper nigrum,* has had a long and interesting history, one that dates back three or four thousand years. Pepper originated in the monsoonal areas of southwest India and from there was brought to the Mediterranean by Arab traders, where it was a much-sought-after commodity.

▶2   The Greeks valued the medical benefits of pepper. **3A** As early as 400 B.C., the Greek physician Hippocrates was prescribing pepper to deal with various medical complaints, and a century later pepper was listed in a medical text as an antidote to poisoning. **3B** During this period, it was quite difficult to get hold of pepper because the Arab traders who dealt with the spice did not want their Mediterranean customers to know where it came from. **3C** The Greeks were willing to pay the exorbitant prices necessary to obtain pepper because it was considered so valuable, but they also put a great deal of effort into determining how to set up trade routes of their own to get pepper. **3D** The Greeks eventually managed to do so.

▶3   Just as the Greeks had held pepper in high regard, the Romans also placed a high value on pepper. However, unlike the Greeks, who had valued pepper for its medicinal properties, the Romans looked at pepper as a highly prized flavoring for food. The value that the Romans placed on pepper can be seen in the prominence of the *Via Piperatica,* or "Pepper Street," in Rome's spice market. Pepper's value can also be seen in the actions of the Visigoths as they laid siege to Rome while the Roman Empire was in a state of decline. In addition to asking the Romans for huge quantities of their gold, silver, and silk to lift the siege, the Visigoths also demanded huge quantities of the Romans' pepper. The Romans paid what the Visigoths asked to be free from the siege.

▶4   During the Middle Ages, pepper retained its position as a valuable commodity. During this era, pepper was used alongside gold as a medium of exchange; in addition, it was possible to pay rents and taxes with pepper or to create dowries for blushing brides with the same. It was a lust for pepper that was, at least in part, responsible for prodding fifteenth-century explorers to head to the East.

▶5   One of the goals of the European explorers at the end of the fifteenth century was the acquisition of pepper. When Christopher Columbus made his voyage to the New World, one of his many goals was to bring spices back to Europe from the East. Upon his arrival in the New World, Columbus was unable to find any *Piper nigrum* plants to take back to Europe; he found another spicy plant, the chili, and named it pepper and took it back to Europe along with the claim that he had found a new kind of pepper. Then, only a few years after Columbus started his explorations, Portuguese explorer Vasco de Gama managed to travel around the Horn of Africa to reach India and the *Piper nigrum* plants there.

▶6   Pepper added an interesting footnote to history in the seventeenth century. In 1672, a young man from New England named Elihu Yale traveled to India to work as a clerk, a low-paying position, at the British East India Company. At the time, the British East India Company was in control of a huge part of the pepper trade between Asia and the West. Over the years that Elihu Yale worked at the British East India Company, he became remarkably wealthy, a rather suspicious result from someone who was working as a clerk and a result that most likely came about because of some rather nefarious dealings on Yale's part. When Yale donated some of his ill-gotten wealth to a small college in Connecticut, the college demonstrated how thankful it was for this donation by changing its name to Yale. Today, Yale is one of the top U.S. universities, in very small part because of pepper.

1. The word "commodity" in paragraph 1 is closest in meaning to
   - Ⓐ prize
   - Ⓑ product
   - Ⓒ demand
   - Ⓓ food

2. According to paragraph 2, it is NOT stated that the Greeks
   - Ⓐ used pepper to treat various illnesses
   - Ⓑ paid dearly to obtain pepper from traders
   - Ⓒ began traveling to India to obtain pepper
   - Ⓓ traded pepper with other Mediterranean countries

3. Look at the four squares [■] that indicate where the following sentence could be added to paragraph 2.

   The Arab traders knew, and the Greeks did not, that pepper was grown in India.

   Where would the sentence best fit? Click on a square [■] to add the sentence to the paragraph.

4. According to paragraph 3, the Romans
   - Ⓐ used pepper as a medicine
   - Ⓑ used pepper as their only food
   - Ⓒ created a street where pepper was grown
   - Ⓓ needed pepper to pay off invaders

5. The author uses the word "also" in paragraph 3 in order to
   - Ⓐ announce a second example of pepper's value to the Romans
   - Ⓑ show a second way the Romans used *Via Piperatica*
   - Ⓒ demonstrate a second way the Romans used pepper
   - Ⓓ indicate a second way the Visigoths demanded payment

6. The expression "a medium" in paragraph 4 could best be replaced by
   - Ⓐ a middle
   - Ⓑ an instrument
   - Ⓒ an average
   - Ⓓ a plan

7. It can be inferred from paragraph 4 that dowries were used
   - Ⓐ to pay for pepper and other spices
   - Ⓑ to make a woman a more attractive marriage partner
   - Ⓒ to pay rent or taxes when there was not enough gold
   - Ⓓ to finance the travels of fifteenth-century explorers

8. The expression "the same" in paragraph 4 refers to
   - Ⓐ pepper
   - Ⓑ gold
   - Ⓒ rents and taxes
   - Ⓓ dowries

9. Which of the sentences below best expresses the essential information in the highlighted sentence in paragraph 5?
   - Ⓐ Because *Piper nigrum* was unavailable in Europe, Columbus found some in the New World and brought it back to Europe.
   - Ⓑ Columbus believed that chili, and not *Piper nigrum,* was actually pepper.
   - Ⓒ Columbus substituted a new plant for pepper and called it a variation of pepper.
   - Ⓓ Columbus mixed *Piper nigrum* with chili to create a new kind of pepper that was popular with Europeans.

10. A "footnote to history" in paragraph 6 is most likely

   Ⓐ a summarized account of an event

   Ⓑ a statement contradicting something that has been said

   Ⓒ an impediment to an action that needs to be taken

   Ⓓ a small but interesting piece of related information

11. It can be inferred from paragraph 6 that Elihu Yale

   Ⓐ attended Yale University

   Ⓑ owned the British East India Company

   Ⓒ dedicated most of his life to improving education

   Ⓓ ended up with more money than he started out with

12. The word "nefarious" in paragraph 6 is closest in meaning to

   Ⓐ underhanded

   Ⓑ brilliant

   Ⓒ importune

   Ⓓ generous

13.

Directions:	Select the appropriate phrases from the answer choices, and match them to the appropriate people. **This question is worth 3 points** (3 points for 5 correct answers, 2 points for 4 correct answers, 1 point for 3 correct answers, and 0 points for 2, 1, or 0 correct answers).
the Greeks	• •
the Romans	• •
Columbus	•

Answer Choices (choose 5 to complete the table):

(1) Used pepper as a medicine

(2) Brought *Piper nigrum* from the Americas to Europe

(3) Used pepper to flavor foods

(4) Eventually found a way to get pepper

(5) Used pepper to pay for an attack on the Visigoths

(6) Brought a substitute for pepper to Europe

(7) Created an area where pepper was traded

Turn to pages 448–450 to *diagnose* your errors and *record* your results.

LISTENING

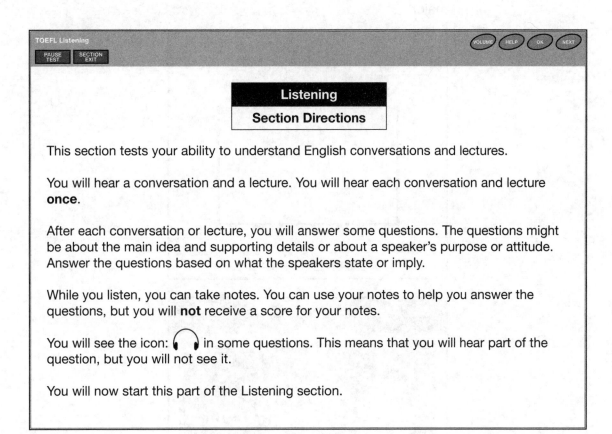

PAUSE
TEST

SECTION
EXIT

VOLUME   HELP   OK   NEXT

Listening
Section Directions

This section tests your ability to understand English conversations and lectures.

You will hear a conversation and a lecture. You will hear each conversation and lecture **once**.

After each conversation or lecture, you will answer some questions. The questions might be about the main idea and supporting details or about a speaker's purpose or attitude. Answer the questions based on what the speakers state or imply.

While you listen, you can take notes. You can use your notes to help you answer the questions, but you will **not** receive a score for your notes.

You will see the icon: 🎧 in some questions. This means that you will hear part of the question, but you will not see it.

You will now start this part of the Listening section.

Questions 1–5

Listen as a student consults with her advisor. The conversation is about her major.

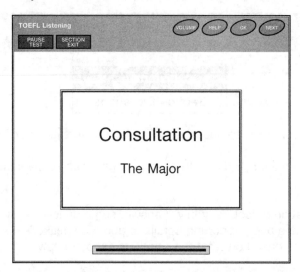

1. What does the student want to do?

Ⓐ Declare a history major

Ⓑ Change her major to history

Ⓒ Change her major from art

Ⓓ Become an art major

2. How does the advisor seem to feel about the student's request at first?

Ⓐ Enthusiastic

Ⓑ Cautious

Ⓒ Unconcerned

Ⓓ Very negative

3. What kind of help does the student want from the advisor?

Ⓐ Help in understanding how much this change will affect her

Ⓑ Help in understanding how to change a major

Ⓒ Help in understanding what it takes to complete a history major

Ⓓ Help in understanding how to major in two subjects

4. Listen again to part of the passage. Then answer the question. 🎧

What does the advisor mean when he says this: 🎧

Ⓐ "Let's postpone this for now."

Ⓑ "Let's take care of this right away."

Ⓒ "Let's try to figure out a better way to do this."

Ⓓ "Let's finish up this appointment now."

5. What arrangement do the student and advisor make?

Ⓐ To meet at exactly three o'clock the next day

Ⓑ To meet just before a three o'clock class

Ⓒ To meet shortly after a class the next day

Ⓓ To meet at three-ten today

Questions 6–11

Listen to a lecture in an engineering class. The professor is talking about the geodesic dome.

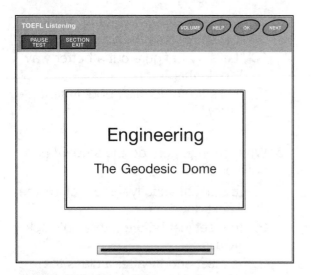

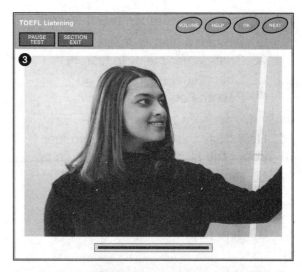

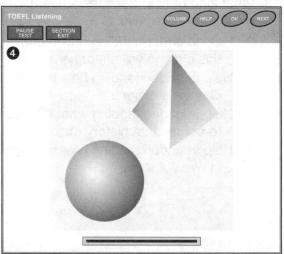

6. Is each of these true about the geodesic dome? **This question is worth 2 points** (2 points for 4 correct answers, 1 point for 3 correct answers, and 0 points for 2, 1, or 0 correct answers).

For each statement, click in the YES or NO column.

	YES	NO
It is relatively light in weight.		
It is relatively heavy in weight.		
It is unable to withstand high stress.		
It is able to withstand high stress.		

7. When was the first geodesic dome created?

Ⓐ In the 1920s
Ⓑ In the 1940s
Ⓒ In the 1960s
Ⓓ In the 1980s

8. What are the characteristics of a sphere?

Click on 2 answers.

Ⓐ Low volume
Ⓑ Low surface area
Ⓒ High volume
Ⓓ High surface area

9. What are the characteristics of a tetrahedron?

Click on 2 answers.

Ⓐ Low volume
Ⓑ Low surface area
Ⓒ High volume
Ⓓ High surface area

10. How do these structures stand up to pressure? **This question is worth 2 points** (2 points for 3 correct answers, 1 point for 2 correct answers, and 0 points for 1 or 0 correct answers).

Click on a phrase. Then drag it to the space where it belongs. Each answer will be used one time only.

Is strongest against internal pressure	Is strongest against both types of pressure	Is strongest against external pressure

A geodesic dome	**A sphere**	**A tetrahedron**

11. Overall, how does the professor seem to feel about the geodesic dome?

Ⓐ She thinks it is interesting but useless.
Ⓑ She thinks it is more abstract than practical.
Ⓒ She thinks it is positive in some respects and negative in others.
Ⓓ She thinks it has numerous positive characteristics.

Turn to pages 451–453 to *diagnose* your errors and *record* your results.

SPEAKING

This section tests your ability to speak about different topics. You will answer six questions. Answer each one as completely as you can.

Questions 1 and 2 will be about familiar topics. Try to speak about the topics clearly and coherently.

Questions 3 and 4 will include reading and listening. First, you will read a short passage. Then the text will disappear, and you will hear a talk about the same topic. Next you will answer a question about the text and the talk. Try to use information from the text and the talk to answer the question clearly and coherently to show that you understood the text and the talk.

Questions 5 and 6 will include part of a conversation or a lecture and a question. Try to answer the question clearly and coherently, using information from the conversation or lecture.

While you read and listen, you can take notes. You can use your notes to help you answer the questions.

Listen closely to the directions for each question. They will not appear on the screen.

Questions 1–6

Question 1

Read the question. Take notes on the main points of a response. Then respond to the question.

> What three adjectives would you use to describe yourself? Use reasons to support your response.

> | Preparation Time: 15 seconds |
> | Response Time: 45 seconds |

INTRODUCTION:

SUPPORTING IDEA 1:

SUPPORTING IDEA 2:

SUPPORTING IDEA 3:

CONCLUSION:

Question 2

Read the question. Take notes on the main points of a response. Then respond to the question.

> Do you plan your life carefully, or do you let things happen as they may? Use examples to support your response.

> | Preparation Time: 15 seconds |
> | Response Time: 45 seconds |

INTRODUCTION:

SUPPORTING IDEA 1:

SUPPORTING IDEA 2:

CONCLUSION:

Question 3

Read the passage. Take notes on the main points of the reading passage.

Reading Time: 45 seconds

A notice posted at the campus cafeteria

A change is taking place in the campus cafeteria in order to better serve the campus community. The campus cafeteria is pleased to announce new hours in the campus cafeteria. The new cafeteria hours will go into effect one week from today. As of Monday, February 1, the campus cafeteria will be open the following hours: 7:00–9:00 A.M., 12:00–2:00 P.M., and 5:00–7:00 P.M. We hope that the campus community is pleased with these new hours.

TOPIC OF READING PASSAGE:

main points about the topic:

-

-

-

Listen to the passage. Take notes on the main points of the listening passage.

TOPIC OF LISTENING PASSAGE:

main points about the topic:

•

•

•

Now answer the following question:

How does the information in the listening passage add to the
ideas in the reading passage?

| Preparation Time: 30 seconds |
| Response Time: 60 seconds |

Question 4

Read the passage. Take notes on the main points of the reading passage.

> Reading Time: 45 seconds

Operant Conditioning

The role of operant conditioning in influencing human behavior is an area of interest of psychologists. Operant conditioning occurs when people learn from the consequences of their behavior. Positive consequences, or positive reinforcement, in reaction to a behavior, whether that behavior is positive or negative, will encourage that behavior to continue. Conversely, negative consequences, or negative reinforcement, in reaction to a behavior, whether that behavior is positive or negative, will discourage that behavior from continuing. Consequences in reaction to behaviors can have a strong impact on whether or not these behaviors continue.

TOPIC OF READING PASSAGE:

main points about the topic:

•

•

Listen to the passage. Take notes on the main points of the listening passage.

TOPIC OF LISTENING PASSAGE:

main points about the topic:

-

-

Now answer the following question:

How does the information in the listening passage add to the ideas in the reading passage?

| Preparation Time: 30 seconds |
| Response Time: 60 seconds |

Question 5

Listen to the passage. Take notes on the main points of the listening passage.

TOPIC OF LISTENING PASSAGE:

<u>main points about the topic</u>:

-

-

-

-

-

-

Now answer the following question:

How do the students seem to feel about Professor Nelson's class?

| Preparation Time: 20 seconds |
| Response Time: 60 seconds |

Question 6

Listen to the passage. Take notes on the main points of the listening passage.

TOPIC OF LISTENING PASSAGE:

main points about the topic:

-

-

-

-

Now answer the following question:

What points does the professor make about the asteroid belt?

Preparation Time: 20 seconds
Response Time: 60 seconds

Turn to pages 454–465 to *assess* the skills used in the test, *score* the test using the Speaking Scoring Criteria, and *record* your results.

WRITING

This section tests your ability to communicate in writing in an academic environment. There are two writing tasks.

In the first writing task, you will read a passage and listen to a lecture. Then you will answer a question using information from the passage and the lecture. In the second task, you will answer a question using your own background knowledge.

Integrated Writing Directions

For this task, you will read a passage about an academic topic. You have **3 minutes** to read the passage, and then the passage will disappear. Then you will hear a lecture about the same topic. You can take notes while you read and listen.

You will then write an answer to a question about the relationship between the reading passage and the lecture. Try to use information from the passage and the lecture to answer the question. You will **not** be asked for your personal opinion. You can see the reading passage again when you are ready to write. You can use your notes to help you. You have **20 minutes** to write your response.

A successful answer will usually be around 150 to 225 words. Try to show that you can write well and give complete, accurate information.

Remember that you can see the passage again when you write your response. As soon as the reading time ends, the lecture will begin.

Independent Writing Directions

In this task, you will write an essay that states, explains, and supports your opinion about an issue. You have **30 minutes** to plan, write, and revise your essay.

A successful essay will usually be at least 300 words. Try to show that you can write well by developing your ideas, organizing your essay, and using language accurately to express your ideas.

Questions 1-2

Question 1
Read the passage. Take notes on the main points of the reading passage.

> Reading Time: 3 minutes

Phrenology is a theory in the field of psychology, one that ascribes to the idea that the human skull carries physical markers of personality traits. It is a theory that was developed by two German psychiatrists, Franz Joseph Gall and Johann Kasper Spurzheim, early in the nineteenth century. According to this theory, different areas of the brain control different aspects of behavior, and certain personality traits are therefore related to specific areas of the brain. This theory, for example, says that a sense of kindness is located in one place in the brain, while a sense of combativeness is in a different place, and a sense of caution is located somewhere else in the brain.

Gall and Spurzheim further believed that the physical marks of bumps and bulges developed on the head as a result of outstanding personality traits. To them, a bump or a bulge in a certain location on the skull might indicate that a person possesses artistic genius, while a bump or bulge in a different location means that someone possesses the personality traits of a serial killer.

Phrenology was extremely popular in the field of psychology in the first half of the nineteenth century. Many leading scientists, doctors, educators, and other famous people believed that phrenology could explain human personality; Queen Victoria of England and American author Edgar Allen Poe were among those who believed that phrenology held the key to human personality. They believed that the first step in the study of human personality traits was to find the locations in the brain that the personality traits were tied to.

TOPIC OF READING PASSAGE:

main points about the topic:

-

-

-

Listen to the passage. Take notes on the main points of the listening passage.

TOPIC OF LISTENING PASSAGE:

main points about the topic:

-

-

-

Now answer the following question:

How does the information in the listening passage cast doubt on the information in the reading passage?

| Preparation Time: 1 minute |
| Response Time: 20 minutes |

Question 2

Read the question. Take notes on the main points of a response. Then write your response.

> Some students have been coming late to class. What should the teacher do about this situation? Use reasons and details to support your response.

> Response Time: 30 minutes

INTRODUCTION:

SUPPORTING PARAGRAPH 1:

SUPPORTING PARAGRAPH 2:

SUPPORTING PARAGRAPH 3:

CONCLUSION:

> Turn to pages 466–472 to *assess* the skills used in the test, *score* the test using the Writing Scoring Criteria, and *record* your results.

APPENDIXES

APPENDIX A
SENTENCE STRUCTURE _____

It is important when you are producing material on the TOEFL *iBT* that you use a variety of correct sentence structures. You should be sure that you know how to use correct simple sentences, compound sentences, and complex sentences.

Appendix A1: USE CORRECT SIMPLE SENTENCES

A simple sentence is a sentence that has only one **clause**. This means that the sentence has one subject and verb.

> The <u>student</u> suddenly <u>jumped</u> out of his chair.
>   SUBJECT   VERB

> The <u>ideas</u> in the paper <u>were</u> unclear.
>   SUBJECT   VERB

The first sentence is correct because it has a subject *student* and a verb *jumped*. The second sentence is correct because it has a subject *ideas* and a verb *were*.

For each simple sentence, you should check that the sentence has both a subject and a verb. Study the following incorrect sentences. (An asterisk [*] indicates that a sentence is not correct.)

> A <u>letter</u> written to her family.*
> SUBJECT

> Usually <u>is</u> necessary to register early.*
>   VERB

> In the first moment at the start of the lecture.*

The first sentence is incorrect because it has the subject *letter* but is missing a verb. The second sentence is incorrect because it has the verb *is* but is missing a subject. The third sentence is incorrect because it is missing both a subject and a verb.

USING CORRECT SIMPLE SENTENCES
1. A simple sentence is a sentence with *one clause*.
2. A simple sentence must have both a *subject* and a *verb*.

APPENDIX EXERCISE A1: Underline the subjects once and the verbs twice. Then indicate if the sentences are correct (C) or incorrect (I).

__I__ 1. Unfortunately <u>forgot</u> to turn in her paper on time.

      (*she forgot*)

_____ 2. The plane took off more than an hour late.

_____ 3. The reason for his late arrival.

_____ 4. My best friends in the world they are coming to visit.

_____ 5. We understand completely.

_____ 6. Behind the first door to the left at the top of the stairs.

_____ 7. The picture is on the wall is very pretty.

_____ 8. The student almost finished the exam on time.

_____ 9. The athlete winning the race at an international competition.

_____ 10. At the end of the first act of the play.

_____ 11. The player hurt himself in the first half of the game.

_____ 12. The chapter in the textbook it was not very interesting.

_____ 13. Gladly accepted first prize in the contest.

_____ 14. The invitation to the party lists the time, the date, and the location.

_____ 15. The program is on television this evening is my favorite program.

Appendix A2: USE CORRECT COMPOUND SENTENCES

A compound sentence is a sentence that has more than one **main clause**. This means that the sentence has more than one subject and verb and that each subject and verb is joined to another subject and verb with a coordinate connector (*and, but, or, so, yet*).

My <u>friends</u> <u><u>will leave</u></u> this evening, **or** <u>they</u> <u><u>will stay</u></u> until tomorrow.
   SUBJECT   VERB   SUBJECT   VERB

The <u>student</u> <u><u>worked</u></u> hard on the project, **but** her <u>grade</u> <u><u>was</u></u> not good.
   SUBJECT   VERB   SUBJECT   VERB

The first sentence is correct because it has two main clauses, *friends will leave* and *they will stay*. These two main clauses are joined with a comma and the coordinate connector *or*. The second sentence is correct because it has two main clauses, *student worked* and *grade was*. These main clauses are joined with the coordinate connector *but*.

For each compound sentence, you should check that each main clause has a subject and a verb. Then you should check that each pair of main clauses is joined with a comma and a coordinate connector. Study the following incorrect sentences.

You <u>need</u> to register for classes, **so** <u>can do</u> this now.*
SUBJECT VERB   VERB

He usually <u>takes</u> the bus, <u>he</u> most likely <u>is</u> on the bus now.*
SUBJECT VERB   SUBJECT VERB

The first sentence is incorrect because it has a complete main clause *you need* and an incomplete main clause *can do*, which are joined by a comma and the coordinate connector *so*. The second sentence is incorrect because it has two main clauses, *he . . . takes* and *he . . . is*, but it is missing a connector.

USING CORRECT COMPOUND SENTENCES

1. A compound sentence is a sentence with two (or more) *main clauses.*
2. Each *main clause* must have a subject and a verb.
3. Each pair of main clauses must be joined with a comma (,) and a coordinate connector (*and, but, or, so, yet*).

APPENDIX EXERCISE A2: Underline the subjects once and the verbs twice in the main clauses. Put parentheses around the punctuation and connectors that join the main clauses. Then indicate if the sentences are correct (C) or incorrect (I).

__I__ 1. Some <u>students</u> <u>were</u> late to class(,) the <u>teacher</u> <u>was</u> very unhappy about this.
(*, and*)

_____ 2. My roommates decided to go out, but I did not go out with them.

_____ 3. I need to leave now, or will not be able to get home on time.

_____ 4. The students did not understand the concept so the teacher gave them another example.

_____ 5. It was really late, yet she did not feel at all sleepy.

_____ 6. The child fell out of the tree, and he broke his arm in three places.

_____ 7. I did not want to take a physics class, but had to anyway.

_____ 8. You need to take your key with you, or you will be locked out of the dormitory.

_____ 9. Traffic was terrible so we decided to wait until later to leave.

_____ 10. The pie looked delicious, yet none of the guests any of it.

_____ 11. I gave you my word I intend to keep it.

_____ 12. He watered the plants regularly, but they still do not look healthy.

_____ 13. The athlete needs to attend daily practices, or she will not do well in the competition.

_____ 14. The boss was out of the office, so the workers did not get much done.

_____ 15. There were no more tickets for the concerts yet many people stayed in the ticket line.

Appendix A3: USE CORRECT COMPLEX SENTENCES

A complex sentence is a sentence that has a main clause and at least one **subordinate clause**. This means that the sentence has a subject and verb in the main clause and another subject and verb in the subordinate clause. It also means that each subordinate clause is joined to the main clause with a subordinate clause connector.

Adverb clauses are one of three types of subordinate clauses (the other two are adjective clauses and noun clauses). Adverb clauses may come either before the main clause or after the main clause. If an adverb clause comes before the main clause, it is followed by a comma. Adverb clauses are introduced by connectors such as *after, as, before, since, until, when, while, because, if, whether, although, even though,* and *though.*

> The <u>student</u> <u>has attended</u> this college **since** <u>he graduated</u> from high school.
>   SUBJECT   VERB   SUBJECT VERB

> **When** <u>you</u> <u>ask</u> for help, <u>you</u> <u>will get</u> a lot of help.
>   SUBJECT VERB   SUBJECT VERB

The first sentence is correct because it has the main clause *student has attended* and the subordinate clause *he graduated,* which is joined to the main clause with the subordinate connector *since*. The second sentence is correct because it has the main clause *you will get* and the subordinate clause *you ask,* which is joined to the main clause with the subordinate connector *when*.

For each complex sentence containing an adverb clause, you should first check that the main clause has a subject and a verb. Then you should check that the adverb clause has a subject and verb and is joined to the main clause with a subordinate connector. You should also check that the adverb clause is followed by a comma if the adverb clause comes before the main clause.

> The <u>teacher</u> <u>graded</u> the papers **after** <u>collected</u> them from the students.*
>   SUBJECT VERB   VERB

> **Because** the <u>car</u> <u>is</u> low on gas <u>we</u> <u>cannot drive</u> into the city.*
>   SUBJECT VERB   SUBJECT   VERB

The first sentence is incorrect because it has a complete main clause *teacher graded* and an incomplete subordinate clause *collected,* which is joined to the main clause with the subordinate connecter *after.* The incomplete subordinate clause needs a subject to be complete. The second sentence has a complete subordinate clause *car is,* which is joined to the main clause *we cannot drive* with the subordinate connector *because.* This sentence is incorrect because the subordinate clause connector comes before the main clause but there is not a comma following the subordinate clause.

USING CORRECT COMPLEX SENTENCES

1. A complex sentence is a sentence with *one main clause* and at least *one subordinate clause.*
2. Each clause must have a *subject* and a *verb.*
3. Each subordinate clause must be joined to the main clause with a *subordinate connector.*
4. An adverb clause may come *before* or *after* the main clause.
5. If an adverb clause comes before the main clause, the adverb clause must be followed by a *comma.*

APPENDIX EXERCISE A3: Underline the subjects once and the verbs twice in the main clauses. Put parentheses around the punctuation and connectors that join the clauses. Then indicate if the sentences are correct (C) or incorrect (I).

__I__ 1. The <u>students</u> <u><u>left</u></u> the room sadly(, after) <u>they</u> <u><u>turned in</u></u> their exam papers.
   (sadly after)

_____ 2. When the guests arrived at the house, they knocked on the door.

_____ 3. You need to do your homework whether want to or not.

_____ 4. I asked the professor several questions, I still did not understand.

_____ 5. We entered the gym just as the game was starting.

_____ 6. Even though I do not want to take the class I still have to anyway.

_____ 7. I am not going to start the next assignment until I see my grade on the last one.

_____ 8. If you turn in the homework on time, you will not lose any points.

_____ 9. I have not had time to do anything enjoyable since got this job.

_____ 10. Before you write the paper you must research the topic thoroughly.

_____ 11. After I saw my grade on the paper.

_____ 12. The mother cried when she heard the good news.

_____ 13. The electricity was turned off, because the bill was not paid for months.

_____ 14. Until you take the introductory course, you are unable to enroll in the advanced course.

_____ 15. He got a good grade on his presentation even he had not prepared very much.

APPENDIX REVIEW EXERCISE (A1–A3): Underline the subjects once and the verbs twice. Put parentheses around the punctuation and connectors that join the clauses. Then indicate if the sentences are correct (C) or incorrect (I).

__I__ 1. Everything in the box it needs to be thrown out.
    (omit *it*)

_____ 2. The professor ended the long lecture, and the students left the lecture hall quickly.

_____ 3. Though the party was scheduled to end at midnight it did not end until 1:00 A.M.

_____ 4. The phone number on the business card turned out to be wrong.

_____ 5. I would like to help you next weekend, I do not have any extra time.

_____ 6. You can visit the professor during office hours if you want to talk to her.

_____ 7. In the classroom at the end of the hall.

_____ 8. The students need to turn in their papers by 4:00 this afternoon, or they will receive failing grades.

_____ 9. Because the television program was enjoyable.

_____ 10. The reason for this behavior seems clear.

_____ 11. They left home ten minutes late this morning, so were ten minutes late to work.

_____ 12. I need to write the number down, before I forget it.

_____ 13. The flowers on the table in the dining room.

_____ 14. It was freezing outside, yet the children still wanted to play in the yard.

_____ 15. While my roommates were at the movies, I was studying in the dormitory.

APPENDIX B

ERROR CORRECTION _____

It is important when you are producing material on the TOEFL *iBT* that your English be grammatically correct. You should be sure that you know how to use agreement, parallel structure, verb forms, nouns and pronouns, and adjectives and adverbs correctly.

Appendix B1: MAKE VERBS AGREE AFTER PREPOSITIONAL PHRASES

It is important to make sure that subjects and verbs agree. This means that a singular subject must have a singular verb, and a plural subject must have a plural verb. There can be confusion in making a subject agree with the verb when a prepositional phrase comes between the subject and the verb. Study the following incorrect sentences.

> The *reason* (for these results) *are** not clear.

> The *directions* (to the event) *is** on the invitation.

In the first example, you might think that *results* is the subject because it comes directly in front of the verb *are*. However, *results* is not the subject because it is the object of the preposition *for*. The subject of the sentence is the singular noun *reason*, so the verb should be changed from the plural *are* to the singular *is*. In the second example, you might think that *event* is the subject because it comes directly in front of the verb *is*. However, *event* is not the subject because it is the object of the preposition *to*. The subject of the sentence is the plural noun *directions*, so the verb should be changed from the singular *is* to the plural *are*.

The following chart outlines the key information you should remember about subject-verb agreement with prepositional phrases.

MAKING VERBS AGREE AFTER PREPOSITIONAL PHRASES
When a *prepositional phrase* comes between the *subject* and the *verb*, be sure that the verb agrees with the *subject* and not with the *object of the preposition*.

APPENDIX EXERCISE B1: Each of the following sentences has one or more prepositional phrases between the subject and the verb. Underline the subjects once and the verbs twice. Put parentheses around the prepositional phrases between the subjects and the verbs. Then indicate if the sentences are correct (C) or incorrect (I).

__I__ 1. The <u>doors</u> (to the room) <u>was</u> both locked.

      (*were*)

_____ 2. The reason for the problems are not clear.

_____ 3. The pictures on the wall to the right are not straight.

_____ 4. The dirt on the windows needs to be cleaned.

_____ 5. The first chapters of the novel takes a long time to read.

_____ 6. The exam on the lectures are scheduled for next Tuesday.

_____ 7. The buildings around the corner were built from brick.

_____ 8. The discussion about the issues starts in one hour.

_____ 9. The words to the song has an interesting story.

_____ 10. The news about the fires in the mountains is not good.

Appendix B2: MAKE VERBS AGREE AFTER EXPRESSIONS OF QUANTITY

It is also important to make sure that subjects and verbs agree when expressions of quantity are used as subjects. An expression of quantity (*all, most, some, half, none*) can be singular or plural, depending on what follows the preposition *of*. Study the following incorrect sentences.

> *All* (of the *books*) *was** on the floor.

> *Most* (of the *book*) *were** really interesting.

> *Some* (of the *music*) *are** wonderful.

In the first example, the singular verb *was* should be changed to the plural verb *were* because the subject *all* refers to the plural noun *books*. In the second example, the singular verb *were* should be changed to the singular verb *was* because the subject *most* refers to the singular noun *book*. In the third example, the plural verb *are* should be changed to the singular verb *is* because the subject *some* refers to the uncountable noun *music*.

The following chart outlines the key information you should remember about subject-verb agreement with expressions of quantity.

MAKING VERBS AGREE AFTER EXPRESSIONS OF QUANTITY
When an expression of quantity using *of* is the subject, the verb agrees with the object of the preposition *of*.

APPENDIX EXERCISE B2: Each of the following sentences has a quantity expression as the subject. Underline the subjects once and the verbs twice. Put parentheses around the prepositional phrases between the subjects and the verbs. Then indicate if the sentences are correct (C) or incorrect (I).

__I__ 1. None (of the reasons) makes any sense.

   (*make*)

_____ 2. Some of the plants need water.

_____ 3. All of the children is playing in the yard now.

_____ 4. Part of the time has to be spent studying.

_____ 5. Half of this chapter covers one theory.

_____ 6. Most of the words was difficult to understand.

_____ 7. None of the movie is very funny at all.

_____ 8. Part of the letter contain good news.

_____ 9. Some of the students have passed the exam.

_____ 10. Half of the food taste good, but not all of it does.

APPENDIX REVIEW EXERCISE (B1–B2): Underline the subjects once and the verbs twice. Put parentheses around the prepositional phrases between the subjects and the verbs. Then indicate if the sentences are correct (C) or incorrect (I).

__I__ 1. The students (in the dormitory) gets little sleep.

   (*get*)

_____ 2. All of the walls was covered in purple paint.

_____ 3. The meeting for freshmen lasts for three hours.

_____ 4. Part of the house is burning in the fire.

_____ 5. The houses along the shore was damaged in the hurricane.

_____ 6. Most of the information has to be explained.

_____ 7. The road through the mountains twists and turns a lot.

_____ 8. Some of the pages of the book was torn.

_____ 9. Several paragraphs in the essay needs to be rewritten.

_____ 10. Half of the people in the room understand the lecture.

Appendix B3: USE PARALLEL STRUCTURE WITH COORDINATE CONJUNCTIONS

It is important to check for parallel structure with coordinate conjunctions. When a coordinate conjunction (*and, but, or*) joins two or more words or expressions, the words or expressions must be equal structures. Study the following incorrect sentences.

> He *came* to the meeting **but** *not saying** anything.

> The girl spilled juice *on her dress* **and** *it was on the floor.**

In the first example, the coordinate conjunction *but* joins the verb *came* and the gerund *not saying*. The verb *did not say* is needed in place of the gerund. In the second example, the coordinate conjunction *and* joins the prepositional phrase *on her dress* and the clause *it was on the floor*. The prepositional phrase *on the floor* is needed in place of the clause.

The following chart outlines the key information that you should remember about parallel structure with coordinate conjunctions.

USING PARALLEL STRUCTURE WITH COORDINATE CONJUNCTIONS		
(same structure)	*and* *but* *or*	(same structure)

APPENDIX EXERCISE B3: Each of the following sentences contains words or groups of words that should be parallel. Put parentheses around the words that indicate that the sentence should have parallel parts. Underline the parts that should be parallel. Then indicate if the sentences are correct (C) or incorrect (I).

__I__ 1. The new teacher is <u>funny</u>, <u>interesting</u>, (and) <u>organize</u>.

    (*organized*)

_____ 2. He came over early but did not offer to help.

_____ 3. Your purse may be in the kitchen or in the dining room.

_____ 4. We are going to the market, the bank, and to the pharmacy.

_____ 5. They drove carefully but quick to the hospital.

_____ 6. Do you prefer classes that are early in the morning or late in the evening?

_____ 7. The mother talked softly and with patience to the naughty child.

_____ 8. The students spent a long time on the assignment but done well on it.

_____ 9. More effort or ability is needed for success in the tournament.

_____ 10. There are stores to the north and the south but not to the east or the west.

Appendix B4: USE PARALLEL STRUCTURE WITH PAIRED CONJUNCTIONS

It is important to check for parallel structure with paired conjunctions. The words or expressions that follow each part of a paired conjunction (*both . . . and, either . . . or, neither . . . nor, not only . . . but also*) must be equal structures. Study the following incorrect sentences.

> The teacher **both** *lectured* **and** *she gave** an exam.

> They are **either** *happy* **or** *are sad** about the news.

> The money is **neither** *on the table* **nor** *the desk.**

> I like **not only** *dancing* **but also** *to sing.**

In the first example, the paired conjunctions *both . . . and* are followed by the verb *lectured* and the subject and verb *she gave.* You can make this parallel by changing the subject and verb *she gave* to the verb *gave.* In the second example, the paired conjunctions *either . . . or* are followed by the adjective *happy* and the verb and adjective *are sad.* You can make this parallel by changing the verb and adjective *are sad* to the adjective *sad.* In the third example, the paired conjunctions *neither . . . nor* are followed by the prepositional phrase *on the table* and the noun *the desk.* You can make this parallel by changing the noun *the desk* to the prepositional phrase *on the desk.* In the last example, the paired conjunctions *not only . . . but also* are followed by the gerund *dancing* and the infinitive *to sing.* You can make this parallel by changing the infinitive *to sing* to the gerund *singing.*

The following chart outlines the key information you should remember about parallel structure with paired conjunctions.

USING PARALLEL STRUCTURE WITH PAIRED CONJUNCTIONS			
both *either* *neither* *not only*	(same structure)	*and* *or* *nor* *but also*	(same structure)

APPENDIX EXERCISE B4: Each of the following sentences contains words or groups of words that should be parallel. Put parentheses around the words that indicate that the sentence should have parallel parts. Underline the parts that should be parallel. Then indicate if the sentences are correct (C) or incorrect (I).

__I__ 1. The students can choose to prepare (either) <u>a paper</u> or <u>choose a presentation</u>. (*or a presentation*)

_____ 2. I lost both the key to my car and the key to my apartment.

_____ 3. He drove neither carelessly nor at a fast speed.

_____ 4. The actor not only sang but also dancing in the movie.

_____ 5. Either one person or the other person must fill out the form.

_____ 6. She is both surprised by and thankful for the award.

_____ 7. I neither lied to you nor to her.

_____ 8. The teacher assigned not only a paper to write but also to read a chapter.

_____ 9. You can work either in the morning or in the afternoon.

_____ 10. She works both in the library and the cafeteria.

APPENDIX REVIEW EXERCISE (B3–B4): Each of the following sentences contains words or groups of words that should be parallel. Put parentheses around the words that indicate that the sentence should have parallel parts. Underline the parts that should be parallel. Then indicate if the sentences are correct (C) or incorrect (I).

__C__ 1. The students worked on the project (not only) <u>in class</u> (but also) <u>at the library</u>.

_____ 2. My sister has studied law but has not become a lawyer.

_____ 3. The lecture was neither amusing nor was it interesting.

_____ 4. This month we can buy a new sofa or a new table.

_____ 5. You may either go home now or you may stay here until later.

_____ 6. She is dedicated, studious, and a hardworking student.

_____ 7. There is food both in the refrigerator and the cabinet.

_____ 8. The injured child has seen a nurse but not a doctor.

_____ 9. My boss expects me to write not only quickly but also to write correctly.

_____ 10. The secretary can give you the answer or at least tell you how to find the answer.

Appendix B5: USE THE PAST PARTICIPLE AFTER *HAVE*

Whenever you see the helping verb *have* in any of its forms (*have, has, had*), it is important to be sure that the verb that follows it is in the past participle form. Study the following incorrect sentences.

> The patient *had took** all the medicine.
>
> An accident *has occurring** on the highway.
>
> We *have* not *saw** that film yet.

In the first example, *took* should be the past participle *taken* because it is after *had*. In the second example, *occurring* should be the past participle *occurred* because it is after *has*. In the third example, *saw* should be the past participle *seen* because it is after *have*.

The following chart outlines the use of verb forms after *have*.

USING THE PAST PARTICIPLE AFTER *HAVE*
have, has, had   +   past participle

APPENDIX EXERCISE B5: Each of the following sentences contains a verb formed with a form of *have*. Underline the complete verbs twice. Then indicate if the sentences are correct (C) or incorrect (I).

__I__   1. I <u>have chose</u> a topic for my paper already.

         (*have chosen*)

_____   2. Everyone has known the date of the exam.

_____   3. They had catch a cold just before their vacation.

_____   4. The children have maked a big mess in the living room.

_____   5. She has lost her glasses often.

_____   6. We have making our best effort to succeed.

_____   7. They have flown to New York to attend a conference.

_____   8. He has driven to the office every day this month.

_____   9. I had forgot to bring all of the necessary equipment.

_____ 10. Have you bought everything you need for the party?

Appendix B6: USE THE PRESENT PARTICIPLE OR PAST PARTICIPLE AFTER *BE*

The verb *be* in any of its forms (*am, is, are, was, were, be, been, being*) can be followed by another verb. It is important to be sure that a verb that follows *be* is in either the present participle or the past participle form. Study the following incorrect sentences.

> The boys *were shout** at each other.
>
> The meal *is* almost *finish.**
>
> I *am leave** on the next flight.
>
> The package is *being send** later today.

In the first example, *shout* should be the present participle *shouting* because it is after *were*. In the second example, *finish* should be the past participle *finished* because it is after *is*. In the third example, *leave* should be the present participle *leaving* because it is after *am*. In the last example, *send* should be the past participle *sent* because it is after *being*.

The following chart outlines the use of verb forms after *be*.

USING THE PRESENT OR PAST PARTICIPLE AFTER *BE*		
am, is, are, was, were, be, been, being +	(1) present participle or (2) past participle	

APPENDIX EXERCISE B6: Each of the following sentences contains a verb formed with a form of *be*. Underline the verbs twice. Then indicate if the sentences are correct (C) or incorrect (I).

__I__ 1. The train <u>is leave</u> the station in five minutes.

   (*is leaving*)

____ 2. The letters were mailed just this morning.

____ 3. I am taking the next semester off from school.

____ 4. The game will be plays on Tuesday.

____ 5. The baby was crying for hours this morning.

____ 6. The books have been placed on the shelf.

____ 7. Classes are be canceled this afternoon.

____ 8. Planes were taking off and landing all day long.

_____ 9. All the children are being reward for their good behavior.

_____ 10. The lecture will be gave by a very famous speaker.

Appendix B7: USE THE BASE FORM AFTER MODALS

Whenever you see a modal such as *will, would, shall, should, can, could, may, might,* or *must,* it is important to be sure that the verb that follows it is in the base form. Study the following incorrect sentences.

> The guests *may arriving** any moment.
>
> The students *should finished** the exam soon.
>
> The employee *can leaves** the office an hour early.

In the first example, *arriving* should be the base form *arrive* because it is after *may*. In the second example, *finished* should be the base form *finish* because it is after *should*. In the third example, *leaves* should be the base form *leave* because it is after *can*.

The following chart outlines the use of verb forms after modals.

USING THE BASE FORM AFTER MODALS
will, would, shall, should, can, could, may, might, must + base form

APPENDIX EXERCISE B7: Each of the following sentences contains a verb formed with a modal. Underline the verbs twice. Then indicate if the sentences are correct (C) or incorrect (I).

__I__ 1. The students <u>will received</u> their grades this afternoon.

(*will receive*)

_____ 2. My friend would never do such a thing.

_____ 3. You can always depending on your friends.

_____ 4. My family should not spends so much time arguing.

_____ 5. The company will mail out checks on the first of the month.

_____ 6. They might leave before midnight.

_____ 7. You must always being prepared for the worst.

_____ 8. I shall offer to help with the plans for the event.

_____ 9. He could not dreamed of winning the lottery.

_____ 10. She may never understands how this can happen.

APPENDIX REVIEW EXERCISE (B5–B7): Underline the verbs twice. Then indicate if the following sentences are correct (C) or incorrect (I).

__I__ 1. The meeting <u>may</u> actually <u>begun</u> on time for once.

   (*may . . . begin*)

____ 2. The student has already takes the final exam.

____ 3. I am always thinking about my family.

____ 4. He can never knows the truth about the situation.

____ 5. The mother had already fed her children by six o'clock.

____ 6. I would not be upset by something like that.

____ 7. The students might had to write papers occasionally.

____ 8. We have not ate for many hours.

____ 9. The house has been sold for a very good price.

____ 10. I would never suspected him of the crime.

Appendix B8: USE CORRECT SINGULAR AND PLURAL NOUNS

It is important to be sure that singular and plural nouns are used correctly. The key words *each, every, single, one,* and *a (an)* indicate that a singular noun should follow. The key words *both, two, many, several,* and *various* indicate that a plural noun should follow. Study the following incorrect sentences.

   I just made *several mistake.**

   We checked *each details** in the report.

In the first example, the singular noun *mistake* should be the plural noun *mistakes* because it follows *several*. In the second example, the plural noun *details* should be the singular noun *detail* because it follows *each*.

The following chart outlines the use of singular and plural nouns following certain key words.

USING SINGULAR AND PLURAL NOUNS	
SINGULAR NOUNS	*Each, every, single, one,* and *a (an)* are used with singular nouns.
PLURAL NOUNS	*Both, two, many, several,* and *various* are used with plural nouns.

APPENDIX EXERCISE B8: Each of the following sentences contains at least one key word to tell you if a noun should be singular or plural. Put parentheses around the key words, and underline the nouns that follow. Then indicate if the sentences are correct (C) or incorrect (I).

__I__ 1. The teacher returned the papers to (every) <u>students</u>.

(*student*)

____ 2. You have given me many interesting ideas.

____ 3. You need to take several placement test for your major.

____ 4. I have a huge favors to ask you.

____ 5. You should try to do the problem both ways.

____ 6. You must sign your name on each page of the document.

____ 7. There are various way to fulfill the requirement.

____ 8. Two people can do this assignment better together.

____ 9. It will take me only one seconds to finish this.

____ 10. I do not have a single cents in my purse.

Appendix B9: USE CORRECT COUNTABLE AND UNCOUNTABLE NOUNS

It is important to be sure that countable and uncountable nouns are used correctly. The key words *many, number, few,* and *fewer* indicate that a countable noun should follow. The key words *much, amount, little,* and *less* indicate that an uncountable noun should follow. Study the following incorrect sentences.

> We do not have *many milk.**

> She has only a small *amount** of *friends.*

In the first example, *many* is incorrect because *milk* is uncountable. This sentence should say *much milk.* In the second example, *amount* is incorrect because *friends* is countable. This sentence should say *number* of *friends.*

The following chart outlines the use of countable and uncountable nouns following certain key words.

USING COUNTABLE AND UNCOUNTABLE NOUNS	
COUNTABLE NOUNS	*Many, number, few,* and *fewer* are used with countable nouns.
UNCOUNTABLE NOUNS	*Much, amount, little,* and *less* are used with uncountable nouns.

APPENDIX EXERCISE B9: Each of the following sentences contains at least one key word to tell you if a noun should be countable or uncountable. Put parentheses around the key words, and underline the nouns that follow. Then indicate if the sentences are correct (C) or incorrect (I).

__I__ 1. He gave me a large (amount) of <u>reasons</u> for his actions.

(*number*)

_____ 2. We have very little time to finish the project.

_____ 3. There are not much chapters left to read.

_____ 4. I have fewer courses to take than you do.

_____ 5. There are less people here today than there were yesterday.

_____ 6. There is little need to say anything else.

_____ 7. We have many ideas but little solutions.

_____ 8. I did not give much importance to her excuse.

_____ 9. How many money are you going to spend today?

_____ 10. There is a large number of applicants, and few of them will be admitted.

APPENDIX REVIEW EXERCISE (B8–B9): Each of the following sentences contains at least one key word to tell you if a noun should be singular or plural, or countable or uncountable. Put parentheses around the key words, and underline the nouns that follow. Then indicate if the sentences are correct (C) or incorrect (I).

__I__ 1. He tried (several) <u>times</u> to make (a) phone <u>calls</u>.

(*call*)

_____ 2. There are less children inside than outside.

_____ 3. There were too many errors in every paragraph.

_____ 4. I invited a large amount of friends to the party.

_____ 5. I completed both assignment in only two hour.

_____ 6. One student received a number of different awards.

_____ 7. Each math problem has a single correct responses.

_____ 8. You have had fewer opportunities than I have had.

_____ 9. We discussed various solution and then chose one solution.

_____ 10. He has not given me much advice that I could use.

Appendix B10: USE CORRECT SUBJECT AND OBJECT PRONOUNS

It is important to be sure that subject pronouns (*I, you, he, she, it, we, they*) and object pronouns (*me, you, him, her, it, us, them*) are used correctly. A subject pronoun is used as the subject of a verb, and an object pronoun is used as the object of a verb or as the object of a preposition. Study the following incorrect sentences.

> My roommate and *me** *are going* to class.
>
> I *saw she and he** at the movie theater.
>
> John gave this present *to you and I.**

In the first example, the object pronoun *me* is incorrect because *my roommate and me* is the subject of the verb *are going*. The object pronoun *me* should change to the subject pronoun *I*. In the second example, the subject pronouns *she* and *he* are incorrect because *she and he* is the object of the verb *saw*. The subject pronouns *she* and *he* should be changed to the object pronouns *her* and *him*. In the third example, the subject pronoun *I* is incorrect because *you and I* is the object of the preposition *to*. The subject pronouns *you* and *I* should be changed to *you* and *me*.

The following chart outlines the use of subject and object pronouns.

USING SUBJECT AND OBJECT PRONOUNS	
SUBJECT PRONOUNS	Subject pronouns (*I, you, he, she, it, we, they*) are used as subjects of verbs.
OBJECT PRONOUNS	Object pronouns (*me, you, him, her, it, us, them*) are used as objects of verbs or as objects of prepositions.

APPENDIX EXERCISE B10: Each of the following sentences contains at least one subject or object pronoun. Put parentheses around the subject and object pronouns. Then indicate if the sentences are correct (C) or incorrect (I).

___I___ 1. (I) did something nice for (him), and (he) did something nice for (I).

   (*for me*)

_____ 2. We saw them in the park, but they did not see us.

_____ 3. Quite possibly, you and him are the best in the class.

_____ 4. This class is quite difficult for me, but it is not very difficult for you.

_____ 5. She helped me with the math problems because I did not understand them

   as well as she did.

_____ 6. The secret is just between you and I. We have to keep this secret.

_____ 7. I have a problem, and I cannot solve it.

_____ 8. Him and me both are doing an extra assignment.

_____ 9. The teacher asked the students to read a chapter because she wanted them to understand the information in it.

_____ 10. This book is for you and I. We have to share it.

Appendix B11: USE CORRECT POSSESSIVE ADJECTIVES AND PRONOUNS

It is important to be sure that possessive adjectives (_my, your, his, her, its, our, their_) and possessive pronouns (_mine, yours, his, hers, ours, theirs_) are used correctly. A possessive adjective describes a noun, so it must accompany a noun. A possessive pronoun takes the place of a noun, so it cannot accompany a noun. Study the following incorrect sentences.

> We are all going to drive _ours*_ cars.
>
> I lost my book, and I would like to borrow _your_.*

In the first example, the possessive pronoun _ours_ is incorrect because it accompanies the noun _cars_. The possessive pronoun _ours_ should be changed to the possessive adjective _our_. In the second example, the possessive adjective _your_ is incorrect because it does not accompany a noun. The possessive adjective _your_ should be changed to the possessive pronoun _yours_.

The following chart outlines the use of possessive adjectives and pronouns.

USING POSSESSIVE ADJECTIVES AND PRONOUNS	
POSSESSIVE ADJECTIVES	Possessive adjectives (_my, your, his, her, its, our, their_) describe nouns, so they must accompany nouns.
POSSESSIVE PRONOUNS	Possessive pronouns (_mine, your, his, hers, ours, theirs_) take the place of nouns, so they cannot accompany nouns.

APPENDIX EXERCISE B11: Each of the following sentences contains at least one possessive pronoun or adjective. Put parentheses around the possessives. Then indicate if the sentences are correct (C) or incorrect (I).

__I__ 1. We can take either (our) car or (your).

(yours)

_____ 2. I have my book, but I do not have his.

_____ 3. Their house is much bigger than our.

_____ 4. I know you have your paper, but do you also have mine?

_____ 5. He is working on his project, but she is not working on her.

_____ 6. The house next door is for sale. Its' owner is really eager to sell it.

_____ 7. I really like mine history class. I hope you like yours.

_____ 8. She is not wearing her own jacket. Instead, she is wearing his.

_____ 9. Our papers are due this week, and theirs are due next week. Ours are due before theirs are.

_____ 10. My opinions are different from yours. You have yours opinions, and I have mines.

Appendix B12: CHECK PRONOUN AND POSSESSIVE REFERENTS

It is important to be sure that pronouns and possessives agree with their referents. A referent is a noun that a pronoun or possessive refers to. Study the following incorrect sentences.

> This *book* is for you, so please take *them*.*

> Each *student* has to turn in *their** paper this afternoon.

In the first example, the plural pronoun *them* is incorrect because it refers to the singular noun *book*. *Them* should be changed to the singular pronoun *it*. In the second example, the plural possessive *their* is incorrect because it refers to the singular noun *student*. *Their* should be changed to the singular possessive *his or her*.

The following chart outlines how to check pronoun and possessive referents.

CHECKING PRONOUNS AND POSSESSIVE REFERENTS	
PRONOUN REFERENTS	Pronouns must agree with their referents. Referents are the nouns that pronouns or possessives refer to.
POSSESSIVE REFERENTS	Possessives must agree with their referents. Referents are the nouns that pronouns or possessives refer to.

APPENDIX EXERCISE B12: Each of the following sentences contains at least one pronoun or possessive. Put parentheses around the pronouns and possessives, and underline the nouns they refer to. Then indicate if the sentences are correct (C) or incorrect (I).

__I__   1. The boys picked up their <u>toys</u> and put (it) in the toy box.

           (*them*)

_____   2. My neighbors rarely mow their lawn, and the grass is very tall.

_____   3. I hope there is more paper because I need to use some of them now.

_____   4. The man has found an error on his bank statement, so he has to contact the bank to discuss it.

_____   5. I read the articles, and then I tried to write a paper about its key points.

_____   6. You need your own book, and I need my own.

_____   7. Has the speaker made a good point, and has he supported it well?

_____   8. The students all had different ideas, so they sat down and tried to discuss it.

_____   9. Mary saw her friends, so she went over to greet them.

_____ 10. Everyone has to bring their own towels to the beach.

APPENDIX REVIEW EXERCISE (B10–B12): Each of the following sentences contains at least one pronoun or possessive. Put parentheses around the pronouns and possessives. Then indicate if the sentences are correct (C) or incorrect (I).

__I__   1. The gift is not for (him) and (her). (It) is for (you) and (I).

           (*me*)

_____   2. Our presentations are not on the same day. Mine is tomorrow, and yours is the day after.

_____   3. I understand the problem, and I am sure that I can help you solve them.

_____   4. I read the first chapter, and he read the second chapter. Then we both discussed the two chapters.

_____   5. Our computer is not as new as theirs is, but it still works as well as theirs does.

_____   6. He has his ideas, and I have mine, and we do not agree about it.

_____ 7. She has been helping him with his paper because she has already finished her.

_____ 8. Could you please show me your notes because I would like to see if my notes are similar to yours.

_____ 9. Our neighbors did a favor for us, and we thanked them for it.

_____ 10. The teacher gave the students topics for theirs research papers, and then she told them when to turn the papers in.

Appendix B13: USE CORRECT BASIC ADJECTIVES AND ADVERBS

It is important to watch out for the correct use of basic adjectives and adverbs. Adjectives and adverbs have very different uses in sentences. Adjectives can describe nouns or pronouns, while adverbs can describe verbs, adjectives, or other adverbs. Study the following incorrect sentences.

> It is a _correctly*_ answer.
>
> _She_ has been _helpfully*_ in answering our question.
>
> The athlete _ran quick*_ down the track.
>
> That was an _awful* nice_ comment.
>
> The man drove _real* fast_ to the hospital.

In the first example, the adverb _correctly_ is incorrect because the adjective _correct_ is needed to describe the noun _answer_. In the second example, the adverb _helpfully_ is incorrect because the adjective _helpful_ is needed to describe the pronoun _she_. In the third example, the adjective _quick_ is incorrect because the adverb _quickly_ is needed to describe the verb _ran_. In the fourth example, the adjective _awful_ is incorrect because the adverb _awfully_ is needed to describe the adjective _nice_. In the last example, the adjective _real_ is incorrect because the adverb _really_ is needed to describe the adverb _fast_.

The following chart outlines the use of basic adjectives and adverbs.

USING BASIC ADJECTIVES AND ADVERBS	
ADJECTIVES	Adjectives describe _nouns_ or _pronouns_.
ADVERBS	Adverbs describe _verbs, adjectives,_ or _adverbs._

APPENDIX EXERCISE B13: Each of the following sentences has at least one adjective or adverb. Put parentheses around the adjectives and adverbs, and indicate the words they describe. Then indicate whether the sentences are correct (C) or incorrect (I).

__I__   1. The students studied the (difficult) material (thorough).

   difficult describes material

   thorough (thoroughly) describes studied

_____   2. He has a real professional résumé.

\
\

_____   3. We arrived unexpectedly early at the party.

\
\

_____   4. He made an obvious mistake in the final paragraph.

\
\

_____   5. I did surprisingly good on the lengthy exam.

\
\

_____   6. She responded politely to my personal question.

\
\

_____   7. You certainly must answer this question correct.

\
\

_____   8. He responded appreciatively to the thoughtful offer of assistance.

\
\

_____   9. There was a suddenly rush of cold air through the open window.

\
\

_____ 10. The teacher spoke extremely softly, and the students listened carefully.

_____

_____

_____

Appendix B14: USE ADJECTIVES AFTER LINKING VERBS

It is important to watch out for the correct use of adjectives following linking verbs. Generally, an adverb rather than an adjective will come directly after a verb because the adverb is describing a verb. However, a linking verb (*appear, be, become, feel, look, seem, smell, taste*) is followed by an adjective because the adjective describes the subject and not the verb. Study the following incorrect sentences.

> The boys *ran quick** to catch the bus.

> The student *feels happily** about the results.

> The choir *sang* the song *enthusiastic.**

> The soup on the stove *smells deliciously.**

In the first example, the adjective *quick* should be the adverb *quickly* because *ran* is not a linking verb and *quickly* describes the verb *ran*. In the second example, the adverb *happily* should be the adjective *happy* because *feels* is a linking verb and *happy* describes the noun *student*. In the third example, the adjective *enthusiastic* should be the adverb *enthusiastically* because *sang* is not a linking verb and *enthusiastically* describes the verb *sang*. In the last example, the adverb *deliciously* should be the adjective *delicious* because *smells* is a linking verb and *delicious* describes the noun *soup*.

The following chart outlines the use of adjectives after linking verbs.

USING ADJECTIVES AFTER LINKING VERBS	
ADVERBS AFTER REGULAR VERBS	A regular verb is followed by an *adverb*. The adverb describes the *verb*.
ADJECTIVES AFTER LINKING VERBS	A linking verb is followed by an *adjective*. The adjective describes the subject. The following verbs are linking verbs: *appear, be, become, feel, look, seem, smell, taste*.

APPENDIX EXERCISE B14: Each of the following sentences has at least one adjective or adverb. Put parentheses around the adjectives and adverbs, and indicate the words they describe. Then indicate whether the sentences are correct (C) or incorrect (I).

<u> I </u>   1. She is (very) (nicely) at this moment.

        <u>*very describes nicely*</u>

        <u>*nicely (nice) describes She*</u>

_____   2. I saw him recently, and he did not appear tired.

_____

_____

_____   3. The romantic movie affected me deeply.

_____

_____

_____   4. I became doubtfully about the new information.

_____

_____

_____   5. They are very eagerly to begin the program.

_____

_____

_____   6. We acted quickly to solve the serious problem.

_____

_____

_____   7. The new perfume smells wonderfully.

_____

_____

_____   8. The house seemed quiet because the children were asleep.

_____

_____

_____   9. I slept soundly through the entire night.

_____

_____

_____ 10. The new dish does not taste as deliciously as it should.

_____

_____

APPENDIX REVIEW EXERCISE (B13–B14): Each of the following sentences has at least one adjective or adverb. Put parentheses around the adjectives and adverbs, and indicate the words they describe. Then indicate whether the sentences are correct (C) or incorrect (I).

__C__ 1. She has a (humorous) way of responding to (negative) comments.

    humorous describes way

    negative describes comments

_____ 2. The room became quiet as the audience waited patiently for the program to start.

_____

_____

_____ 3. The situation was completely impossibly.

_____

_____

_____ 4. The homework appeared unusual difficult to the sad students.

_____

_____

_____

_____ 5. She apologized sincerely, and he generously accepted her sincere apology.

_____

_____

_____

_____ 6. The teacher seemed really happily about the rapid progress his students were making.

_____

_____

_____

_____ 7. He behaved truly irrational for no apparent reason.

_____

_____

_____

_____ 8. I felt really emotional when I heard the positive results.

_____

_____

_____

_____ 9. She eats incredibly unhealthy food, but she stills looks incredibly healthy.

_____

_____

_____

_____

_____ 10. He looked extremely happily, but he was actually feeling sadly.

_____

_____

_____

_____

DIAGNOSIS, ASSESSMENT, AND SCORING

OVERALL SCORES

The highest possible score on the TOEFL *iBT* is 120. Each of the four sections (Reading, Listening, Speaking, Writing) receives a scaled score from 0 to 30. The scaled scores from the four sections are added together to determine the overall scores.

The following chart shows how overall scores on the TOEFL *iBT* can be compared with overall scores on the paper TOEFL test.

iBT Internet-Based Test	PBT Paper-Based Test
120	677
115	650
110	637
105	620
100	600
95	587
90	577
85	563
80	550
75	537
70	523
65	513
60	497
55	480
50	463
45	450
40	433
35	417
30	397
25	377
20	350

READING DIAGNOSIS AND SCORING

For Reading test sections in this book, it is possible to do the following:

- *diagnose* errors in the Pre-Test, Post-Test, Mini-Tests, Complete Test, and TOEFL-Level Test
- *score* the TOEFL-Level Test
- *record* your test results

DIAGNOSING READING ERRORS

Every time you take a Reading test section of a Pre-Test, Post-Test, Mini-Test, Complete Test, or TOEFL-Level Test, you should use the following chart to diagnose your errors.

Circle the number of each of the questions on the test that you *answered incorrectly* or *were unsure of*. Then you will see which skills you should focus on.

	PRE-TEST	POST-TEST	MINI-TESTS 1	2	3	4	COMPLETE TEST 1–13	14–26	27–39	TOEFL-LEVEL TEST 1–13
SKILL 1	2 10	4 6	1 5 7 10	2 4 6 9	2 9 12	1 4 9	1 7 9 11	14 19 21 25	27 30 36	1 6 10 12
SKILL 2	4 9	7 12	11	10	4	10	12	23	31	8
SKILL 3	6 8	10 13	3	12	7	8	3	17	37	9
SKILL 4	5 15	3 15	8	11	10	7	6	18	32	3
SKILL 5	13 14	1 16	2	5	3 8	6 12	2 4	20	29 35	4
SKILL 6	1 16	2 8	4	3	1 11	3	8	24	28	2
SKILL 7	3 7	5 11	9 12	1 7	6	2 11	5	15 22	33	7 11
SKILL 8	11 12	9 14	6	8	5	5	10	16	34 38	5
SKILL 9	17	17	13			13			39	
SKILL 10	18	18		13	13		13	26		13

SCORING THE READING TOEFL-LEVEL TEST

In this book, it is possible to determine your Reading Scaled Score on the Reading section of the TOEFL-Level Test. You cannot determine a scaled score on the Reading sections of the Pre-Test, Post-Test, Mini-Tests, and Complete Test because they are below the level of the TOEFL iBT.

To determine a scaled score on the Reading section of the TOEFL-Level Test, you must first determine the number of points you received in the section. You must determine the number of points you received on the last question before you can determine the total number of points. The last question is worth 3 points and has 5 correct answers. You get 3 points for 5 correct answers, 2 points for 4 correct answers, 1 point for 3 correct answers, and 0 points for 2, 1, or 0 correct answers. After you have determined the number of points you have earned on the last question, add this number to the number correct on questions 1 through 12 to determine your total points out of 15. When you know the total points you received on the Reading section of the TOEFL-Level Test, you can refer to the following chart to determine your scaled score out of 30 for this section.

TOTAL POINTS	READING SCALED SCORE	TOTAL POINTS	READING SCALED SCORE
15	30	7	8
14	28	6	7
13	25	5	5
12	22	4	4
11	19	3	2
10	16	2	1
9	14	1	1
8	11	0	0

RECORDING YOUR READING TEST RESULTS

Each time you complete a Reading Pre-Test, a Post-Test, a Mini-Test, Complete Test section, or a TOEFL-Level Test section, you should record the results in the chart that follows. In this way, you will be able to keep track of the progress you are making.

READING TEST RESULTS	
PRE-TEST	_____ out of 21 possible points
POST-TEST	_____ out of 21 possible points
MINI-TEST 1	_____ out of 14 possible points
MINI-TEST 2	_____ out of 15 possible points
MINI-TEST 3	_____ out of 14 possible points
MINI-TEST 4	_____ out of 15 possible points
COMPLETE TEST, READING 1	_____ out of 14 possible points
COMPLETE TEST, READING 2	_____ out of 15 possible points
COMPLETE TEST, READING 3	_____ out of 14 possible points
TOEFL-LEVEL TEST	_____ out of 15 possible points

LISTENING DIAGNOSIS AND SCORING

For Listening test sections in this book, it is possible to do the following:

- *diagnose* errors in the Pre-Test, Post-Test, Mini-Tests, Complete Test, and TOEFL-Level Test
- *score* the TOEFL-Level Test
- *record* your test results

DIAGNOSING LISTENING ERRORS

Every time you take a Listening test section of a Pre-Test, Post-Test, Mini-Test, Complete Test, or TOEFL-Level Test, you should use the following chart to diagnose your errors.

Circle the number of each of the questions on the test that you *answered incorrectly* or *were unsure of*. Then you will see which skills you should focus on.

	PRE-TEST	POST-TEST	MINI-TESTS 1	MINI-TESTS 2	MINI-TESTS 3	MINI-TESTS 4	COMPLETE TEST 1–10	COMPLETE TEST 11–22	COMPLETE TEST 23–34	TOEFL-LEVEL TEST 1–5	TOEFL-LEVEL TEST 6–11
SKILL 1	1, 7	1, 7	1	1, 6	1, 6	1	1, 6	11, 17		1	
SKILL 2	2, 8	4, 9	2, 3, 7, 8	7, 8, 11	3, 5, 8	3, 4, 5, 8, 9	2, 5, 9, 10	13, 16, 18	23, 25, 27, 31, 34	3, 5	7, 8, 9
SKILL 3	4, 11	3, 8	4, 11	5	2, 9	7	7	14, 20	26, 29, 33	4	
SKILL 4	3, 9	2, 12	5	2, 4, 10		2	3, 8		24	2	11
SKILL 5	6, 12	6, 10	6, 9	3, 9	4, 7, 10	6, 10		12, 21, 22	28, 30, 32		6, 10
SKILL 6	5, 10	5, 11	10		11	11	4	15, 19			

SCORING THE LISTENING TOEFL-LEVEL TEST

In this book, it is possible to determine your Listening Scaled Score on the Listening section of the TOEFL-Level Test. You cannot determine a scaled score on the Listening sections of the Pre-Test, Post-Test, Mini-Tests, and Complete Test because they are below the level of the TOEFL iBT.

To determine a scaled score on the Listening section of the TOEFL-Level Test, you must first determine the number of points you received in the section. In Listening, you simply need to count the number of questions you answered correctly (out of 13) because the number of points is the number of questions you answered correctly. When you know the total points you received on the Listening section of the TOEFL-Level Test, you can refer to the following chart to determine your scaled score out of 30 for this section.

TOTAL POINTS	LISTENING SCALED SCORE	TOTAL POINTS	LISTENING SCALED SCORE
13	30	6	12
12	28	5	10
11	25	4	8
10	23	3	6
9	20	2	4
8	17	1	2
7	14	0	0

RECORDING YOUR LISTENING TEST RESULTS

Each time you complete a Listening Pre-Test, a Post-Test, a Mini-Test, Complete Test section, or TOEFL-Level Test section, you should record the results in the chart that follows. In this way, you will be able to keep track of the progress you are making.

LISTENING TEST RESULTS	
PRE-TEST	_____ out of 14 possible points
POST-TEST	_____ out of 14 possible points
MINI-TEST 1	_____ out of 13 possible points
MINI-TEST 2	_____ out of 13 possible points
MINI-TEST 3	_____ out of 13 possible points
MINI-TEST 4	_____ out of 13 possible points
COMPLETE TEST, LISTENINGS 1–2	_____ out of 10 possible points
COMPLETE TEST, LISTENINGS 3–4	_____ out of 15 possible points
COMPLETE TEST, LISTENINGS 5–6	_____ out of 15 possible points
TOEFL-LEVEL TEST	_____ out of 13 possible points

SPEAKING ASSESSMENT AND SCORING _____

For Speaking test sections in this book, it is possible to do the following:

- *assess* the skills used in the Pre-Test, Post-Test, Mini-Tests, Complete Test, and TOEFL-Level Test
- *score* the Pre-Test, Post-Test, Mini-Tests, Complete Test, and TOEFL-Level Test using the Speaking Scoring Criteria
- *record* your test results

ASSESSING SPEAKING SKILLS

After you complete each Speaking task on a Pre-Test, Post-Test, Mini-Test, Complete Test, or TOEFL-Level Test, put checkmarks in the appropriate boxes in the following Skill-Assessment Checklists. This will help you assess how well you have used the skills presented in the textbook.

	SKILL-ASSESSMENT CHECKLIST ASSESSMENT OF THE SPEAKING INDEPENDENT TASKS, FREE CHOICE: SKILLS 1–2						
		PRE-TEST, Question 1	REVIEW EXERCISE (Skills 1–2)	POST-TEST, Question 1	MINI-TEST 1, Question 1	MINI-TEST 3, Question 1	COMPLETE TEST, Question 1	TOEFL-LEVEL TEST, Question 1
SKILL 1	I read the **question** carefully.							
SKILL 1	I included an introduction, supporting ideas, and a conclusion in my **plan**.							
SKILL 2	I began with an **introduction**.							
SKILL 2	I used strong **supporting ideas**.							
SKILL 2	I ended with a **conclusion**.							

SKILL-ASSESSMENT CHECKLIST **ASSESSMENT OF THE SPEAKING INDEPENDENT TASKS,** **PAIRED CHOICE: SKILLS 3–4**							
	PRE-TEST, Question 2	REVIEW EXERCISE (Skills 3–4)	POST-TEST, Question 2	MINI-TEST 2, Question 1	MINI-TEST 4, Question 1	COMPLETE TEST, Question 2	TOEFL-LEVEL TEST, Question 2
SKILL 3 I read the **question** carefully.							
SKILL 3 I included an introduction, supporting ideas, and a conclusion in my **plan**.							
SKILL 4 I began with an **introduction**.							
SKILL 4 I used strong **supporting ideas**.							
SKILL 4 I ended with a **conclusion**.							

	SKILL-ASSESSMENT CHECKLIST ASSESSMENT OF THE SPEAKING INTEGRATED TASKS, READING AND LISTENING: SKILLS 5–8	PRE-TEST, Question 3	REVIEW EXERCISE (Skills 5–8)	POST-TEST, Question 3	MINI-TEST 1, Question 2	MINI-TEST 3, Question 2	COMPLETE TEST, Question 3	TOEFL-LEVEL TEST, Question 3
SKILL 5	I noted the **main points** of the **reading passage**.							
SKILL 6	I noted the **main points** of the **listening passage**.							
SKILL 7	I read the **question** carefully.							
SKILL 7	I included a topic statement and supporting ideas in my **plan**.							
SKILL 8	I began with an overall **topic statement**.							
SKILL 8	I used strong **supporting ideas**.							

	SKILL-ASSESSMENT CHECKLIST ASSESSMENT OF THE SPEAKING INTEGRATED TASKS, READING AND LISTENING: SKILLS 9–12						
	PRE-TEST, Question 4	REVIEW EXERCISE (Skills 9–12)	POST-TEST, Question 4	MINI-TEST 2, Question 2	MINI-TEST 4, Question 2	COMPLETE TEST, Question 4	TOEFL-LEVEL TEST, Question 4
SKILL 9 I noted the **main points** of the **reading passage**.							
SKILL 10 I noted the **main points** of the **listening passage**.							
SKILL 11 I read the **question** carefully.							
SKILL 11 I included a topic statement and supporting ideas in my **plan**.							
SKILL 12 I began with an overall **topic statement**.							
SKILL 12 I used strong **supporting ideas**.							

SKILL-ASSESSMENT CHECKLIST ASSESSMENT OF THE SPEAKING INTEGRATED TASKS, LISTENING: SKILLS 13–15							
	PRE-TEST, Question 5	REVIEW EXERCISE (Skills 13–15)	POST-TEST, Question 5	MINI-TEST 2, Question 3	MINI-TEST 4, Question 3	COMPLETE TEST, Question 5	TOEFL-LEVEL TEST, Question 5
SKILL 13 I noted the **main points** of the **listening passage**.							
SKILL 14 I read the **question** carefully.							
SKILL 14 I included a topic statement and key details in my **plan**.							
SKILL 15 I began with an overall **topic statement**.							
SKILL 15 I used **key details**.							

	SKILL-ASSESSMENT CHECKLIST ASSESSMENT OF THE SPEAKING INTEGRATED TASKS, LISTENING: SKILLS 16–18						
	PRE-TEST, Question 6	REVIEW EXERCISE (Skills 16–18)	POST-TEST, Question 6	MINI-TEST 1, Question 3	MINI-TEST 3, Question 3	COMPLETE TEST, Question 6	TOEFL-LEVEL TEST, Question 6
SKILL 16 I noted the **main points** of the **listening passage**.							
SKILL 17 I read the **question** carefully.							
SKILL 17 I included a topic statement and key details in my **plan**.							
SKILL 18 I began with an overall **topic statement**.							
SKILL 18 I used **key details**.							

SCORING THE SPEAKING TESTS USING THE SCORING CRITERIA

You may use the Speaking Scoring Criteria to score your Speaking tasks on the Pre-Test, Post-Test, Mini-Tests, Complete Test, and TOEFL-Level Test. You will receive a score of 0 through 4 for each Speaking task; this score of 0 through 4 will then be converted to a scaled score out of 30. The criteria for Speaking scores of 0 through 4 are listed below.

SPEAKING SCORING CRITERIA		
4	ANSWER TO QUESTION	The student answers the question thoroughly.
	COMPREHENSIBILITY	The student can be understood completely.
	ORGANIZATION	The student's response is well organized and developed.
	FLUENCY	The student's speech is generally fluent.
	PRONUNCIATION	The student has generally good pronunciation.
	GRAMMAR	The student uses advanced grammatical structures with a high degree of accuracy.
	VOCABULARY	The student uses advanced vocabulary with a high degree of accuracy.
3	ANSWER TO QUESTION	The student answers the question adequately but not thoroughly.
	COMPREHENSIBILITY	The student can generally be understood.
	ORGANIZATION	The student's response is organized basically and is not thoroughly developed.
	FLUENCY	The student's speech is generally fluent, with minor problems.
	PRONUNCIATION	The student has generally good pronunciation, with minor problems.
	GRAMMAR	The student uses either accurate easier grammatical structures or more advanced grammatical structures with some errors.
	VOCABULARY	The student uses either accurate easier vocabulary or more advanced vocabulary with some errors.

2	ANSWER TO QUESTION	The student discusses information from the task but does not answer the question directly.
	COMPREHENSIBILITY	The student is not always intelligible.
	ORGANIZATION	The student's response is not clearly organized and is incomplete or contains some inaccurate points.
	FLUENCY	The student's speech is not very fluent and has a number of problems.
	PRONUNCIATION	The student's pronunciation is not very clear, with a number of problems.
	GRAMMAR	The student has a number of errors in grammar or uses only very basic grammar fairly accurately.
	VOCABULARY	The student has a number of errors in vocabulary or uses only very basic vocabulary fairly accurately.
1	ANSWER TO QUESTION	The student's response is only slightly related to the topic.
	COMPREHENSIBILITY	The student is only occasionally intelligible.
	ORGANIZATION	The student's response is not clearly organized and is only minimally on the topic.
	FLUENCY	The student has problems with fluency that make the response difficult to understand.
	PRONUNCIATION	The student has problems with pronunciation that make the response difficult to understand.
	GRAMMAR	The student has numerous errors in grammar that interfere with meaning.
	VOCABULARY	The student has numerous errors in vocabulary that interfere with meaning.
0	The student either says nothing or fails to answer the question.	

The following chart shows how a score of 0 through 4 on a Speaking task is converted to a scaled score out of 30.

SPEAKING SCORE (0–4)	SPEAKING SCALED SCORE (0–30)
4.00	30
3.83	29
3.66	28
3.50	27
3.33	26
3.16	24
3.00	23
2.83	22
2.66	20
2.50	19
2.33	18
2.16	17
2.00	15
1.83	14
1.66	13
1.50	11
1.33	10
1.16	9
1.00	8
0.83	6
0.66	5
0.50	4
0.33	3
0.16	1
0.00	0

Scaled scores on each of the Speaking tasks on a test are averaged to determine the scaled score for the test.

RECORDING YOUR SPEAKING TEST RESULTS

Each time that you complete a Speaking Pre-Test, Post-Test, Mini-Test, Complete Test section, or TOEFL-Level Test section, you should record your results in the chart that follows. In this way, you will be able to keep track of the progress you are making.

SPEAKING TEST RESULTS	
PRE-TEST	Speaking Task 1 _____ Speaking Task 2 _____ Speaking Task 3 _____ Speaking Task 4 _____ Speaking Task 5 _____ Speaking Task 6 _____ **Overall Speaking Score** _____
POST-TEST	Speaking Task 1 _____ Speaking Task 2 _____ Speaking Task 3 _____ Speaking Task 4 _____ Speaking Task 5 _____ Speaking Task 6 _____ **Overall Speaking Score** _____
MINI-TEST 1	Speaking Task 1 _____ Speaking Task 2 _____ Speaking Task 3 _____ **Overall Speaking Score** _____
MINI-TEST 2	Speaking Task 1 _____ Speaking Task 2 _____ Speaking Task 3 _____ **Overall Speaking Score** _____
MINI-TEST 3	Speaking Task 1 _____ Speaking Task 2 _____ Speaking Task 3 _____ **Overall Speaking Score** _____

MINI-TEST 4	Speaking Task 1 _____
	Speaking Task 2 _____
	Speaking Task 3 _____
	Overall Speaking Score _____
COMPLETE TEST	Speaking Task 1 _____
	Speaking Task 2 _____
	Speaking Task 3 _____
	Speaking Task 4 _____
	Speaking Task 5 _____
	Speaking Task 6 _____
	Overall Speaking Score _____
TOEFL-LEVEL TEST	Speaking Task 1 _____
	Speaking Task 2 _____
	Speaking Task 3 _____
	Speaking Task 4 _____
	Speaking Task 5 _____
	Speaking Task 6 _____
	Overall Speaking Score _____

WRITING ASSESSMENT AND SCORING _____

For Writing test sections in this book, it is possible to do the following:

- *assess* the skills used in the Pre-Test, Post-Test, Mini-Tests, Complete Test, and TOEFL-Level Test
- *score* the Pre-Test, Post-Test, Mini-Tests, Complete Test, and TOEFL-Level Test using the Writing Scoring Criteria
- *record* your test results

ASSESSING WRITING SKILLS

After you complete each Writing task on a Pre-Test, Post-Test, Mini-Test, Complete Test, or TOEFL-Level Test, put checkmarks in the appropriate boxes in the following Skill-Assessment Checklists. This will help you assess how well you have used the skills presented in the textbook.

SKILL-ASSESSMENT CHECKLIST **ASSESSMENT OF THE WRITING INTEGRATED TASKS, SKILLS 1–8**							
	PRE-TEST, Question 1	REVIEW EXERCISE (Skills 1–8)	POST-TEST, Question 1	MINI-TEST 1, Question 1	MINI-TEST 3, Question 1	COMPLETE TEST, Question 1	TOEFL-LEVEL TEST, Question 1
SKILL 1 I noted the **main points** of the **reading passage**.							
SKILL 2 I noted the **main points** of the **listening passage**.							
SKILL 3 I included a topic statement and supporting ideas in my **plan**.							
SKILL 4 I began with an overall **topic statement**.							
SKILL 5 I wrote a unified **supporting paragraph** on reading.							
SKILL 6 I wrote a unified **supporting paragraph** on listening.							
SKILL 7 I checked the **sentence structure** in my response.							
SKILL 8 I checked the **grammar** in my response.							

SKILL-ASSESSMENT CHECKLIST
ASSESSMENT OF THE WRITING INDEPENDENT TASKS, SKILLS 9–14

	PRE-TEST, Question 2	REVIEW EXERCISE (Skills 9–14)	POST-TEST, Question 2	MINI-TEST 2, Question 1	MINI-TEST 4, Question 1	COMPLETE TEST, Question 2	TOEFL-LEVEL TEST, Question 2
SKILL 9 I used careful **planning** to outline my response.							
SKILL 10 I included the topic and organization in the **introduction**.							
SKILL 11 I wrote unified **supporting paragraphs**.							
SKILL 12 I summarized the main points in the **conclusion**.							
SKILL 13 I checked the **sentence structure** in my response.							
SKILL 14 I checked the **grammar** in my response.							

SCORING THE WRITING TESTS USING THE SCORING CRITERIA

You may use the Writing Scoring Criteria to score your Writing tasks on the Pre-Test, Post-Test, Mini-Tests, Complete Test, and TOEFL-Level Test. You will receive a score of 0 through 5 for each Writing task; this score of 0 through 5 will then be converted to a scaled score out of 30. The criteria for Writing scores of 0 through 5 are listed below.

WRITING SCORING CRITERIA		
5	ANSWER TO QUESTION	The student answers the question thoroughly.
	COMPREHENSIBILITY	The student can be understood completely.
	ORGANIZATION	The student's response is maturely organized and developed.
	FLOW OF IDEAS	The student's ideas flow cohesively.
	GRAMMAR	The student uses advanced grammatical structures with a high degree of accuracy.
	VOCABULARY	The student uses advanced vocabulary with a high degree of accuracy.
4	ANSWER TO QUESTION	The student answers the question adequately but not thoroughly.
	COMPREHENSIBILITY	The student can generally be understood.
	ORGANIZATION	The student's response is adequately organized and developed.
	FLOW OF IDEAS	The student's ideas generally flow cohesively.
	GRAMMAR	The student uses either accurate easier grammatical structures or more advanced grammatical structures with a few errors.
	VOCABULARY	The student uses either accurate easier vocabulary or more advanced vocabulary with some errors.

3	ANSWER TO QUESTION	The student gives a basically accurate response to the question.
	COMPREHENSIBILITY	The student's basic ideas can be understood.
	ORGANIZATION	The student's response is organized basically and is not thoroughly developed.
	FLOW OF IDEAS	The student's ideas flow cohesively sometimes and at other times do not.
	GRAMMAR	The student has a number of errors in grammar or uses only very basic grammar fairly accurately.
	VOCABULARY	The student has a number of errors in vocabulary or uses only very basic vocabulary fairly accurately.
2	ANSWER TO QUESTION	The student discusses information from the task but does not answer the question directly.
	COMPREHENSIBILITY	The student's ideas are not always intelligible.
	ORGANIZATION	The student's response is not clearly organized and is incomplete or contains some inaccurate points.
	FLOW OF IDEAS	The student's ideas often do not flow cohesively.
	GRAMMAR	The student has numerous errors in grammar that interfere with meaning.
	VOCABULARY	The student has numerous errors in vocabulary that interfere with meaning.
1	ANSWER TO QUESTION	The student's response is only slightly related to the topic.
	COMPREHENSIBILITY	The student's ideas are occasionally intelligible.
	ORGANIZATION	The student's response is only slightly related to the topic.
	FLOW OF IDEAS	The student's ideas do not flow smoothly.
	GRAMMAR	The student has very little grammatically correct language.
	VOCABULARY	The student uses very little vocabulary correctly.
0	The student either writes nothing or fails to answer the question.	

The following chart shows how a score of 0 through 5 on a Writing task is converted to a scaled score out of 30.

WRITING SCORE (0–5)	WRITING SCALED SCORE (0–30)
5.00	30
4.75	29
4.50	28
4.25	27
4.00	25
3.75	24
3.50	22
3.25	21
3.00	20
2.75	18
2.50	17
2.25	15
2.00	14
1.75	12
1.50	11
1.25	10
1.00	8
0.75	7
0.50	5
0.25	4
0.00	0

Scaled scores on each of the Writing tasks on a test are averaged to determine the scaled score for the test.

RECORDING YOUR WRITING TEST RESULTS

Each time that you complete a Writing Pre-Test, Post-Test, Mini-Test, Complete Test section, or TOEFL-Level Test section, you should record your results in the chart that follows. In this way, you will be able to keep track of the progress you are making.

WRITING TEST RESULTS	
PRE-TEST	Writing Task 1 _____ Writing Task 2 _____ **Overall Writing Score** _____
POST-TEST	Writing Task 1 _____ Writing Task 2 _____ **Overall Writing Score** _____
MINI-TEST 1	Writing Task 1 _____ **Overall Writing Score** _____
MINI-TEST 2	Writing Task 1 _____ **Overall Writing Score** _____
MINI-TEST 3	Writing Task 1 _____ **Overall Writing Score** _____
MINI-TEST 4	Writing Task 1 _____ **Overall Writing Score** _____
COMPLETE TEST	Writing Task 1 _____ Writing Task 2 _____ **Overall Writing Score** _____
TOEFL-LEVEL TEST	Writing Task 1 _____ Writing Task 2 _____ **Overall Writing Score** _____

RECORDING SCRIPT

LISTENING DIAGNOSTIC PRE-TEST

Questions 1 through 6. Listen as two students have a conversation. The conversation is on an economics class.

(man) Hey, Lynn. How's your economics class going?

(woman) Not very well, I'm afraid.

(man) Why not? Why isn't your economics class going well? I took the same class before, and I enjoyed it.

(woman) I'm glad you enjoyed it when you took it, but I'm not enjoying it now. I guess the problem is that I don't always understand everything the professor says in class.

(man) Do you ask questions when you don't understand?

(woman) No, I never do.

(man) Why not?

(woman) Because I don't understand. Everyone else seems to understand everything, and I don't.

(man) I'm sure that other students don't understand everything, either.

(woman) I'm not sure of that. I think I'm the only one who doesn't understand.

(man) Well, maybe you are the only one who doesn't understand . . . But I doubt that. Then you should ask the questions outside of class. You can talk to the professor after class or during office hours, or maybe ask other students after class, but just ask questions when you don't understand. . . . How does that sound? Can you try that?

(woman) I'll try.

1. WHY IS THE WOMAN TALKING WITH THE MAN?
2. WHAT IS STATED IN THE CONVERSATION ABOUT THE ECONOMICS CLASS?
3. HOW DOES THE WOMAN SEEM TO FEEL ABOUT THE ECONOMICS CLASS?
4. LISTEN AGAIN TO PART OF THE PASSAGE. THEN ANSWER THE QUESTION.

(woman) I think I'm the only one who doesn't understand.

(man) Well, maybe you are the only one who doesn't understand. . . . But I doubt that. Then you should ask the questions outside of class.

WHAT DOES THE MAN MEAN WHEN HE SAYS THIS:

(man) But I doubt that.

5. IT CAN BE INFERRED THAT THE MAN WOULD MOST LIKELY NOT SUGGEST WHICH OF THE FOLLOWING TO THE WOMAN?
6. IS EACH OF THESE DISCUSSED IN THE PASSAGE?

Questions 7 through 12. Listen to a discussion in a geography class. The discussion is on Antarctica.

(professor) ❶ Today, we'll be discussing the continent of Antarctica, which is the place with the coldest climate on Earth. How big is Antarctica? Is Antarctica the smallest continent? Meg?

(Meg) No, Antarctica isn't the smallest continent. It's the fifth largest continent.

(professor) And which continents are smaller than Antarctica?

(Meg) Australia is the smallest continent, and Asia's the largest. Both Australia and Europe are smaller than Antarctica. North America, South America, Africa, and Asia are all larger than Antarctica, so Antarctica is the fifth largest of seven continents.

(professor) That's right. Now, the focus of our discussion today is on the American bases on Antarctica. ❷ Let's look at a map of Antarctica. How many American bases are there on Antarctica? John?

(John) Uh, . . . I'm not sure. . . . Let me think about that for a minute. . . .

(professor) Just look at the map, John. . . . You can just count the number of bases.

(John) Oh, I see. There are three bases.

(professor) Very good, John. But it did take you a while. Yes, there are three American bases on Antarctica. They are Palmer, Amundsen-Scott, and McMurdo. ❸ Let's talk about the base at Palmer first. What can you tell me about the base at Palmer, Pat?

(Pat) Palmer is located on an island just off the Antarctic Peninsula, in the western half of Antarctica. The Antarctic Peninsula is, of course, the curved hook of land out in the ocean. Palmer is used mainly for the scientific study of the animals of Antarctica.

(professor) Yes, the main purpose of Palmer is the study of the wildlife of Antarctica. ❹ Now, what about Amundsen-Scott? Meg?

(Meg) Amundsen-Scott is very close to the geographic South Pole. It's so cold at Amundsen-Scott during the winter that no one can get in or out from February through October.

(professor) And now for the third base. ❺ What's this third base, John?

(John) Ummmm . . .

(professor) Just look at the map again, John. . . . You really need to pay more attention, John. . . . Now, the third base?

(John) The third base is McMurdo.

(professor) That's right, John. And where's McMurdo located?

(John) McMurdo is on an island in the eastern part of Antarctica.

(professor) That's right, too, John. It's close to Mount Erebus, which is Antarctica's most active volcano. . . . Now, let's ask someone other than John. . . . Pat, you seem to know what you're talking about. How would you describe the base at McMurdo, Pat?

(Pat) McMurdo is the largest American base in Antarctica. During the summer months, there are over a thousand people living there, and it looks like a regular town.

7. WHAT IS THE LECTURE MAINLY ABOUT?

8. WHAT IS STATED ABOUT THE RELATIVE SIZES OF THE CONTINENTS?

9. LISTEN AGAIN TO PART OF THE PASSAGE. THEN ANSWER THE QUESTION.

(professor) How many American bases are there on Antarctica? John?

(John) Uh, . . . I'm not sure. . . . Let me think about that for a minute. . . .

(professor) Just look at the map, John. . . . You can just count the number of bases.

(John) Oh, I see. There are three bases.

(professor) Very good, John. But it did take you a while.

HOW DOES THE PROFESSOR SEEM TO FEEL ABOUT JOHN'S RESPONSE?

10. WHEN WOULD SOMEONE BE MOST LIKELY TO GET INTO AMUNDSEN-SCOTT?

11. LISTEN AGAIN TO PART OF THE PASSAGE. THEN ANSWER THE QUESTION.

(professor) Now, let's ask someone other than John. . . . Pat, you seem to know what you're talking about.

WHAT DOES THE PROFESSOR MEAN WHEN HE SAYS THIS?

12. HOW COULD EACH OF THESE BE DESCRIBED?

LISTENING EXERCISE 1

PASSAGE ONE

Page 108

Questions 1 and 2. Listen as two students have a conversation. The conversation is on an exam.

(woman) Mark, do you have a minute? I need to ask you a question.

(man) Sure. What's your question?

(woman) It's about the exam.

(man) Which exam? The one we just took in math class?

(woman) No, not the math exam we just took. My question's about the exam we're going to have in English class.

(man) Oh, that exam. The one we're having next Wednesday.

(woman) That's right. . . . Do you know what's on the exam? I know it's on Chapter 9 in the textbook, but is that all?

(man) No, that's not all. The exam's not just on Chapter 9 in the textbook. It's also on Chapters 10 and 11.

(woman) So it's on a lot more than I thought. . . . I have a lot of studying to do.

1. WHY DOES THE WOMAN WANT TO TALK WITH THE MAN?

2. WHAT IS COVERED ON THE EXAM?

PASSAGE TWO

Page 109

Questions 3 and 4. Listen as a student consults with a professor. The conversation is about a reading assignment.

(student) I have a question about the reading assignment you gave in today's class.

(professor) Yes, what's your question?

(student) I believe you said that we were supposed to read some articles.

(professor) That's right.

(student) You listed some articles on the board, and we're supposed to finish reading all of the articles that you listed on the board. You listed seven of them.

(professor) Yes, that's right, too.

(student) And did you also say that we're supposed to finish reading all of the articles, all seven articles, by this coming Monday?

(professor) No, not by this coming Monday. It's way too much reading for one weekend. No, I said to finish them by a week from Monday, by Monday the tenth.

(student) Oh, I'm glad I asked. I thought you said this coming Monday. It's too much reading for one weekend.

(professor) It certainly is. That's why you have more than a week to read all of it.

3. WHY DOES THE STUDENT GO TO SEE THE PROFESSOR?

4. WHAT IS THE STUDENT MAINLY CONFUSED ABOUT?

PASSAGE THREE

Page 110

Questions 5 and 6. Listen to a lecture in an astronomy class. The lecture is on sunspots.

(professor) Today, I'm going to talk about our Sun. You should understand this material clearly because it's going to be on the exam on Friday.

The Sun has a number of dark-colored and irregularly shaped patches called sunspots. The number of sunspots doesn't remain the same. The number of sunspots increases and then decreases in a regular pattern. This regular pattern of increasing and decreasing numbers of sunspots is called the sunspot cycle. The sunspot cycle occurs every eleven years.

Sunspots appear dark because they're cooler than the surface of the Sun around them. Sunspots are approximately five thousand degrees cooler than the rest of the surface of the Sun, which averages temperatures of ten thousand degrees. There are very strong magnetic fields that cause the sunspots to remain cooler than the rest of the surface of the Sun.

Is all of this clear to you? You should ask questions if it isn't clear . . . because you will need to show me that you know it on Friday.

5. WHY IS THE PROFESSOR DISCUSSING THIS MATERIAL?
6. WHAT IS THE TALK MAINLY ABOUT?

LISTENING EXERCISE 2

PASSAGE ONE

Page 114

Questions 1 through 4. Listen as two students have a conversation. The conversation is about a recital.

(woman) What is that you're carrying?
(man) It's a tuba.
(woman) A tuba?
(man) It's a musical instrument.
(woman) I know. You play the tuba?
(man) Yes. That's why I'm carrying a tuba around. I'm going to the Music Building.
(woman) That makes sense. Are you going to the Music Building to practice?
(man) No, I'm not going to the Music Building to practice. I'm going there because I'm playing in a recital.
(woman) You're in a recital this afternoon?
(man) Yeah, it starts in about an hour and a half. You should come.
(woman) The recital is over in the Music Building?
(man) Yes, it is.
(woman) Will it last very long?
(man) Only about a half hour.
(woman) I can take a half hour off from studying. I'll be there.
(man) You'll enjoy the recital. I'm sure.

1. WHAT IS THE MAN DOING DURING THE CONVERSATION?
2. WHY IS THE MAN GOING TO THE MUSIC BUILDING?
3. WHAT DOES THE MAN STATE ABOUT THE RECITAL?
4. WHAT IS THE WOMAN GOING TO DO?

PASSAGE TWO

Page 115

Questions 5 through 10. Listen to a lecture in a geography class. The lecture is on the Carlsbad Caverns.

(professor) Today, I'll be talking about Carlsbad Caverns. Are any of you familiar with Carlsbad Caverns? . . . Well, Carlsbad Caverns is a huge series of caves. This huge series of caves is in the state of New Mexico. It's located in the southeastern corner of New Mexico. This extremely large maze of caves was formed 200 million years ago when the Rocky Mountains were only small hills. Today

the Rocky Mountains are huge mountains and not small hills.

The caves in Carlsbad Caverns extend for miles, and it isn't possible to count the caves because there are so many of them. Many of the caves haven't been explored yet because there are just so many caves.

The largest of the caves is called the Big Room. The Big Room is as long as ten football fields and is as high as a twenty-story building. Picture ten football fields, and picture a building with twenty stories. That's how large the Big Room is, and that's a pretty big cave.

5. IN WHICH STATE IS CARLSBAD CAVERNS LOCATED?
6. IN WHICH PART OF THE STATE IS CARLSBAD CAVERNS LOCATED?
7. HOW LONG AGO WAS CARLSBAD CAVERNS FORMED?
8. WHAT IS TRUE ABOUT THE NUMBER OF CAVES IN CARLSBAD CAVERNS?
9. WHAT IS THE NAME OF THE LARGEST CAVE?
10. WHAT IS STATED ABOUT THE LARGEST CAVE?

PASSAGE THREE

Page 116

Questions 11 through 16. Listen to a discussion in a zoology class. The discussion is on the grouper.

(professor) The next type of fish we need to discuss is the grouper. What type of fish is a grouper? Does it live in rivers, in lakes, or in the ocean? Mark?
(Mark) The grouper lives in the ocean. It generally lives close to the shore. It doesn't live out in the deep part of the ocean, away from the shore.
(professor) And what does the grouper look like? Ellen?
(Ellen) It's easy to recognize the grouper from the shape of its mouth.
(professor) And what does its mouth look like?
(Ellen) It has a very large mouth. Its mouth is huge in relation to the rest of the fish.
(professor) And why does it need such a large mouth? Sam?
(Sam) It needs a large mouth because it feeds on other fish. It swallows other fish whole. It needs a large mouth to swallow other fish.
(professor) Now, you should have read something about male and female grouper fish. What's unusual about male and female grouper fish? Mark?
(Mark) What's unusual about male and female grouper fish is that all grouper fish are born as females.
(professor) Exactly. When grouper fish are born, they're all females. Then what happens to them? Ellen?
(Ellen) Later, as grouper fish age, they change from female to male.

(Sam) So all groupers are females when they're born, and they change to males when they're older?

(professor) That's exactly right. It's quite unusual, isn't it? . . . Now, for something exciting. We're going to be watching a film. . . . Does that sound good? . . . But I hope you're not expecting a comedy, or a love story, or a musical. . . . We're going to be watching a documentary on . . . you guessed it . . . grouper fish.

11. WHAT IS A GROUPER?
12. WHERE DO GROUPERS LIVE?
13. WHAT PART OF THE GROUPER IS LARGER IN RELATION TO THE REST OF THE BODY?
14. WHAT DOES A GROUPER EAT?
15. WHAT IS STATED ABOUT THE GROUPER?
16. WHAT ARE THE STUDENTS GOING TO DO NEXT?

LISTENING REVIEW EXERCISE (Skills 1 and 2)

Page 117

Questions 1 through 9. Listen to a lecture in an architecture class. The professor is talking about the London Bridge.

(professor) ❶ Today, we're going to talk about the London Bridge. The London Bridge is covered in your text, on page 122 (*one hundred twenty-two*). I'm going to talk a little about this topic today, and you can also read about it in your text.

There is something important that you need to understand about the London Bridge. The London Bridge isn't actually in London anymore, but it used to be there.

❷ You can see the London Bridge when it was in London. The bridge crossed the Thames River, which is in the middle of London. The London Bridge is made of granite, and it's an arch bridge; you can see the five curved arches in the bridge. The London Bridge was built in the first half of the nineteenth century. When it was built, it was a very difficult project. It took 800 men seven years to build the bridge.

❸ In 1968, the city of London decided that it needed a new bridge. The London Bridge was too narrow; a wider bridge with six lanes was needed. The city didn't tear the bridge down and throw it away. Instead, the city found a buyer and sold the bridge.

❹ Here's the bridge in its new home. Do you know where this is? It's Lake Havasu in Arizona. The company that bought the London Bridge paid a lot of money for it. The company paid two and a half million dollars for the London Bridge. Then the company took the bridge apart stone by stone, put it into crates, transported it across the Atlantic, and rebuilt it in its new home. The London Bridge is now far from its original home, on a lake in the southwest United States.

1. WHAT IS THE TOPIC OF THE LECTURE?
2. WHAT DOES THE PROFESSOR MAINLY DISCUSS ABOUT THE BRIDGE?
3. WHY DOES THE PROFESSOR DISCUSS THIS TOPIC?
4. HOW MANY ARCHES DOES THE LONDON BRIDGE HAVE?
5. WHEN WAS THE LONDON BRIDGE ORIGINALLY BUILT?
6. WHAT IS TRUE ABOUT THE BUILDING OF THE ORIGINAL LONDON BRIDGE?
7. WHY WAS THE LONDON BRIDGE REPLACED?
8. HOW MUCH MONEY WAS PAID FOR THE BRIDGE?
9. WHERE IS THE LONDON BRIDGE LOCATED TODAY?

LISTENING EXERCISE 3

PASSAGE ONE

Page 123

Questions 1 and 2. Listen as two students have a conversation. The conversation is about a professor's grading.

(woman) I think it's so unfair!
(man) Uh . . . what do you mean? What's unfair?
(woman) Professor Kim's grading. The way he's going to give grades in our economics class.
(man) But he said that grades would be based on the final exam. That doesn't sound so unfair to me.
(woman) How can you say that? Grades shouldn't be based just on the final exam. Grades should also be based on things like attendance, participation, and effort . . . that sort of stuff.
(man) But the professor is saying that all he cares about is the grade on the final exam, and I think that's just fine.

1. LISTEN AGAIN TO PART OF THE PASSAGE. THEN ANSWER THE QUESTION.
   (woman) I think it's so unfair!
   (man) Uh . . . what do you mean? What's unfair?
   WHY DOES THE MAN SAY THIS:
   (man) Uh . . . what do you mean?

2. LISTEN AGAIN TO PART OF THE PASSAGE. THEN ANSWER THE QUESTION.
   (man) But he said that grades would be based on the final exam. That doesn't sound so unfair to me.
   (woman) How can you say that?
   WHAT DOES THE WOMAN MEAN WHEN SHE SAYS THIS:
   (woman) How can you say that?

PASSAGE TWO

Page 124

Questions 3 through 5. Listen as a student consults with a bookstore clerk. The conversation is about finding a book.

(student) Excuse me. . . . Are you free for a moment?
(worker) Sure. What can I do for you?
(student) I'm trying to find a book.
(worker) What book are you trying to find?
(student) It's Introduction to Philosophy, by Smith. It's the required textbook for my philosophy class.
(worker) That book should be right here on the bottom shelf. Books are organized alphabetically by the author's last name. The shelf for authors with last names beginning with "S" is right here.
(student) But I've checked this shelf again and again. . . . Are you sure the book's not somewhere else?
(worker) If the book's not on the shelf, then it's probably out of stock now.
(student) You mean, it's not in the store now?
(worker) That's right.
(student) Oh, no! I really need the book for my philosophy class, and I need it really soon.
(worker) I know what you mean. I think some more will be coming in soon. I can check the computer and see when the book will be here.
(student) You could? Thanks.

3. LISTEN AGAIN TO PART OF THE PASSAGE. THEN ANSWER THE QUESTION.
(student) Excuse me. . . . Are you free for a moment?
WHY DOES THE STUDENT SAY THIS?

4. LISTEN AGAIN TO PART OF THE PASSAGE. THEN ANSWER THE QUESTION.
(worker) That book should be right here on the bottom shelf. Books are organized alphabetically by the author's last name. The shelf for authors with last names beginning with "S" is right here.
(student) But I've checked this shelf again and again. . . . Are you sure the book's not somewhere else?
WHAT DOES THE STUDENT MEAN WHEN SHE SAYS THIS:
(student) But I've checked this shelf again and again.

5. LISTEN AGAIN TO PART OF THE PASSAGE. THEN ANSWER THE QUESTION.
(student) Oh, no! I really need the book for my philosophy class, and I need it really soon.
(worker) I know what you mean.
WHAT DOES THE WORKER MEAN WHEN HE SAYS THIS:
(worker) I know what you mean.

PASSAGE THREE

Page 125

Questions 6 through 8. Listen to a discussion from a geography class. The discussion is about rivers.

(professor) Today, we're going to talk about the parts of a river: the head, the mouth, and the

delta. First of all, what's the difference between the head of a river and the mouth of a river? Gail?
(Gail) The mouth of a river is the place where a river starts, and the head of a river is the place where the river ends.
(professor) Try again, Gail.
(Gail) Oh, did I have that backwards?
(professor) You did. A river starts at its head and ends at its mouth. . . . Now the last part of a river that we need to discuss is the delta. . . . Can anyone tell me what shape a delta is? Steve?
(Steve) Uh . . .
(professor) Steve seems to need some help. Can anyone help Steve out? Yes, Tom.
(Tom) A delta is a triangular shape.
(professor) Yes, and what about a river delta? What exactly is a river delta, Tom?
(Tom) A river delta is a triangular piece of land that may appear at the mouth of a river. A river delta forms when sand and soil are pushed from the riverbanks downriver to the mouth of the river.
(professor) You seem to understand this material well, Tom . . . unlike some of the other students.

6. LISTEN AGAIN TO PART OF THE PASSAGE. THEN ANSWER THE QUESTION.
(Gail) The mouth of a river is the place where a river starts, and the head of a river is the place where the river ends.
(professor) Try again, Gail.
WHAT DOES THE PROFESSOR MEAN WHEN SHE SAYS THIS:
(professor) Try again, Gail.

7. LISTEN AGAIN TO PART OF THE PASSAGE. THEN ANSWER THE QUESTION.
(professor) Can anyone tell me what shape a delta is? Steve?
(Steve) Uh . . .
(professor) Steve seems to need some help. Can anyone help Steve out?
WHY DOES THE PROFESSOR SAY THIS:
(professor) Steve seems to need some help. Can anyone help Steve out?

8. LISTEN AGAIN TO PART OF THE PASSAGE. THEN ANSWER THE QUESTION.
(professor) You seem to understand this material well, Tom . . . unlike some of the other students.
WHAT DOES THE PROFESSOR MEAN WHEN SHE SAYS THIS?

LISTENING EXERCISE 4

PASSAGE ONE

Page 130

Questions 1 and 2. Listen as two students have a conversation. The conversation is about a meeting.

(man) Are you coming to the meeting?
(woman) The meeting?
(man) The meeting of the Service Club.

(woman) The Service Club?

(man) It's a great club, and it'll be a great meeting.

(woman) Well, I'm not sure. . . . When is the meeting? . . . I'm sure I'll . . . uh . . . be busy . . . whenever the meeting is.

(man) The meeting starts in a few minutes, and you seem to be free now.

(woman) Well, I'm . . . uh . . . going somewhere . . . somewhere . . . uh . . . really important.

(man) Well, if you can't come to this meeting of the Service Club, then maybe you can come to the next meeting. It's in a week, a week from today.

(woman) Oh, of course, I'll try to come then, but . . . uh . . . I just might be busy then, too.

1. LISTEN AGAIN TO PART OF THE PASSAGE. THEN ANSWER THE QUESTION.

(man) Are you coming to the meeting?

(woman) The meeting?

(man) The meeting of the Service Club.

(woman) The Service Club?

(man) It's a great club, and it'll be a great meeting.

WHICH OF THE FOLLOWING MIGHT THE MAN SAY ABOUT THE MEETING?

2. LISTEN AGAIN TO PART OF THE PASSAGE. THEN ANSWER THE QUESTION.

(man) The meeting starts in a few minutes, and you seem to be free now.

(woman) Well, I'm . . . uh . . . going somewhere . . . somewhere . . . uh . . . really important.

(man) Well, if you can't come to this meeting of the Service Club, then maybe you can come to the next meeting. It's in a week, a week from today.

(woman) Oh, of course, I'll try to come then, but . . . uh . . . I just might be busy then, too

HOW DOES THE WOMAN SEEM TO FEEL ABOUT THE MEETING?

PASSAGE TWO
Page 131

Questions 3 through 5. Listen as a student consults with a professor. The conversation is about turning in a late paper.

(student) I know we're supposed to turn our papers in today, . . . but I don't . . . uh . . . have mine.

(professor) I really don't want to hear a lot of excuses about why you don't have your paper. I told you the due date. I told all the students the due date many times.

(student) Is there anything I can do about this, or will I receive a failing grade on the paper?

(professor) Well . . . I'll give you one extra week to complete the paper.

(student) Oh, thank you. I can finish the paper easily in one week.

(professor) But I am going to lower the grade on your paper by one letter grade because the paper is late.

(student) Thanks so much. It's better to have a lowered grade than a failing grade.

(professor) You're welcome. But, please understand. I will do this only one time. I won't do this

a second time. If any of your other papers are late you will receive failing grades on them.

(student) I understand. Thank you again.

3. LISTEN AGAIN TO PART OF THE PASSAGE. THEN ANSWER THE QUESTION.

(student) I know we're supposed to turn our papers in today . . . but I don't . . . uh . . . have mine.

(professor) I really don't want to hear a lot of excuses about why you don't have your paper. I told you the due date. I told all the students the due date many times.

HOW DOES THE PROFESSOR SEEM TO FEEL ABOUT THE STUDENT'S SITUATION?

4. LISTEN AGAIN TO PART OF THE PASSAGE. THEN ANSWER THE QUESTION.

(professor) Well . . . I'll give you one extra week to complete the paper.

(student) Oh, thank you. I can finish the paper easily in one week.

(professor) But I am going to lower the grade on your paper by one letter grade because the paper is late.

(student) Thanks so much. It's better to have a lowered grade than a failing grade.

HOW DOES THE STUDENT SEEM TO FEEL ABOUT THE PROFESSOR'S OFFER?

5. LISTEN AGAIN TO PART OF THE PASSAGE. THEN ANSWER THE QUESTION.

(professor) You're welcome. But, please understand. I will do this only one time. I won't do this a second time. If any of your other papers are late you will receive failing grades on them.

WHICH OF THE FOLLOWING MIGHT THE PROFESSOR SAY?

PASSAGE THREE
Page 132

Questions 6 through 8. Listen as a professor begins a lecture. The professor is making some announcements.

(professor) I have a few announcements to make before I start today's lecture.

First of all, I'd like to tell you—regretfully—that I cannot return your papers today. I'm sorry that I was not quite able to finish reading and grading them. However, I have almost finished with them, and I will definitely return them to you next week. Again, please understand that I sincerely regret this.

I have already spent a lot of time reading your papers, and I can tell you today that I'm really pleased with them. It's clear to me that you all did a lot of work on your term papers, and you even went way beyond what I expected of you. It has been a pleasure for me to read your term papers.

Now, on a more serious note, I'd like to say something about attendance. A number of you have been absent from class more than once, and I want you to understand that this is not acceptable. Remember what's on the class syllabus. The class syllabus clearly states that attendance is counted as part of your grade in this course. Please pay more attention to attendance because it will affect your grade.

Okay, that's all of the announcements for today. Next, I'll start today's lecture.

6. LISTEN AGAIN TO PART OF THE PASSAGE. THEN ANSWER THE QUESTION.

(professor) First of all, I'd like to tell you—regretfully—that I cannot return your papers today. I'm sorry that I was not quite able to finish reading and grading them. However, I have almost finished with them, and I will definitely return them to you next week. Again, please understand that I sincerely regret this.

HOW DOES THE PROFESSOR SEEM TO FEEL ABOUT NOT RETURNING THE PAPERS?

7. LISTEN AGAIN TO PART OF THE PASSAGE. THEN ANSWER THE QUESTION.

(professor) I have already spent a lot of time reading your papers, and I can tell you today that I'm really pleased with them. It's clear to me that you all did a lot of work on your term papers, and you even went way beyond what I expected of you. It has been a pleasure for me to read your term papers.

WHICH OF THE FOLLOWING MIGHT THE PROFESSOR SAY ABOUT THE TERM PAPERS?

8. LISTEN AGAIN TO PART OF THE PASSAGE. THEN ANSWER THE QUESTION.

(professor) Now, on a more serious note, I'd like to say something about attendance. A number of you have been absent from class more than once, and I want you to understand that this is not acceptable. Remember what's on the class syllabus. The class syllabus clearly states that attendance is counted as part of your grade in this course. Please pay more attention to attendance because it will affect your grade.

HOW DOES THE PROFESSOR SEEM TO FEEL ABOUT THE STUDENTS' ATTENDANCE?

LISTENING EXERCISE (Skills 3 and 4)

Page 133

Questions 1 through 5. Listen as a student consults with her advisor. The conversation is about a music class.

(student) Hi, Mr. Roberts. Do you have a minute? I'd like to ask you a question.

(advisor) Sure, I have a moment before my next appointment. What's your question?

(student) It's about the music class.

(advisor) The music class? I'm not sure what you're talking about.

(student) I mean, it's about the requirement to take a music class. Everyone must take a music class?

(advisor) Yes, that's right. It's a requirement; everyone must take a music class. You don't want to take a music class?

(student) Well, I mean, I don't play a musical instrument, and I don't sing. . . . How can I take a music class?

(advisor) Oh, that's not really a problem. You can take a music class where you play a musical instrument or sing, if you want to, but you don't have to take that kind of music class.

(student) Really? I don't have to? What kind of music class can I take?

(advisor) There are several music classes you can take where you don't have to sing or play a musical instrument. There's Music History, where you study the history of music, there's Famous Composers, where you study famous composers, and there's Modern Music, where you study the music of today.

(student) Oh, some of those courses sound really interesting.

(advisor) You can say that again!

(student) It'll be okay . . . just as long as I don't need to play a musical instrument or sing.

1. LISTEN AGAIN TO PART OF THE PASSAGE. THEN ANSWER THE QUESTION.

(advisor) What's your question?

(student) It's about the music class.

(advisor) The music class? I'm not sure what you're talking about.

WHAT DOES THE ADVISOR MEAN WHEN HE SAYS THIS:

(advisor) I'm not sure what you're talking about.

2. LISTEN AGAIN TO PART OF THE PASSAGE. THEN ANSWER THE QUESTION.

(student) Everyone must take a music class?

(advisor) Yes, that's right. It's a requirement; everyone must take a music class. You don't want to take a music class?

(student) Well, I mean, I don't play a musical instrument, and I don't sing. . . . How can I take a music class?

HOW DOES THE STUDENT SEEM TO FEEL ABOUT THE MUSIC REQUIREMENT IN THIS PART OF THE PASSAGE?

3. LISTEN AGAIN TO PART OF THE PASSAGE. THEN ANSWER THE QUESTION.

(advisor) You can take a music class where you play a musical instrument or sing, if you want to, but you don't have to take that kind of music class.

(student) Really? I don't have to?

WHAT DOES THE STUDENT MEAN WHEN SHE SAYS THIS:

(student) Really? I don't have to?

4. LISTEN AGAIN TO PART OF THE PASSAGE. THEN ANSWER THE QUESTION.

(advisor) There are several music classes you can take where you don't have to sing or play a musical instrument. There's Music History, where you study the history of music, there's Famous Composers, where you study famous composers, and there's Modern Music, where you study the music of today.

(student) Oh, some of those courses sound really interesting.

(advisor) You can say that again!

WHAT DOES THE ADVISOR MEAN WHEN HE SAYS THIS:

(advisor) You can say that again!

5. LISTEN AGAIN TO PART OF THE PASSAGE. THEN ANSWER THE QUESTION.

(student) Oh, some of those courses sound really interesting.

(advisor) You can say that again!

(student) It'll be okay . . . just as long as I don't need to play a musical instrument or sing.

WHAT MIGHT THE STUDENT SAY ABOUT THE MUSIC REQUIREMENT AT THE END OF THE CONVERSATION?

LISTENING REVIEW EXERCISE (Skills 1 through 4)

Page 134

Questions 1 through 8. Listen to a lecture in a literature class. The professor is talking about James Fenimore Cooper.

(professor) ❶ In today's class, I'll be talking about another author. The author for today is one who was quite popular in the first half of the nineteenth century.

❷ The man in this portrait is James Fenimore Cooper. He was born in 1789, and he died in 1851. He wrote more than thirty different novels. The most famous of his novels was a group of five novels which, as a group, was called *The Leatherstocking Tales*.

❸ All of the five Leatherstocking novels had the same main character. This main character was known by a number of different names. He was, of course, called Leatherstocking, but he was also known by two other names. He was known by the name of Hawkeye, and he was also known by the name Natty Bumpo. This character was a skilled outdoorsman and courageous hero. How many of you know about this character? . . . A show of hands, please? . . . Yes, I see many of you do.

❹ On the board, you can see the names of the five novels that were called *The Leatherstocking Tales*. They are *The Deerslayer, The Pathfinder, The Last of the Mohicans, The Pioneers,* and *The Prairie,* and they all feature the character known as Leatherstocking, Hawkeye, or Natty Bumpo. You can see from the list that the books are not listed on the board in the order that they were written. Instead, the books are listed in the order that they take place. Cooper didn't write the books in chronological order. You can see, for example, that *The Pioneers* was the first of *The Leatherstocking Tales* to be written, in 1823, but it took place later in Leatherstocking's life. You can also see that *The Deerslayer* was the last of *The Leatherstocking Tales* to be written, in 1841, but it describes the earliest part of Leatherstocking's life.

❺ Okay, that's all for today on James Fenimore Cooper and the five novels of the many novels that he wrote, which together are called *The Leatherstocking Tales*. You should be working on the assignment, the assignment to read all of *The Leatherstocking Tales*. I know this is quite an assignment, but you do need to finish it by, by next class. I hope you've already started it and are well into it. If not, you've got quite a lot of work in front of you.

1. WHAT IS THE MAIN TOPIC OF THIS TALK?
2. APPROXIMATELY HOW MANY NOVELS DID JAMES FENIMORE COOPER WRITE?
3. WHAT WAS TRUE ABOUT THE LEATHERSTOCKING NOVELS?
4. BY WHAT OTHER NAMES WAS LEATHERSTOCKING KNOWN?
5. LISTEN AGAIN TO PART OF THE PASSAGE. THEN ANSWER THE QUESTION.

(professor) This main character was known by a number of different names. He was, of course, called Leatherstocking, but he was also known by two other names. He was known by the name of Hawkeye, and he was also known by the name Natty Bumpo. This character was a skilled outdoorsman and courageous hero. How many of you know about this character? . . . A show of hands, please? . . . Yes, I see many of you do.

WHAT DOES THE PROFESSOR MEAN WHEN SHE SAYS THIS:

(professor) A show of hands, please?

6. WHAT IS TRUE ABOUT HOW COOPER WROTE *THE LEATHERSTOCKING TALES*?
7. LISTEN AGAIN TO PART OF THE PASSAGE. THEN ANSWER THE QUESTION.

(professor) Okay, that's all for today on James Fenimore Cooper and the five novels of the many novels that he wrote, which together are called *The Leatherstocking Tales.*

WHY DOES THE PROFESSOR SAY THIS?

8. LISTEN AGAIN TO PART OF THE PASSAGE. THEN ANSWER THE QUESTION.

(professor) You should be working on the assignment, the assignment to read all of *The Leatherstocking Tales*. I know this is quite an assignment, but you do need to finish it by, by next class. I hope you've already started it and are well into it. If not, you've got quite a lot of work in front of you.

HOW DOES THE PROFESSOR SEEM TO FEEL ABOUT THE ASSIGNMENT?

LISTENING EXERCISE 5

PASSAGE ONE
Page 143

Questions 1 through 3. Listen to a discussion about a history class. The discussion is on the city of Chicago.

(woman 1) Wasn't that an interesting lecture that we just heard on the history of Chicago?

(man) It certainly was. I hadn't understood that Chicago was such a young city, less than 200 years old.

(woman 2) Yes, and that the army fort, Fort Dearborn, was built in 1803 in the place that would become Chicago. Chicago didn't officially become a town until thirty years later, in 1833.

(woman 1) And when it officially became a town in 1833, it was very small. It had a population of only, uh, 350.

(man) Then, after Chicago had grown, much of it was destroyed in a fire. When was the Great Chicago Fire, do you know?

(woman 2) The Great Chicago Fire was in 1871. Chicago wasn't even forty years old at the time, but it had grown much bigger. The fire destroyed a large part of the city.

(woman 1) Yet only twenty-two years later, in 1893, Chicago was able to host a World's Fair.

(man) Yes, Chicago had been rebuilt after the fire and was eager to show itself off to the rest of the world at the World's Fair in 1893.

1. HOW IS THE INFORMATION IN THE PASSAGE ORGANIZED?
2. IN THE LECTURE, THE PROFESSOR DISCUSSES EVENTS IN THE HISTORY OF CHICAGO. PUT THESE EVENTS IN THE ORDER THAT THEY OCCURRED.
3. WHICH OF THESE ARE DISCUSSED IN THE LECTURE?

PASSAGE TWO
Page 144

Questions 4 through 6. Listen to a lecture in an astronomy class. The lecture is on Alpha Centauri.

(professor) The nearest star system to our Sun is the Alpha Centauri system. Alpha Centauri isn't just one star. Instead, it's three stars. These three stars are called Alpha Centauri A, Alpha Centauri B, and Proxima Centauri.

Alpha Centauri A is a star much like our Sun. It's brighter than the other two stars in this system. The other two stars orbit around Alpha Centauri A.

Alpha Centauri B isn't quite as bright as Alpha Centauri A. Alpha Centauri B orbits around Alpha Centauri A. It takes about eighty years for Alpha Centauri B to orbit around Alpha Centauri A.

Proxima Centauri is the dimmest of the three stars in the system. This very faint star orbits around the other two stars in the system. It orbits around both Alpha Centauri A and Alpha Centauri B. It takes Proxima Centauri about a million years to orbit around the other two stars in the three-star system.

4. HOW IS THE INFORMATION IN THE PASSAGE ORGANIZED?
5. IS EACH OF THESE MENTIONED IN THE PASSAGE?
6. WHICH STARS ORBIT THE OTHERS?

PASSAGE THREE
Page 145

Questions 7 through 10. Listen to a discussion about a political science course. The discussion is on the course syllabus.

(man 1) Let's look over the syllabus from our political science class.

(woman) It looks like there are three units of study during the twelve-week course.

(man 2) That's right. The three units of study are on the three branches of the U.S. government: the executive branch, the legislative branch, and the judicial branch.

(man 1) Let's see. . . . The legislative branch is the part of government that includes the Congress.

(woman) And we'll be discussing the legislative branch in the first four weeks of the course.

(man 2) Then there's the judicial branch of the government. This is the part of the government that includes the courts.

(man 1) We'll be discussing the judicial branch of government during the second four weeks of the course, weeks five through eight.

(woman) And that leaves the executive branch of government for the last four weeks of the course.

(man 2) The executive branch is the part of the government that includes the president. So, we'll be discussing the president of the United States in the last part of the course, in weeks nine through twelve.

7. HOW IS THE INFORMATION IN THE DISCUSSION ORGANIZED?
8. IS EACH OF THESE COVERED IN THE DISCUSSION?
9. WHAT WILL BE THE TOPIC OF EACH OF THESE PARTS OF THE COURSE?

10. WHAT ARE THE THREE MAIN BRANCHES OF
    THE U.S. GOVERNMENT?

LISTENING EXERCISE 6

PASSAGE ONE

Page 148

Questions 1 and 2. Listen as a student consults with a professor. The conversation is about a missed exam.

(student)   Hello, Professor.
(professor) Hello, Mary. What happened to you last Friday? Were you really sick? You missed the exam I gave on Friday. Are you feeling better today?
(student)   Oh, I wasn't sick last Friday.
(professor) But you missed the exam. Why did you miss the exam last Friday?
(student)   Oh, some friends of mine were going skiing, and the weather was so beautiful, and they wanted me to go skiing with them. I just had to go.
(professor) You missed an exam because you went skiing?
(student)   Yeah, so I was hoping I could make the exam up, maybe tomorrow.
(professor) You missed an exam because you went skiing, and you think you're going to be able to make it up?
(student)   Yeah.
(professor) Don't count on it.

1. WHAT CAN BE INFERRED FROM THE
   CONVERSATION?
2. WHAT IS IMPLIED ABOUT THE STUDENT IN THE
   CONVERSATION?

PASSAGE TWO

Page 149

Questions 3 and 4. Listen to a lecture from a zoology class. The lecture is on the robin.

(professor) A robin is a type of bird that's known for its singing. When a robin sings, it isn't to relax or to entertain other birds or people. Instead, a robin sings to defend its territory.

Robins are territorial birds. This means that they select a certain location for their family and they don't allow other birds to enter the location. The way that they tell other robins that they've taken a certain location as their own is to sing. When one robin hears another robin singing, this means "This is my territory. Don't enter it."

The territory that one robin family takes can be one tree or a group of trees. And why do you think that a robin protects its territory from other birds? That's easy. It protects its territory from other birds in order to have a better chance of raising its family safely and having enough food for its family.

3. WHEN WOULD A ROBIN MOST LIKELY SING?
4. IN WHAT SITUATION WOULD A ROBIN MOST
   PROBABLY BEGIN TO SING?

PASSAGE THREE

Page 150

Questions 5 through 7. Listen to a discussion from an astronomy class. The discussion is on auroras.

(professor) Today, we're going to discuss auroras. First of all, what's an aurora, Tom?
(Tom)   An aurora is a natural show of colored light in the night sky.
(professor) And what colors are in the auroras?
(Tom)   The auroras are usually white with a bit of green. Other colors may appear in the auroras, such as yellow or red.
(professor) And where are the auroras found? Pam?
(Pam)   The auroras are found mainly in the high latitudes of both hemispheres.
(professor) That's right. Now, Pam, can you explain which parts of the world are in the higher latitudes?
(Pam)   The higher latitudes are in the far north and far south.
(professor) Exactly. The auroras can be seen mainly in the northernmost and the southernmost parts of the world. . . . Now, Marie, how often do auroras occur?
(Marie)   They occur about twenty-four times a year.
(professor) And are these twenty-four occurrences of the auroras spread out equally during the year?
(Marie)   No, they're not spread out equally throughout the year. They occur more often in the spring and the fall. They occur less often in the summer and the winter.
(professor) That's exactly right. It's much more common to see auroras during the spring and the fall than it is during the summer and the winter.

5. WHEN WOULD AN AURORA MOST PROBABLY
   OCCUR?
6. WHERE WOULD AN AURORA MOST LIKELY BE
   VISIBLE?
7. IT IS IMPLIED THAT WHICH OF THE FOLLOWING
   IS QUITE UNUSUAL?

LISTENING EXERCISE (Skills 5 and 6)

Page 151

Questions 1 though 5. Listen to a discussion about a business class. The discussion is on the Harley-Davidson Company.

(woman 1)   ❶ We're giving our presentation next week on the Harley-Davidson Company.
(man)   Yes, there are three distinct phases in the history of Harley-Davidson. I think we should each talk about one of the three phases in our presentation.
(woman 2)   Excuse me, but what do you mean by three phases in the history of Harley-

(man) Davidson? I'm not sure that I understand what you mean.

(man) Well, the first phase is the period from 1903 to 1969, when the company was family owned. The next period was from 1969 to 1980, when the company was owned by a corporation. And the third period was from 1980 to the present, when some former executives bought the company back from the corporation.

(woman 2) Oh, now I see what you mean by three phases. Which phase would each of you like to discuss?

(woman 1) ❷ I'd like to discuss the first period from 1903 to 1969. I'll talk about how the company was started in 1903 by William Harley and three Davidson brothers. I'll also talk about how they built the first motorbikes in the backyard. I'll talk about this period of time when the company was owned by the Harley and Davidson families.

(man) ❸ Then I guess I can talk about the second phase. This phase started in 1969, when the family-owned company was bought by a corporation. Harley-Davidson didn't do very well under the corporation. By 1980, it was almost bankrupt.

(woman 2) ❹ Then that leaves the third phase for me. This began in 1980, when a group of former executives bought Harley-Davidson from the corporation. Harley-Davidson was bought by a group of people who had worked for Harley-Davidson earlier and didn't want to see Harley-Davidson go out of business. This last group managed to turn Harley-Davidson around. Since 1980, the company has been very successful.

1. HOW IS THE INFORMATION IN THE PASSAGE ORGANIZED?
2. WHO OWNED HARLEY-DAVIDSON DURING EACH OF THESE PERIODS?
3. WHAT IS IMPLIED ABOUT THE CHANGE IN OWNERSHIP FROM FAMILY TO CORPORATION?
4. WHAT MOST LIKELY HAPPENED WHEN THE FORMER EXECUTIVES BOUGHT THE COMPANY?
5. IN THE LECTURE, THE PROFESSOR DISCUSSES EVENTS IN THE HISTORY OF HARLEY-DAVIDSON. PUT THESE EVENTS IN THE CORRECT ORDER.

LISTENING REVIEW EXERCISE (Skills 1 through 6)

Page 153

Questions 1 through 7. Listen to a lecture in an oceanography class. The professor is talking about the Mid-Atlantic Ridge.

(professor) ❶ Can you tell me the most important mountain ranges in the world? The Himalayas are taller than any other mountain range, and the Appalachians are one of the oldest mountain ranges.

But which mountain range is the longest mountain range in the world? Do you think it's the Himalayas, or the Rockies, or the Andes? Well, the longest mountain range in the world is one you might not have heard of. It's one called the Mid-Atlantic Ridge.

❷ You can see the Mid-Atlantic Ridge on this map. The Mid-Atlantic Ridge extends from the Arctic Circle in the north to Antarctica in the south. It's 7,000 miles in length.

Let me explain how the Mid-Atlantic Ridge was formed. Two hundred million years ago, the Atlantic Ocean didn't exist. The continents of Europe and Africa were touching the Americas. Then the continents began moving apart.

❸ It's important to understand how the material moved. As the continents moved apart, the older material moved toward the continents. New material came from inside the Earth and pushed up to create the Mid-Atlantic Ridge.

❹ Let me say this point again because you really need to get it. As the continents continue to move apart, new material pushes up from inside the Earth along the Mid-Atlantic Ridge. This means that the oldest material is found close to the continents. The youngest part of the crust is found in the middle of the ocean, along the Mid-Atlantic Ridge.

1. WHAT DOES THE PROFESSOR MAINLY DISCUSS IN THE LECTURE?
2. LISTEN AGAIN TO PART OF THE PASSAGE. THEN ANSWER THE QUESTION.
   (professor) But which mountain range is the longest mountain range in the world? Do you think it's the Himalayas, or the Rockies, or the Andes? Well, the longest mountain range in the world is one you might not have heard of. It's one called the Mid-Atlantic Ridge.
   HOW DOES THE PROFESSOR SEEM TO FEEL THE STUDENTS WILL RESPOND TO THIS QUESTION:
   (professor) Do you think it's the Himalayas, or the Rockies, or the Andes?
3. WHAT IS STATED ABOUT THE MID-ATLANTIC RIDGE?
4. LISTEN AGAIN TO PART OF THE PASSAGE. THEN ANSWER THE QUESTION.
   (professor) Let me say this point again because you really need to get it.
   WHY DOES THE PROFESSOR SAY THIS?
5. WHICH MOUNTAIN RANGES ARE DISCUSSED IN THE LECTURE?
6. WHAT IS IMPLIED IN THE LECTURE ABOUT THE CRUST ALONG THE EAST COAST OF SOUTH AMERICA?

7. IN THE LECTURE, THE PROFESSOR DISCUSSES EVENTS IN THE CREATION OF THE MID-ATLANTIC RIDGE. PUT THESE EVENTS IN THE CORRECT ORDER.

LISTENING POST-TEST

Page 156

Questions 1 through 6. Listen as a student consults with her professor. The conversation is about an exam.

(student)	Hi, Professor Hall.
(professor)	Oh, hi, Sandy.
(student)	Do you have a minute? I'd like to ask you about something.
(professor)	Sure. What do you want to ask me?
(student)	Well, it's . . . uh . . . about my grade on the exam.
(professor)	What was your grade?
(student)	It was a grade of C. I got 75 percent.
(professor)	75 percent, a C. That's not so good. It could be better. It should be better.
(student)	I wanted to ask you about this. I mean, I studied. I really studied a lot. I studied all three chapters that were on the exam, and I'm sure I knew all the material from the chapters.
(professor)	That's good. But did you study your lecture notes?
(student)	My lecture notes?
(professor)	The notes you took during the lectures.
(student)	Well . . . um . . . I didn't . . . exactly . . . take any notes during the lectures.
(professor)	Okay, so now we know what the problem is. The exams cover the textbook chapters and the lectures. It's important to take notes on the lectures and then study your lecture notes to prepare for the exams.
(student)	You mean, if I just study the chapters, it's not enough?
(professor)	That's exactly right. You also need to take good notes during the lectures and study your lecture notes, too, if you want to get high grades on the exams.

1. WHY DOES THE STUDENT GO TO SEE THE PROFESSOR?
2. LISTEN AGAIN TO PART OF THE PASSAGE. THEN ANSWER THE QUESTION.
   (professor) What was your grade?
   (student) It was a grade of C. I got 75 percent.
   (professor) 75 percent, a C. That's not so good. It could be better. It should be better.
   HOW DOES THE PROFESSOR SEEM TO FEEL ABOUT THE EXAM GRADE?

3. LISTEN AGAIN TO PART OF THE PASSAGE. THEN ANSWER THE QUESTION.
   (professor) But did you study your lecture notes?
   (student) My lecture notes?
   (professor) The notes you took during the lectures.
   WHAT DOES THE STUDENT MEAN WHEN SHE SAYS THIS:
   (student) My lecture notes?

4. WHAT PROBLEM DID THE STUDENT HAVE ON THE EXAM?
5. WHAT CAN BE INFERRED FROM THE CONVERSATION?
6. IS EACH OF THESE TRUE, BASED ON THE CONVERSATION?

Page 158

Questions 7 through 12. Listen to a group of students discussing information from a history class. The discussion is on the Roosevelts.

(man 1)	❶ We're having a quiz in history class today, and I'm confused about all the Roosevelts.
(woman)	Me, too. I need to understand this before the quiz.
(man 2)	Okay. There are three Roosevelts that we need to know. They are Theodore Roosevelt, Franklin Roosevelt, and Eleanor Roosevelt.
(man 1)	❷ Now, this picture shows Theodore Roosevelt, who was also known as Teddy. He was president of the United States early in the nineteenth century, wasn't he?
(woman)	Uh . . . that's a little bit off. He was vice-president when McKinley was president. He became president in 1901 when McKinley was assassinated.
(man 2)	Was he the one who was sick and in a wheelchair while he was president?
(man 1)	No, that was Franklin. Teddy Roosevelt was very sickly when he was a child, but he was very healthy and active as an adult.
(man 2)	❸ Okay, now this is Franklin Roosevelt. Was he the one who got polio when he was an adult?
(woman)	Yes, he became sick with polio when he was 39. It was after he got polio that he was elected president of the United States.
(man 1)	And when was he president?
(woman)	He was president in the 1930s and 1940s. He was president during the Great Depression and during World War II.
(man 2)	Was he related to Teddy Roosevelt?
(man 1)	They were distantly related. They were fifth cousins.
(woman)	❹ Now, for the third of the Roosevelts we need to know about. This is Eleanor Roosevelt, and she was married to Franklin Roosevelt.
(man 2)	She was also related to Franklin Roosevelt. Her father was Teddy Roosevelt's younger brother. So she was Teddy Roosevelt's niece.
(woman)	That means that, before she was married, her last name was Roosevelt because her father's last name was Roosevelt. After she was married, her last name was Roosevelt because her husband's name was Roosevelt.
(man 1)	Exactly. And she was very active as the wife of the president because her husband had polio while he was in the White House. She gave many speeches and did a lot of traveling for her husband. After his death,

she even became a delegate to the United Nations.

(woman) ❺ I hope I've got this all sorted out.

(man 2) Me, too.

(man 1) I hope we all do because we have a quiz in a few minutes.

7. WHY ARE THESE STUDENTS DISCUSSING THE ROOSEVELTS?
8. LISTEN AGAIN TO PART OF THE PASSAGE. THEN ANSWER THE QUESTION.

   (man 1) ❷ Now, this picture shows Theodore Roosevelt, who was also known as Teddy. He was president of the United States early in the nineteenth century, wasn't he?

   (woman) Uh . . . that's a little bit off. He was vice-president when McKinley was president. He became president in 1901 when McKinley was assassinated.

   WHAT DOES THE WOMAN MEAN WHEN SHE SAYS THIS:

   (woman) Uh . . . that's a little bit off.

9. HOW WERE THE ROOSEVELTS RELATED?
10. WHICH ROOSEVELT ACCOMPLISHED THE FOLLOWING?
11. WHAT IS IMPLIED IN THE DISCUSSION ABOUT TEDDY, FRANKLIN, AND ELEANOR ROOSEVELT?
12. HOW DO THE STUDENTS SEEM TO FEEL ABOUT THE MATERIAL?

SPEAKING DIAGNOSTIC PRE-TEST

Page 165
Question 3

Listen to the passage. Take notes on the main points of the listening passage.

(man) Hey, Jane, did you see the announcement?

(woman) Which announcement?

(man) The announcement about the dorm, the one saying the dorm is closing on June 4 at five o'clock.

(woman) Oh, I did see that announcement. . . .

(man) It sounds like it's not a problem for you that the dorm is closing on June 4 at five o'clock.

(woman) No, it's not a problem for me.

(man) You don't have any exams on June 4?

(woman) No, my last exam is on June 3, so it won't be difficult for me to move out by five o'clock on June 4. . . . But it does sound like it's a problem for you to move out by then.

(man) It is.

(woman) Why? When's your last exam?

(man) My last exam's on June 4.

(woman) Really?

(man) And that's not the worst of it. My last exam starts at three o'clock on June 4. It goes from three o'clock to five o'clock on June 4.

(woman) And you have to be out of the dormitory by five o'clock.

(man) That's right. That means I need to move out of the dorm before I take my last exam.

(woman) That sounds like a problem to me.

(man) It really sounds like a problem to me, too.

HOW IS THE INFORMATION IN THE LISTENING PASSAGE RELATED TO THE INFORMATION IN THE READING PASSAGE?

Page 167
Question 4

Listen to the passage. Take notes on the main points of the listening passage.

(professor) I'd like to talk about why so many tornadoes occur in the area called Tornado Alley. It's not just a coincidence. There is good reason why so many tornadoes occur there.

Tornadoes occur when cold, dry air and warm, wet air come together. In the middle of the United States, there is a big wide area of flat land. This flat land, the central plains, stretches all the way from the northern part of the country to the southern part of the country. In the north there is cold and dry arctic weather, while in the south there is warm and wet tropical weather.

So many tornadoes occur in the central plains because the central plains are so big and because cold, dry air from the north and warm, wet air from the south can meet there.

HOW IS THE INFORMATION IN THE LISTENING PASSAGE RELATED TO THE INFORMATION IN THE READING PASSAGE?

Page 168
Question 5

Listen to the passage. Take notes on the main points of the listening passage.

(man) I don't know if I can take much more of this class.

(woman) You don't like our biology class?

(man) Not really. You do like it?

(woman) Yes, I really do like the biology class.

(man) How can you like it? I mean, the professor is so boring. He talks in such a quiet voice, and he just goes on and on, class after class.

(woman) I know he's not a really lively speaker. I mean. . . . Uh . . . I know his lectures aren't really exciting or anything.

(man) Then why do you like the class so much, if you agree with me that the lectures are pretty boring?

(woman) The lectures aren't very exciting, but I like the class because the professor's so organized. I like professors that are very organized. I like professors that are very clear about the material in the course, about the assignments, about course requirements.

(man)	Okay, so our professor is very organized. I'll agree with you on that. But his lectures are pretty boring. . . .
(woman)	His lectures are clear and organized, and that's what I like.

WHAT ARE THE STUDENTS DISCUSSING?

Page 169
Question 6

Listen to the passage. Take notes on the main points of the listening passage.

(professor)	Clams are sea animals that live in shells. Some clams can grow to be very large. These very large clams have sometimes been called man-eating clams. Here's how some very large clams have come to be called man-eating clams.
	A clam often sits in the water with its shell open. A clam has a two-part shell that it can open very wide. If an underwater diver swims by the clam, parts of the diver's body might touch the shell or enter into it. This could happen by accident, it could happen because the diver is too interested in exploring the clam and gets too close, or it could happen because the diver is hoping to find a pearl in the clam shell. When the clam senses something getting too close, it feels that it's a danger. As a result of this feeling of danger, the clam closes its shell to protect itself. Sometimes it may close its shell on the arm or leg of a diver. Because of this, the giant clam has gotten the name of man-eating clam even though it doesn't actually eat the person it has caught.

WHAT DOES THE PROFESSOR SAY ABOUT CLAMS?

SPEAKING EXERCISE 6

Page 185
1. Listen to the passage. Take notes on the main points of the listening passage.

(man)	It's great, isn't it!
(woman)	What's great?
(man)	That Professor Jones isn't here for two days. I mean, it's not great that he's sick. I'm sorry he's sick. But it's nice to get a little time off from class.
(woman)	Well, I'm not sure it's so great.
(man)	Why not? Couldn't you use some time off?
(woman)	But I'm not sure we really get any time off.
(man)	What do you mean? Classes are canceled for two days.
(woman)	But we still have to learn the material that's on the syllabus for the classes on those two days. I think it would be easier to go over the material in class than to learn it on our own. I think it's not much of a vacation.

(man)	Well, I still think it's going to give us some extra time to relax, and I'm still very happy about it.

Page 186
2. Listen to the passage. Take notes on the main points of the listening passage.

(man)	Did you see the notice from the Literature Department?
(woman)	The one about schedule forms?
(man)	Yeah.
(woman)	I did see it.
(man)	Did you happen to notice the dates?
(woman)	What about the dates?
(man)	Today's May 1, isn't it?
(woman)	It is.
(man)	And the memo has the date May 1 on it.
(woman)	It does. . . . Oh, I see the problem. The memo tells us to turn the forms in by April 30.
(man)	And that was yesterday.
(woman)	It looks like we'll be late turning the forms in.
(man)	It looks like the memo was a bit late, too.

Page 186
3. Listen to the passage. Take notes on the main points of the listening passage.

(woman)	Did you see the notice posted in the library?
(man)	The notice about the part-time jobs that are available there?
(woman)	Yeah. That notice. It sounds like you saw it.
(man)	Yeah, I did see it.
(woman)	Are you going to apply for one of the jobs?
(man)	No, I can't apply for one.
(woman)	Why not?
(man)	I'm not available during the day to work.
(woman)	But you don't have to be available during the day to work. There are jobs in the evening and on weekends.
(man)	Really? I thought the notice said something about nine o'clock to five o'clock Monday through Friday.
(woman)	That's when you need to talk to the head librarian about a job, but the jobs are in the evenings and on weekends.
(man)	Okay, so I am available to work when the jobs are available . . . but, I have another problem, too.
(woman)	What's the other problem?
(man)	I think the jobs are for full-time students.
(woman)	And you're not a full-time student?
(man)	Not quite.
(woman)	Then these jobs aren't for you. But they look great for me. I'm going over to the library to talk to the head librarian right now.

SPEAKING REVIEW EXERCISE (Skills 5 through 8)

Page 192

Listen to the passage. Take notes on the main points of the listening passage.

(man)   Have you finished the assignment for business class?

(woman) Sure, I've finished the assignment. Have you finished yours?

(man)   No, I haven't even started the assignment.

(woman) Why not? Why haven't you done the assignment yet? It was so easy. It didn't take much time at all.

(man)   It was easy? It didn't take much time?

(woman) No, I finished the assignment in about 30 minutes. All we have to do for the assignment is to write two paragraphs. It took me about a half hour to write the two paragraphs.

(man)   Two paragraphs? You wrote only two paragraphs?

(woman) Sure.

(man)   But the assignment doesn't say to write two paragraphs. It says to write six paragraphs.

(woman) Six paragraphs? No, it says to write only two paragraphs.

(man)   Listen. The assignment says "Choose three strengths and write one paragraph about each of the strengths."

(woman) You mean, the assignment doesn't say, "Write one paragraph about the strengths"?

(man)   No, it doesn't say that. That would mean to write one paragraph about the strengths. But it says, "Write one paragraph about each. . . ."

(woman) So that means we should write three paragraphs about the strengths.

(man)   And three paragraphs about the weaknesses, for a total of six paragraphs.

(woman) That also means that I need to go back to the library and do the assignment over again.

(man)   I'll go over to the library with you now. I need to work on the assignment, too.

HOW IS THE INFORMATION IN THE LISTENING PASSAGE RELATED TO THE INFORMATION IN THE READING PASSAGE?

SPEAKING EXERCISE 10

Page 197

1. Listen to the passage. Take notes on the main points of the listening passage.

(professor) I'm going to talk today about why the surface temperature of Venus is so high. The surface temperature of Venus is so high because of the thick atmosphere that surrounds the planet. Venus is surrounded by a thick layer of carbon dioxide. The thick layer of gases surrounding Venus traps the heat of the Sun inside it. The trapped heat can't escape because the atmosphere is so thick. The temperature of Venus barely drops at all, even at night. Venus can never cool down because the thick atmosphere around it traps the Sun's heat and doesn't allow it to escape.

2. Listen to the passage. Take notes on the main points of the listening passage.

(professor) Let me give you an example that demonstrates this point. If you think of a situation where there are two mountains with similar heights, one of them may have permanent snow on it, while the other doesn't. The mountain with permanent snow on it would be the one that's farther from the equator, and the mountain that doesn't have permanent snow on it would be the one that's closer to the equator.

A certain mountain in Norway that is 6,500 feet high always has snow on it because Norway is far from the equator. A certain mountain in Spain that is 6,500 feet high doesn't always have snow on it because Spain's much closer to the equator than Norway is.

3. Listen to the passage. Take notes on the main points of the listening passage.

(professor) I'd like to talk today about the information you just read on honeybees. While most of the information you read is correct, one part isn't completely true.

It is true that honeybees sting humans. That part is true. However, not all honeybees sting humans. Worker bees sting people to protect their colonies, but queen bees and drone bees do not. It's only the worker bees that sting humans.

There are three kinds of honeybees: the queen, the drones, and the worker bees. It's not completely accurate to say that they all sting humans when only the worker bees—and not the queen or the drone—do.

SPEAKING REVIEW EXERCISE (Skills 9 through 12)

Page 204

Listen to the passage. Take notes on the main points of the listening passage.

(professor) Now, I'd like to talk about mercantilism. I'd like to talk about how having colonies could make a mother country more successful. I'd like to talk about three ways that colonies helped a mother country.

One way that a colony could help its mother country to become more successful was to provide raw materials to the mother country. A colony could give raw materials like wood, or gold, or cotton to the mother country.

Another way that a colony could help its mother country to become more successful was by buying the mother country's manufactured products. The mother country would be more successful because the people in its colony would purchase the mother country's manufactured products.

There is a third way that having colonies helped a mother country to be more successful. The third way is that the colony would take people the mother country did not want to keep. The mother country could send criminals or mentally ill people or poor people to its colonies. This would also help to make the mother county more successful.

HOW IS THE INFORMATION IN THE LISTENING PASSAGE RELATED TO THE INFORMATION IN THE READING PASSAGE?

SPEAKING EXERCISE 13

Page 207

1. Listen to the passage. Take notes on the main points of the listening passage.

(woman)	I was late to class this morning, again.
(man)	I saw that.
(woman)	You did? You saw that I was late to class?
(man)	Yes, I did see that . . . but, something that's more important is that the professor saw it.
(woman)	He did?
(man)	Yes, the professor saw that you weren't there when he started class. He said something about it.
(woman)	He said something? What did he say?
(man)	He said, "Lynn's late for class, one more time."
(woman)	The professor knows that I'm late to class all the time?
(man)	Yes, he does.
(woman)	I think I need to try really hard to get to class on time from now on.
(man)	I think that would be a very good idea.

Page 208

2. Listen to the passage. Take notes on the main points of the listening passage.

(woman)	Jeff, did you take good notes today in history class?
(man)	I think so.
(woman)	Well, could I look at your notes?
(man)	You want to see my notes?
(woman)	Yes, I do.
(man)	Why do you need to see my notes? You were in class today. I saw you in class today.
(woman)	I was in class, but I didn't take notes. That's why I need to see your notes.
(man)	You were in class, but you didn't take any notes?
(woman)	That's right. I was in class, but I didn't take any notes.

(man)	Why didn't you take any notes?
(woman)	It's a little bit silly, but I didn't take notes because I didn't have a pen or pencil with me.
(man)	You forgot to bring a pen or pencil to class?
(woman)	That's right. It's silly, isn't it? So that's why I need to see your notes.
(man)	It is a really silly reason, but, yes, you may see my notes.

Page 209

3. Listen to the passage. Take notes on the main points of the listening passage.

(woman)	Hi, Tom.
(man)	Oh, hi, Beth.
(woman)	Listen, Tom, I've been looking for you. I have a question for you.
(man)	Well, you've found me. What's your question?
(woman)	It's about the economics course.
(man)	I'm not taking an economics course. . . .
(woman)	Oh, I know you're not taking an economics course now. I want to know about the economics course you took last semester.
(man)	Oh, yeah, I did take an economics course last semester. What do you want to know about the economics course?
(woman)	Well, I'm thinking about taking the same course next semester, and I wanted to know what you thought about it.
(man)	I don't think you should take the course. I didn't like it very much.
(woman)	You didn't like it? Why not?
(man)	Well, all the professor did was lecture, day after day after day. He's a pretty good lecturer, but I prefer classes where the students participate more. I thought that class was really boring.
(woman)	A course like that doesn't sound bad to me. In fact, I kind of like courses where the professor lectures, if the professor is a good lecturer. You can pay attention to the professor, but you don't have to say anything.
(man)	Well, then, maybe it's a good course for you, but I didn't really like it.
(woman)	I think it's a good course for me.

SPEAKING REVIEW EXERCISE (Skills 13 through 15)

Page 214

Listen to the passage. Take notes on the main points of the listening passage.

(man)	Hey, Anne, do you want to get together Thursday evening to prepare for the exam?
(woman)	Uh . . . Thursday evening?
(man)	Yeah, you know, we have a math exam on Friday. And the last time we had a math exam, we prepared for the exam together. We both did well on the exam, so I thought maybe you would want to do the same thing again.
(woman)	Uh, I'm sorry, Joe, but I can't.
(man)	You're not going to prepare for the exam?

(woman) I <u>am</u> going to prepare for the exam, but not on Thursday evening. I'm going to a concert on Thursday evening.

(man) You're going to a concert the evening before a math exam?

(woman) Yes, I am. It's a really important concert. I'm going to have to prepare for the exam, but not on Thursday evening because that's when the concert is . . . listen, are you free on Wednesday evening?

(man) I am. Are you thinking that maybe we can prepare for the exam on Wednesday evening?

(woman) Yeah. If it's okay with you, let's prepare for the exam on Wednesday evening instead of Thursday evening.

(man) That works for me.

(woman) That works for me, too.

WHAT DO THE STUDENTS HAVE TO SAY ABOUT PREPARING FOR THE EXAM?

SPEAKING EXERCISE 16

Page 217

1. Listen to the passage. Take notes on the main points of the listening passage.

(professor) Today, we're going to discuss the bald eagle. The bald eagle became a symbol of the United States soon after the nation was born.

The bald eagle isn't exactly a bald bird. Instead, it has a different color of feathers on its head and its tail than it does on the rest of its body. Its head and tail feathers are white, while the feathers on the rest of its body are dark brown.

The bald eagle is one of the world's largest and most powerful hunting birds. It's so large that, when its wings are extended, it can measure eight feet from one tip, or end, of the wing to the other wingtip. To hunt, it extends its talons, the sharp claws on its feet. The bald eagle is so big and powerful that it's able to capture and kill prey with the sharp talons on its feet.

Page 218

2. Listen to the passage. Take notes on the main points of the listening passage.

(professor) Today, I'm going to talk about hot-air balloons. Hot-air balloons are large, gas-filled balloons with baskets. People can climb into the baskets and fly through the air in hot-air balloons. The people who fly in hot-air balloons are called balloonists.

When balloonists fly in hot-air balloons, they can't control the direction they're going to fly. Balloons are pushed by the wind, so balloons travel in the directions the wind is blowing. Balloonists can't make their balloons fly into the wind.

Though balloonists can't control the direction they fly, they can control how high or low the balloon is. There is a burner in the balloon to provide heat. To make the balloon rise, the balloonist must heat the balloon. To make the balloon descend, the balloonist must cool the balloon.

Page 219

3. Listen to the passage. Take notes on the main points of the listening passage.

(professor) The chapter you just read described the "dark days." Do you understand what happened on these dark days? Well, on the dark days, the skies in the northeastern part of the United States got dark during the middle of the day.

Now, how did people feel when the sky became dark during the middle of the day? Well, as you would expect, the people became frightened when the dark days occurred.

Next, let's talk about how often have these dark days occurred. The dark days occurred eighteen times in a period of 200 years. And when was this period of time when the dark days occurred? The dark days occurred eighteen times over a 200-year period from the beginning of the 1700s until the beginning of the 1900s.

We understand today why these eighteen dark days occurred in the northeast from early in the 1700s through the early 1900s. These dark days in the northeastern part of the United States occurred because of forest fires in the northwestern part of the United States. The smoke and soot from the fires was carried by the weather from the northwest to the northeast. The forest fires occurred in the northwest and the smoke and soot caused the sky to darken in the northeast.

SPEAKING REVIEW EXERCISE (Skills 16 through 18)

Page 223

Listen to the passage. Take notes on the main points of the listening passage.

(professor) Today, I'm going to be talking about the human brain, and the point I'd like to make clearly about the human brain, your brain, is that it's a big energy user. That's right . . . your brain needs a lot of energy to function.

Let me give you some statistics that show just how much of an energy user the brain is. The brain, on average, is one fiftieth of the weight of the human body. This means that the brain is one part to fifty parts of the body's weight. But it uses more than one fiftieth of the body's energy, a lot more. The brain uses one fifth, or one part out of five parts, of the body's energy. The conclusion that can be drawn is that, overall, the human brain uses ten times more energy than the rest of the body. Your brain really needs a lot of energy to function.

WHAT POINT DOES THE PROFESSOR MAKE ABOUT THE HUMAN BRAIN?

SPEAKING POST-TEST

Page 227
Question 3

Listen to the passage. Take notes on the main points of the listening passage.

(man)	I wonder why this notice is posted.
(woman)	I know why.
(man)	You do?
(woman)	At least, I think I do.
(man)	Why do you think this notice is posted?
(woman)	I think it's here because some students have pets in the dormitory.
(man)	They do? I don't know anyone who has a pet in the dorm.
(woman)	Well, I do. I know someone who has cats in the dorm.
(man)	Cats? How many cats?
(woman)	I'm not sure, but she has several. I've seen a black cat, a gray cat, and a white cat.
(man)	That's at least three different cats. And she keeps them in her dorm room? How does she do that?
(woman)	She has a first-floor room, and she just leaves the window open. The cats go in and out through the open window.
(man)	I can't believe that. Now I understand why the notice is up.

HOW DOES THE INFORMATION IN THE LISTENING PASSAGE ADD TO THE IDEAS IN THE READING PASSAGE?

Page 229
Question 4

Listen to the passage. Take notes on the main points of the listening passage.

(professor)	I'd like to talk now about why Los Angeles grew so suddenly from a small town to a city. There is an interesting explanation why Los Angeles grew suddenly and quickly. The explanation has to do with the railroads. In the 1880s, the railroads were competing for business. One of the ways that the railroads competed for business was to lower fares. One railroad lowered the amount of money that it cost to ride, and then another railroad lowered the fare even more. In the 1880s, the railroads competed so strongly that fares got really low. Fares were so low that it cost only a dollar, just one dollar, to travel across the country to Los Angeles.

Because of the low fares on the railroads in the 1880s, the population of Los Angeles grew tremendously then.

HOW IS THE INFORMATION IN THE LISTENING PASSAGE RELATED TO THE INFORMATION IN THE READING PASSAGE?

Page 230
Question 5

Listen to the passage. Take notes on the main points of the listening passage.

(man)	How are your classes going, Jane?
(woman)	Not too well, particularly my English class.
(man)	Do you know what the problem is in your English class?
(woman)	Not really. I turn in all the work. We have to write a lot of papers. I turn in all the papers . . . but my grades on the papers aren't very good.
(man)	You know, if you don't know why the grades on your papers aren't very good, then maybe you should talk to your professor. You could go see your professor during his office hours.
(woman)	Her office hours.
(man)	Okay, you can go see your English professor during her office hours.
(woman)	But I don't know when the professor has office hours.
(man)	Then, ask the professor when she has office hours.
(woman)	Ask the professor about office hours? During class? I can't do something like that during class.
(man)	Not during class. Right after class. Go up to the professor right after class and ask her when she has office hours.
(woman)	But the professor leaves right after class.
(man)	Well, you need to try something. You need to find out why the grades on your papers aren't as high as you want them to be.

WHAT ARE THE TWO STUDENTS DISCUSSING?

Page 231
Question 6

Listen to the passage. Take notes on the main points of the listening passage.

(professor)	Our Earth is constantly changing. Our world today is quite different from what it was like in the past. I'd like to give you a few examples now that will show you just how much the Earth has changed over time.
	Let's talk about a period 65 million years ago. At that time 65 million years ago, a lot of what is land today was covered by water.
	First, let's talk about Europe. The southern half of Europe was covered by a large sea 65 million years ago. Northern Europe was a landmass, but southern Europe was under water.

Now, let's talk about North America. The North American continent was also very different 65 million years ago. There was a huge sea through the middle 65 million years ago. What is today North America was divided into two parts by a giant body of water.

Today's continents of Asia and Africa were also partially under water 65 million years ago. The northern part of today's Africa and the southern part of today's Asia were covered by water 65 million years ago.

WHAT DOES THE PROFESSOR SAY ABOUT THE PERIOD 65 MILLION YEARS AGO?

WRITING DIAGNOSTIC PRE-TEST

Page 236
Question 1

Listen to the passage. Take notes on the main points of the listening passage.

(professor) Do you know that Old World monkeys are not the only monkeys? There are also New World monkeys, and New World monkeys are quite different from Old World monkeys. New World monkeys live in the Americas rather than in Africa or Asia. They live in Central America and South America.

New World monkeys are easily differentiated from Old World monkeys because they have very wide nostrils, or noses. The wide nostrils of New World monkeys are very different from the thin nostrils of Old World monkeys.

Another difference is that New World monkeys are herbivores. This means that they eat only plants; they don't eat meat as the omnivore Old World monkeys do.

A final difference is that New World monkeys generally have prehensile tails, which means that they can use their tails to grip, or hold onto, tree branches. They use their prehensile tails a lot because they spend most of their time in trees. This is unlike Old World monkeys, which do not have prehensile tails and spend most of their time on the ground.

HOW DOES THE INFORMATION IN THE LISTENING PASSAGE ADD TO THE IDEAS IN THE READING PASSAGE?

WRITING EXERCISE 2

Page 247
1. Listen to the passage. Take notes on the main points of the listening passage.

(professor) Now, I'd like to talk about the situation in agriculture today and how it has changed since 1900. The situation in agriculture today is quite different from what it was then.

Today, only 2 percent of the U.S. labor force is involved in agriculture. This is quite a drop from the 40 percent of the population that was involved in agriculture in 1900. The percentage of the population that was involved in agriculture decreased considerably in that period of time.

Another difference is that farms today tend to be owned by corporations. Farming today is big business. Family-owned farms are generally something from the past; few farms today are family owned.

Now I'd like to talk about a final huge difference between the farms of today and the farms of 1900. This huge difference between the farms of today and the farms of 1900 is that today's corporate-owned farms are considerably more productive than the farms of the past. Farmers today are able to be more productive because of greatly improved farm machinery. A typical farmer today produces food for an average of 75 to 100 people. This is a huge increase over the productivity of a farmer in 1900.

Page 248
2. Listen to the passage. Take notes on the main points of the listening passage.

(professor) Dolphins may be extraordinarily intelligent beings, but the facts that are stated in the reading passage do not necessarily prove this. Let's look at each fact, one by one.

First, dolphins do have larger brains than humans, but dolphins are also larger than humans. When you compare a dolphin's brain to its body size, a dolphin's brain does not seem so large. This may not indicate that dolphins have extraordinary intelligence.

Now let's talk about the behaviors that seem to be almost human. Dolphins may not be reaching out to humans when they save drowning people. Instead, such a behavior may be natural to dolphins. A group of dolphins will save a dolphin that is drowning. Perhaps when a group of dolphins saves a drowning person, the dolphins mistake the drowning person for an injured dolphin. This behavior may not prove that dolphins have human-like intelligence.

Finally, let's talk about the commands that dolphins learn. It is true that dolphins can learn commands, but does this indicate extraordinary intelligence? Other animals, dogs, for example, can learn to follow commands. The ability to follow some commands does not prove extraordinary intelligence.

Please understand my main point because this is important. I'm not saying dolphins are unintelligent. The point I'm making is that the points in the reading passage do not prove with certainty that dolphins are intelligent.

Page 249

3. Listen to the passage. Take notes on the main points of the listening passage.

(professor) The reading passage discussed conclusions that Leonardo da Vinci drew about what it would take for man to fly. The passage discussed two conclusions Leonardo drew. You should have understood the conclusions in the reading passage. One conclusion was about the size of the wings that would be needed to carry a man in flight. The other conclusion was about how much power would be needed to lift a man into flight.

Well, let's talk now about whether or not Leonardo's conclusions were correct. Do you think Leonardo da Vinci's conclusions were correct? . . . Well, one of the conclusions was correct, and the other conclusion was not. . . . Do you know which conclusion was correct and which conclusion was not?

The conclusion about the size of the wings needed to carry a man in flight was the conclusion that was correct. Leonardo da Vinci was accurate in determining how large the wings needed to be to keep a man in flight.

It was the other of Leonardo's conclusions that was not correct. The conclusion that Leonardo drew about how much power would be needed to lift a man into flight was not at all correct. Leonardo da Vinci thought that a man had enough power in his legs to push himself into flight, but this was not accurate. It takes far more power than a man has in his legs to push him into flight.

WRITING REVIEW EXERCISE (Skills 1 through 8)

Page 267

Listen to the passage. Take notes on the main points of the listening passage.

(professor) Let me tell you what happened when Company X decided to use centralized decision-making. Well, it was a disaster. The company was not able to function at all. Let me tell you why centralized decision-making was not a good decision for this company. A company needs to consider several things when it decides whether to have centralized or decentralized decision-making.

One thing a company needs to think about is the distance between the main office and the local managers. If the local managers are close to the main office, then perhaps centralized decision-making is better. If local managers are far away from the main office, then perhaps decentralized decision-making is better. In Company X, the local managers are far away from the main office, so perhaps decentralized decision-making is best.

A second thing a company needs to think about is whether local decisions are needed. If no local decisions are needed, then perhaps centralized decision-making is better for a company. If local decisions are needed, then decentralized decision-making is better. In Company X, local decisions are needed, so perhaps decentralized decision-making is best.

A third thing a company needs to think about is whether local managers are capable of making decisions. If local managers are not capable of making decisions, then centralized decision-making is better. If local managers are capable of making decisions, then decentralized decision-making is better. Company X has very capable managers, so decentralized decision-making is best.

HOW DOES THE INFORMATION IN THE LISTENING PASSAGE CAST DOUBT ON THE DECISION IN THE READING PASSAGE?

WRITING POST-TEST

Page 285

Question 1

Listen to the passage. Take notes on the main points of the listening passage.

(professor) A large group of parents and teachers came to a school district meeting to discuss this proposed change in the school year from a nine-month school year to a twelve-month school year. This group of parents and teachers strongly opposed the change. This group wanted to keep the traditional nine-month school year. The group of parents and teachers presented their reasons against the change at the meeting with the school district.

The first reason that the parents and teachers gave was about the school district's claim that students forget too much over the long summer vacation. The parents and teachers brought up a number of studies to show that the reason given by the school district was not good. The studies show that there is not better memory of material in a twelve-month school year than there is in a nine-month school year.

The second reason that the parents and teachers gave was about the school district's claim that costs would be reduced because summer school would be cut. While the parents and teachers agree that there would be a cost savings if summer school is cut, they believe strongly that it is a bad decision to cut summer school. Many students need summer school. They need summer school because they need to catch up on courses they need or to get ahead in their studies.

The third reason that parents and teachers gave was about the school district's claim that families would have more opportunities for vacations. If the twelve-month school year goes into effect in the elementary school district, families with students in high school or in college will not be able to take vacations because high schools and colleges are not on the same schedule.

HOW DOES THE INFORMATION IN THE LISTENING PASSAGE CHALLENGE THE PROPOSAL IN THE READING PASSAGE?

MINI-TEST 1

LISTENING

Page 292

Questions 1 through 5. Listen as a student consults with his professor. The conversation is about the professor's attendance policy.

(student) Professor, can you tell me what your policy on attendance is? . . . I mean, what happens if a student is absent from class? You see, I need to know because I need to miss a class next week.

(professor) Well, any time you miss a class, you need to ask other students what we covered in class. You also need to get good notes from one of the students who was in class.

(student) Oh, I can certainly ask some other students what was covered in class. I can also get notes from someone. But will there be a penalty for missing a class? Will something happen if I miss a class?

(professor) There's no penalty for missing one class. But watch it! There is a penalty for missing three or more classes. If you miss three or more classes, then your final grade will be lowered.

(student) That's fine. That won't be a problem for me. I have to miss one class next week. But after that, I don't intend to miss any more classes.

1. WHY DOES THE STUDENT GO TO SEE THE PROFESSOR?
2. WHAT HAPPENS IF A STUDENT MISSES ONE CLASS?
3. WHAT HAPPENS IF A STUDENT MISSES MORE THAN TWO CLASSES?
4. LISTEN AGAIN TO PART OF THE PASSAGE. THEN ANSWER THE QUESTION.
   (professor) There's no penalty for missing one class. But watch it! There is a penalty for missing three or more classes.
   WHAT DOES THE PROFESSOR MEAN WHEN SHE SAYS THIS:
   (professor) But watch it!
5. HOW DOES THE STUDENT SEEM TO FEEL BY THE END OF THE CONVERSATION?

Page 294

Questions 6 through 11. Listen to a lecture in a geography class. The professor is talking about waterfalls.

(professor) ❶ Today, we'll be looking at some of the most impressive of the world's waterfalls. You may have heard of the waterfalls we'll be discussing. They are Angel Falls, Victoria Falls, and Niagara Falls. After this lecture, you should be able to describe what makes each of these waterfalls so impressive.

Which of these, Angel Falls, Victoria Falls, or Niagara Falls, do you think is the tallest? ❷ The answer to that question is the waterfall in this photo. This is Angel Falls in southeastern Venezuela. It drops more than 3,000 feet. The descent of 3,000 feet is actually in two falls, an upper falls and a lower falls. The upper falls are much higher than the lower falls.

❸ Now, we'll go on to discuss another waterfall. Do you recognize this waterfall? Of course, this is Victoria Falls on the Zambezi River in southern Africa. The falls are more than a mile wide at the top, but they narrow considerably at the bottom. These falls are much shorter than Angel Falls, but they're also much wider than Angel Falls. In fact, they're only 355 feet high, compared with the over 3,000-foot Angel Falls.

❹ Now, we'll move on to the last of the waterfalls we'll be discussing. These falls are, of course, Niagara Falls. These falls are actually divided into two falls side by side. Goat Island divides the falls into the American Falls and Horseshoe Falls. As we've seen, Niagara Falls isn't the tallest waterfall in the world. In fact, it's not even close to being the tallest waterfall. Angel Falls is the tallest at over 3,000 feet, Victoria Falls is far shorter at a height of 355 feet, and Niagara Falls is only half the height of Victoria Falls at a mere 167 feet. What makes Niagara Falls so impressive is its width. Niagara Falls is wider than Angel Falls and Victoria Falls. Because

Niagara Falls is so wide, a higher volume of water passes over each of these falls than over any other waterfall.

❺ That's it for today. That's all on these three very famous waterfalls. Be sure to read the next chapter in the textbook and be prepared for a quiz on Friday. See you then.

6. WHICH WATERFALLS ARE DISCUSSED IN THE LECTURE?
7. WHAT IS STATED ABOUT VICTORIA FALLS?
8. WHY IS NIAGARA FALLS SO IMPRESSIVE?
9. HOW TALL IS EACH OF THESE FALLS?
10. WHAT CAN BE INFERRED FROM THE LECTURE?
11. LISTEN AGAIN TO PART OF THE PASSAGE. THEN ANSWER THE QUESTION.

(professor) That's it for today. That's all on these three very famous waterfalls.

WHAT DOES THE PROFESSOR MEAN WHEN HE SAYS THIS:

(professor) That's it for today.

SPEAKING

Page 299

Question 2

Listen to the passage. Take notes on the main points of the listening passage.

(man) I can't believe it!
(woman) I know. The library's closed. And I think I know why it's closed.
(man) Why is the library closed?
(woman) Because the key to the library is lost.
(man) The key is lost? So no one can open the door of the library?
(woman) That's right.
(man) How do you know this?
(woman) I work in the library. I went to the library to work this morning, and someone told me then.
(man) So you couldn't work this morning?
(woman) I couldn't work . . . because the library was locked and no one could find the key!

HOW DOES THE INFORMATION IN THE LISTENING PASSAGE ADD TO THE IDEAS IN THE READING PASSAGE?

Page 300

Question 3

Listen to the passage. Take notes on the main points of the listening passage.

(professor) The next artist in the chapter is George Catlin. George Catlin was painting in the first half of the nineteenth century. He became famous for his paintings of the Iroquois and other Native American tribes.

He studied art and began his career painting portraits of rich people who lived in the city, but he wasn't happy doing that. So he decided he wanted to travel out west and paint.

He was influenced by stories his mother told him. Did you read the part of the chapter about what happened to his mother when she was a child? . . . Well, when Catlin's mother was a little girl, she was captured by the Iroquois and lived with them for a while. The Iroquois took good care of her and then sent her back to her family. Catlin's mother had a good experience living with the Iroquois when she was young, and she told her son George about the good experience.

What you should understand is that when George grew up and became an artist, he began by painting portraits of wealthy people. But then he changed his mind and spent the rest of his career painting pictures of Native Americans, including the Iroquois, the tribe that had taken care of his mother.

WHAT POINTS DOES THE PROFESSOR MAKE ABOUT CATLIN?

WRITING

Page 303

Listen to the passage. Take notes on the main points of the listening passage.

(professor) You may be wondering how these wild ponies came to be on the island. The ponies are not native to the island; the wild ponies have not been on the island since the beginning of time. Instead, the ponies were brought to the island. People brought the ponies to the island.

There is a story about how the ponies came to the island. It is a story; no one knows for sure if this story really happened. However, this story quite possibly really did take place.

According to the story, the ponies came from a Spanish ship. The Spanish truly brought ponies with them when they came to the Americas. The story says that there was a shipwreck in the ocean close to Assateague Island. A Spanish ship carrying ponies was damaged during a storm, and the ship broke apart and sank to the bottom of the ocean. At least some of the ponies were able to escape from the ship and swim to safety on the island. According to the story, the descendents of the ponies from the Spanish ship are still living on Assateague Island today.

MINI-TEST 2

LISTENING

Page 310

Questions 1 through 5. Listen as a student consults with his advisor. The conversation is about a math class.

(*advisor*) Hi, Steve. Come on in.

(*student*) Thanks.

(*advisor*) Do you have a question for me?

(*student*) I sure do.

(*advisor*) What's your question?

(*student*) It's about my math class.

(*advisor*) What about it? How's your math class going?

(*student*) It's not going very well . . . not very well at all. I was wondering if I could drop the class . . . drop my math class. . . . I think an advisor needs to sign a paper so that a student can drop a class, and that's why I'm here.

(*advisor*) Steve, you're right that you need your advisor's signature to drop a class. . . .

(*student*) I thought so.

(*advisor*) But I have some bad news for you.

(*student*) Bad news? Oh, no! What's the bad news?

(*advisor*) The bad news is that it's too late to drop a class.

(*student*) It's too late?

(*advisor*) That's right. October first was the last day to drop a class, and now it's October fifteenth.

(*student*) So it's too late to drop my math class?

(*advisor*) That's right.

(*student*) And there's no way I can drop it now?

(*advisor*) No way at all. You really need to put a lot of effort into your math class because there's no way you can drop it at this late date. Sorry I can't be any more help than that.

(*student*) Thanks, anyway.

(*advisor*) You're welcome, anyway.

1. WHY DOES THE STUDENT GO TO SEE THE ADVISOR?
2. HOW DOES THE STUDENT SEEM TO FEEL ABOUT HIS MATH CLASS?
3. IS EACH OF THESE SOMETHING THE ADVISOR SAYS IN RESPONSE TO THE STUDENT'S REQUEST?
4. LISTEN AGAIN TO PART OF THE PASSAGE. THEN ANSWER THE QUESTION.
   (*advisor*) But I have some bad news for you.
   (*student*) Bad news? Oh, no! What's the bad news?
   HOW DOES THE STUDENT SEEM TO FEEL?

5. LISTEN AGAIN TO PART OF THE PASSAGE. THEN ANSWER THE QUESTION.
   (*student*) And there's no way I can drop it now?
   (*advisor*) No way at all.
   WHAT DOES THE ADVISOR MEAN WHEN SHE SAYS THIS:
   (*advisor*) No way at all.

Page 312

Questions 6 through 11. Listen to a discussion from a history class. The discussion is on Stone Mountain.

(*professor*) ❶ Today, we're going to discuss Stone Mountain, which is the largest smooth-sided rock dome in North America. This huge rock has a carving of three men on it. We'll be focusing mainly on the historical events that Stone Mountain shows. ❷ Let's look at a photograph of Stone Mountain. Who can tell me where Stone Mountain is located? What about you, Tom?

(*Tom*) Stone Mountain is in the state of Georgia, in the southeastern part of the United States.

(*professor*) And who are the three men carved into the side of Stone Mountain? Nan?

(*Nan*) The three men carved into the side of Stone Mountain are three famous Southern leaders. That's Jefferson Davis on the left, Robert E. Lee in the middle, and Stonewall Jackson on the right.

(*professor*) That's exactly right. And when did these three Southern leaders live? Matt?

(*Matt*) These three Southern leaders lived during the period of the Civil War, which was in the 1860s, in the second half of the nineteenth century. They were leaders of the Southern Confederacy during the Civil War.

(*professor*) ❸ Now, let's look more closely at the men carved into the side of the mountain. As you said, Jefferson Davis is the one on the left. What was his role during the Civil War? Tom?

(*Tom*) Jefferson Davis was the president of the Southern Confederacy during the Civil War.

(*professor*) And the other two? Nan?

(*Nan*) The other two, Robert E. Lee in the middle and Stonewall Jackson on the right, were generals in the Confederate Army.

(*professor*) That's right. Robert E. Lee was the general in chief, and Stonewall Jackson was a general who served under Lee. . . . Yes, Matt?

(*Matt*) I just wanted to add that Lee is riding his horse Traveller.

(*professor*) Oh, I wasn't expecting that, Matt. So you're familiar with Traveller, Matt?

(*Matt*) Sure. I've read a lot about the Civil War. Lee rode Traveller throughout the entire Civil War, and every story of Lee in history books seems to mention Lee's horse Traveller.

6. WHAT IS THE PROFESSOR MAINLY DISCUSSING?
7. WHERE IS STONE MOUNTAIN LOCATED?
8. WHEN WAS THE CIVIL WAR?
9. WHO ARE THESE PEOPLE?

10. LISTEN AGAIN TO PART OF THE PASSAGE. THEN ANSWER THE QUESTION.

(Matt)   I just wanted to add that Lee is riding his horse Traveller.

(professor)   Oh, I wasn't expecting that, Matt. So you're familiar with Traveller, Matt?

HOW DOES THE PROFESSOR SEEM TO FEEL ABOUT THE STUDENT'S RESPONSE?

11. WHAT IS TRAVELLER?

SPEAKING

Page 317

Question 2

Listen to the passage. Take notes on the main points of the listening passage.

(professor)   Okay, so we understand that there can be foreshocks, or smaller earthquakes leading up to a major earthquake. Well, there can also be smaller earthquakes after a major earthquake, and these smaller earthquakes following a major earthquake are called—you guessed it—aftershocks. A related point that should make sense to you is that larger earthquakes tend to have more aftershocks. If an earthquake is not so big, then it usually does not have so many aftershocks.

HOW DOES THE INFORMATION IN THE LISTENING PASSAGE ADD TO THE IDEAS IN THE READING PASSAGE?

Page 318

Question 3

Listen to the passage. Take notes on the main points of the listening passage.

(woman)   You don't look too happy.

(man)   I'm not very happy.

(woman)   Why aren't you happy? What's the problem?

(man)   Oh, I just finished an exam.

(woman)   And the exam didn't go well?

(man)   No, the exam was awful.

(woman)   What was so awful about the exam?

(man)   Well, the whole exam consisted of just one question. And the question was so vague that I really didn't know how to deal with it.

(woman)   The whole exam was just one question?

(man)   That's right.

(woman)   Was it a short exam? After all, there was only one question.

(man)   No, it was a long exam. The exam was two hours long. We were supposed to write on this one question for two hours. And it was a vague question.

(woman)   You mean, the question wasn't clear?

(man)   That's right. The question was vague. It wasn't very clear. I wasn't sure what to write because the question wasn't clear.

(woman)   So what did you do?

(man)   I just wrote and wrote. I wrote pages and pages that weren't very clear or organized . . . because I didn't understand what the question was asking.

(woman)   So you just wrote a lot without really answering the question or organizing your response?

(man)   That's exactly what happened. That's why the exam was so awful.

(woman)   I understand.

WHAT DO THE STUDENTS HAVE TO SAY ABOUT THE EXAM?

MINI-TEST 3

LISTENING

Page 326

Questions 1 through 5. Listen as a student consults with a librarian. The conversation is about some library books.

(student)   I'd like to check these books out, please.

(librarian)   I'm sorry, but these books cannot be checked out.

(student)   Excuse me? Books can't be checked out of the library?

(librarian)   Oh, some books can be checked out, but these books can't.

(student)   Why not?

(librarian)   Well, they're reference books. The reference books here on the first floor of the library cannot be checked out. Reference books must be used here in the library.

(student)   How can you tell that these books are reference books and cannot be checked out?

(librarian)   You look at the call number, which is the number used to identify the book. The first letter of the call number, or identification number, is R. Each book in the library has a call number on the cover. The R in the call number on the book stands for "reference."

(student)   So, if I want to use these books, I have to use them in the library? I can't check them out?

(librarian)   Yes, that's right. Any of the books from the reference section cannot be checked out.

(student)   So, any book with an R at the beginning of the call number can't be checked out?

(librarian)   That's right. And the reference books, the ones with R in the call number, are the ones on the first floor.

1. WHY DOES THE STUDENT GO TO SEE THE LIBRARIAN?
2. LISTEN AGAIN TO PART OF THE PASSAGE. THEN ANSWER THE QUESTION.

(librarian)   I'm sorry, but these books cannot be checked out.

(student)   Excuse me? Books can't be checked out of the library?

WHAT DOES THE STUDENT MEAN WHEN SHE SAYS THIS:

(student)   Excuse me?

3. WHAT DOES THE LIBRARIAN SAY ABOUT THE REFERENCE BOOKS?
4. IS EACH OF THESE TRUE ABOUT CALL NUMBERS?
5. HOW CAN SOMEONE KNOW WHICH BOOKS ARE REFERENCE BOOKS?

Page 328

Questions 6 though 11. Listen to a lecture in an American history class. The professor is talking about Leland Stanford.

(professor) ❶ The topic for today is Leland Stanford, a nineteenth-century politician, businessman, and philanthropist. As a politician, he was deeply involved in government and held a number of public offices. As a businessman, he was very successful in establishing the railroads. As a philanthropist, he gave away a lot of money to start a university.

❷ This is Leland Stanford, the man who was a successful politician, businessman, and philanthropist. First, we'll talk about his success in politics. Leland Stanford served as governor of the state of California in the 1860s. Some twenty years later, he represented the state of California in the United States Congress.

❸ Now, we'll go on to talk about Leland Stanford as a businessman. This map shows the Central Pacific Railroad. The Central Pacific Railroad was the western part of the country's first transcontinental railroad, and Leland Stanford was president of the company when the transcontinental railroad was completed. He made millions of dollars in his business with the railroads.

❹ Stanford was accomplished not just as a politician and a businessman. He was also quite a philanthropist. As a philanthropist, Leland Stanford gave away millions of dollars of the money he earned from the Central Pacific Railroad to start a university. The university in this photo is the university that was started by Leland Stanford. It is, of course, Stanford University.

The university is actually named after Leland Stanford's son, Leland Stanford, Junior. Leland Stanford, Junior was Leland Stanford's only child, and he died in 1884 at the age of fifteen. Leland Stanford decided to start the university to honor his son who had died. Because the university is a memorial to Stanford's son, the official name of the university is actually Leland Stanford Junior University, but most people just call it Stanford.

❺ That's all for today on Leland Stanford. I hope you have a good idea of Leland Stanford's contributions, not only as a politician and as a businessman but also as a philanthropist.

6. WHAT IS THE TOPIC OF THE LECTURE?
7. HOW IS THE INFORMATION IN THE PASSAGE ORGANIZED?
8. WHAT WAS STATED ABOUT THE CENTRAL PACIFIC RAILROAD?
9. LISTEN AGAIN TO PART OF THE PASSAGE. THEN ANSWER THE QUESTION.

(professor) Stanford was accomplished not just as a politician and a businessman. He was also quite a philanthropist. As a philanthropist, Leland Stanford gave away millions of dollars of the money he earned from the Central Pacific Railroad to start a university.

WHY DOES THE PROFESSOR SAY THIS?

(professor) Stanford was accomplished not just as a politician and a businessman.

10. IN THE LECTURE, THE PROFESSOR DISCUSSES A SERIES OF EVENTS IN LELAND STANFORD'S LIFE. PUT THESE EVENTS IN THE CORRECT ORDER.
11. BASED ON THE LECTURE, WHAT IS MOST LIKELY TRUE?

SPEAKING

Page 333

Question 2

Listen to the passage. Take notes on the main points of the listening passage.

(woman) Where are you going, Matt?

(man) I'm going to turn in my lab report.

(woman) Well, you're too late.

(man) Too late? But it's only four o'clock. I thought we could turn our lab reports in until five o'clock.

(woman) I thought so, too. But I just went to the professor's office to turn my report in, and there's a notice posted on the door.

(man) What does the notice say?

(woman) It says that lab reports were due by three o'clock.

(man) But I'm sure the professor said that they were due by five o'clock.

(woman) I thought so, too. I went to turn my report in at four o'clock, and I thought I was an hour early. Instead, I was an hour late. And the notice says that we're going to get failing grades on our lab reports because we're late turning them in.

(man) Oh, no, that's terrible. I worked so hard on this report, and I don't think it's late. . . . Look! I even wrote down five o'clock in my notes. The professor must have said five o'clock in class because I wrote down five o'clock in my notes.

(woman) Well, there's nothing we can do now because the professor's not in his office. But we can certainly talk to him tomorrow.

(man) Yeah. We can't be the only students who had this problem.

HOW DOES THE INFORMATION IN THE LISTENING PASSAGE ADD TO THE IDEAS IN THE READING PASSAGE?

Page 334
Question 3

Listen to the passage. Take notes on the main points of the listening passage.

(*professor*) For the quiz tomorrow in this health class, you need to understand different types of injuries. You need to understand sprains, strains, and bruises. Do you understand sprains, and strains, and bruises? Briefly, a sprain is an injury to a joint, while a strain is an injury to a muscle . . . and a bruise is an injury to blood vessels.

A sprain is an injury to a joint, like an ankle or an elbow . . . or a knee or a wrist. And when a joint is sprained, there's swelling over the sprained joint.

Now, what about a strain? As I said, a strain is an injury to a muscle. So, if a muscle is strained, what happens? If a muscle is strained, it's very stiff and painful. You must know what that feels like. A strained muscle is stiff, so it doesn't move very easily, and it hurts if you try to move it.

Now, the last type of injury is a bruise. A bruise is an injury to a blood vessel. The blood vessels break beneath the skin, and the skin becomes discolored. It's a bruise when the skin turns all sorts of colors. This happens when the blood vessels are broken beneath the skin.

I hope this material is very clear now. It had better be because there is a quiz tomorrow.

WHAT DOES THE PROFESSOR HAVE TO SAY ABOUT INJURIES?

WRITING

Page 337
Listen to the passage. Take notes on the main points of the listening passage.

(*professor*) So, up until 1977, scientists believed that there was no life at the bottom of the ocean. They believed this because there was no light at the bottom of the ocean.

Well, in 1977, scientists got a big surprise. In 1977, a small submarine went down to the bottom of the Pacific Ocean. There was no light at the bottom of the ocean because it was so far away from the surface of the water. The bottom of the Pacific Ocean was more than 2 kilometers away from the surface of the ocean.

There was no natural light at the bottom of the ocean, but the submarine had brought lights. When the scientists in the submarine looked out of the submarine into the light coming from the submarine, they got a huge surprise. The surprise was that the water at the bottom of the Pacific Ocean was full of all kinds of living beings.

Up to that time, scientists thought that it was necessary to have sunlight in order to have life. But after the trip to the bottom of the ocean in the submarine, the scientists knew for sure that life can exist where there is no light at the bottom of the ocean.

HOW DOES THE INFORMATION IN THE LISTENING PASSAGE CHALLENGE THE INFORMATION IN THE READING PASSAGE?

MINI-TEST 4

LISTENING

Page 344
Questions 1 through 5. Listen as a student consults with her professor. The conversation is about an assignment.

(*student*) Excuse me, Professor Walker.
(*professor*) Oh, hi, Jean, come on in. You have a question for me?
(*student*) Yes, I do.
(*professor*) Well, what's your question?
(*student*) My question, uh . . . it's about the . . . uh . . . writing assignment.
(*professor*) The writing assignment?
(*student*) Yes, the writing assignment for your class.
(*professor*) There's a writing assignment for my class? You think there's a writing assignment for my class?
(*student*) No, really. You talked about it in class yesterday.
(*professor*) I talked about a writing assignment yesterday in class? . . . No, I didn't. There isn't a writing assignment in that class, so I'm sure I didn't talk about any writing assignment yesterday in class.
(*student*) No, really, Professor Walker. You did talk about a writing assignment. Or, at least I thought you did. You talked about an article. You said we are supposed to write an article.
(*professor*) Oh, okay. Now I see what the problem is. Yesterday in class, I <u>did</u> talk about an article.
(*student*) See, I thought you did. . . .
(*professor*) Yes, I did talk about an article, but I didn't say you have to <u>write</u> an article.
(*student*) You didn't?
(*professor*) No, I talked about some articles you were supposed to <u>read</u>.
(*student*) We're supposed to <u>read</u> an article, and not <u>write</u> one?

(professor)	You're supposed to read <u>three</u> articles. I wrote the names of the articles on the board yesterday.
(student)	Yes, I wrote down the names of the articles. I thought we were supposed to <u>write</u> an article like those three articles.
(professor)	No, you're just supposed to read the articles.
(student)	That's a much easier assignment.
(professor)	Yes, it is.
(student)	Thank you for your help, Professor Walker.
(professor)	You're quite welcome.

1. WHY DOES THE STUDENT GO TO SEE THE PROFESSOR?
2. LISTEN AGAIN TO PART OF THE PASSAGE. THEN ANSWER THE QUESTION.

(student)	My question, uh . . . it's about the . . . uh . . . writing assignment.
(professor)	The writing assignment?
(student)	Yes, the writing assignment for your class.
(professor)	There's a writing assignment for my class? You think there's a writing assignment for my class?

HOW DOES THE PROFESSOR SEEM TO FEEL?

3. WHAT DOES THE STUDENT THINK THE PROFESSOR SAID IN CLASS?
4. WHAT DID THE PROFESSOR ACTUALLY TELL THE STUDENTS TO DO IN CLASS?
5. WHAT DID THE PROFESSOR WRITE ON THE BOARD?

Page 346

Questions 6 through 11. Listen to a discussion from an astronomy class. The discussion is on the planet Neptune.

(professor)	❶ Today, we'll be talking about Neptune, which is the eighth planet from the Sun in our solar system. ❷ Let's look at this picture of Neptune. Neptune is bluish-green in color. Now, can you tell me, is Neptune visible from Earth? Charles?
(Charles)	No, Neptune isn't visible from Earth.
(professor)	And why is that?
(Charles)	Neptune is quite far from Earth, so it can only be seen with a telescope.
(professor)	❸ Now, I'd like to talk about Neptune's moons. Who knows how many moons Neptune has? Betty?
(Betty)	Neptune has six moons.
(professor)	Six moons? Are you sure, Betty?
(Betty)	Did I say six moons? I meant eight moons.
(professor)	That's right. Now for the hard question. Which of Neptune's eight moons is the largest?
(Betty)	The largest of Neptune's eight moons is Triton.
(professor)	Not bad, Betty. I didn't think you'd get that. ❹ Now, what can you tell me about the size of Neptune? Dave?
(Dave)	Neptune is a much bigger planet than Earth.

(professor)	That's true. And just how much bigger than Earth is Neptune?
(Dave)	The diameter of Neptune is four times the diameter of Earth. Four Earths could be lined up along Neptune's diameter.
(professor)	❺ And now, what is the length of a year on Neptune? Charles?
(Charles)	A year on Neptune is much longer than a year on Earth. This is because Neptune takes much longer than the Earth to move around the Sun.
(professor)	And just how long is a year on Neptune? Betty?
(Betty)	It takes 165 Earth-years for Neptune to move around the Sun once. This means that one year on Neptune is equal to 165 years on Earth.
(professor)	❻ Now, let's talk about the length of a day on Neptune. We've seen that a year on Neptune is much longer than a year on Earth. Is a day on Neptune also much longer than a day on Earth? Dave?
(Dave)	A year on Neptune may be much longer than a year on Earth, but a day on Neptune is much shorter. A day on Neptune is only 18 hours long, compared with a 24-hour day on Earth.
(professor)	And what does it mean that a day on Neptune is only 18 hours long?
(Dave)	This means that it takes only 18 hours for Neptune to rotate on its axis, while it takes 24 hours for Earth to rotate on its axis. This means that a day on Neptune is six hours shorter than a day on Earth.

6. WHICH OF THESE ARE TRUE ABOUT THE PLANET NEPTUNE?
7. LISTEN AGAIN TO PART OF THE PASSAGE. THEN ANSWER THE QUESTION.

(professor)	That's right. Now for the hard question. Which of Neptune's eight moons is the largest?
(Betty)	The largest of Neptune's eight moons is Triton.
(professor)	Not bad, Betty. I didn't think you'd get that.

WHAT DOES THE PROFESSOR MEAN WHEN SHE SAYS THIS:

| (professor) | Not bad, Betty. |

8. WHAT IS TRITON?
9. WHAT ARE THE RELATIVE SIZES OF EARTH AND NEPTUNE?
10. IS EACH OF THESE FACTS TRUE ABOUT NEPTUNE?
11. WHAT IS IMPLIED IN THE DISCUSSION ABOUT THE ROTATION OF NEPTUNE ON ITS AXIS?

SPEAKING

Page 351
Question 2

Listen to the passage. Take notes on the main points of the listening passage.

(professor) I'd like to talk now about the stories on how Abraham Lincoln wrote the Gettysburg Address. Well, history shows that the stories aren't true.

First, it's not true that Lincoln waited until the last moment to write the speech. He actually wrote it before he left on the trip; he didn't write it on the train.

Second, Lincoln didn't write the speech on the back of an envelope. He wrote the speech in the White House before he left on the trip, and he had paper available in the White House. He wrote the Gettysburg Address on presidential paper before he left on the trip.

HOW DOES THE INFORMATION IN THE LISTENING PASSAGE CHALLENGE THE INFORMATION IN THE READING PASSAGE?

Page 352
Question 3

Listen to the passage. Take notes on the main points of the listening passage.

(man) Where are you going, Erin? You seem to be rushing somewhere.

(woman) I'm going to the library.

(man) And you're in a hurry to get to the library?

(woman) Yes. I have to get there soon. I have a lot of work to do. I have a research paper due on Friday.

(man) You have a research paper due on Friday? Are you almost finished with it?

(woman) Finished, no. I'm just starting. I'm going over to the library to start on the research paper now.

(man) The research paper is due on Friday, and you're just starting it on Monday? . . . When did the professor assign the research paper?

(woman) Oh, the professor assigned the paper more than a month ago . . . maybe five or six weeks ago.

(man) And you didn't do any work on the paper until now?

(woman) That's right. I always work this way. I never get work done until the last possible moment.

(man) Oh, I don't like to work that way. I wouldn't say that I get papers done really early, but I don't wait until the last possible moment, like you do.

(woman) I work best this way. When it's early, I don't feel any pressure. When it's late, I feel a lot of pressure and I work very hard.

(man) Well, I think I should let you get going now.

(woman) Yeah, I should get going now. I have a lot of work to get done by Friday.

(man) You certainly do.

WHAT ARE THE STUDENTS DISCUSSING?

COMPLETE TEST

LISTENING

Page 368
Questions 1 through 5. Listen as a student consults with her professor. The conversation is about the topic for a research paper.

(student) Excuse me. Do you have some time when I could discuss the topic of my research paper?

(professor) Let's see. Now's not a good time for me to talk with you. I'm heading to another class.

(student) Okay. When would be a good time to talk?

(professor) The best time for me is during my office hours.

(student) When are your office hours?

(professor) You don't know when I have office hours? I told all the students on the first day of class, and it's also in the syllabus. You should know when I have office hours. . . . Anyway, I have office hours Wednesday afternoon, from two o'clock to five o'clock.

(student) Then, is it possible for me to meet with you tomorrow in your office at three o'clock?

(professor) That's a good plan. I'll see you here in my office tomorrow at three o'clock, and we can discuss the topic of your research paper.

1. WHAT DOES THE STUDENT WANT TO TALK ABOUT?
2. WHY IS THE PROFESSOR UNABLE TO TALK NOW?
3. LISTEN AGAIN TO PART OF THE PASSAGE. THEN ANSWER THE QUESTION.
   (professor) You don't know when I have office hours? I told all the students on the first day of class, and it's also in the syllabus. You should know when I have office hours.
   HOW DOES THE PROFESSOR SEEM TO FEEL?

4. ON WHICH DAY DOES THIS CONVERSATION MOST LIKELY TAKE PLACE?
5. WHEN ARE THE STUDENT AND PROFESSOR SCHEDULED TO MEET?

Page 370
Questions 6 through 10. Listen as a student consults with his professor. The consultation is about an assignment.

(student) Hi, professor. Can I talk with you for a moment?

(professor) Certainly. What's your question?

(student)   It's about the assignment. The assignment that you, uh, returned in class this morning.

(professor) Sure. What's your question?

(student)   Well, I didn't do very well on the assignment, and I'd, I'd like to know why.

(professor) Did you turn the assignment in on time?

(student)   Yes, I did.

(professor) Well, then, that's not the reason for the low grade. . . . Do you have the assignment with you?

(student)   Yes, here it is.

(professor) Okay, then. . . . Let me look it over . . .umm . . . Okay, I see what the problem is . . . Listen . . . I asked you to write an essay on a certain topic.

(student)   Yes, that's what I thought I did.

(professor) But what was the topic that I asked you to write about?

(student)   The topic was the Civil War. You asked us to write an essay about the Civil War.

(professor) That's not exactly right, and that's what the problem is. The topic that I asked you to write about was not exactly the Civil War. The topic was the causes of the Civil War. You wrote about the Civil War, but you never discussed the causes of the war.

(student)   So I didn't write about the exact topic you asked us to write about?

(professor) That's right. When I give you a topic to write about, it's important to write about the exact topic that I assign.

(student)   Okay, that's clear to me now. Thanks for your help.

6. WHY DOES THE STUDENT GO TO SEE THE PROFESSOR?
7. LISTEN AGAIN TO PART OF THE PASSAGE. THEN ANSWER THE QUESTION.
    (professor) Do you have the assignment with you?
    (student)   Yes, here it is.
    (professor) Okay, then. . . . Let me look it over . . . umm . . . Okay, I see what the problem is . . .
    WHAT DOES THE PROFESSOR MEAN WHEN SHE SAYS THIS:
    (professor) Okay, I see what the problem is . . .
8. HOW DID THE STUDENT SEEM TO THINK HE DID ON THE ASSIGNMENT?
9. WHAT PROBLEM DID THE STUDENT HAVE?
10. WHAT MESSAGE DOES THE PROFESSOR WANT THE STUDENT TO UNDERSTAND?

Page 372

Questions 11 through 16. Listen to a lecture in a government class. The lecture is on the Pentagon.

(professor) ❶ Today, we'll be talking about the Pentagon Building. The Pentagon Building is one of the largest office buildings in the world. It's where the United States has its Department of Defense. About 25,000 people work in the Pentagon Building.

❷ Let's look now at a photograph of the Pentagon Building. I'm sure I don't need

to tell you this . . . but the word pentagon refers to the number five. The number five is very important in the structure of the Pentagon Building. The Pentagon Building is a five-sided building. There are actually five rings of buildings around a central courtyard, and the buildings have five stories.

❸ Many people are surprised when they learn how quickly the Pentagon Building was built. It's such a big building, so you might think that it took a long time to build. However, it was actually completed rather quickly. It was started in 1941, and it was completed early in 1943.

11. WHAT DOES THE PROFESSOR MAINLY DISCUSS?
12. WHICH OF THESE ARE TRUE ABOUT THE PENTAGON?
13. APPROXIMATELY HOW MANY PEOPLE WORK IN THE PENTAGON?
14. LISTEN AGAIN TO PART OF THE PASSAGE. THEN ANSWER THE QUESTION.
    (professor) I'm sure I don't need to tell you this . . . but the word pentagon refers to the number five.
    WHAT DOES THE PROFESSOR MEAN WHEN HE SAYS THIS:
    (professor) I'm sure I don't need to tell you this . . .
15. WHAT IS A "PENTAD" MOST LIKELY TO BE?
16. IN WHICH DECADE WAS THE PENTAGON CONSTRUCTED?

Page 374

Questions 17 through 22. Listen to a lecture in a theater course. The lecture is on the musical The Unsinkable Molly Brown.

(professor) ❶ Today, we'll talk about a famous musical. More specifically, we'll be talking about how this musical got its name.

❷ The musical we'll be discussing is *The Unsinkable Molly Brown*. Molly Brown was a real woman who lived in Denver, Colorado, around a century ago. Her name became known many years after her death as the title character of the musical.

❸ Molly Brown and her husband started out very poor, but they became rich when Molly's husband discovered gold in Colorado. The newly rich Molly decided to use some of her husband's wealth to travel to Europe. Molly was on her way back to Denver from Europe on the *Titanic* when the ship sank. You've heard of the *Titanic*, haven't you? And you must've seen the movie based on the *Titanic*. Molly was one of the few survivors of the *Titanic* disaster in 1912. From this, she received the nickname of "the unsinkable Molly Brown." This was because she did not sink when the *Titanic* went down.

❹ Many years later, in 1960, a musical about Molly Brown was presented on Broadway, in New York City. This very successful Broadway show, named *The Unsinkable Molly Brown*, was about a woman who succeeded and survived against all odds.

17. WHAT IS THE TOPIC OF THIS TALK?
18. WHAT DOES THE PROFESSOR SAY ABOUT MOLLY BROWN?
19. WHAT IS IMPLIED IN THE LECTURE ABOUT MOLLY BROWN?
20. LISTEN AGAIN TO PART OF THE PASSAGE. THEN ANSWER THE QUESTION.

(professor) Molly was on her way back to Denver from Europe on the *Titanic* when the ship sank. You've heard of the *Titanic*, haven't you? And you must've seen the movie based on the *Titanic*.

WHAT DOES THE PROFESSOR MEAN WHEN SHE SAYS THIS:

(professor) You've heard of the *Titanic*, haven't you? And you must've seen the movie based on the *Titanic*.

21. IN THE LECTURE, THE PROFESSOR DISCUSSES EVENTS IN MOLLY'S LIFE. PUT THESE EVENTS IN THE CORRECT ORDER.
22. WHAT HAPPENED IN EACH OF THESE PLACES?

Page 376

Questions 23 through 28. Listen to a discussion in an astronomy class. The discussion is on Olympus Mons.

(professor) ❶ Today we're going to be discussing Olympus Mons. Can you tell me what Olympus Mons is? Judy?

(Judy) Olympus Mons is the largest known volcano in our solar system.

(professor) And where is Olympus Mons located, Al?

(Al) It's located on the planet Mars.

(professor) Is it bigger than Mount Everest? Mark?

(Mark) Yes, it's three times higher than, uh, Mount Everest.

(professor) ❷ Let's look now at this photo of Olympus Mons. Can you see the caldera on Olympus Mons? Judy, what's a caldera?

(Judy) Uh . . . I think . . . umm . . . it's a crater, isn't it?

(professor) Yes, that's right. It's a crater, and the caldera, or crater, on Olympus Mons is more than two miles deep. How does this compare with the depth of the Grand Canyon? Al?

(Al) The Grand Canyon's about a mile deep, so the caldera on Olympus Mons is twice as deep as the Grand Canyon.

(professor) What kind of volcano is this? Mark?

(Mark) Olympus Mons looks like a shield volcano. A shield volcano is one that is spread out wide and has very gently sloping sides.

(professor) And what other shield volcanoes are you familiar with? Judy?

(Judy) The volcanoes of the Hawaiian Islands are also shield volcanoes.

(professor) ❸ Okay, now let's take a moment and go back over some of the comparisons we've just made. First of all, Olympus Mons is taller than any other volcano in our solar system. What else?

(Al) It's three times as high as Mount Everest.

(Mark) Its caldera is twice as deep as the Grand Canyon.

(Judy) And it's the same type of volcano, a shield volcano, as the volcanoes in the Hawaiian Islands.

(professor) Very good. These are all the important points.

23. WHERE IS OLYMPUS MONS LOCATED?
24. LISTEN AGAIN TO PART OF THE PASSAGE. THEN ANSWER THE QUESTION.

(professor) Judy, what's a caldera?

(Judy) Uh . . . I think . . . umm . . . it's a crater, isn't it?

HOW DOES JUDY SEEM TO FEEL ABOUT HER RESPONSE?

25. WHAT IS STATED ABOUT THE CALDERA ON OLYMPUS MONS?
26. LISTEN AGAIN TO PART OF THE PASSAGE. THEN ANSWER THE QUESTION.

(professor) Okay, now let's take a moment and go back over some of the comparisons we've just made.

WHY DOES THE PROFESSOR SAY THIS?

27. WHICH OF THE FOLLOWING HAS A SHIELD VOLCANO?
28. IS EACH OF THESE TRUE ACCORDING TO THE LECTURE?

Page 378

Questions 29 through 34. Listen to a lecture in an engineering class. The professor is talking about dams.

(professor) ❶ Today we're going to be talking about different kinds of dams. You need to pay careful attention today because this is one of those topics that require special attention.

Dams are large structures built across rivers to control large amounts of water. Today, we'll be doing two things. First, we'll look at three theoretical types of dams. Then we'll look in depth at one actual dam.

❷ The first type of dam that we'll look at is a gravity dam. A gravity dam is built in a straight line across a river. This type of dam must be built of very strong material such as concrete. The wall needs to be very strong to hold back the weight of the water that's pushing against it.

❸ The next drawing shows an arch dam. An arch dam is not built in a straight line. Instead, an arch dam has a curve. The purpose of the curve in the arch dam is to transfer the weight of some of the water from the middle of the dam to the sides of the dam.

❹ The last of the three types of dams is a buttress dam. A buttress dam has buttresses to support the wall. The buttresses help to balance the weight of the water pushing against the wall.

❺ Now, we'll look at one well-known dam. The dam in this photograph is today known as Hoover Dam. It used to be called Boulder Dam. You can see in the photo that Hoover Dam is an arch dam. In fact, it's the biggest arch dam in the United States. It's located on the Colorado River, near Boulder City, Nevada. When it was first named, it was named Boulder Dam because it's near Boulder City. Later, it was named Hoover Dam after a president of the United States, Herbert Hoover. It was started in 1931, soon after the start of the Great Depression. The purpose of this dam-building project was to create jobs for workers who needed jobs because of the Great Depression.

❻ I hope you understand the three basic kinds of dams we've looked at today, the gravity dam, the arch dam, and the buttress dam. It should also be clear to you that the Hoover Dam is an example of one of these three, the arch dam. In the next class, we'll have a quiz on the material we covered today. See you then.

29. LISTEN AGAIN TO PART OF THE PASSAGE. THEN ANSWER THE QUESTION.
   (professor) You need to pay careful attention today because this is one of those topics that require special attention.
   WHAT DOES THE PROFESSOR MEAN?

30. HOW IS EACH TYPE OF DAM DESCRIBED IN THE LECTURE?

31. WHAT IS THE PURPOSE OF THE ARCH IN AN ARCH DAM?

32. WHICH OF THESE ARE TRUE ABOUT HOOVER DAM?

33. WHY DOES THE PROFESSOR MENTION THE GREAT DEPRESSION IN A PASSAGE ON DAMS?

34. WHAT IS STATED ABOUT THE NAME OF THE DAM DISCUSSED IN THE LECTURE?

SPEAKING

Page 383

Question 3

Listen to the passage. Take notes on the main points of the listening passage.

(man) You saw the syllabus from our math class?
(woman) Yes, I did.
(man) Are you going to stay in the class?
(woman) Yes, I'm going to stay in the class.
(man) But it sounds like a lot of work.
(woman) There is a lot of work in the class.
(man) Then why do you want to stay in the class?

(woman) Because it's a good class. One of my friends took the class, and she said it was really good.
(man) I think it's a lot more work than I want to do. I think I want to change to a different class. . . . You're going to stay in this one?
(woman) I'm going to stay.

HOW DOES THE INFORMATION IN THE LISTENING PASSAGE ADD TO THE IDEAS IN THE READING PASSAGE?

Page 385

Question 4

Listen to the passage. Take notes on the main points of the listening passage.

(professor) Do you know what happened to the Dutch settlement in Manhattan? Well, the Dutch settlement was captured by the British. The British captured the Dutch settlement in 1664.

When the British captured the settlement in 1664, they decided to rename the settlement because they didn't want to have control of a settlement that was named after a Dutch city. The British decided to rename the city after the brother of the king, who was known as the Duke of York. You can guess, I'm sure, that the settlement of New Amsterdam was renamed New York.

After the British took control of New York, the settlement began to spread. It spread way beyond the eastern tip of the island of Manhattan to much of the rest of the island after the British took control of it.

HOW DOES THE INFORMATION IN THE LISTENING PASSAGE ADD TO THE IDEAS IN THE READING PASSAGE?

Page 386

Question 5

Listen to the passage. Take notes on the main points of the listening passage.

(woman) Hey, Joe, are you going to be using your math book tonight?
(man) I'm not sure. Why are you asking about this?
(woman) Well, I was hoping that you wouldn't need your math book tonight.
(man) Why is that?
(woman) Because I've misplaced my math book.
(man) You've lost your math book?
(woman) It's not exactly lost. I've just misplaced it. I've put it somewhere, and I just don't remember where I put it.
(man) That means the book is lost.
(woman) But maybe I'll find it . . . and, umm, until I find my book, I need to use someone else's book . . . just until I find my book.
(man) Well, I may need my book tonight. We do have an assignment due on Friday, and I

don't want to wait until the last minute to work on the assignment.

(woman) I understand that. . . .

(man) Listen, I do need my math book tonight, but I'm not using it this afternoon. Would you like to use my math book this afternoon?

(woman) That would be great! You're not going to need your math book this afternoon?

(man) No, I won't need it this afternoon. I'm going to be in the lab all afternoon, so I won't be using my math book then.

(woman) It would be great if I could use your math book this afternoon. I don't have any classes this afternoon, so I could work on math all afternoon.

(man) But I'll need the math book back this evening. Let's meet in the library at seven o'clock this evening.

(woman) Thank you very much. I'll meet you in the library at seven o'clock and return the book to you then. Thanks again!

WHAT ARE THE STUDENTS SAYING ABOUT THEIR MATH BOOKS?

Page 387

Question 6

Listen to the passage. Take notes on the main points of the listening passage.

(professor) Today, we'll be talking about the Continental Divide of North America. The Continental Divide separates the waters that flow to the east and the waters that flow to the west on this continent.

Let's look at this map of the United States. The Continental Divide, or Great Divide as it is known, runs along the Rocky Mountains. Waters to the east of the Rocky Mountains flow to the east, and waters to the west of the Rocky Mountains flow to the west.

First, let's talk about the waters to the east of the Continental Divide. Most of the waters to the east of the Continental Divide actually flow to the Gulf of Mexico before they reach the Atlantic Ocean. One of the great routes for water to reach the Gulf of Mexico is the Mississippi River system and all of the tributaries feeding into it.

Now, let's look at what happens to waters west of the Continental Divide. Much of the water to the west of the Continental Divide follows one of two river systems to the ocean. Water to the west of the Continental Divide flows either through the Columbia River to the Pacific Ocean or through the Colorado River to the Gulf of California and then out to the Pacific Ocean.

Today, we've looked at the Continental Divide, and we've seen how water flows to the east and to the west of the Continental Divide. That's all for today. I'll see you in class tomorrow.

WHAT DOES THE PROFESSOR HAVE TO SAY ABOUT THE CONTINENTAL DIVIDE?

WRITING

Page 390

Question 1

Listen to the passage. Take notes on the main points of the listening passage.

(professor) I'd like to talk now about what happened when Sylvia began telecommuting instead of going into the office. Sylvia was not happy with it. It was not what Sylvia had expected.

First of all, she had thought she would have more time for work because she was not going to be driving to and from the office each day. But she did not have more time. There were always things going on at home. The neighbors came over, the phone kept ringing; she had things to take care of at home; the children were at home after school.

The next problem she had was with her co-workers, or, actually, with a lack of co-workers. When she was working at home, she never saw her co-workers, and she never had anyone to talk with about her work. She did not like working alone at home without any co-workers to talk with.

A final problem she had was with only a limited amount of feedback from her boss. At home, she heard from her boss only once in a while. This meant that she did not really know what her boss was thinking about her work.

Because of these problems, Sylvia was not really happy with her telecommuting experience. She had thought it was going to be really great, but it did not turn out that way for her.

HOW DOES THE INFORMATION IN THE LISTENING PASSAGE CHALLENGE THE INFORMATION IN THE READING PASSAGE?

TOEFL-LEVEL TEST

LISTENING

Page 398

Questions 1 through 5. Listen as a student consults with her advisor. The conversation is about her major.

(student) Hi.

(advisor) Hello. What can I do for you?

(student) I'd like to talk with you about my major. . . . I'd like to . . . uh . . . have a different major. . . . I'd like to change my major.

(advisor) What year are you in? You're a junior, aren't you?

(student) That's right. You got it. I'm in my junior year.

(advisor) Well, you're quite far along in your studies, you know, as a junior. . . . It's kind of difficult to change your major now.

(student) Difficult? . . . But not impossible?

(advisor) That's right, difficult, really difficult, but not impossible. . . . Now, what did you want to change your major to?

(student) I'm thinking of changing my major to art.

(advisor) To art? . . . From what?

(student) My major's history now. I'd like to change my major from history to art.

(advisor) From history to art? That's quite a big change. An art major requires a very different program from a history major. You need to think carefully before making this decision. Because history and art require such different courses of study and because you're already close to the end of your junior year, it would be a big decision to change your major.

(student) I do want to think carefully before making this decision.

(advisor) You really need to. . . . Listen, can I help you somehow with this decision?

(student) Well, let me think about that. . . . I do need some help . . . umm . . . What I really would like help in doing is in figuring out just how this change would affect my program of studies.

(advisor) Sure, I can help you with that. But that's a bit much to look at now. Why don't you make an appointment, and we can figure this out at a later date.

(student) I'd like to talk about this pretty soon.

(advisor) Yes, that's important. . . . Listen, I have some time tomorrow afternoon, around three o'clock. Are you free then?

(student) Uh . . . yeah . . . actually, I have a class until three o'clock, and I can make it to your office in about ten minutes.

(advisor) That'll work out well. I'll see you a little after three o'clock tomorrow, then.

(student) Perfect. I'll see you then. Thanks.

1. WHAT DOES THE STUDENT WANT TO DO?
2. HOW DOES THE ADVISOR SEEM TO FEEL ABOUT THE STUDENT'S REQUEST AT FIRST?
3. WHAT KIND OF HELP DOES THE STUDENT WANT FROM THE ADVISOR?
4. LISTEN AGAIN TO PART OF THE PASSAGE. THEN ANSWER THE QUESTION.

    (student) What I really would like help in doing is in figuring out just how this change would affect my program of studies.

    (advisor) Sure, I can help you with that. But that's a bit much to look at now. Why don't you make an appointment, and we can figure this out at a later date.

    WHAT DOES THE ADVISOR MEAN WHEN HE SAYS THIS:

    (advisor) But that's a bit much to look at now. Why don't you make an appointment, and we can figure this out at a later date.

5. WHAT ARRANGEMENT DO THE STUDENT AND ADVISOR MAKE?

Page 400

Questions 6 through 11. Listen to a lecture in an engineering class. The professor is talking about the geodesic dome.

(professor) ❶ Today in our engineering class, we'll be talking about the geodesic dome. This type of structure is interesting in a study of engineering because, even though it's relatively lightweight, it's able to withstand high stresses.

❷ You can see a geodesic dome in this photograph. The first geodesic dome was designed by Buckminster Fuller for the Montreal Exposition in 1967. Fuller held a patent on this invention.

Let's talk about why this dome is called a geodesic dome. What makes it geodesic is that all of the elements in the dome are connected with the shortest possible lines. The lines intersect to form a framework of three-way, or triangular, shapes that produce uniform stress on all its members. This type of framework is able to absorb and, uh, distribute pressure loads evenly.

❸ Now we're going to talk about what makes this type of structure able to withstand high pressure. To do this, we'll look at two structures that are related to the geodesic dome, the sphere and the tetrahedron.

❹ The two structures in this drawing are the sphere, on the left, and the tetrahedron, on the right. We're looking at these two structures because the geodesic dome takes positive characteristics from each of these two structures. The sphere contains the greatest volume with the least surface area. The volume of what's inside a sphere is very large in relation to the surface area of the sphere. Because of this, the sphere is the strongest structure against internal pressure. And the tetrahedron contains the least volume with the greatest surface area. The volume of what's inside a tetrahedron is very low in relation to the surface area of the tetrahedron. Because of this, the tetrahedron is the strongest structure against external pressure.

❺ The geodesic dome is a combination of both these two structures. It combines the best of the sphere and the tetrahedron. The sphere is the strongest structure against internal pressure, the tetrahedron is the strongest structure against external pressure, and the geodesic dome is the strongest structure against a combination of internal and external pressure.

6. IS EACH OF THESE TRUE ABOUT A GEODESIC DOME?
7. WHEN WAS THE FIRST GEODESIC DOME CREATED?
8. WHAT ARE THE CHARACTERISTICS OF A SPHERE?
9. WHAT ARE THE CHARACTERISTICS OF A TETRAHEDRON?
10. HOW DO THESE STRUCTURES STAND UP TO PRESSURE?
11. OVERALL, HOW DOES THE PROFESSOR SEEM TO FEEL ABOUT THE GEODESIC DOME?

SPEAKING

Page 405
Question 3

Listen to the passage. Take notes on the main points of the listening passage.

(man) Can you believe that notice?
(woman) Which notice?
(man) The one about the new cafeteria hours.
(woman) You don't sound very happy about the notice.
(man) I'm not.
(woman) Why not?
(man) First of all, I don't like the change in hours.
(woman) Are the hours changing a lot?
(man) Yes, the cafeteria used to be open for a lot more hours. It used to be open three hours in the morning, three hours at lunchtime, and three hours for dinner.
(woman) Oh, now I see. After the hours change, the cafeteria will be open for only two hours for each meal.
(man) That's right. The cafeteria used to be open for nine hours a day, and now it's open for only six hours a day.
(woman) I can see why you're not exactly pleased with this change. . . .
(man) But that's not all. Something else really bothers me.
(woman) What? What else bothers you?
(man) Something that really bothers me is the tone of the notice. I don't like the way the notice is worded. The notice says that they aim to serve the campus community and they're pleased to announce the change. That sounds like they're announcing something good, something that will help the campus community. Instead, they're doing something that hurts the campus community, something that limits the hours that meals are available in the campus cafeteria.
(woman) So, it sounds like you don't like the message itself, and you also don't like the way the message was delivered.
(man) That's exactly right!

HOW DOES THE INFORMATION IN THE LISTENING PASSAGE ADD TO THE IDEAS IN THE READING PASSAGE?

Page 407
Question 4

Listen to the passage. Take notes on the main points of the listening passage.

(professor) Let's look now at the effect of operant conditioning in a couple of situations. In each of these situations, a child is misbehaving and a mother is reacting to the child's bad behavior.

In the first situation, the mother sees the child's extreme misbehavior and reacts to the misbehavior with negative consequences. She gives the child a time-out, or restricts the child from playing with friends or with toys or from watching television for a period of time. The child learns from this that there will be negative consequences for his misbehavior. This has an impact on his future behavior; the child makes an effort not to misbehave because he doesn't want to face the negative consequences that result from his bad behavior.

In the second situation, the mother sees the child's extreme misbehavior and reacts to the misbehavior with positive consequences. She hugs the child and is affectionate with him after he misbehaves. The child learns from this that there will be positive consequences for his misbehavior. This has an impact on his future behavior; the child makes an effort to misbehave because he enjoys the positive consequences that result from his bad behavior.

HOW DOES THE INFORMATION IN THE LISTENING PASSAGE ADD TO THE IDEAS IN THE READING PASSAGE?

Page 408
Question 5

Listen to the passage. Take notes on the main points of the listening passage.

(man) Are you enjoying Professor Nelson's class?
(woman) Uh . . . not really.
(man) Why not? It's such a great class. I took it last quarter, you know, and I really enjoyed it. Why don't you like it?
(woman) Well, it's just that . . . umm . . . Professor Nelson says some things that . . . he says some things that don't make sense to me. I think that some of the things he says are completely wrong.
(man) Yes, I know what you mean. . . . Professor Nelson does say some things that are completely wrong, but he does this for a reason.
(woman) He says things that are incorrect for a reason? Why does he say things that are incorrect on purpose? Why does he do this?
(man) He says things that are incorrect on purpose because he wants you to challenge him.

(woman) He wants us to do <u>what</u>?

(man) To challenge him. He wants you to question whether something is correct or not and tell him what you think is correct.

(woman) He really does this? He really says things that are incorrect on purpose because he wants the students to question him, to challenge him, to ask him if these things are really correct?

(man) Yes, that's exactly what he does.

(woman) Okay, now I think I understand what Professor Nelson is doing in class. . . . You really think I should challenge him? I should ask him if what he's saying is correct?

(man) Yes, absolutely. . . . That's what he wants. . . . Listen, are any of the other students in the class challenging him?

(woman) No . . . no one has done that.

(man) Well, then, you can be the first one to challenge him.

(woman) You're sure that's what he wants?

(man) I'm absolutely positive.

HOW DO THE STUDENTS SEEM TO FEEL ABOUT PROFESSOR NELSON'S CLASS?

Page 409
Question 6

Listen to the passage. Take notes on the main points of the listening passage.

(professor) The topic for today's lecture is asteroids, particularly the asteroids found in the asteroid belt. An asteroid is a rocky body orbiting around the Sun. Because asteroids orbit around the Sun, they're sometimes called "small planets." Asteroids can be very small: one asteroid that has been catalogued is only 7 <u>feet</u> in diameter. Asteroids can also be very large. The largest known asteroid is Ceres, which is almost 600 miles in diameter; its diameter is about one-quarter of the diameter of our Moon.

The asteroid belt is a region between Jupiter and Mars that contains a large number of asteroids. Not all known asteroids are in the asteroid belt, but a high percentage of them are. The first detailed pictures of asteroids in the asteroid belt were obtained by NASA's *Galileo* spacecraft. The *Galileo* spacecraft entered the asteroid belt in 1991 on its way to Jupiter; it took several more years for *Galileo* to traverse the asteroid belt, and *Galileo* went into orbit around Jupiter in 1995.

Now, I'd like to discuss some theories about how the asteroid belt came into existence. Scientists aren't sure how the main belt of asteroids came to exist. There are two theories about the origin of the asteroid belt. According to one theory, there used to be another planet in orbit between Mars and Jupiter. This planet broke up into pieces that are orbiting around the Sun between Mars and Jupiter. According to the other theory, the asteroids are the material from another planet that never formed or that was in the process of forming. So, according to these two theories, either another planet actually existed between Mars and Jupiter, or another planet was in the process of forming between Mars and Jupiter.

WHAT POINTS DOES THE PROFESSOR MAKE ABOUT THE ASTEROID BELT?

WRITING

Page 412
Question 1

Listen to the passage. Take notes on the main points of the listening passage.

(professor) Now, I'd like to talk a little about some studies on phrenology. You know, phrenology was the theory that different personality traits are related to certain areas of the brain and that physical markers of human personality traits could be seen on human skulls. This theory was very popular in the nineteenth century.

Well, since the nineteenth century, a lot of research has been done on phrenology, you know, to find out if there is a relationship between personality traits and locations in the brain and markers on the skull. And guess what! Studies over the last century have shown—clearly shown—that there is no relationship between a certain personality trait and a single location in the brain. . . . That's right . . . Even though this theory was quite popular in the nineteenth century and many leading scientists believed it, studies have shown that this theory was wrong.

Scientists now know that there is no relationship between a single personality trait and one specific area of the brain. Instead, they know that the brain is far more complex than the phrenologists believed. Different parts of the brain also do have different functions, but a single personality trait involves numerous functions, perhaps an uncountable number of functions. A single personality trait therefore cannot be tied to just one location in the brain.

HOW DOES THE INFORMATION IN THE LISTENING PASSAGE CAST DOUBT ON THE INFORMATION IN THE READING PASSAGE?

ANSWER KEY

READING

READING DIAGNOSTIC PRE-TEST   Page 2

1. B	5. B	9. B	13. D
2. A	6. A	10. D	14. C
3. D	7. A	11. C	15. A
4. C	8. D	12. A	16. B

17. (6) (2) (4)

18. in education: (2)
in solving a problem in cotton farming: (5) (6)
in solving a problem in the production of peanuts:
(1) (7)

Note: These answers may be in any order.

READING EXERCISE 1   Page 14

1. B	6. D	11. A	16. D	21. D
2. C	7. A	12. D	17. B	
3. D	8. C	13. D	18. B	
4. A	9. B	14. A	19. C	
5. B	10. C	15. A	20. C	

READING EXERCISE 2   Page 19

1. A	4. B	7. C	10. A
2. B	5. B	8. B	11. A
3. A	6. C	9. A	12. C

READING EXERCISE (Skills 1–2)   Page 22

1. B	3. D	5. C	7. B	9. D
2. A	4. B	6. B	8. A	10. A

READING EXERCISE 3   Page 26

1. A	3. C	5. D	7. A	9. B
2. D	4. B	6. C	8. D	

READING EXERCISE 4   Page 31

1. D	3. C	5. B	7. C
2. C	4. B	6. C	8. D

READING EXERCISE (Skills 3–4)   Page 34

1. C	2. B	3. A	4. D	5. C

READING REVIEW EXERCISE (Skills 1–4)   Page 36

1. D	3. C	5. B	7. C	9. A
2. B	4. C	6. A	8. C	10. C

READING EXERCISE 5   Page 40

1. D	5. C	9. B	13. B	17. A
2. B	6. D	10. C	14. A	18. D
3. A	7. D	11. A	15. D	19. C
4. D	8. A	12. B	16. D	

READING EXERCISE 6   Page 47

1. B	4. D	7. C	10. B	13. D
2. D	5. C	8. D	11. A	
3. A	6. B	9. D	12. C	

READING EXERCISE (Skills 5–6)   Page 50

1. C	3. A	5. D	7. C
2. B	4. D	6. B	

READING REVIEW EXERCISE (Skills 1–6)   Page 51

1. A	3. C	5. B	7. A	9. B
2. D	4. C	6. D	8. B	10. D

READING EXERCISE 7   Page 55

1. A	3. C	5. A	7. A	9. D
2. B	4. D	6. C	8. C	

READING EXERCISE 8   Page 60

1. B	4. D	7. D	10. C
2. D	5. A	8. D	11. D
3. A	6. C	9. B	12. A

READING EXERCISE (Skills 7–8)   Page 63

1. A	3. C	5. A	7. A
2. D	4. B	6. B	

READING REVIEW EXERCISE (Skills 1–8)   Page 65

1. A	3. D	5. A	7. B	9. D
2. B	4. C	6. C	8. C	10. B

READING EXERCISE 9   Page 70

1. (2) (4) (6)
2. (2) (4) (5)
3. (1) (2) (6)

READING EXERCISE 10   Page 76

1. Romans: (4) (6) (7)
English: (2) (5)

2. the first group of Virginia colonists: (1) (4)
the second group of Virginia colonists: (5) (8)
the third group of Virginia colonists: (2) (6) (9)

3. Venus: (1) (2) (8) (9)
Earth: (3) (5) (7)

READING EXERCISE (Skills 9–10)   Page 80

1. (1) (3) (6)

2. Mercury flights: (4) (7)
Gemini flights: (2) (6)
Apollo flights: (3)

3. (1) (4) (5)   4. (2) (5) (6)

5. command module in the spacecraft: (3) (7)
service module in the spacecraft: (4) (6)
lunar module in the spacecraft: (1)

READING REVIEW EXERCISE (Skills 1–10) Page 84

1. D	3. D	5. B
2. A	4. C	6. A

7. *James and the Giant Peach:* (3) (5) (9)
   Charlie and the Chocolate Factory: (1) (6)
   George's Marvelous Medicine: (4) (7)

8. A   10. B
9. B   11. (2) (3) (6)

READING POST-TEST Page 89

1. D	5. A	9. D	13. C
2. C	6. D	10. A	14. A
3. B	7. A	11. B	15. C
4. B	8. C	12. B	16. D

17. (3) (6) (1)

18. what it was: (2)
    why it happened: (6) (7)
    how it happened: (4) (1)

LISTENING

LISTENING DIAGNOSTIC PRE-TEST Page 98

1. A	5. C	9. B
2. B, C	6. N, Y, Y, N	10. A, D
3. B	7. B	11. C
4. D	8. D	

12. Palmer: Is used mainly for wildlife studies
    Amundsen-Scott: Is nearest the South Pole
    McMurdo: Is the biggest American base

LISTENING EXERCISE 1 Page 108

1. A	3. B	5. A
2. D	4. C	6. B

LISTENING EXERCISE 2 Page 114

1. B	5. B	9. B	13. A
2. D	6. B	10. A, D	14. B
3. B, C	7. C	11. D	15. B, C
4. A	8. C, D	12. B, C	16. D

LISTENING EXERCISE (Skills 1–2) Page 117

1. D	4. C	7. B
2. A	5. C	8. D
3. B	6. A, D	9. A, C

LISTENING EXERCISE 3 Page 123

1. C	3. D	5. C	7. B
2. B	4. A	6. C	8. A

LISTENING EXERCISE 4 Page 130

1. C	3. B	5. A	7. B
2. A	4. D	6. B	8. C

LISTENING EXERCISE (Skills 3–4) Page 133

1. C	3. A	5. B
2. B	4. D	

LISTENING REVIEW EXERCISE (Skills 1–4) Page 134

1. C	3. A	5. A	7. C
2. D	4. B, D	6. D	8. B

LISTENING EXERCISE 5 Page 143

1. C

2. Fort Dearborn was built.
   Chicago became a town.
   A fire destroyed much of Chicago.
   Chicago hosted a world's fair.

3. A, D, E
4. D
5. N, Y, N, Y

6. Alpha Centauri A: Has two stars orbiting around it
   Alpha Centauri B: Orbits around one of the other stars
   Proxima Centauri: Orbits around the two other stars

7. D
8. Y, Y, Y, N

9. The executive branch: Is covered in weeks 9–12
   The legislative branch: Is covered in weeks 1–4
   The judicial branch: Is covered in weeks 5–8

10. A, C, E

LISTENING EXERCISE 6 Page 148

1. A	3. D	5. A	7. B, C
2. D	4. C	6. B, C	

LISTENING EXERCISE (Skills 5–6) Page 151

1. A

2. Former executives: Owned the company from 1980 to
   the present
   The families: Owned the company from 1903 to 1969
   A corporation: Owned the company from 1969-1980

3. B   4. D

5. Harley and the Davidsons built bikes in their yard.
   The Harley and Davidson families sold the business.
   The company almost went bankrupt.
   Former executives turned the company around.

LISTENING REVIEW EXERCISE (Skills 1–6) Page 153

1. D	3. A, D	5. B, C, D
2. B, D	4. A	6. D

7. No Atlantic Ocean existed.
   The continents started separating.
   Older crust moved toward the continents.
   Newer crust pushed up along the Mid-Atlantic Ridge.

LISTENING POST-TEST Page 155

1. D	4. D	7. C
2. A	5. C	8. D
3. B	6. N, Y, N, N	9. A, B

10. Teddy: Was married to a president
    Franklin: Was president early in the 20th century
    Eleanor: Was married to a president

11. D
12. C

SPEAKING

SPEAKING DIAGNOSTIC PRE-TEST Page 162

Question 1 Page 163

Sample Notes

INTRODUCTION:
  kinds of material I read

SUPPORTING IDEA 1:
  first kind
  • newspapers
  • because I like to know about the world

SUPPORTING IDEA 2:
  second kind
  • history books
  • because I like to know about the past

CONCLUSION:
  I like to read newspapers and history books

Sample Response

I read two kinds of material most often. These two kinds of material are newspapers and history books.

I read newspapers all the time. I read newspapers because I like to know about the world. I can learn about the world from newspapers.

Another kind of material that I read often is history books. I read history books because I like to know about the past. I think we can learn a lot about today if we understand the past, and I can learn about the past in history books.

These two kinds of reading material are the kinds of material that I read the most.

Question 2 Page 163

Sample Notes

INTRODUCTION:
  better to live in the mountains because of the weather

SUPPORTING IDEA 1:
  first reason
  • like snow in winter

SUPPORTING IDEA 2:
  second reason
  • like warm (but not hot) weather in summer

CONCLUSION:
  prefer to live in mountains because of weather

Sample Response

If I have to choose between a life in the mountains or a life by the ocean, I'll choose a life in the mountains. I have two reasons for choosing a life in the mountains, and they are related to the weather in the mountains.

The first reason I prefer the weather in the mountains is that I like snow in the winter. In the mountains, there is usually snow in the winter.

The second reason I prefer the weather in the mountains is that I like warm but not hot weather in the summer. In the mountains, the weather is usually warm but not hot in the summer.

I would choose to live in the mountains rather than the ocean because I like these two things about the weather in the mountains.

Question 3 Page 164

Sample Notes

TOPIC OF READING PASSAGE: announcement about closing of campus dormitory

main points about the topic:
• dormitory will close at 5:00 P.M. on June 4
• all students must be out of the dormitory by then

TOPIC OF LISTENING PASSAGE: student discussion about announcement

main points about the topic:
• woman does not have a problem with the announcement, but man does
• man has final exam from 3:00–5:00 on June 4
• man must move out of dormitory before his last final exam

Sample Response

In this set of materials, the reading passage is an announcement about the closing of a campus dormitory. Two students discuss the announcement in the listening passage.

The announcement in the reading passage says that the dormitory will close at 5:00 P.M. on June 4. All students must be out of the dormitory by then.

In the listening passage, two students discuss this announcement. The woman doesn't have a problem with it, but the man does. The man has a final exam from 3:00 to 5:00 on June 4. This means that the man must move out of the dormitory before he takes his last final exam, and he's not happy about this.

Question 4 Page 166

Sample Notes

TOPIC OF READING PASSAGE: tornado alley

main points about the topic:
• is name of area where many tornadoes occur
• is in flat area in middle of U.S.
• has almost all of U.S.'s 800–900 yearly tornadoes

TOPIC OF LISTENING PASSAGE: why tornadoes occur in tornado alley

main points about the topic:
• tornadoes occur where cold, dry air and warm, wet air meet
• central plains extend from north to south
• cold, dry air from north and warm, wet air from south meet there

Sample Response

In this set of materials, the reading discusses an area where tornadoes occur. The listening passage explains why tornadoes occur there.

The reading passage describes an area called Tornado Alley. Tornado Alley is a flat area in the middle of the United States, and many tornadoes occur there. Almost half of the United States' 800 to 900 yearly tornadoes occur there.

The listening passage explains why so many tornadoes occur in Tornado Alley. Tornadoes occur where cold, dry air and warm, wet air meet. Tornado Alley is in the central plains, and the central plains extend from north to south of the country. Cold, dry air from the north and warm, wet air from the south meet in the central plains and cause tornadoes.

Question 5 Page 168

Sample Notes

TOPIC OF LISTENING PASSAGE: discussion about biology class

main points about the topic:
- man does not like biology class, and woman does
- man thinks class is boring (even though it is organized)
- woman likes professor's organization (even though it is not exciting)

Sample Response

In this listening passage, two students are discussing a biology class they are taking. They have very different ideas about the class.

The man doesn't like the class, but the woman does. The man thinks that the class is too boring, while the woman likes the way that the professor organizes the class. The woman agrees that the class isn't exciting, but she still likes it. The man agrees that the class is organized well, but he still doesn't like it.

Question 6 Page 169

Sample Notes

TOPIC OF LISTENING PASSAGE: why large clams are called man-eating clams

main points about the topic:
- diver touches part of open clam
- clam feels danger and closes shell, maybe on part of diver
- clam isn't really eating diver but it seems as if it is

Sample Response

In this listening passage, the professor talks about why large clams are called man-eating clams. Clams are sea animals that have two-part shells. Sometimes a diver in the ocean touches part of an open clam. The clam thinks it's in danger and closes its shell, perhaps on part of the diver. The clam really isn't eating the diver; it's just trying to close its shell. But it seems as if the clam is eating the diver, so it's called a man-eating clam.

SPEAKING EXERCISE 1 Page 174

Sample Notes

1. INTRODUCTION:
   things I do when I am feeling sad
   SUPPORTING IDEA 1:
   first thing
   - go visit family
   SUPPORTING IDEA 2:
   second thing
   - go visit friends
   CONCLUSION:
   visit family and friends when sad

2. INTRODUCTION:
   December is favorite month
   SUPPORTING IDEA 1:
   first reason
   - is a month when there is a holiday season
   SUPPORTING IDEA 2:
   second reason
   - is a month when my family gets together
   CONCLUSION:
   December is favorite month

3. INTRODUCTION:
   my classmates are friendly
   SUPPORTING IDEA 1:
   first example
   - greeting me when I come to class
   SUPPORTING IDEA 2:
   second example
   - helping me when I don't understand
   CONCLUSION:
   classmates are friendly because they greet and help me

SPEAKING EXERCISE 2 Page 176

Sample Responses

1. Sometimes I do feel sad. I've learned that I need to be with people I care about, like my family or my friends, when I'm sad.
   When I'm feeling sad, the first thing I like to do is to visit my family and talk with my family. This is something that can make me forget my sadness.
   If family members aren't close by when I'm sad, then I go visit friends and talk with them. This can also make me forget my sadness.
   When I'm sad, I know that the best thing for me is to go and talk with my family or my friends. This helps me get over my sadness.

2. Of all the months of the year, I think that December is my favorite month. This is because December is a month when there is a big holiday, and it's also a month when my family gets together.
   I like December because it's the month when there is a holiday season. I like the holiday season a lot because everyone is friendly and kind, and people always think about others.
   I also like December because this is the month when my family gets together. I have a large family. I have a mother and father, brothers and sisters, and nieces and nephews. During the holiday season in December, all of my family gets together.
   Because there is a holiday season and because my family gets together then, I think December is my favorite month of the year.

3. I like my classmates a lot, and there are many things that I like about them. It's difficult to choose one thing that I like about them, but I guess the thing I like most about them is that they're very friendly. I can tell you about two situations that show how friendly they are.
   The first thing that shows how friendly my classmates are happens each time I come to class. My classmates always greet me happily when I come into the classroom. This makes me feel so relaxed.

The second thing that shows how friendly my classmates are happens when the lesson is difficult for me. Sometimes I don't understand the material in class, and someone always helps me. I really appreciate this a lot.

You can see from the greetings and the help that my classmates are really friendly. This is something that I like about them very much.

SPEAKING EXERCISE 3   Page 178
Sample Notes

1. INTRODUCTION:
   choose to be a musician

   SUPPORTING IDEA 1:
   first reason
   • wonderful to have musical talent

   SUPPORTING IDEA 2:
   second reason
   • fun to perform in front of a lot of people

   CONCLUSION:
   choose to be musician for two reasons

2. INTRODUCTION:
   I always wait to get work done

   SUPPORTING IDEA 1:
   first example
   • English class paper

   SUPPORTING IDEA 2:
   second example
   • science class assignment

   CONCLUSION:
   I don't get work done early

3. INTRODUCTION:
   better to have love than money

   SUPPORTING IDEA 1:
   first reason
   • love makes you happy

   SUPPORTING IDEA 2:
   second reason
   • money doesn't make you happy

   CONCLUSION:
   better to choose love over money

SPEAKING EXERCISE 4   Page 179
Sample Responses

1. If I can be an astronaut or a famous musician, I'll choose to be a famous musician. I have two reasons why I'll choose to be a musician.

   The first reason I'll choose to be a famous musician over an astronaut is that it would be wonderful to have musical talent. I'd like to have a great singing voice, and I'd also like to be able to play several musical instruments really well.

   The second reason I'll choose to be a famous musician over an astronaut is that it would be fun to perform in front of a lot of people. I'd love to have a lot of fans who enjoy music and come to see me in concerts.

   For these two reasons, I'll choose to be a famous musician over an astronaut.

2. Unfortunately, I am the kind of student who gets work done at the last possible moment. Examples

from my English class and my science class will show you that this is true.

In my English class recently, I waited until the last day to write a paper. The teacher gave us two weeks to write a paper, but I waited until the day before the paper was due to start it. I had to stay up really late the night before the paper was due to finish it.

In my science class recently, I was even worse. The teacher gave us a huge science assignment and gave us a week to do it. I didn't even start the assignment the day before it was due. Instead, I waited until the morning the assignment was due to start it. I had to hurry through the assignment, and I didn't do well on it because I hurried.

You can see from these two examples that I am not a student who gets work done early.

3. If I have to choose between love and money, I think I'll choose love. I have two reasons for choosing love over money.

The first reason that I'll choose love over money is about love. Love makes you happy. If you have people who love you, this is the greatest happiness.

The second reason that I'll choose love over money is about money. Money doesn't make you happy. Lots of people who have money aren't happy.

For these two reasons, I think I'll choose love over money.

SPEAKING REVIEW EXERCISE (Skills 1–4)   Page 180

Question 1   Page 180
Sample Notes

INTRODUCTION:
activities on the beach

SUPPORTING IDEA 1:
first kind
• really active activities (swimming, surfing, playing games, walking or jogging)

SUPPORTING IDEA 2:
second kind
• really relaxing activities (sitting on the beach, talking with friends, watching the sunset, having a picnic)

CONCLUSION:
many different activities on beach

Sample Response

My hometown is near the beach, so people in my hometown generally enjoy different kinds of activities at the beach. They enjoy things that are active and things that are relaxing.

Some of the activities that people enjoy at the beach are really active activities. They enjoy swimming or surfing, playing games like football, and walking or jogging on the beach.

Some of the activities that people enjoy at the beach are really relaxing. They enjoy just sitting on the beach and talking with friends or watching a beautiful sunset. They also enjoy having a nice picnic or barbecue on the beach.

There are many enjoyable things to do on the beach. Some of them are very active, while others can be very relaxing.

Question 2 Page 180

Sample Notes

INTRODUCTION:
prefer lecture classes over discussion classes

SUPPORTING IDEA 1:
first reason
• professor is more knowledgeable than students

SUPPORTING IDEA 2:
second reason
• I don't have to talk

CONCLUSION:
prefer lectures over discussions for two reasons

Sample Response

In college there are lecture classes and discussion classes. If I get to choose, I prefer to choose lecture classes over discussion classes. There are two reasons why I prefer lecture classes.

The first reason that I prefer lecture classes over discussion classes is that the professor is more knowledgeable than the students. I like to listen to the professor's ideas more than the ideas of the other students.

The second reason that I prefer lecture classes over discussion classes is that I don't have to talk so much. I'm not very comfortable talking in a classroom, so I prefer classes where the professor does most of the talking.

For these two reasons, I prefer to take lecture classes instead of discussion classes.

SPEAKING EXERCISE 5 Page 182

Sample Notes

1. TOPIC OF READING PASSAGE: note on door of professor's classroom about professor's absence

main points about the topic:
• professor will be absent on Thursday and Friday because of illness
• professor expects to return next Monday

2. TOPIC OF READING PASSAGE: memo from Literature Department on schedule forms

main points about the topic:
• memo is dated May 1
• schedule forms must be turned in by April 30
• schedule forms will not be accepted after April 30

3. TOPIC OF READING PASSAGE: notice about part-time jobs in library

main points about the topic:
• jobs available evenings and weekends
• jobs for full-time students only
• contact head librarian 9–5 Monday–Friday to see about jobs

SPEAKING EXERCISE 6 Page 185

Sample Notes

1. TOPIC OF LISTENING PASSAGE: student discussion of the note

main points about the topic:
• man is happy that two classes are canceled
• woman is not happy because they must still learn the material from the canceled classes

2. TOPIC OF LISTENING PASSAGE: student discussion about problem in memo

main points about the topic:
• man notices date of May 1 on memo
• is impossible to turn in schedule forms by April 30 because it was yesterday

3. TOPIC OF LISTENING PASSAGE: student discussion about notice

main points about the topic:
• man can't apply because he's not full-time (he is available)
• woman is going to apply (must be available and must be full-time)

SPEAKING EXERCISE 8 Page 191

Sample Responses

1. In this set of materials, the reading passage is a note on the door of a professor's classroom. Two students discuss the note in the listening passage.

   The note in the reading passage states that the professor will be absent from class on Thursday and Friday because of illness. The note also states that the professor is expected to return to class next Monday.

   Two students discuss this note in the listening passage. The man is happy that two classes are canceled because he wants some time off. The woman isn't happy about the canceled classes because the students must still learn the material from the canceled classes.

2. In this set of materials, the reading passage is a memo. Two students discuss a problem with the memo in the listening passage.

   The reading passage is a memo that is dated May 1. According to this memo, schedule forms must be turned in by April 30. They will not be accepted after April 30.

   In the listening passage, the man has noticed a problem with the memo. The memo is dated with today's date of May 1. It is impossible to do what the memo says. It is impossible to turn in schedule forms by April 30 because that was yesterday.

3. In this set of materials, the reading passage describes a notice. Two students discuss the notice in the listening passage.

   The notice in the reading passage is about part-time jobs that are available in the library. The jobs are available evenings and weekends, and they're for full-time students only. Students who want these jobs must contact the head librarian between 9:00 and 5:00 Monday through Friday to see about the jobs.

   In the listening passage, two students have a discussion about the notice. The man would like to apply for the jobs and he's available to work evenings and weekends. However, he can't apply because he isn't a full-time student. The woman wants one of the jobs, and she's going to apply. This must mean that she's available to work evenings and weekends and that she's a full-time student.

SPEAKING REVIEW EXERCISE (Skills 5–8) Page 191

Sample Notes

TOPIC OF READING PASSAGE: assignment on leader in business class

main points about the topic:
- students must choose leader from textbook
- students must describe three strengths (one paragraph each)
- students must describe three weaknesses (one paragraph each)

TOPIC OF LISTENING PASSAGE: student discussion about a problem with assignment

main points about the topic:
- woman completed assignment
- man explains that woman completed assignment incorrectly
- woman wrote two paragraphs instead of six
- woman misunderstood "one paragraph about each . . ."
- woman needs to redo assignment

Sample Response

In this set of materials, the reading passage is a description of an assignment in a business class. Two students discuss a problem one of them had with the assignment in the listening passage.

The reading passage describes a writing assignment on a leader that was given in a business class. According to this assignment, the students are supposed to choose a leader from their textbook. They are to write three paragraphs on the leader's strengths and three paragraphs on the leader's weaknesses, for a total of six paragraphs.

Two students discuss this assignment in the listening passage. The woman thinks that she has already completed the assignment, but the man explains to her that she did it incorrectly. The woman wrote only two paragraphs instead of six because she misunderstood the meaning of "one paragraph about each . . . ." She needs to redo the assignment now.

SPEAKING EXERCISE 9 Page 194

Sample Notes

1. TOPIC OF READING PASSAGE: high temperature on planet Venus

   main points about the topic:
   - has an extraordinarily high surface temperature
   - has a surface temperature of 890°F, or 470°C
   - has a warmer surface temperature than the planet Mercury, which is closer to the sun

2. TOPIC OF READING PASSAGE: relationship between mountains and permanent snow

   main points about the topic:
   - height of mountains isn't only factor
   - distance from equator is other factor

3. TOPIC OF READING PASSAGE: honeybees

   main points about the topic:
   - live in a colony with queen bee, some male drones, and a lot of female workers
   - sting people and animals to protect colony
   - sting can be painful and can even kill

SPEAKING EXERCISE 10 Page 197

Sample Notes

1. TOPIC OF LISTENING PASSAGE: cause of high temperature on Venus

   main points about the topic:
   - Venus has thick atmosphere
   - thick atmosphere traps heat of Sun so it can't escape

2. TOPIC OF LISTENING PASSAGE: example about relationship between mountains and permanent snow

   main points about the topic:
   - two mountains of equal height may not both have permanent snow
   - mountain in Norway has permanent snow (is far from equator)
   - mountain in Spain doesn't have permanent snow (is closer to equator)

3. TOPIC OF LISTENING PASSAGE: clarification about one point on honeybees

   main points about the topic:
   - not completely true that all honeybees sting people
   - only workers (and not queen or drones) sting

SPEAKING EXERCISE 11 Page 200

1. reading passage describes *a certain situation on the planet Venus*; listening passage discusses *the cause of this situation*

2. reading passage discusses *the relationship between mountains and permanent snow*; listening passage provides *an example of the relationship*

3. reading passage describes *a certain kind of bee*; listening passage *clarifies the information given in the reading passage*

SPEAKING EXERCISE 12 Page 203

Sample Responses

1.   In this set of materials, the reading passage discusses a certain situation on the planet Venus. The listening passage discusses the cause of this situation.

   The reading passage discusses the high temperature on the planet Venus. Venus has a surface temperature of 890 degrees Fahrenheit, or 470 degrees Centigrade, which is an extraordinarily high temperature. Venus even has a higher surface temperature than the planet Mercury, which is closer to the Sun than Venus.

   The listening passage explains the cause of the high temperature on Venus. The cause of the high temperature on Venus is the thick atmosphere that surrounds the planet. The thick atmosphere traps the heat of the Sun and doesn't allow it to escape.

2.   In this set of materials, the reading passage discusses the relationship between mountains and permanent snow. The listening passage provides an example.

   The reading passage says that there are two factors that determine if a mountain has permanent snow on it. One factor is the height of the mountain, but that isn't the only factor. The distance of the mountain from the equator is the other factor.

The listening passage provides an example. In this example, the professor discusses two mountains with equal height. The mountain in Norway has permanent snow on it because it's far from the equator. The mountain in Spain doesn't have permanent snow on it because it's closer to the equator.

3. In this set of materials, the reading passage describes a certain kind of bee, and the listening passage clarifies the information given in the reading passage.

The reading passage describes honeybees. Honeybees live in a colony with one queen bee, some male drones, and a lot of female worker bees. Honeybees sting people and animals to protect their colony. The sting can be painful and can even kill a human.

The listening passage clarifies some of the information in the reading passage. According to the listening passage, it's not completely true that all honeybees sting people. Instead, only the worker bees sting humans. The queen bee and the drones don't sting humans.

SPEAKING REVIEW EXERCISE (Skills 9–12) Page 203
Sample Notes

TOPIC OF READING PASSAGE: definition of mercantilism

main points about the topic:
- mother countries have colonies
- business from colonies can help mother country
- business for mother country from colonies is mercantilism

TOPIC OF LISTENING PASSAGE: ways mercantilism helps mother country

main points about the topic:
- colony provides raw materials
- colony buys mother country's products
- colony takes people mother country doesn't want

Sample Response

In this set of materials, the reading passage defines mercantilism. The listening passage describes the benefits of mercantilism.

Mercantilism is defined in the reading passage. Mother countries have colonies, and business from the colonies can help the mother country. This business for the mother country from the colonies is called mercantilism.

The listening passage describes the ways that mercantilism can help the mother countries. The passage describes three ways. The first way that a colony can help its mother country is by providing raw materials. The second way a colony can help its mother country is by buying the country's products. The third way the colony can help its mother country is by taking people the mother country doesn't want.

SPEAKING EXERCISE 13 Page 207
Sample Notes

1. TOPIC OF LISTENING PASSAGE: student discussion about woman's tardiness to class

    main points about the topic:
    - woman was late to class
    - man says professor saw her and said something about it
    - woman knows she must come on time from now on

2. TOPIC OF LISTENING PASSAGE: discussion about history class notes

    main points about the topic:
    - woman wants to borrow man's notes from class today
    - woman was in class but did not take notes for silly reason (nothing to write with)
    - man agrees this is silly but also agrees to lend her his notes

3. TOPIC OF LISTENING PASSAGE: student discussion about an economics course

    main points about the topic:
    - woman wants to know about the course because she is thinking about taking it
    - man has already taken the course
    - man suggests not taking the course because the professor lectured too much
    - woman thinks she might like that kind of course

SPEAKING EXERCISE 15 Page 213
Sample Responses

1. In this listening passage, two students are having a discussion about the woman's tardiness to class.

    The woman was late to class this morning. The man knows that the professor saw her come in late to class, and the man also knows that the professor said something about her tardiness. The woman knows that it's important to come to class on time from now on, and the man strongly agrees with her.

2. In this listening passage, two students are having a discussion about the notes from a history class earlier today.

    The woman wants to borrow the man's notes from class. She was in class, but she didn't take any notes because she didn't have anything to write with.

    Both students agree that the woman has a silly excuse for not taking any notes. The man does agree to let the woman borrow his notes even though her excuse was silly.

3. In this listening passage, two students have a discussion about an economics class.

    In the discussion, the woman wants to know about the course because she's thinking about taking it. The man has already taken the course, and he didn't like it because the professor lectured too much. He suggests to the woman that for this reason she shouldn't take the course.

    The woman doesn't want to follow the man's suggestion. She thinks that she might like that kind of course, so she may take it.

SPEAKING REVIEW EXERCISE (Skills 13–15)   Page 214

Sample Notes

TOPIC OF LISTENING PASSAGE: discussion of preparation for math exam on Friday

main points of the discussion:
- man wants to prepare with woman on Thursday evening
- woman can't prepare on Thursday because of concert
- they decide to prepare on Wednesday evening

Sample Response

In this listening passage, the two students are discussing how to prepare for a math exam. The math exam will be on Friday.

The man wants to prepare for the math exam with the woman on Thursday evening. However, the woman can't prepare for the math exam on Thursday evening because she's going to a concert.

In the end, the two students decide to prepare earlier for the exam. They decide to work together to prepare for the exam on Wednesday evening instead of Thursday evening.

SPEAKING EXERCISE 16   Page 217

Sample Notes

1. TOPIC OF LISTENING PASSAGE: bald eagle

   main points about the topic:
   - is symbol of U.S.
   - is not bald
   - has white feathers on head and dark brown feathers on body
   - has wide wings (8 feet from tip to tip)
   - is strong hunter
   - has strong claws (talons) on its feet

2. TOPIC OF LISTENING PASSAGE: hot-air balloons

   main points about the topic:
   - balloonists can't control direction (balloons are pushed by wind)
   - balloonists can control height (heat to rise and cool to descend)

3. TOPIC OF LISTENING PASSAGE: "dark days"

   main points about the topic:
   - sky became dark during middle of day
   - happened in northeastern U.S.
   - happened from beginning of 1700s to beginning of 1900s
   - occurred 18 times
   - were caused by forest fires in northwestern U.S.

SPEAKING EXERCISE 18   Page 223

Sample Responses

1. In this listening passage, the professor discusses the bald eagle, which is the symbol of the United States. The bald eagle isn't really bald but has coloring that makes it look bald. The bald eagle has a wide wing span of eight feet from tip to tip. It uses its strong claws, or talons, to hunt.

2. In this listening passage, the professor discusses hot-air balloons. Balloonists are people who fly in hot-air balloons. Balloonists are unable to control the direction their balloons fly because balloons are pushed by the wind. Balloonists are able to control how high their balloons fly. They heat the air in the balloon to make it rise, and they cool the air in the balloon to make it descend.

3. In this listening passage, the professor discusses the dark days. During the dark days, the sky became dark during the middle of the day. This happened eighteen times in the northeastern part of the United States from the beginning of the 1700s to the beginning of the 1900s. Today we know that the dark days were caused by forest fires in the northwestern part of the United States.

SPEAKING REVIEW EXERCISE (Skills 16–18)   Page 223

Sample Notes

TOPIC OF LISTENING PASSAGE: energy used by human brain

main points about the topic:
- brain is 1/50 of weight of human body
- brain uses 1/5 of energy of human body
- brain uses 10 times more energy than rest of human body

Sample Response

In this listening passage, the professor discusses the human brain and the large amount of energy it uses. The brain is one fiftieth of the weight of the human body, but it uses one fifth of the energy of the human body. This means that the brain uses ten times more energy than the rest of the human body.

SPEAKING POST-TEST   Page 224

Question 1   Page 225

Sample Notes

INTRODUCTION:
   dream job as airline pilot

SUPPORTING IDEA 1:
   first reason
   - want to learn to fly

SUPPORTING IDEA 2:
   second reason
   - want to see many places

CONCLUSION:
   dream job is to be airline pilot for two reasons

Sample Response

There is one job that I've always dreamed of having. My dream job is to be an airline pilot. There are two reasons why this is my dream job.

The first reason that I dream of being an airline pilot is that I want to learn to fly an airplane. I think it would be wonderful to be up in the clouds flying a plane.

The second reason that I dream of being an airline pilot is that I want to see many different places in the world. If I can be a pilot, then I can see a lot of different places when I fly.

Because I want to learn to fly an airplane and because I want to see many different places in the world, being an airline pilot is my dream job.

Question 2 Page 225

Sample Notes

> INTRODUCTION:
> I am forgetful
>
> SUPPORTING IDEA 1:
> first example
>   • forgot mother's birthday
>
> SUPPORTING IDEA 2:
> second example
>   • forgot economics exam
>
> CONCLUSION:
> I am forgetful about important things

Sample Response

Some people are forgetful, while others remember everything. Unfortunately, I am one of the forgetful ones. Here are some examples that show you how forgetful I am.

The first example that shows that I'm forgetful is about my mother's birthday. My mother's birthday was last week, but I forgot about it. She reminded me yesterday when she called me. I'm really sorry I forgot about her birthday.

The second example that shows that I'm forgetful is about an economics exam. I had an economics exam this morning, but I forgot about it. I wasn't prepared for the exam at all when I came to class this morning, and I'm sure I didn't do well on it.

I think you can see from these examples about my mother's birthday and my economics exam that I'm quite forgetful about important things.

Question 3 Page 226

Sample Notes

> TOPIC OF READING PASSAGE: notice in dormitory about policy against pets
>
> main points about the topic:
> • no pets allowed in dormitory
> • anyone who breaks rule must leave dormitory
>
> TOPIC OF LISTENING PASSAGE: student discussion about notice
>
> main points about the topic:
> • man does not know why notice was posted, but woman thinks she does
> • woman knows someone who has at least three cats in dormitory
> • person with cats lives on first floor of dormitory and leaves window open for cats

Sample Response

In this set of materials, the reading passage is a notice posted in a dormitory. Two students discuss this notice in the listening passage.

The notice posted in the dormitory is about the dormitory's policy on pets. The policy is that absolutely no pets are allowed in the dormitory. Any student who breaks this rule must move out of the dormitory and live somewhere else.

In the listening passage, two students discuss this notice. The man doesn't know why the notice was posted, but the woman thinks she does know why. The woman knows someone who has at least three

cats living in the dormitory. The person with the cats lives on the first floor of the dormitory and leaves the window open for the cats. This may be why the notice about pets was posted.

Question 4 Page 228

Sample Notes

> TOPIC OF READING PASSAGE: city of Los Angeles
>
> main points about the topic:
> • started as small town in 1781
> • remained small for a century
> • then grew very suddenly
>
> TOPIC OF LISTENING PASSAGE: why city grew suddenly
>
> main points about the topic:
> • railroads competed for business by lowering fares
> • fare across country to L.A. was $1
> • many people traveled to L.A.
> • population grew rapidly

Sample Response

In this set of materials, the reading passage describes something interesting that happened in the history of a city. The listening passage explains why this happened.

The reading passage describes the history of the city of Los Angeles. Los Angeles started as a small town in 1781, and it remained small for a century.

The listening passage explains why the city of Los Angeles grew so suddenly. The reason for the sudden growth was that the railroads were competing for business by lowering fares. The fare across the country to Los Angeles dropped to one dollar. Because of this low fare, many people traveled to Los Angeles, and the population grew rapidly.

Question 5 Page 230

Sample Notes

> TOPIC OF LISTENING PASSAGE: discussion about woman's English class
>
> main points about the topic:
> • woman is having problem in class
> • woman turns in papers but gets bad grades
> • man suggests seeing professor during office hours
> • woman does not like man's idea
> • man says woman has to do something

Sample Response

In this listening passage, two students are discussing an English class that the woman is taking.

The woman is having a problem in this class. She turns in all of the papers that are assigned, but she gets bad grades on them.

The man suggests that the woman should see the professor during the professor's office hours, but the woman doesn't seem to want to do this. The man then says that she needs to do something about this situation.

Question 6 Page 231

Sample Notes

TOPIC OF LISTENING PASSAGE: water covering parts of the continents 65 million years ago

main points about the topic:
- water covering today's southern Europe
- water dividing today's North America
- water covering today's northern Africa
- water covering today's southern Asia

Sample Response

In this listening passage, the professor discusses the water that was covering parts of the continents 65 million years ago.

According to the listening passage, there were many big differences then. Sixty-five million years ago, there was water covering today's southern Europe, today's northern Africa, and today's southern Asia. There was also water dividing today's North America.

WRITING

WRITING DIAGNOSTIC PRE-TEST Page 234

Question 1 Page 235

Sample Notes

TOPIC OF READING PASSAGE: Old World monkeys (in Africa and Asia)

main points about the topic:
- have narrow nostrils, or noses
- eat insects and animals as well as plants (omnivores)
- do not have prehensile tails (gripping tails) and spend most of their time on the ground

TOPIC OF LISTENING PASSAGE: New World monkeys (in Central and South America)

main points about the topic:
- have wide nostrils
- eat plants only (herbivores)
- most have prehensile tails (gripping tails) and spend most of their time in trees

Sample Response

In this set of materials, the reading passage discusses one kind of animal. The listening passage adds to the reading passage by discussing a kind of animal with opposite characteristics.

The reading passage describes Old World monkeys, which live in Africa and Asia. Old World monkeys have narrow nostrils, or noses; they eat insects and animals as well as plants, so they are omnivores. They do not have prehensile tails to grip tree branches, and they spend most of their time on the ground.

The listening passage describes New World monkeys, which are monkeys that are very different from Old World monkeys. Unlike Old World monkeys, which live in Africa and Asia, New World monkeys live in Central and South America. New World monkeys have wide nostrils, which are different from the narrow nostrils of the Old World

monkeys, and unlike Old World monkeys, they are herbivores, which means that they eat only plants. Another difference is that most New World monkeys have prehensile tails, and they spend most of their time in trees.

Question 2 Page 237

Sample Notes

TOPIC: spring is favorite season of the year

Why
- winter is cold, and sky is gray, and you feel sad
- spring is warm, and sky is blue, and you feel happy

Sample Response

There are four different seasons of the year, and there are reasons to like each one. For me, I have a strong preference for the spring season because of how I feel when winter turns to spring.

I live in a place that has cold and cloudy winters. During the winter months, it is cold, and there is usually a lot of snow on the ground. During the winter months, the sun never comes out, and the sky is always gray. It is easy to feel sad in the winter because of the cold weather and dark sky.

In spring in my hometown, everything changes dramatically. In spring, the weather starts to warm up, and the sky is blue. Day after day in the spring, the sun shines in a clear blue sky. This is a particularly welcome change because it comes after the cold, gray winter. It is impossible to feel sad in the spring in my hometown.

Spring is really my favorite time of year. It is a time to say goodbye to the sad, cold, gray winter and to say a cheerful hello to the blue sky of spring.

WRITING EXERCISE 1 Page 242

1. TOPIC OF READING PASSAGE: agriculture in 1900 in the U.S.

   main points about the topic:
   - 40% of labor force in agriculture
   - farms generally owned by individual families
   - not very productive (typical farmer grew food for 5 people)
   - a lot of manual labor, horse-drawn plows

2. TOPIC OF READING PASSAGE: reasons why dolphins are very intelligent

   main points about the topic:
   - brain size (larger than human brains)
   - dolphins reach out to humans (saving drowning humans)
   - ability to learn commands (some dolphins learn dozens)

3. TOPIC OF READING PASSAGE: Leonardo's conclusions about human flight, based on observations of birds in flight

   main points about the topic:
   - one conclusion about size of wings needed to support man in flight
   - one conclusion about power needed to push a man into flight

WRITING EXERCISE 2   Page 247

1. TOPIC OF LISTENING PASSAGE: agriculture today in the U.S.

   main points about the topic:
   - 2% of labor force in agriculture
   - farms generally owned by corporations rather than families
   - more productive (typical farmer grows food for 75–100 people)
   - efficient farm machinery to increase yield

2. TOPIC OF LISTENING PASSAGE: reasons for dolphin intelligence are not so good

   main points about the topic:
   - brain is not so big (in comparison to body size)
   - behavior may be natural (have nothing to do with humans)
   - learning some commands may not show extreme intelligence (dogs learn commands)

3. TOPIC OF LISTENING PASSAGE: whether or not Leonardo's conclusions were correct

   main points about the topic:
   - conclusion about wing size was correct
   - conclusion about power was not correct (much more power needed)

WRITING EXERCISE 3   Page 252

1. reading passage describes a *situation in the past*
   listening passage describes the *situation today*

2. reading passage describes *reasons something is true*
   listening passage says *the reasons are not good*

3. reading passage describes *conclusions by a certain person*
   listening passage discusses *whether or not the conclusions are correct*

WRITING EXERCISE 4   Page 256

1. TOPIC STATEMENT: In this set of materials, the reading passage describes a certain situation in the past. The listening passage adds to the ideas in the reading passage by describing this situation today.

2. TOPIC STATEMENT: In this set of materials, the reading passage discusses reasons that a certain animal is intelligent. The listening passage casts doubt on the ideas in the reading passage by explaining that the reasons are not very good.

3. TOPIC STATEMENT: In this set of materials, the reading passage describes certain conclusions made by a certain famous person. The listening passage supports one conclusion and challenges the other.

WRITING EXERCISE 5   Page 258

1. supporting paragraph on reading:
   The reading passage describes the situation in agriculture in the United States in 1900. At this time, 40 percent of the U.S. labor force was involved in agriculture. Farms were generally owned by families and were not very productive because work was done through manual labor, except for help from horse-drawn plows. A typical farmer was able to grow food for only an average of 5 people.

2. supporting paragraph on reading:
   The reading passage explains that dolphins are very intelligent. The reasons are that a dolphin's brain is larger than a human's brain, that a dolphin reaches out to humans, and that it has the ability to learn dozens of commands.

3. supporting paragraph on reading:
   The reading passage describes two conclusions that Leonardo da Vinci made about human flight. The first conclusion was about the size of the wings that would be needed to support a man in flight. The second conclusion was about the amount of power that would be needed to push a man into flight.

WRITING EXERCISE 6   Page 261

1. supporting paragraph on listening:
   The listening passage describes the situation in agriculture in the United States today. This situation is very different from the situation in the past. Today, the percentage of the labor force that is involved in agriculture has dropped from 40 percent to only 2 percent, and farms are generally owned by corporations rather than families. Farms today are also considerably more productive; a typical farmer is able to grow food for 75 to 100 people instead of 5 people. This is because the farmer of today has efficient farm machinery to increase yield, and these were not available to the farmer in 1900, who worked with only horse-drawn plows.

2. supporting paragraph on listening:
   The listening passage explains that the reasons that are given to demonstrate the dolphin's intelligence are not very good. The dolphin may be intelligent, but there are not good reasons to prove this in the reading passage. First, the dolphin may have a large brain, but it also has a very large body. In comparison to the body, the brain is not so large. Second, the behavior that seems to be human may actually be natural to a dolphin. When a dolphin saves a drowning human, for example, it may think it is saving a drowning dolphin. Third, the dolphin can learn some commands, but learning some commands may not show extreme intelligence. A dog can learn to follow some commands, so this does not show that a dolphin is any more intelligent than a dog.

3. supporting paragraph on listening:
   The listening passage discusses the accuracy of Leonardo's conclusions. It supports one conclusion and challenges the other. The conclusion about the size of the wing that would be needed to support a man in flight was correct. The conclusion about the amount of power that would be needed to push a man into flight was not correct. Much more power would be needed than the amount that Leonardo described.

WRITING EXERCISE 7   Page 263

1. In this set of materials, the reading passage presents a traditional **story. The** listening passage discusses this traditional story. The traditional **story** is not generally accepted today.

2. The reading passage **describes** a traditional story about the origin of the word "news." According to this traditional story, the word "news" came from

the first letters of compass directions. Compass directions are north, east, west, and **south. The** first letters of each of these compass directions make up the word "news." Since news seems to come from all directions at the same **time, a** traditional story arose. According to this story, the word "news" was created **because it represents** the idea of the four directions, north, east, west, and south.

3.   According to the listening passage, this traditional story about the origin of the word "**news**" **is not** true. Though it makes a nice and interesting **story, the** actual origin of the **word is** not so exotic. As you might be able to guess, the word "news" actually developed from the Latin word that meant "new." The news, **indeed, is a** description of new events just **after they have** occurred.

WRITING EXERCISE 8   Page 265

1.   In this set of materials, the reading passage discusses a concept. The listening passage gives an example of the concept.

2.   The reading passage discusses the "halo effect." A halo is a large number of **bands** of light around the head of an angel, and the "halo effect" is something that can **occur** when a business manager **is hiring** someone to work in a company. The "halo effect" occurs when an applicant for a position has one quality that is **truly** outstanding and a manager hires that person because of this one outstanding quality. Because the manager sees only this one quality, he or **she** does not see the applicant's other qualities, and each of these other qualities **is** not guaranteed to be good.

3.   An example of the concept of the "halo effect" **is** provided in the listening passage. This example concerns a young woman named Ms. Owen. Ms. Owen had good test scores when **she** completed her university studies; in fact, all of her test scores **were** extremely good. When she applied for her first job after finishing **her** studies, the manager who interviewed her thought that she seemed **perfect** for the job because of her test scores. In fact, because he was so impressed with her test scores, he did not ask about anything else. He did not learn that Ms. Owen is someone who **rarely** gets work done on time. Because the manager saw only one of Ms. Owen's good qualities and did not find out about **many** of her other qualities, he made a **careless** and quick hiring decision. Since she was hired, Ms. Owen **has had** a lot of problems on the job. The problems she had were not only her fault but **also the** fault of the manager. The manager had not done a good job in hiring Ms. Owen because of the halo effect.

WRITING REVIEW EXERCISE (Skills 1–8)   Page 266

Sample Notes

TOPIC OF READING PASSAGE: decision of Company X to use centralized decision-making

main points about the topic:
• managers are far apart
• local decisions are needed
• local managers are capable

TOPIC OF LISTENING PASSAGE: wrong decision-making choice

main points about the topic:
• decentralized decision-making better when local managers are far from main office
• decentralized decision-making better when local decisions are needed
• decentralized decision-making better when local managers are capable

Sample Answer

In this set of materials, the reading passage describes a choice about decision-making in a certain company. The listening passage casts doubt on the information in the reading passage by explaining why the company made the wrong choice.

The reading passage discusses Company X. In Company X, the managers are far from the main office, local decisions are needed, and the local managers are capable. Company X has chosen centralized decision-making.

The listening passage explains why centralized decision-making was a bad choice for Company X. First, decentralized decision-making is better when the local managers are far from the main office. The local managers are far from the main office in Company X. Second, decentralized decision-making is better when local decisions are needed. Local decisions are needed in Company X. Third, decentralized decision-making is better when local managers are capable. The local managers in Company X are very capable.

WRITING EXERCISE 9   Page 269

1. INTRODUCTION:
   I like my English teacher's humor
   SUPPORTING PARAGRAPH 1:
   first reason why
   • makes class enjoyable
   SUPPORTING PARAGRAPH 2:
   second reason why
   • makes students feel relaxed about speaking English
   CONCLUSION:
   humor can really help a classroom

2. INTRODUCTION:
   writing a paper by myself and not with other students
   SUPPORTING PARAGRAPH 1:
   first reason why
   • hard to agree on ideas
   SUPPORTING PARAGRAPH 2:
   second reason why
   • hard to agree on style
   CONCLUSION:
   may seem better to write a paper with others, but not for me

3. INTRODUCTION:
   won a million dollars in the lottery

   SUPPORTING PARAGRAPH 1:
   first thing to do with it
   • spend some on me

   SUPPORTING PARAGRAPH 2:
   second thing to do with it
   • spend some on my parents

   SUPPORTING PARAGRAPH 3:
   third thing to do with it
   • invest a lot of it

   CONCLUSION:
   will spend some but will save most

WRITING EXERCISE 10   Page 272

1. I am taking an English class now, and I am learning a lot of English. It may surprise you that what I like most about this class is not so much the English I am learning; instead, it is the teacher's humor. I can explain why this is.

2. Sometimes a teacher will assign a paper and will tell the students that they can write the paper by themselves or with other students. It may be surprising to you, but in that situation I am certain that I will decide to write the paper by myself. I will decide this because of the ideas and the writing style in the paper.

3. Lotteries are held all the time, and someone has to win them. Maybe I just won a million dollars in a lottery, so I need to figure out what I am going to do with it. I know I will spend some of it, but I will not spend most of it.

WRITING EXERCISE 11   Page 274

1. first supporting paragraph:
   The first reason that I like my teacher's humor is that it makes the class enjoyable. The teacher says a lot of funny things during class, and we laugh a lot. We really enjoy coming to this class.

   second supporting paragraph:
   The second and most important reason that I like my teacher's humor is that it makes the students feel more relaxed. Then we are not afraid to try to speak English even if we make a lot of mistakes.

2. first supporting paragraph:
   The first reason that I will decide to write the paper by myself is the ideas. Everyone has different ideas, and it is difficult for a group of people to decide on the ideas in a paper. It is much easier and takes less time for me to decide on the ideas alone.

   second supporting paragraph:
   The second reason that I will decide to write the paper by myself is the writing style. It is hard to write in the same writing style if each person in the group writes one part of the paper. Then the group needs to spend a lot of time deciding on a writing style. It is much easier and takes much less time to write the paper alone.

3. first supporting paragraph:
   First, I will spend some of the money on things I need. I will buy a new car for myself because the car I am driving now is old and breaks down all the time.

Then, I will move to a better apartment because I do not like the one where I am living now very much.

second supporting paragraph:
   I will also give some money to my parents. My parents do not have very much money, but they have always done everything they can for me. I am an only child, so I need to take care of my parents now. It will be nice to give them some money, for a change.

third supporting paragraph:
   I will not spend most of the money, however. Instead, I will save most of it. I will learn how to invest money carefully, and then I will invest most of my lottery winnings for my future.

WRITING EXERCISE 12   Page 277

1. Humor in the classroom can really help a class. It makes the class enjoyable, and it also makes the students feel relaxed. My English teacher understands this, so she uses a lot of humor in class.

2. At first, it may seem easier to write a paper with other students instead of writing it alone. However, if you think about the ideas and the writing style, maybe you will decide that it is easier to write the paper alone. I certainly think it is.

3. If I am lucky and I win the lottery, I do want to spend some of my money, on myself and on my parents. However, I want to invest most of it because I want to plan for my future.

WRITING EXERCISE 13   Page 279

1. There is no question about it. **I am a** really messy **person. You** just need to look in the kitchen sink, on the floor of my bedroom, or on my desk to know that this is true.

2. **Whenever I use** dishes, I put the dirty dishes in the kitchen sink and leave them there for two or three weeks. I wash them **only when I** really need to use a dish and there are not any clean dishes. **This is** one way that shows how messy I am.

3. You can also see how messy I am by the dirty clothes all over the floor of my bedroom. Whenever I take clothes **off, I** just drop them on the floor of my bedroom. The dirty clothes **stay** on the floor for a long time. **There are piles** of clothes on the floor of my bedroom.

4. **You can** also see how messy I am by looking at the papers all over my desk. Whenever I write something on a piece of paper or print something from my **computer, I** put the papers on my desk. Right now, my **desk is** covered with so many piles of paper. I cannot sit down at my desk to **work because** there are so many papers on my desk.

5. From these examples, you can see my **point. I** am not a very neat person. The dirty dishes in the sink, the dirty clothes all over the bedroom floor, and the piles of papers all over my **desk clearly** prove this point.

WRITING EXERCISE 14   Page 281

1. There are many possible ways to spend free time, and every person **has** different ways of doing this. I spend my free time in two different ways. Both of the

ways that I spend my free time involve **either** moving a lot or not moving at all.

2.   One way that I spend my free time is to move a lot. I enjoy tennis, volleyball, swimming, running, bicycling, and hiking in the hills. I have always **enjoyed** these sports and others. Whenever I am not **working** and I have some free time, I sometimes like to be very **active**. Either I will get involved in one of those activities with a **few** of my friends, or maybe my friends and **I** will get involved in more than one of **them**.

3.   I do not spend all of **my** free time moving a lot, however. Another way that I spend my free time is by not moving at all. In some of my free time, I like to sit quietly and not think very much. Maybe I sit quietly and **listen** to music, or maybe I sit quietly and watch a television program. When I am sitting quietly and not thinking, I can **relax completely**.

4.   I spend my free time in two very **different** ways. One of the ways **involves** a lot of movement, and the other way does not. These two ways of spending my free time **are** necessary for me to have a good life.

WRITING REVIEW EXERCISE (Skills 9–14)   Page 282

Sample Notes

INTRODUCTION:
      prefer going to bed and getting up late but cannot do this

SUPPORTING PARAGRAPH 1:
      I want something
      • going to bed and getting up late means I can do a lot in the evening and get all the sleep I want

SUPPORTING PARAGRAPH 2:
      I cannot do it
      • going to bed and getting up late is not possible for my career

CONCLUSION:
      not possible for me to do what I want

Sample Response

Some people prefer to go to bed early and get up early, while other people like to go to bed late and get up late. I strongly prefer one of these, but, unfortunately, I have to do the other.

It sounds wonderful to me to go to bed late and get up late. If I go to bed late, I can stay up as late as I want in the evening and go out, or watch television, or talk with my family, or read. Then, I can stay in bed and sleep as much as I want and get up when I feel like it.

Even though it sounds wonderful to me to stay up late at night and sleep late in the morning, this is something that I just cannot do. I have a successful career in business, and I work in a company that opens for business at 7 o'clock in the morning. This means that I need to get up at 5 o'clock in the morning to get ready for work and get to the office before 7 o'clock.

It is not always possible to live as one chooses. If I could choose, I would stay up all night and sleep during the day. However, this is not something I can choose and still have the career I want.

WRITING POST-TEST   Page 283

Question 1   Page 284

Sample Notes

TOPIC OF READING PASSAGE: reasons to support proposal by school district to change to a 12-month school year

main points about the topic:
• better memory of material by students
• cost savings because summer school would be cut
• more opportunities for family vacations

TOPIC OF LISTENING PASSAGE: reasons parents and teachers are against proposal

main points about the topic:
• studies showing that students do not forget a lot over a long summer break
• lack of summer school when many students need summer school to catch up or get ahead
• not more opportunities for family vacations because high schools and colleges are not on the same schedule

Sample Response

In this set of materials, the reading passage describes a proposal by a school district. The listening passage challenges the information in the reading passage by explaining why a group of parents and teachers is against the proposal.

The reading passage states that a school district has decided to change to a 12-month school year. The school district wants to do this because it believes there will be better memory of material by the students, a cost savings because summer school would be cut, and more opportunities for family vacations.

The listening passage explains that some parents and teachers are against the plan. They believe that the reasons the school district gave are not good. First, the school district claimed that the students would remember material better without a long summer vacation. The parents and teachers discussed studies that showed that the school district's claim was not valid. Second, the school district claimed that there would be a cost savings in the 12-month school year because there would not be any summer school. The parents and teachers said that it was not a good idea to end summer school because many students need summer school. Third, the school district claimed that there would be more opportunities for family vacations in the 12-month school year. The parents and teachers said that there would not be more opportunities for family vacations because high schools and colleges would not be on the same schedule.

Question 2   Page 286

Sample Notes

INTRODUCTION:
      see a classmate cheating on an exam

SUPPORTING PARAGRAPH 1:
      first thing to do
      • should talk to teacher

SUPPORTING PARAGRAPH 2:
  second thing to do
  • should talk to student
SUPPORTING PARAGRAPH 3:
  third thing to do
  • easier to do nothing
CONCLUSION:
  there are good things to do but it is easier to be silent

Sample Response

I am sure that students cheat on exams all the time. Maybe one day, I will see a classmate cheating on an exam. What will I do? There are some things I know I should do, but will I be able to do them?

One thing I know I should do if I see a classmate cheating on an exam is to talk with the teacher after the exam. I know that this is the right thing to do, but maybe it is too hard for me to do. Maybe my classmates will find out about this and will be upset with me. I am not sure if I will do this.

Another thing I know I should do if I see a classmate cheating on an exam is to talk to the student who was cheating. I know that this is also a good thing to do, but maybe it is also very difficult. Maybe the student will get really angry with me. I am not sure if I will do this.

I know it is not good to be silent if I see a classmate cheating on an exam. However, it is the easy thing to do to be silent. It is much easier than talking to the teacher. It is much easier than talking to the student. It is not right, but it is easy.

MINI-TEST 1   Page 287

READING   Page 287

1. B	4. D	7. D	10. B
2. D	5. C	8. C	11. A
3. C	6. A	9. A	12. C

13. (2) (4) (6)

LISTENING   Page 291

1. C	3. B	5. B	7. A
2. A	4. D	6. A, B, C	8. B, D

9. Angel Falls: Is 3,000 feet tall
   Victoria Falls: Is 355 feet tall
   Niagara Falls: Is 167 feet tall

10. B
11. C

SPEAKING   Page 296

Question 1   Page 297

Sample Notes

INTRODUCTION:
  favorite sport is tennis
SUPPORTING IDEA 1:
  first reason
  • because I like to play tennis
SUPPORTING IDEA 2:
  second reason
  • because I like to watch tennis

CONCLUSION:
  because I like to play and watch it, tennis is favorite sport

Sample Response

My favorite sport is tennis. Tennis is my favorite sport because I like to play it and because I like to watch it.

I play tennis two times every week with some friends of mine. We play every Tuesday and every Thursday. We have a lot of fun when we play even though we don't play very well.

I also like to watch tennis matches. I watch tennis matches on television a lot, and I also go to watch professional tennis matches whenever I can. I really enjoy sitting in the stands or even sitting in front of the television and watching an exciting tennis match.

Because I play tennis all the time and also watch it a lot, you can see that tennis is really my favorite sport.

Question 2   Page 298

Sample Notes

TOPIC OF READING PASSAGE: notice on library door announcing that the library is closed

main points about the topic:
• library is closed unexpectedly
• library may open later today or tomorrow

TOPIC OF LISTENING PASSAGE: student discussion about closed library

main points about the topic:
• man is surprised library is closed
• woman thinks she knows why library is closed
• woman thinks it is because the key to the library is lost

Sample Response

In this set of materials, the reading passage is a notice on the door of the library. Two students discuss the notice in the listening passage.

The notice on the door of the library announces that the library is closed unexpectedly. It also announces that the library may reopen later today or tomorrow.

In this listening passage, two students discuss this notice. The man is surprised that the library is closed, but the woman thinks she knows why it's closed. The woman thinks that the library is closed because someone lost the key to the library.

Question 3   Page 300

Sample Notes

TOPIC OF LISTENING PASSAGE: artist George Catlin

main points about the topic:
• lived in first half of nineteenth century
• was painter
• started painting portraits of rich people
• went west to paint
• was influenced by mother (who was captured by Native Americans and had a good experience)

Sample Response

In this listening passage, the professor discusses artist George Catlin. George Catlin lived in the first half of the nineteenth century. He was a painter who started his career painting portraits of rich people. He later went west to paint because he had been influenced by an experience his mother had. His mother had been captured by Native Americans when she was young, and she had had a good experience.

WRITING Page 301

Sample Notes

TOPIC OF READING PASSAGE: Assateague Island (and the ponies on it)

main points about the topic:
- is long, thin barrier island off east coast of U.S.
- has many wild ponies living there

TOPIC OF LISTENING PASSAGE: how ponies possibly got to island

main points about the topic:
- Spanish ship wrecked close to Assateague Island
- ponies from ship swam to island
- descendants of ponies live on island today

Sample Response

In this set of materials, the reading passage describes an unusual situation. The listening passage adds to the information in the reading passage by explaining how this unusual situation possibly came to be.

The reading passage discusses Assateague Island. The island is a long, thin barrier island just off the east coast of the United States. Something unusual about this island is that there are many wild ponies living on the island. It is unusual to have so many wild ponies living on a barrier island.

The listening passage discusses how the ponies possibly got to the island, although no one is completely sure how this happened. It is possible that a Spanish ship wrecked close to Assateague Island several centuries ago, and it is possible that there were ponies on the ship. When the ship wrecked, the ponies got off the ship and swam to Assateague Island. Today, descendants of the original ponies from the Spanish ship may be the wild ponies living on the island.

MINI-TEST 2 Page 304

READING Page 304

1. B	4. B	7. D	10. C
2. A	5. D	8. B	11. D
3. D	6. C	9. C	12. A

13. from France: (2)
from Spain: (4) (7)
from the West Indies: (1) (6)

LISTENING Page 309

1. C	4. A	7. C
2. D	5. C	8. D
3. Y, N, N, Y	6. A	

9. Robert E. Lee: Was general in chief
Jefferson Davis: Was president of the Confederacy
Stonewall Jackson: Was a general under the chief
10. A
11. B

SPEAKING Page 314

Question 1 Page 315

Sample Notes

INTRODUCTION:
sometimes better to lie

SUPPORTING IDEA 1:
first reason
- does not hurt someone's feelings

SUPPORTING IDEA 2:
second reason
- is easier

CONCLUSION:
there are two times when it's better to lie

Sample Response

I always like to tell the truth when I can. But sometimes I think it's better to lie, if you have good reasons.

One reason that I think it can be better to lie sometimes is in a situation when the truth might hurt someone's feelings. If a lie doesn't hurt the person's feelings, then maybe a lie is better.

Another reason that I might lie sometimes is in a situation when it's difficult for me to tell the truth. When it's really difficult to tell someone the truth, it can be much easier for me to tell a little lie.

Two times when it may be better to tell a lie are when it's better for someone else or when it's easier for me.

Question 2 Page 316

Sample Notes

TOPIC OF READING PASSAGE: foreshocks (before earthquake)

main points about the topic:
- are smaller earthquakes before a major earthquake
- happen when tectonic plates first begin to move

TOPIC OF LISTENING PASSAGE: aftershocks (after earthquake)

main points about the topic:
- are smaller earthquakes after major earthquake
- occur more after really large earthquakes

Sample Response

In this set of materials, the reading passage discusses something that happens before a major earthquake. The listening passage discusses something that happens after a major earthquake.

The reading passage discusses foreshocks. Foreshocks are smaller earthquakes that happen before a major earthquake. They happen when tectonic plates first begin to move.

The listening passage discusses aftershocks. Aftershocks are smaller earthquakes that happen after a major earthquake. Really large earthquakes tend to have more aftershocks.

Question 3 | Page 318

Sample Notes

TOPIC OF LISTENING PASSAGE: student discussion about an exam the man took

main points about the topic:
- man thinks exam was awful because it was only one vague question in two hours
- man's response was long, disorganized, unclear because of the exam question
- woman agrees the exam was awful

Sample Response

In this listening passage, two students are discussing an exam the man just took.

The man thinks that the exam was awful. It was awful because it consisted of only one vague question, and the man had to write for two hours on this one question. He wrote a response that was long, disorganized, and unclear because of the kind of question he was given.

The woman agrees with the man about the exam. She, too, thinks that an exam like this is just awful.

WRITING | Page 319

Sample Notes

INTRODUCTION:
prefer natural spot for a vacation

SUPPORTING PARAGRAPH 1:
first reason
- live in a big city

SUPPORTING PARAGRAPH 2:
second reason
- enjoy outdoor activities

CONCLUSION:
there are reasons why a natural spot is best for me

Sample Response

It is possible to take a vacation in a big city or in a natural spot. I strongly prefer to take vacations in natural places. This is because of where I live and because of what I enjoy.

One reason that I prefer a vacation in a natural spot is that I live in a big city, so I spend most of my time in the city. Most of the time, I do not get to see much nature. There is a little park in my city, but that is all the nature there is. I do not get to see very much nature in my daily life, so when I take a vacation, I want to see a lot of nature.

Another reason that I prefer a vacation in a natural spot is that I enjoy outdoor activities. I enjoy things like hiking in the woods, camping, fishing, and swimming in lakes or rivers. These are not things that I can do in my daily life in the city, so when I take a vacation, I want to do them.

Some people may prefer city vacations, but for me the best vacation is a vacation in a natural location. Because of my life in the city and because of my enjoyment of outdoor activities, a vacation in nature is my preference.

MINI-TEST 3 | Page 321

READING | Page 321

1. D	4. A	7. B	10. C
2. A	5. C	8. C	11. D
3. D	6. A	9. A	12. A

13. (1) (6) (5)

LISTENING | Page 325

1. A	4. Y, N, Y, N	7. C
2. B	5. B	8. A, B
3. D	6. D	9. D

10. *Stanford started a railroad.*
Stanford made millions.
Stanford's son died.
Stanford started a university.

11. C

SPEAKING | Page 330

Question 1 | Page 331

Sample Notes

INTRODUCTION:
things to do when we go out

SUPPORTING IDEA 1:
first thing
- go to movies

SUPPORTING IDEA 2:
second thing
- go to concerts

SUPPORTING IDEA 3:
third thing
- go dancing

CONCLUSION:
three things we do most—go to movies, go dancing, go to concerts

Sample Response

My friends and I go out all the time. When we go out, there are different things we like to do.

The first thing we like to do when we go out is to go to the movies. We like to see new movies a lot, and we usually go to see a new movie about once a week.

The second thing we like to do when we go out is to go to concerts. There are concerts in my hometown about every month, and my friends and I like to go to concerts when we can.

Another thing we like to do when we go out is to go dancing. There is a nice club near my home, and we go there when there is nothing else to do. When we're at the club, we always dance a lot.

When my friends and I go out, we really like to do different things. The three things we do most are go to movies, go to concerts, and go dancing.

Question 2 | Page 332

Sample Notes

TOPIC OF READING PASSAGE: notice about lab reports

main points about the topic:
- notice posted on professor's door
- lab reports due at 3:00
- failing grade on any late lab reports

TOPIC OF LISTENING PASSAGE: student discussion about notice

main points about the topic:
- notice says lab reports due at 3:00
- professor said lab reports due at 5:00
- students took report to office at 4:00
- students worried about failing grades
- students to talk with professor in class

Sample Response

In this set of materials, the reading passage describes a notice. Two students discuss the notice in the listening passage.

The notice in the reading passage is about lab reports that are due. The notice is posted on the professor's door. The notice says the lab reports are due at 3:00 and that any lab reports that are late will receive failing grades.

In the listening passage, two students discuss the notice. The notice says that lab reports were due at 3:00, but the professor said in class that lab reports were due at 5:00. The students took their reports to the professor's office at 4:00, and they thought they were early. Instead, they were late and were worried about failing grades on their reports. The students decide to talk with the professor in the next class.

Question 3 Page 334
Sample Notes

TOPIC OF LISTENING PASSAGE: various kinds of injuries

main points about the topic:
- sprain (injury to joint, such as ankle, elbow, knee, wrist)
- strain (injury to muscle, muscle is stiff and painful)
- bruise (injury to blood vessel, blood vessel breaks and skin discolors)

Sample Response

In this listening passage, the professor discusses various kinds of injuries. She discusses sprains, strains, and bruises. A sprain is an injury to a joint, such as an ankle, an elbow, a knee, or a wrist. A strain is an injury to a muscle. A strained muscle is stiff and painful. A bruise is an injury to a blood vessel. A bruise is caused when a blood vessel breaks and the skin discolors.

WRITING Page 335
Sample Notes

TOPIC OF READING PASSAGE: beliefs, before 1977

main points about the topic:
- belief that light is necessary for life
- belief that there is no light at the bottom of the ocean
- belief that there is no life at bottom of ocean because of lack of light

TOPIC OF LISTENING PASSAGE: contradictory facts, learned in 1977 (from a submarine sent to the bottom of the ocean)

main points about the topic:
- learned that there is a lot of life at bottom of ocean
- learned that there is no light at the bottom of the ocean
- learned that life is possible without light

Sample Response

In this set of materials, the reading passage discusses certain early beliefs that scientists held. The listening passage challenges the information in the reading passage by discussing contradictory facts that were learned later.

The reading passage discusses certain beliefs that scientists held prior to 1977. Before 1977, scientists believed that light was necessary for life to exist. Because there is no light at the bottom of the ocean, they believed that there could not be any life at the bottom of the ocean.

The listening passage discusses contradictory facts that were learned in 1977 from a submarine. In 1977, a submarine went down to the bottom of the ocean, and scientists learned a lot from this. They learned that it was true that there was no light at the bottom of the ocean. However, they also learned that there is a lot of life at the bottom of the ocean, where there is no light. From this, scientists also learned that light is not necessary for life to exist.

MINI-TEST 4 Page 338

READING Page 338
1. B	4. A	7. D	10. A
2. C	5. B	8. A	11. C
3. D	6. D	9. C	12. D

13. (1) (5) (4)

LISTENING Page 343
1. A	4. D	7. B	10. N, Y, N, Y
2. B	5. D	8. B	11. D
3. C	6. A, C, E	9. D	

SPEAKING Page 348
Question 1 Page 349
Sample Notes

INTRODUCTION:
   prefer to write a paper

SUPPORTING IDEA 1:
   first reason
- can check work to make sure it's good

SUPPORTING IDEA 2:
   second reason
- can share ideas only with teacher

CONCLUSION:
   because I can check work and share ideas, prefer to write paper

Sample Response

If I have to choose between writing a paper and giving an oral presentation, I'll choose to write a paper. There are two reasons why I'll choose to write a paper.

The first reason that I'll choose to write a paper instead of giving a presentation is that you can check your work to make sure it's OK when you write a paper. When you give an oral presentation, you do not have the chance to check your work.

The second reason that I'll choose to write a paper instead of giving a presentation is that you share your ideas only with the teacher when you write a paper. When you give an oral presentation, you have to share your ideas with the other students.

For these two reasons, I prefer to write a paper instead of giving an oral presentation.

Question 2   Page 350

Sample Notes

TOPIC OF READING PASSAGE: stories about Gettysburg Address

main points about the topic:
- was given by U.S. president Lincoln in 1863 (during Civil War)
- was written on an envelope during train trip to Gettysburg, according to stories

TOPIC OF LISTENING PASSAGE: untruth of stories about address

main points about the topic:
- was not written on the train (was written in White House)
- was not written on an envelope (was written on paper)

Sample Response

In this set of materials, the reading passage discusses some stories from American history. According to the listening passage, these stories aren't true.

The reading passage describes some stories about the Gettysburg Address. The Gettysburg Address was written by United States president Abraham Lincoln in 1863, during the Civil War. According to traditional stories, Lincoln wrote the address on an envelope while he was traveling by train to Gettysburg.

According to the listening passage, the stories about the Gettysburg Address aren't true. The professor states in the listening passage that the address wasn't written on the train and wasn't written on an envelope. Instead, it was written in the White House on presidential paper before the trip.

Question 3   Page 352

Sample Notes

TOPIC OF LISTENING PASSAGE: a research paper the woman has to write

main points about the topic:
- paper was assigned more than a month ago and is due on Friday
- woman is just starting paper
- man doesn't work this way

Sample Response

In the listening passage, the students discuss a research paper the woman has to write. The paper was assigned more than a month ago, and the paper is due on Friday. The woman is just starting the

paper now because this is how she always works. She always waits until it's late to start assignments because she needs pressure to work hard.

The man is a very different kind of student. The man doesn't work in the same way as the woman. He doesn't wait until the last moment to get work done.

WRITING   Page 353

Sample Notes

INTRODUCTION:
    perfect boss

SUPPORTING PARAGRAPH 1:
    first characteristic
    - be polite

SUPPORTING PARAGRAPH 2:
    second characteristic
    - be direct

CONCLUSION:
    my current boss has these two characteristics and is a great boss

Sample Response

I have worked for three different bosses, and I know from these experiences that there are some very important characteristics in a boss. Two of the most important characteristics to me are politeness and directness.

First, a boss should be nice and polite to all employees. Just because someone is the boss, it is still not acceptable to yell and scream at other people. I had a boss who shouted all the time. I no longer work for this boss.

Secondly, a boss should be very direct when he or she is giving directions to employees. It is not fair to say something very general to an employee and then expect that the employee will do something very specific. I had a boss like this, and I also no longer work for that boss.

I am now working for my third boss, and I am very happy to be working for him. He is always polite and kind with everyone, and he always tells me very directly what I should do. This boss is very happy with my work, and I am very happy to be working for this boss.

COMPLETE TEST   Page 355

READING 1   Page 355

1. D	4. B	7. B	10. D
2. B	5. C	8. A	11. B
3. A	6. C	9. D	12. D

13. (3) (4) (2)

READING 2   Page 359

14. B	17. D	20. B	23. A
15. C	18. C	21. A	24. D
16. A	19. C	22. B	25. C

26. **early scientists:** (4)
    Lord Kelvin: (2) (7)
    20th-century scientists: (3) (6)

READING 3 `Page 363`

27. A	30. D	33. A	36. A
28. D	31. B	34. C	37. D
29. C	32. C	35. C	38. C

39. (5) (4) (3)

LISTENING `Page 367`

1. B	8. D	15. A
2. D	9. D	16. C
3. A	10. A	17. B
4. B	11. D	18. C, D
5. C	12. B, C, E	19. A
6. C	13. C	20. D
7. A	14. A	

21. *Molly became rich.*
Molly traveled to Europe.
Molly survived a ship disaster.
A musical about Molly was created.

22. Denver: Was where Molly lived
Europe: Was where Molly traveled
New York: Was where a show about Molly was presented

23. D	25. B, D	27. D	29. C
24. C	26. D	28. N, Y, N, Y	

30. An arch dam: Is a curved dam
A buttress dam: Is a dam with supports
A gravity dam: Is a straight dam without supports

31. B	33. A
32. C, D, E	34. A, D

SPEAKING `Page 380`

Question 1 `Page 381`

Sample Notes

INTRODUCTION:
    gift I want to receive is tuition
SUPPORTING IDEA 1:
    first reason
    • tuition is really high
SUPPORTING IDEA 2:
    second reason
    • I don't have much money
CONCLUSION:
    need gift of tuition for two reasons

Sample Response

The gift that I would like to receive most is a big one. I would like to receive a gift of university tuition.

The first reason I really need a gift of university tuition is because the tuition at my university is really high. I am attending a private university, and the tuition at private universities is very expensive.

The second reason I really need a gift of university tuition is because I don't have very much money. I need to work to pay for my tuition, and it's really difficult to work a lot and also go to the university.

Because tuition is expensive and I don't have very much money, I would really like to have a gift of university tuition.

Question 2 `Page 381`

Sample Notes

INTRODUCTION:
    better to say nothing
SUPPORTING IDEA 1:
    first reason
    • the person would be happy (if you say something)
SUPPORTING IDEA 2:
    second reason
    • situation could become worse (if you say something)
CONCLUSION:
    sometimes better to say nothing

Sample Response

Sometimes someone might say something mean to me. In this situation, I think it's better to say nothing in response instead of saying something. I have two reasons for thinking this.

The first reason I think it's better to say nothing is that the person who said the mean thing might be happy about that. If someone says something mean, I think he or she wants a response. So it's better in this situation to say nothing.

The second reason I think it's better to say nothing is that the situation could become worse. If someone says something mean and I say something in response, a big argument could develop. So, again, it's better in this situation to say nothing.

For these two reasons, I think it's better to say nothing in response when someone says something mean to me.

Question 3 `Page 382`

Sample Notes

TOPIC OF READING PASSAGE: part of syllabus describing hard work in math class

main points about the topic:
• many quizzes
• many homework assignments
• exam every week

TOPIC OF LISTENING PASSAGE: student discussion about syllabus

main points about the topic:
• woman decides to stay in class even though there is a lot of work
• man wants to change to different class because of hard work

Sample Response

In this set of materials, the reading passage describes part of a syllabus from a math class. Two students discuss this syllabus in the listening passage.

The part of the syllabus from the math class says that there is a lot of hard work in the class. There are many quizzes and many homework assignments, and there is an exam every week.

In the discussion, the two students react differently to the syllabus. The woman decides to stay in the math class even though there is a lot of work in the class. The man wants to change to a different math class because of all the hard work in this class.

Question 4 Page 384

Sample Notes

> TOPIC OF READING PASSAGE: Dutch settlement on island of Manhattan
>
> main points about the topic:
> - was settled in 1612
> - was named after city in homeland
> - was on only eastern tip of Manhattan
>
> TOPIC OF LISTENING PASSAGE: British settlement on island of Manhattan
>
> main points about the topic:
> - was captured in 1664
> - was renamed New York
> - spread beyond eastern tip of island

Sample Response

In this set of materials, the reading passage talks about a certain settlement before 1664. The listening passage talks about the same settlement after 1664.

The reading passage describes the Dutch settlement on the island of Manhattan. The Dutch created a settlement on the island of Manhattan in 1612 and named the settlement New Amsterdam after a city in their homeland. The Dutch settlement was small; it was on only the eastern tip of the island of Manhattan.

The listening passage describes what happened to the Dutch settlement on the island of Manhattan. The British captured the island and took over the settlement in 1664. After the British captured the settlement, they renamed it New York. The settlement under the British spread way beyond the tiny Dutch settlement on the eastern tip of the island.

Question 5 Page 386

Sample Notes

> TOPIC OF LISTENING PASSAGE: student discussion about missing math book
>
> main points about the topic:
> - woman wants to borrow man's math book this evening because she lost hers
> - man needs book this evening but agrees to lend it to her this afternoon
> - woman is delighted with man's offer
> - woman agrees to return book to man at the library at 7:00 P.M.

Sample Response

In this listening passage, two students are discussing a math textbook.

The woman wants to borrow the man's math book this evening because she has misplaced hers. The man needs the book this evening, so he can't lend it to her then. However, he does offer to lend her the book for the afternoon.

The woman is delighted with the man's offer because she can use the book in the afternoon. She does borrow the book for the afternoon and agrees to return it to the man at the library at 7 o'clock that evening.

Question 6 Page 387

Sample Notes

> TOPIC OF LISTENING PASSAGE: Continental Divide
>
> main points about the topic:
> - separates waters flowing to east and waters flowing to west in North America
> - waters flowing to east mostly flow through Mississippi River to Gulf of Mexico
> - waters flowing to west mostly flow through Columbia River or Colorado River to Pacific Ocean

Sample Response

In this listening passage, the professor discusses the Continental Divide, which separates waters flowing to the east and waters flowing to the west in North America. Waters that flow to the east mostly flow through the Mississippi River to the Gulf of Mexico. Waters that flow to the west mostly flow through the Columbia River or the Colorado River to the Pacific Ocean.

WRITING Page 388

Question 1 Page 389

Sample Notes

> TOPIC OF READING PASSAGE: possible advantages of telecommuting
>
> main points about the topic:
> - no time commuting, more time for work
> - no interruptions from co-workers in the office
> - inability of the boss to check on her so much
>
> TOPIC OF LISTENING PASSAGE: actual problems in telecommuting
>
> main points about the topic:
> - difficulty of working at home (neighbors, telephone, children)
> - lack of social contacts with co-workers
> - lack of information from boss

Sample Response

In this set of materials, the reading passage discusses the possible advantages of telecommuting in a certain situation. The listening passage challenges the ideas in the reading passage by discussing actual problems that occurred in this situation.

The reading passage describes a woman named Sylvia. Sylvia was considering telecommuting. She thought that telecommuting would be good for three reasons. The first reason was that there would be more time for work. The second reason was that there would be no interruptions from her co-workers in the office. The third reason was that there would be few interruptions from her boss.

The listening passage shows that Sylvia's expectations were not correct. First, she had thought that she would have more time for work, but she did not. It was difficult for her to work at home because of problems with the neighbors, the children, and the telephone. Second, she had thought she would enjoy working without co-workers, but she did not. She missed talking to her co-workers. Finally, she had thought her boss was checking on her too much, but she found that she needed more information. She wanted to know more about her boss's thoughts on her work.

Question 2 `Page 391`

Sample Notes

> INTRODUCTION:
> prefer to go out in the evening

> SUPPORTING PARAGRAPH 1:
> first reason
> • am usually at home during the day

> SUPPORTING PARAGRAPH 2:
> second reason
> • like to try new things

> CONCLUSION:
> there are reasons why it is good for me to go out sometimes

Sample Response

Every evening people make decisions about going out or staying home with friends. It can be relaxing to stay home in the evening. However, most evenings I prefer to go out with friends. This is because of the kind of life I have during the day and because of the kind of person I am.

I like to go out in the evenings because of the kind of life I have. I am usually at home during the day. Because I am at home so much during the day, I like to go out in the evenings. I go out in the evenings whenever I have the chance to do so.

I also like to go out in the evenings because I am the kind of person who likes to try new things. When I am at home, I always do the same things. There is more chance to try new things if I go out. Maybe I can go to a new restaurant or club, or maybe see a new movie or play, or maybe meet new people. These new things will not happen when I stay home; maybe they will happen when I go out.

Some people may prefer to stay home in the evenings, but I like to go out in the evenings. Because I am at home so much during the day and because I like to try new things all the time, it is best for me to go out often in the evenings.

TOEFL-LEVEL TEST `Page 392`

READING `Page 392`

1. B	4. D	7. B	10. D
2. D	5. A	8. A	11. D
3. C	6. B	9. C	12. A

13. the Greeks: (1) (4)
the Romans: (3) (7)
Columbus: (6)

LISTENING `Page 397`

1. D	4. A	7. C
2. B	5. C	8. B, C
3. A	6. Y, N, N, Y	9. A, D

10. A geodesic dome: Is strongest against both types of pressure
A sphere: Is strongest against internal pressure
A tetrahedron: Is strongest against external pressure

11. D

SPEAKING `Page 402`

Question 1 `Page 403`

Sample Notes

> INTRODUCTION:
> three adjectives to describe myself

> SUPPORTING IDEA 1:
> first adjective
> • sincere

> SUPPORTING IDEA 2:
> second adjective
> • considerate

> SUPPORTING IDEA 3:
> third adjective
> • well-intentioned

> CONCLUSION:
> three examples show why I would use the adjectives

Sample Response

It's an interesting question to talk about which adjectives would best describe me. I think that maybe the three adjectives I would use to describe myself are *sincere, considerate,* and *well-intentioned.*

First, I would use the adjective *sincere* to describe myself. I always try to be sincere with people around me, with my friends, my classmates, and my family. I like people who are always sincere with me, and I always try to be that way myself.

Second, I would use the adjective *considerate* to describe myself. I always think about what people around me want and need. I was raised to be considerate of others. My parents are always considerate of others, and I always try to act that way myself.

Third, I would use the adjective *well-intentioned* to describe myself. I always have good intentions; I always think about doing the right thing. I don't always succeed in doing the right thing, but my intentions are always good.

From these examples, you can see why I would use the adjectives *sincere, considerate,* and *well-intentioned* to describe myself.

Question 2 `Page 403`

Sample Notes

> INTRODUCTION:
> sometimes plan and sometimes don't

> SUPPORTING IDEA 1:
> first example
> • careful planning in professional life (lists)

> SUPPORTING IDEA 2:
> second example
> • no planning in personal life (no lists)

> CONCLUSION:
> plan in professional life and not in personal life

Sample Response

Some people plan their lives carefully, while other people let things happen as they may. I am the kind of person who plans carefully in one part of my life but doesn't plan at all in the other.

In my professional life, I plan every single detail carefully. Every morning at work, I make a list of everything I need to do and when I'm going to do it. I check things off the list as soon as they're done, and I don't leave work until every single item has been crossed off the list even if I have to stay several extra hours on the job to get them done.

In my personal life, I just don't plan the way I do in my professional life. I don't make lists at home the way I do at work, and, in fact, I don't make plans at all. I don't make shopping lists when I go shopping, I don't make a schedule when I run errands, and I don't plan my itinerary when I go on vacation.

These examples show you that I live my life very differently in my professional and personal lives. I do a tremendous amount of planning in one and almost no planning in the other.

Question 3   Page 404

Sample Notes

TOPIC OF READING PASSAGE: notice about change in hours of campus cafeteria

main points about the topic:
- new hours will go into effect in one week (on February 1)
- new hours are 7:00–9:00 A.M., 12:00–2:00 P.M., 5:00–7:00 P.M.
- campus cafeteria is pleased with announcement

TOPIC OF LISTENING PASSAGE: student discussion about notice

main points about the topic:
- man is not happy with notice and explains why to woman
- man is not happy about reduction of hours from nine per day to six per day
- man is not happy with tone of announcement (saying campus cafeteria is pleased when it is actually doing something negative)

Sample Response

In this set of materials, the reading passage presents a notice about a change at the campus cafeteria, and two students discuss this notice in the listening passage.

The reading passage describes a change in the hours of operation of the campus cafeteria; the change will go into effect in one week, on February 1. The new hours are 7:00 to 9:00 A.M., 12:00 to 2:00 P.M., and 5:00 to 7:00 P.M. The campus cafeteria is quite pleased to be announcing this change.

Two students discuss this announcement in the listening passage. The man isn't at all happy with the announcement, and he explains why he's upset with it to the woman. He's unhappy about the announcement for two reasons. First of all, the number of hours that the campus cafeteria will be in operation is being reduced from nine hours per day to six hours per day. Second of all, the man isn't happy with the tone of the announcement. He's upset that the campus cafeteria is saying it's pleased when it's actually doing something negative.

Question 4   Page 406

Sample Notes

TOPIC OF READING PASSAGE: operant conditioning (when people learn from consequences of behavior)

main points about the topic:
- positive consequences for a behavior tend to cause the behavior to continue
- negative consequences for a behavior tend to cause the behavior to end

TOPIC OF LISTENING PASSAGE: examples showing effect of operant conditioning (mother and misbehaving child)

main points about the topic:
- negative consequences for negative behavior (and negative behavior ends)
- positive consequences for negative behavior (and negative behavior continues)

Sample Response

In this set of materials, the reading passage defines a certain concept, while the listening passage provides two opposing examples of the concept.

The reading passage defines the concept of operant conditioning, which occurs when people learn from the consequences of their behavior. If there are positive consequences for a behavior, the positive consequences tend to cause the behavior to continue. If there are negative consequences for a behavior, the negative consequences tend to cause the behavior to end.

The listening passage provides two opposing examples showing the effect of operant conditioning, both of which involve a mother and a child who is misbehaving. In the first example, the child behaves in a negative way, and there are negative consequences for the negative behavior. In this situation, the negative behavior ends because of the negative consequences. In the second example, the child behaves in a negative way, and there are positive consequences for the negative behavior. In this second situation, the negative behavior continues because of the positive consequences.

Question 5   Page 408

Sample Notes

TOPIC OF LISTENING PASSAGE: student discussion about a class

main points about the topic:
- woman is taking Professor Nelson's class and is not enjoying it
- she thinks professor says incorrect things
- man already took class and enjoyed it
- he explains that professor says incorrect things on purpose
- he explains that professor wants students to challenge him
- he suggests that the woman should begin challenging the professor

Sample Response

In this listening passage, two students are having a discussion about Professor Nelson's class. The woman is taking the class, and she isn't enjoying it. The man already took the class, and he did enjoy it.

The reason that the woman isn't enjoying the class is that she thinks the professor repeatedly says incorrect things. The man understands the situation. He explains to the woman that the professor says incorrect things on purpose. The reason the professor says incorrect things is that he wants the students to challenge what he says. The man suggests to the woman that she should start challenging the professor when he says incorrect things.

Question 6 Page 409

Sample Notes

TOPIC OF LISTENING PASSAGE: asteroids and asteroid belt

main points about the topic:
- asteroids are large or small rocky bodies orbiting the Sun
- many asteroids in asteroid belt, region between Mars and Jupiter
- one theory about origin of asteroid belt is that there was another planet
- another theory about origin of asteroid belt is that another planet was beginning to form

Sample Response

In this listening passage, the professor discusses asteroids and the asteroid belt. Asteroids are large or small rocky bodies that orbit the Sun. There are many asteroids in the asteroid belt, a region between the planets Mars and Jupiter. There are two theories about the origin of the asteroid belt. One theory is that there was another planet that broke up. Another theory is that another planet was beginning to form from the rocky bodies there.

WRITING Page 410

Question 1 Page 411

Sample Notes

TOPIC OF READING PASSAGE: a description of phrenology (the idea that there is a relationship between personality traits and locations in the brain)

main point about the topic:
- indicates that bumps and marks on skull are due to personality traits
- was developed in nineteenth century
- was believed by well-known people (Queen Victoria, Poe)

TOPIC OF LISTENING PASSAGE: validity of phrenology

main points about the topic:
- no relationship between single personality trait and single location in brain
- no indication that bumps and marks on skull are due to personality traits
- single personality trait involves many functions and many brain locations

Sample Response

In this set of materials, the reading passage describes a certain theory in psychology, while the listening passage casts doubt on the ideas in the reading passage by discussing the validity of this theory.

The reading passage describes the theory of phrenology, which indicates that there is a relationship between a certain personality trait and a specific location in the brain. This theory, in addition, indicates that each bump and mark on the human skull is due to a specific personality trait. This theory was developed in the nineteenth century and was quite a popular theory. A number of well-known people, including Queen Victoria of England and American author Edgar Allan Poe, followed this theory.

The listening passage discusses beliefs today about the validity of the theory of phrenology. Studies today have shown that there is no relationship between a single personality trait and a single location in the brain as was believed in the nineteenth century. Studies have also shown that there is no relationship between bumps and marks on the skull and personality traits, as was also believed in the nineteenth century. Instead, a single personality trait involves numerous functions that take place in a variety of areas of the brain and cannot be linked to a single location in the brain.

Question 2 Page 413

Sample Notes

INTRODUCTION:
  ways of dealing with students who come late to class

SUPPORTING PARAGRAPH 1:
  first way
- let class as a whole know that there is a problem

SUPPORTING PARAGRAPH 2:
  second way
- speak to individuals privately

SUPPORTING PARAGRAPH 3:
  third way
- take decisive action

CONCLUSION:
  one of these ways will definitely work

Sample Response

It is a common situation for a teacher to find that students are coming late to class day after day. In this situation, the teacher needs to take action; after all, if the teacher fails to take action, the situation is going to continue and will perhaps even deteriorate. There are several steps that a teacher can take to deal with this problem once and for all.

It is very important as a first step for the teacher to make sure that the class as a whole understands that the repeated tardiness is a problem. This is something that does not need to be serious; it can, in fact, be done quite effectively with humor. It is quite simply important that the message is delivered to the students. The teacher can ask, for example, if the students understand when class actually begins, because some of them seem to think that class begins at ten or fifteen minutes past the hour. The teacher can also make funny comments when students come into class late.

If humor to the class as a whole does not solve the problem, then the teacher needs to do something more. Because humor to the whole group has not worked, the teacher needs to speak seriously and directly to the individuals who are causing the problem. The teacher needs to explain in a serious way that it is not acceptable to come late to class. This explanation can be made privately after class with the students involved.

If these first two steps do not work to solve the problem, then the teacher needs to take really decisive action. This decisive action needs to show the tardy students once and for all that continued tardiness will no longer be accepted. Such decisive action could consist of something as simple as locking the door to the classroom and not allowing any tardy students to enter the classroom. It could also involve giving the students failing grades for any days that they are tardy to class. By taking such decisive action, the teacher is clearly demonstrating to the students that there will be no further tardiness.

Repeated tardiness is something that the teacher needs to deal with. The teacher can try using humor with the class as a whole or speaking quietly with the students who are repeatedly coming late to class. If this does not work, then more serious steps can be taken until the problem is solved.

APPENDIX

APPENDIX EXERCISE A1 Page 418

1. I forgot
   (she forgot)
2. C plane took off
3. I reason
   (is good)
4. I friends . . . they are coming
   (omit they)
5. C We understand
6. I (It is)
7. I picture is . . . is
   (omit is)
8. C student . . . finished
9. I athlete
   (won)
10. I (It is)
11. C player hurt
12. I chapter . . . it was
   (omit it)
13. I accepted
   (She)
14. C invitation . . . lists
15. I program is . . . is
   (omit is)

APPENDIX EXERCISE A2 Page 419

1. I students were . . . (,) . . . teacher was
   (, and)
2. C roommates decided . . . (, but) I did . . . go
3. I I need . . . (, or) will . . . be
   (or I will)
4. I students did . . . understand . . . (so) . . . teacher gave
   (, so)

5. C It was . . . (, yet) she did . . . feel
6. C child fell . . . (, and) he broke
7. I I did . . . want . . . (, but) had
   (I had)
8. C You need . . . (, or) you will be locked
9. I Traffic was . . . (so) we decided
   (, so)
10. I pie looked . . . (, yet) none . . .
   (guests ate)
11. I I gave . . . ( ) I intend
   (, and)
12. C He watered . . . (, but) they . . . do . . . look
13. C athlete needs . . . (, or) she will . . . do
14. C boss was . . . (, so) . . . workers did . . . get
15. I were . . . tickets . . . (yet) . . . people stayed
   (, yet)

APPENDIX EXERCISE A3 Page 421

1. I students left . . . (, after) they turned in
   (sadly after)
2. C (When) . . . guests arrived . . . (,) they knocked
3. I You need . . . (whether) want
   (you want)
4. I I asked . . . (,) I . . . did . . . understand
   (After I)
5. C We entered . . . (just as) . . . game was starting
6. I (Even though) I do . . . want . . . ( ) I . . . have
   (class,)
7. C I am . . . going . . . (until) I see
8. C (If) you turn in . . . (,) you will . . . lose
9. I I have . . . had . . . (since) got
   (I got)
10. I (Before) you write . . . ( ) you must research
   (paper,)
11. I (After) I saw
   (paper, I cried.)
12. C mother cried (when) she heard
13. I electricity was . . . (, because) . . . bill was . . . paid
   (off because)
14. C (Until) you take . . . (,) you are
15. I He got . . . (even) he had . . . prepared
   (even though)

APPENDIX REVIEW EXERCISE (A1–A3) Page 422

1. I Everything . . . it needs
   (omit it)
2. C professor ended . . . (, and) . . . students left
3. I (Though) . . . party was scheduled . . . ( ) it did . . . end
   (midnight,)
4. C number . . . turned out
5. I I would like . . . (,) I do . . . have
   (, but I)
6. C You can visit . . . (if) you want
7. I (It is)
8. C students need . . . (, or) they will receive
9. I (Because) . . . program was
   (, I watched it)
10. C reason . . . seems
11. I They left . . . (, so) were
   (, so they)
12. I I need . . . (, before) I forget
   (down before)
13. I flowers
   (flowers are)

14. C It was . . . (, yet) . . . children . . . wanted
15. C (While) . . . roommates were . . . (,) I was studying

APPENDIX EXERCISE B1   Page 423

1. I <u>doors</u> (to the room) <u>was</u>
   (were)
2. I <u>reason</u> (for the problems) <u>are</u>
   (is)
3. C <u>pictures</u> (on the wall) (to the right) <u>are</u>
4. C <u>dirt</u> (on the windows) <u>needs</u>
5. I <u>chapters</u> (of the novel) <u>takes</u>
   (take)
6. I <u>exam</u> (on the lectures) <u>are scheduled</u>
   (is scheduled)
7. C <u>buildings</u> (around the corner) <u>were built</u>
8. C <u>discussion</u> (about the issues) <u>starts</u>
9. I <u>words</u> (to the song) <u>has</u>
   (have)
10. C <u>news</u> (about the fires) (in the mountains) <u>is</u>

APPENDIX EXERCISE B2   Page 425

1. I <u>None</u> (of the reasons) <u>makes</u>
   (make)
2. C <u>Some</u> (of the plants) <u>need</u>
3. I <u>All</u> (of the children) <u>is playing</u>
   (are playing)
4. C <u>Part</u> (of the time) <u>has</u>
5. C <u>Half</u> (of this chapter) <u>covers</u>
6. I <u>Most</u> (of the words) <u>was</u>
   (were)
7. C <u>None</u> (of the movie) <u>is</u>
8. I <u>Part</u> (of the letter) <u>contain</u>
   (contains)
9. C <u>Some</u> (of the students) <u>have passed</u>
10. I <u>Half</u> (of the food) <u>taste</u>
    (tastes)

APPENDIX REVIEW EXERCISE (B1–B2)   Page 425

1. I <u>students</u> (in the dormitory) <u>gets</u>
   (get)
2. I <u>All</u> (of the walls) <u>was</u>
   (were)
3. C <u>meeting</u> (for freshmen) <u>lasts</u>
4. C <u>Part</u> (of the house) <u>is burning</u>
5. I <u>houses</u> (along the shore) <u>was damaged</u>
   (were damaged)
6. C <u>Most</u> (of the information) <u>has</u>
7. C <u>road</u> (through the mountains) <u>twists . . . turns</u>
8. I <u>Some</u> (of the pages) (of the book) <u>was</u>
   (were)
9. I <u>paragraphs</u> (in the essay) <u>needs</u>
   (need)
10. C <u>Half</u> (of the people) (in the room) <u>understand</u>

APPENDIX EXERCISE B3   Page 426

1. I <u>funny, interesting,</u> (and) <u>organize</u>
   (organized)
2. C <u>came</u> . . . (but) <u>did</u> . . . <u>offer</u>
3. C <u>in the kitchen</u> (or) <u>in the dining room</u>
4. I <u>to the market, the bank,</u> (and) <u>to the pharmacy</u>
   (to the bank)
5. I <u>carefully</u> (but) <u>quick</u>
   (quickly)
6. C <u>early in the morning</u> (or) <u>late in the evening</u>

7. I <u>softly</u> (and) <u>with patience</u>
   (patiently)
8. I <u>spent</u> . . . (but) <u>done</u>
   (did)
9. C <u>effort</u> (or) <u>ability</u>
10. C <u>the north</u> (and) <u>the south</u> (but) . . . <u>the east or the west</u>

APPENDIX EXERCISE B4   Page 428

1. I (either) <u>a paper</u> (or) <u>choose a presentation</u>
   (or a presentation)
2. C (both) <u>the key to my car</u> (and) <u>the key to my apartment</u>
3. I (neither) <u>carelessly</u> (nor) <u>at a fast speed</u>
   (nor fast)
4. I (not only) <u>sang</u> (but also) <u>dancing</u>
   (but also danced)
5. C (Either) <u>one person</u> (or) <u>the other person</u>
6. C (both) <u>surprised by</u> (and) <u>thankful for</u>
7. I (neither) <u>lied to you</u> (nor) <u>to her</u>
   (nor lied to her)
8. I (not only) <u>a paper to write</u> (but also) <u>to read a chapter</u>
   (but also a chapter to read)
9. C (either) <u>in the morning</u> (or) <u>in the afternoon</u>
10. I (both) <u>in the library</u> (and) <u>the cafeteria</u>
    (and in the cafeteria)

APPENDIX REVIEW EXERCISE (B3–B4)   Page 428

1. C (not only) <u>in class</u> (but also) <u>at the library</u>
2. C <u>has studied</u> . . . (but) <u>has</u> . . . <u>become</u>
3. I (neither) <u>amusing</u> (nor) <u>was it interesting</u>
   (nor interesting)
4. C <u>a new sofa</u> (or) <u>a new table</u>
5. I (either) <u>go home</u> . . . (or) <u>you may stay here</u>
   (or stay here)
6. I <u>dedicated, studious,</u> (and) <u>a hardworking student</u>
   (and hardworking)
7. I (both) <u>in the refrigerator</u> (and) <u>the cabinet</u>
   (and in the cabinet)
8. C <u>a nurse</u> (but) . . . <u>a doctor</u>
9. I (not only) <u>quickly</u> (but also) <u>to write correctly</u>
   (but also correctly)
10. C <u>give you</u> . . . (or) . . . <u>tell you</u>

APPENDIX EXERCISE B5   Page 429

1. I <u>have chose</u>
   (have chosen)
2. C <u>has known</u>
3. I <u>had catch</u>
   (had caught)
4. I <u>have maked</u>
   (have made)
5. C <u>has lost</u>
6. I <u>have making</u>
   (have made)
7. C <u>have flown</u>
8. C <u>has driven</u>
9. I <u>had forgot</u>
   (had forgotten)
10. C <u>Have</u> . . . <u>bought</u>

APPENDIX EXERCISE B6 Page 430

1. I is leave
      (is leaving)
2. C were mailed
3. C am taking
4. I will be plays
      (will be played)
5. C was crying
6. C have been placed
7. I are be canceled
      (are being canceled)
8. C were taking off . . . landing
9. I are being reward
      (are being rewarded)
10. I will be gave
       (will be given)

APPENDIX EXERCISE B7 Page 431

1. I will received
      (will receive)
2. C would . . . do
3. I can . . . depending
      (can . . . depend)
4. I should . . . spends
      (should . . . spend)
5. C will mail out
6. C might leave
7. I must . . . being
      (must . . . be)
8. C shall offer
9. I could . . . dreamed
      (could . . . dream)
10. I may . . . understands
       (may . . . understand)

APPENDIX REVIEW EXERCISE (B5–B7) Page 432

1. I may . . . begun
      (may . . . begin)
2. I has . . . takes
      (has . . . taken)
3. C am . . . thinking
4. I can . . . knows
      (can . . . know)
5. C had . . . fed
6. C would . . . be
7. I might had
      (might have)
8. I have . . . ate
      (have . . . eaten)
9. C has been sold
10. I would . . . suspected
       (would . . . suspect)

APPENDIX EXERCISE B8 Page 433

1. I (every) students
      (student)
2. C (many) . . . ideas
3. I (several) . . . test
      (tests)
4. I (a) . . . favors
      (favor)
5. C (both) ways
6. C (each) page
7. I (various) way
      (ways)

8. C (Two) people
9. I (one) seconds
      (second)
10. I (single) cents
       (cent)

APPENDIX EXERCISE B9 Page 434

1. I (amount) . . . reasons
      (number)
2. C (little) time
3. I (much) chapters
      (many)
4. C (fewer) courses
5. I (less) people
      (fewer)
6. C (little) need
7. I (many) ideas
      (little) solutions
      (few)
8. C (much) importance
9. I (many) money
      (much)
10. C (large) number
       (few) . . . them

APPENDIX REVIEW EXERCISE (B8–B9) Page 434

1. I (several) times
      (a) . . . calls
      (call)
2. I (less) children
      (fewer)
3. C (many) errors
      (every) paragraph
4. I (amount) . . . friends
      (number)
5. I (both) assignment
      (assignments)
      (two) hour
      (hours)
6. C (number) . . . awards
7. I (each) . . . problem
      (single) . . . responses
      (response)
8. C (fewer) opportunities
9. I (various) solution
      (solutions)
      (one) solution
10. C (much) advice

APPENDIX EXERCISE B10 Page 435

1. I (I) . . . (him) . . . (he) . . . (I)
      (for me)
2. C (We) . . . (them) . . . (they) . . . (us)
3. I (you) . . . (him)
      (you and he)
4. C (me) . . . (it) . . . (you)
5. C (She) . . . (me) . . . (I) . . . (them) . . . (she)
6. I (you) . . . (I). . . (We)
      (you and me)
7. C (I) . . . (I) . . . (it)
8. I (Him) . . . (me)
      (He and I)
9. C (she) . . . (them) . . . (it)
10. I (you) . . . (I) . . . (We) . . . (it)
       (you and me)

APPENDIX EXERCISE B11 Page 436

1. I   (our) . . . (your)
      (yours)
2. C   (my) . . . (his)
3. I   (Their) . . . (our)
      (ours)
4. C   (your) . . . (mine)
5. I   (his) . . . (her)
      (hers)
6. I   (Its')
      (Its)
7. I   (mine) . . . (yours)
      (my)
8. C   (her) . . . (his)
9. C   (Our) . . . (theirs) . . . (Ours) . . . (theirs)
10. I   (My) . . . (yours) . . . (yours) . . . (mines)
      (your opinions . . . mine)

APPENDIX EXERCISE B12 Page 438

1. I   toys . . . (it)
      (them)
2. C   neighbors . . . (their)
3. I   paper . . . (them)
      (it)
4. C   man . . . (his)
      error . . . (it)
5. I   articles . . . (its)
      (their)
6. C   You . . . (your)
      I . . . (my)
7. C   speaker . . . (he)
      point . . . (it)
8. I   students . . . (they)
      ideas . . . (it)
      (them)
9. C   Mary . . . (her)
      Mary . . . (she)
      friends . . . (them)
10. I   Everyone . . . (their)
      (his or her)

APPENDIX REVIEW EXERCISE (B10–B12) Page 438

1. I   (him) . . . (her) . . . (It) . . . (you) . . . (I)
      (me)
2. C   (Our) . . . (Mine) . . . (yours)
3. I   (I) . . . (I) . . . (I) . . . (them)
      (it)
4. C   (I) . . . (he) . . . (we)
5. C   (Our) . . . (theirs) . . . (it) . . . (theirs)
6. I   (He) . . . (his) . . . (I) . . . (mine) . . . (we) . . . (it)
      (them)
7. I   (She) . . . (him) . . . (his) . . . (she) . . . (her)
      (hers)
8. C   (you) . . . (me) . . . (your) . . . (I) . . . (my) . . . (yours)
9. C   (Our) . . . (us) . . . (we) . . . (them) . . . (it)
10. I   (theirs) . . . (she) . . . (them)
      (their)

APPENDIX EXERCISE B13 Page 440

1. I   (difficult) . . . (thorough)
      (thoroughly)
      difficult describes *material*
      thorough *(thoroughly)* describes *studied*

2. I   (real) (professional)
      (really)
      real *(really)* describes *professional*
      professional describes *résumé*
3. C   (unexpectedly) (early)
      unexpectedly describes *early*
      early describes *arrived*
4. C   (obvious) . . . (final)
      obvious describes *mistake*
      final describes *paragraph*
5. I   (surprisingly) (good)
      (well)
      surprisingly describes *good (well)*
      good *(well)* describes *did*
6. C   (politely) . . . (personal)
      politely describes *responded*
      personal describes *question*
7. I   (certainly) . . . (correct)
      (correctly)
      certainly describes *must answer*
      correct *(correctly)* describes *must answer*
8. C   (appreciatively) . . . (thoughtful)
      appreciatively describes *responded*
      thoughtful describes *offer*
9. I   (suddenly) . . . (cold) . . . (open)
      (sudden)
      suddenly *(sudden)* describes *rush*
      cold describes *air*
      open describes *window*
10. C   (extremely) (softly) . . . (carefully)
      extremely describes *softly*
      softly describes *spoke*
      carefully describes *listened*

APPENDIX EXERCISE B14 Page 442

1. I   (very) (nicely)
      (nice)
      very describes *nicely*
      nicely *(nice)* describes *She*
2. C   (recently) . . . (tired)
      recently describes *saw*
      tired describes *he*
3. C   (romantic) . . . (deeply)
      romantic describes *movie*
      deeply describes *affected*
4. I   (doubtfully) . . . (new)
      (doubtful)
      doubtfully *(doubtful)* describes *I*
      new describes *information*
5. I   (very) (eagerly)
      (eager)
      very describes *eagerly (eager)*
      eagerly *(eager)* describes *They*
6. C   (quickly) . . . (serious)
      quickly describes *acted*
      serious describes *problem*
7. I   (new) . . . (wonderfully)
      (wonderful)
      new describes *perfume*
      wonderfully *(wonderful)* describes *perfume*
8. C   (quiet) . . . (asleep)
      quiet describes *house*
      asleep describes *children*

9. C (soundly) . . . (entire)
   soundly describes *slept*
   entire describes *night*
10. I (new) . . . (deliciously)
   (delicious)
   new describes *dish*
   deliciously (delicious) describes *dish*

APPENDIX REVIEW EXERCISE (B13–B14) Page 443

1. C (humorous) . . . (negative)
   humorous describes *way*
   negative describes *comments*
2. C (quiet) . . . (patiently)
   quiet describes *room*
   patiently describes *waited*
3. I (completely) (impossibly)
   (impossible)
   completely describes *impossibly (impossible)*
   impossibly (impossible) describes *situation*
4. I (unusual) (difficult) . . . (sad)
   (unusually)
   unusual (unusually) describes *difficult*
   difficult describes *homework*
   sad describes *students*
5. C (sincerely) . . . (generously) . . . (sincere)
   sincerely describes *apologized*
   generously describes *accepted*
   sincere describes *apology*

6. I (really) (happily) . . . (rapid)
   (happy)
   really describes *happily (happy)*
   happily (happy) describes *teacher*
   rapid describes *progress*
7. I (truly) (irrational) . . . (apparent)
   (irrationally)
   truly describes *irrational (irrationally)*
   irrational (irrationally) describes *behaved*
   apparent describes *reason*
8. C (really) (emotional) . . . (positive)
   really describes *emotional*
   emotional describes *I*
   positive describes *results*
9. C (incredibly) (unhealthy) . . . (incredibly) (healthy)
   incredibly describes *unhealthy*
   unhealthy describes *food*
   incredibly describes *healthy*
   healthy describes *she*
10. I (extremely) (happily) . . . (actually) . . . (sadly)
   (happy . . . sad)
   extremely describes *happily (happy)*
   happily (happy) describes *He*
   actually describes *was . . . feeling*
   sadly (sad) describes *he*

Single User License Agreement:

IMPORTANT: READ CAREFULLY

WARNING: BY OPENING THE PACKAGE YOU AGREE TO BE BOUND BY THE TERMS OF THE LICENSE AGREEMENT BELOW

This is a legally binding agreement between You (the user or purchaser) and Pearson Education, Inc. By retaining this license, any software media or accompanying written materials or carrying out any of the permitted activities You agree to be bound by the terms of the license agreement below. If You do not agree to these terms, then promptly return the entire publication (this license and all software, written materials, packaging and any other components received with it) with Your sales receipt to Your supplier for a full refund.

SINGLE USER LICENSE AGREEMENT

❏ YOU ARE PERMITTED TO:

✓ Use (load into temporary memory or permanent storage) a single copy of the software on only one computer at a time. If this computer is linked to a network then the software may only be installed in a manner such that it is not accessible to other machines on the network.

✓ Use the software with a class provided it is only installed on one computer

✓ Transfer the software from one computer to another provided that you only use it on one computer at a time

✓ Print out individual screen extracts from the disk for (a) private study or (b) to include in Your essays or classwork with students

✓ Photocopy individual screen extracts for Your schoolwork or classwork with students

❏ YOU MAY NOT:

✗ Rent or lease the software or any part of the publication

✗ Copy any part of the documentation, except where specifically indicated otherwise

✗ Make copies of the software, even for backup purposes

✗ Reverse engineer, decompile or disassemble the software or create a derivative product from the contents of the databases or any software included in them

✗ Use the software on more than one computer at a time

✗ Install the software on any networked computer or server in a way that could allow access to it from more than one machine on the network

✗ Include any material or software from the disk in any other product or software materials except as allowed under "You are permitted to"

✗ Use the software in any way not specified above without prior written consent of the Publisher

✗ Print out more than one page at a time

ONE COPY ONLY

This license is for a single user copy of the software. THE PUBLISHER RESERVES THE RIGHT TO TERMINATE THIS LICENSE BY WRITTEN NOTICE AND TO TAKE ACTION TO RECOVER ANY DAMAGES SUFFERED BY THE PUBLISHER IF YOU BREACH ANY PROVISION OF THIS AGREEMENT.
The Publisher owns the software. You only own the disk on which the software is supplied.

LIMITED WARRANTY

The Publisher warrants that the disk or CD-ROM on which the software is supplied is free from defects in materials and workmanship under normal use for ninety (90) days from the date You received them. This warranty is limited to You and is not transferable. The Publisher does not warrant that the functions of the software meet Your requirements or that the media is compatible with any computer system on which it is used or that the operation of the software will be unlimited or error free.

You assume responsibility for selecting the software to achieve Your intended results and for the installation of, the use of, and the results obtained from the software. The entire liability of the Publisher and Your only remedy shall be replacement free of charge of the components that do not meet this warranty.

This limited warranty is void if any damage has resulted from accident, abuse, misapplication, service or modification by someone other than the Publisher. In no event shall the Publisher or its suppliers be liable for any damages whatsoever arising out of installation of the software, even if advised of the possibility of such damages. The Publisher will not be liable for any loss or damage of any nature suffered by any part as a result of reliance upon or reproduction of any errors in the content of the publication.

The Publisher does not limit its liability for death or personal injury caused by its negligence. This license agreement shall be governed by and interpreted and construed in accordance with New York State law.

For technical assistance, you may call (877) 546-5408 or e-mail epsupport@pearson.com.